Religion and Prevention in Mental Health: Research, Vision, and Action

Religion and Prevention in Mental Health: Research, Vision, and Action

Kenneth I. Pargament
Kenneth I. Maton
Robert E. Hess
Editors

The Haworth Press, Inc.
New York • London • Norwood (Australia)

Religion and Prevention in Mental Health: Research, Vision, and Action has also been published as *Prevention in Human Services*, Volume 9, Number 2 and Volume 10, Number 1 1991.

The Haworth Press, Inc., 10 Alice Street, Binghamton, NY 13904-1580 USA

Library of Congress Cataloging-in-Publication Data

Religion and prevention in mental health : research, vision, and action / Kenneth I. Pargament, Kenneth I. Maton, Robert E. Hess, editors.
    p. cm.
Includes bibliographical references and index.
ISBN 1-56024-225-6 (alk. paper). — ISBN 1-56024-226-4 (pbk. : alk. paper)
    1. Mental health—Religious aspects. 2. Psychology and religion. I. Pargament, Kenneth I. (Kenneth Ira), 1950- . II. Maton, Kenneth I. III. Hess, Robert, 1948- .
BL65.M45R46 1991
261.8'322—dc20   92-5887
                                                            CIP

Religion and Prevention in Mental Health: Research, Vision, and Action

CONTENTS

ABOUT THE EDITORS

Kenneth I. Pargament, PhD, currently Professor at Bowling Green State University, has published widely in community psychology and in the psychology of religion. In 1987, he received the William James Award from Division 36 of the American Psychological Association for exellence in research in the psychology of religion. He is the author of a forthcoming book on the psychology of religion and coping.

Kenneth I. Maton, PhD, is Associate Professor of Psychology at the University of Maryland Baltimore County. He has published widely in community psychology and in the psychology of religion. His current research has focused on spiritual support and religious settings as buffers of life stress.

Robert E. Hess, PhD, is Chief of the Bureau of Mental Health in Boise, Idaho. He has received several national awards in prevention, has published extensively in the field, and has served on and chaired various organizations devoted to furthering the philosophy of prevention. He is past Chair of the Division of Prevention of the National Council of Community Mental Health Centers. Dr. Hess is editor of *Prevention in Human Services*.

Religion as a Resource for Preventive Action: An Introduction

Kenneth I. Maton

University of Maryland Baltimore County

Kenneth I. Pargament

Bowling Green State University

At first glance, a book on the topic of religion and prevention may seem strange, even farfetched. After all, some of us respond to words like "faith," "prayer," "spirituality," "ritual," "church," or "synagogue" with a yawn, sigh, or shudder. Others of us, who see more value to religion, view it as a resource to people *after* they have encountered problems. The congregation can provide food to the poor; the minister can counsel the member in crisis; the individual can pray to God for strength and guidance in times of turmoil. It is true that religions have a long tradition of helping people back on their feet after they have run into trouble. But the helping tradition is only one part of a broader religious mission and legacy.

At their heart, the religions of the world try to bring the person closer to God, however the deity may be conceived. For thousands of years, Hindus and Buddhists have sought Nirvana, Christians have tried to let Jesus Christ into their hearts, Moslems have embraced Allah, and Jews have tried to know God. The religions of the world have also constructed in rich detail a set of paths to guide the person in the effort to find and stay with God. These paths prescribe values in living, courses of conduct, ways of thinking, and standards for relating to others throughout the lifespan.

What has been overlooked has been the fact that these paths do not simply offer direction to people *after* problems arise. Instead, they offer

1

an overarching framework for living, one which carries with it implications for anticipating, avoiding, or modifying problems *before* they develop.

Listen to the preventive chords running through this illustrative religious material:

- Proverbs such as "Wisdom is the principal thing; therefore get wisdom: and with all thy getting get understanding" (Proverbs 4:7); "Better it is to be of an humble spirit with the lowly; than to divide the spoil with the proud" (Proverbs 16:18); "A good name is rather to be chosen than great riches, and loving favour rather than silver and gold" (Proverbs 22:1).
- The Islamic concept of "sharia" (translated as pathway to water), which prescribes appropriate human conduct or the way to God. This comprehensive term designates acceptable law, moral behavior, rational thought, mystical experience, and personal piety (Crim, Bullard, & Shinn, 1989).
- The declaration of Quakers originally made to Charles II in 1661 and still affirmed today: "We utterly deny all outward wars and strife and fightings with outward weapons, for any end or under any pretense whatsoever. . . . The spirit of Christ, which leads us into all Truth, will never move us to fight and war against any man with outward weapons, neither for the kingdom of Christ nor for the kingdoms of this world (Rosten, 1975, p. 229).
- The Noble Eightfold Path of Buddhism through which the causes of suffering can be eliminated: Right Belief, Right Attitude, Right Speech, Right Bodily Action, Right Livelihood, Right Effort, Right Self-Awareness, and Right Meditation (Smart, 1989).

As these examples show, preventive concerns can become wrapped up in the broader system of religious beliefs and practices.

This is not to say that the sole or even primary goal of religion is prevention. It is important to stress that the religious mission goes beyond this concept. Further, some of the assumptions underlying certain religious perspectives depart from those at the core of the prevention orientation. For example, many religious traditions see the state of sin as basic to the human condition. Although it can be transcended through spiritual growth, there can be no "primary prevention" of sin. Similarly, apocalyptic forecasts of life soon coming to an end or visions of a world at the mercy of an unpredictable God are incompatible with an important assumption of prevention: that the world is at least somewhat stable, orderly, predictable, and manageable by human hands. Finally, even among those religious traditions with world views and values more consistent with the goals of prevention, it remains to be seen how effectively these values are implemented.

Thus, religious systems should not be mistaken for prevention centers. But in the pursuit of its unique mission, religion can harmonize well with the goals and values of prevention by selectively encouraging and discouraging particular frameworks for living. It is in this sense that religion can serve as a resource for preventive action.

Given the implications of religious life for prevention, it is surprising that, with some exceptions (e.g., Whitlock, 1973), relatively little has been said or written about the topic by human services professionals. This oversight may reflect several factors. For one, there is a gap between the religious orientations of people in the larger community and those of human service providers. Psychologists in particular are considerably less religious than the general community (Beit-Hallahmi, 1974). As a result, they may underestimate the scope and power of religion in society. Second, a physical gap also exists between human service and religious communities. Members of the two communities often travel in different circles; when they do connect it is most often within the context of traditional mental health concerns (Carson, 1976). The clergy will refer a difficult case to a clinician or a mental health center will provide consultation or clinical training to clergy, but the larger reservoir of religious resources remains untapped. Finally, and perhaps most importantly, there is a tension between the world views of religion and those of the human service professional. While the religious world generally emphasizes the limits of personal control and individual agency, the human service community stresses the power of people to effect changes in their lives. It is easy to distort either of these positions. Religion can be viewed as simply an attempt to anesthetize the individual, relieving him/her from any responsibility in life. On the other hand, the mental health community can be dismissed as morally corrupt, promoting hedonistic self-indulgence and self-worship at the expense of more ultimate concerns.

In spite of these divisive factors, there are a number of good reasons for taking a closer look at religion as a resource for prevention. First, perhaps the most basic of all axioms of prevention is that preventive activities must be nested in the settings, systems, and events most central to people. Thus, we find prevention programs directed towards families, schools, work settings, neighborhoods, and larger communities, and at critical points in life—prenatal, early childhood, the transition to school, marriage, a change in working conditions, aging, or widowhood (Edelstein & Michelson, 1986). Religion is another central part of individual and institutional life in our culture as some of the following figures reveal. Nine out of ten Americans report they have never doubted the existence of God (Gallup & Castelli, 1989); 56% indicate that religion is very important to them (Princeton Religion Research Center, 1984); there are approximately 340,000 religious congregations in the United States with over 143 million members; 42% of the population reports congregation attendance within the last seven days (Jacquet, 1989). Religion, as a personal and social force, also has a close association with particularly significant occasions. It provides a set of rituals to mark, interpret, and deal with key moments through the lifespan such as birth, transitions to adulthood, marriage, divorce, tragedy, and death. The conclusion to be drawn from this discussion is that the religious realm represents another "nesting ground" for people and another natural site for preventive efforts.

Second, religious communities have several distinct advantages over the mental health community when it comes to prevention. While human service professionals have a tradition of waiting for people to come to them with problems, religious communities have greater natural access to people. Through their ongoing participation in church/synagogue life, members often establish long-term relationships with other members and leaders of the congregation. In these sustained relationships, worrisome changes and potential problems can be identified early in the process of development. Religious communities also have greater social sanction to reach out to people in need, even if they have not come to the congregation for help. Regular calls by clergy on their members are allowed and even expected within many congregations. Congregation members allow clergy and others to reach out to them before trouble occurs or when the first signs of problems arise. And it is particularly important to stress that the access of religion is greatest among those groups least connected to traditional human services. The congregation, the minister, or the healer have long stood at the center of community life providing a sense of identity, meaning, belonging, optimism, power, and concrete services to minorities, the disenfranchised, and those often at the margin of society (e.g., Frazier, 1964).

There is one further reason why it makes sense to examine religion as a resource for prevention. As we have noted elsewhere, religious world views and practices have several unique things to add to secular perspectives and approaches to the prevention of problems and the promotion of well-being (Maton & Pargament, 1987).

1. Religious leaders have at times been particularly successful in articulating visions of what their communities can and should become, and what each individual is "called" to do with his/her special talents in life. For instance, the Reverend Martin Luther King Junior formed a powerful link between the realities of racism in America and a spiritually-based vision of freedom and hope and, through this linkage, generated an intense passion and commitment to social justice among hundreds of thousands of people.
2. Religious systems can also provide human service professionals with models for the development of communities which share a commitment to a set of values, a tradition of symbols and rituals, and an identity which locate and mark them within the continuous flow of time and the myriad possibilities of experience.
3. The human service community might take note of certain central values within the religious world, such as the notion of "servant," helping others even at the possible cost to oneself, or "spirituality," the connection and commitment of the person to a force, being, or phenomena which goes beyond humankind.
4. Finally, the world views of religious and human service communities may complement rather than conflict with each other. Although it is easy to exaggerate either position, there are some basic truths bound up in both views of the world. It is true (as psychologists say) that people are capable of creating and constructing unique approaches to life, but it is just as true (as religions say) that our resources, control, and lives themselves are finite commodities. The critical question of concern to us all is how we live in a world characterized both by possibilities and by limitations. And the question is hard enough that it deserves more than one answer. Thus, it should not be troubling to us that, in their answer, psychologists have had quite a bit to say about maximizing the power we do have in life, or that, in their answer, religions have had a lot to say about the way we come to grips with our mortality. Neither answer is wrong, but then again neither answer is complete. Both are necessary as we consider the character of life in its fullest sense.

The purpose of this book is to make a case for the value of religion as a resource for preventive action. In focussing on religion as a *resource*, we are not trying to deny the dysfunctional, burdensome, even crippling roles religion can play in life. But the human service audience is already quite familiar with psychological discussions of religion's "dark side" (e.g., Ellis, Freud). Less systematic attention has been paid to the resources religion can bring to bear to the realm of prevention and promotion. That will be our focus in this book. From the outset, it is important to admit that we are not talking about a well-established literature here. Instead, through these papers, we hope to highlight the promise of conceptual, empirical and practical work in this area, and build a foundation for future efforts.

PART ONE:
RELIGION AS A RESOURCE FOR PREVENTIVE ACTION: CONCEPTUAL AND EMPIRICAL FOUNDATIONS

The first part of this book lays a general foundation for preventive work in the religious arena. The papers survey and distill a far-reaching and important literature on the nature of religion as a personal and social force in American society. They draw out important implications for the interface of religion with individual life, community functioning, and prevention.

Setting the stage, the first two papers provide a sociocultural analysis of the role of religion. Spilka and Bridges focus on the role of modernist and traditionalist religious theologies in legitimating social, economic, and political power in society. They conclude that whereas traditionalist religious theology tends to protect the existing social system and support individualistic preventive views and actions, modernist theology is more likely to challenge the status quo and support transactional and context-sensitive prevention activities.

Roberts examines the influence of various religion-cultural megatrends in society in terms of their implications for religion and mental health. In particular, he argues that secularization, and individualization of culture and religion, have diminished the traditional potential of religion to combat anomie and alienation, and to provide the foundation for a psychological sense of community in social life. The implications for interventions to counteract these megatrends are addressed.

The next three papers are comprehensive reviews of large, empirical literatures. Payne, Bergin, Bielema, and Jenkins review the empirical literature concerning the relationship between religion and mental health. They conclude from their review that the empirical evidence for a positive influence of religion is relatively strong concerning general well-being, personal adjustment, family cohesion, and lifestyle, and relatively weak or nonexistent concerning serious mental illness.

Levin and Vanderpool review the literature in the area of religion, physical health, and illness. Like Payne, Bergin, Bielema, and Jenkins they conclude that there is empirical evidence in support of a salutary influence of religion on health. In particular, they find that religion is positively associated with a variety of subjective and clinical health outcomes, regardless of the aspect of religiosity assessed (e.g., attendance, prayer, subjective religiosity).

Koenig reviews the research linking religion to adaptive health outcomes among the elderly. Evidence is mounting, he concludes, that religious beliefs and practices buffer the particular stresses of life which become increasingly common with age.

As is clear even from these brief summaries, the papers in this section encompass a diversity of topics and perspectives on the interface of religion and prevention. For instance, they address a wide array of potential preventive outcomes, including mental and physical health (Levin & Vanderpool; Payne, Bergin, Bielema, & Jenkins), populations (Koenig), social issues (Spilka & Bridges), and psychological sense of community (Roberts). They also vary in regard to the pathways of religious influence explored, ranging from personal religion as a source of adaptive beliefs and practices (Koenig), to denominational teachings as a directive for behavioral lifestyle (Levin & Vanderpool) to theological religion as a foundation for societal power arrangements (Spilka & Bridges). Paralleling this latter source of variation, the papers vary widely in their implications for intervention; for instance, they suggest a range of levels of prevention intervention strategies from the individual to the congregational to the sociocultural. Finally, the papers vary in the extent of optimism about religion as a preventive resource. Payne, Bergin, Bielema, and Jenkins, Levin and Vanderpool and Koenig appear the most optimistic about religion as a salutary influence, Spilka and Bridges present a mixed perspective, and Roberts appears the least hopeful.

The variety of perspectives and foci represented in the five papers underscore the complexity and diversity of religion in general, and of the interface of religion and prevention in particular. This indeed is an important understanding to be gained from these papers and this book more generally: simplistic, undifferentiated understanding of religion, of prevention, and of religion as a resource for preventive action will likely prove counterproductive.

The complexity and diversity notwithstanding, an important, convergent theme can be discerned across these five papers: religion is a potentially important, little understood, underutilized, and unique resource in the preventive intervention arena. Religion is different than the human services; religiously based intervention has both strengths and weaknesses distinctly different from those of the human services. And yet religion shares with the human services a concern for the well-being of people and society.

PART TWO:
RELIGION AS A RESOURCE FOR PREVENTIVE ACTION:
TOWARD THE PROMISED LAND

Having laid a conceptual and empirical foundation for religion as a preventive resource, we continue the effort to describe this promising, yet largely unexplored landscape for social scientists and practitioners in the second part of the book. The papers of this section focus more specifically and more concretely on programs, processes, and populations which hold important implications for preventive and promotive action. As in the first section, the papers are wide-ranging in style and focus. Together, however, they underscore important themes and provide an important guide through the landscape of religion, prevention, and promotion.

The Lay of the Land

The papers describe something of the terrain the researcher or practitioner interested in religion and prevention finds him or herself in. The map of this terrain is marked by several features. First of all, it is *enduring*, a point made clear by Thom Moore in his detailing of the long history and evolution of the black church as an instrument of empowerment and social change for African-Americans.

The terrain is not only enduring, it is *diverse*, ranging from the formal religious programs of the kind designed by established congregations and denominations (Cohen, Mowbray, Gillette, & Thompson), the private process embodied in the nontraditional setting, illustrated by Klass' study of the religious aspects of solace among bereaved parents who are members of Compassionate Friends, to the multiple pathways of religious influence in the coping process described by Hathaway and Pargament.

While this terrain is not a completely alien one, it is in some respects *unique*. Through their interviews with mainstream Christian workers, Anderson, Maton, and Ensor delineate several distinctive features of religious preventive and promotive work, including notions such as the sanctity and continuity of religious actions, and the critical contributions of faith and religious community. In the same vein, Rappaport and Simkins underscore the special healing and empowering role religious narratives can play for individuals and communities.

Finally, like other landscapes, there are potential *barriers* and *pitfalls* to the individual interested in prevention and promotion. As Malony discusses in his paper on congregational consultation, mistrust, misunderstanding, stereotyping, coaptation, and failed promises are some of the dangers that arise when religious and human service communities come together to prevent or solve problems.

The Promise: Religion as a Preventive Resource

As each of the chapters in this section attest, religion has been, and can be, an effective and empowering force. However, the chapters vary greatly in the perspective through which religion and religious action are viewed as a preventive resource. The first three chapters primarily adopt a psychological perspective; the next three attempt to capture the religious perspective; and the last four chapters focus on issues of religion-human services partnership and action.

The psychological perspective. The Hathaway and Pargament chapter focuses in depth on one particularly important mechanism of religious influence — the role of religion in the coping process. The authors define a variety of points of interface between religion and the coping process, including critical situations, appraisals, the forces guiding coping, specific coping activities, and the outcomes of the coping process. The authors emphasize the complexity of religion as it interfaces with the coping process, and draw out implications for interventions which focus on preventing negative events, cognitive stress inoculation, competency building, and resource provision.

The chapter by Klass focuses on religion, broadly defined, in an explicitly nonreligious setting — Compassionate Friends, a self-help group for bereaved parents. In a poignant portrayal of parental coping with child loss, Klass argues that achieving solace is the key, religious task for the bereaved parent. The near universality of belief in the child's existence in an afterlife, and the importance of support from similar others in achieving solace, are also emphasized. The chapter exemplifies the importance for religious and human service professionals of learning how people, in community contexts, cope with the difficulties of life.

In his chapter, Jenkins considers the preventive implications of religion for people with cancer. Jenkins highlights religion as a coping resource, as a source of adaptive lifestyles and behaviors, and as providing social support through church involvement. He argues that collaboration between secular and religious workers can enhance the health-promotion and illness-prevention potential of religion and religious settings.

Diverse as they are, the papers by Hathaway and Pargament, Klass, and Jenkins all take a psychological perspective on religion as a preventive influence. The next three chapters consider religion and preventive more from the vantage point of religion.

The religious perspective. Anderson, Maton and Ensor present a religious perspective on prevention, based on exploratory interviews with a select group of religious workers. The religious workers' holistic view of persons and of problems, encompassing spiritual, social, material and psychological components, is emphasized as a distinctive preventive resource. The promotion of individual well-being, broadly defined, is described as the salient goal guiding social ministry work. The authors suggest that religion and the human services constitute distinctly different cultures, but are hopeful that cross-cultural dialogue and joint endeavors will contribute to viable collaboration.

Rappaport and Simkins propose that the empowering potential of religion resides in part in the powerful nature of the "community narratives" told in the religious setting. They describe key community narratives which appear successful in healing and empowering members in a specific, non-denominational congregation. Narratives described include "you are lovable and you are valuable"; "we are all broken and all capable of being healed"; "you are a gift"; and "God wastes nothing in moving toward the goal of building character."

Moore highlights the history of the black church, delineating how it has served as a buffer, resource, social change agent, and empowering community for African-Americans in a larger, alien society. He suggests that knowledge of the successful self-development of the church can prove a valuable resource for blacks today, and underscores the importance of mutual help, rather than external professional intervention, as central to viable, future church evolution.

Religion-human services partnership and action. The final four chapters in the book focus on some of the very different ways religion can come to life through preventive action. The first two of these chapters deal with prevention in churches and synagogues. Thorsheim and Roberts illustrate the potential empowering role of congregations, highlighting the importance of leadership and personal narrative. Specifically, they emphasize the importance of reciprocal ministry, in which clergy provide opportunities for congregational members to take part in meaningful, sharing, mutual empowering activity. The authors encourage human service providers to get to know clergy on an informal basis, to listen to their stories, and to encourage them to engage members in mutual empowerment and meaningful activity.

Malony, in contrast to the previous authors, presents a more critical view of religion as a resource for preventive action. Adopting an explicitly organizational perspective, he delineates ways that the survival concerns of religious settings limit their potential. Malony highlights potential resources for prevention, and encourages organizational consultants to help mobilize that potential.

The final two chapters consider preventive programs of partnership between religions and human service systems. In their chapter on the black church, Eng and Hatch focus on the church as a "mediating structure" for black citizens in society. Specifically, they underscore the church's potential for preventing physical illness in black citizens. They demonstrate the value of a "lay health advisor" model in which members of local congregations are recruited, trained and supported in bringing knowledge about illness-prevention behaviors into the local church setting. They also outline the challenges for church-human services collaboration in prevention work.

Finally, Cohen, Mowbray, Gillette and Thompson focus on religious institutions' involvement in a pressing social task—preventing homelessness. The authors present examples of action projects in which religious organizations have contributed to this effort through advocacy, community investment, and community development. Cohen and his colleagues also discuss barriers which impede collaboration between religious and secular groups in such endeavors, and the importance of "painstaking, incremental trust-building" to the development of viable religious-secular partnerships.

PATHWAYS TO THE PROMISED LAND: TEN COMMANDMENTS FOR PREVENTION AND PROMOTION IN RELIGIOUS SETTINGS

What are the practical lessons to be drawn from these theoretical, conceptual, and action-oriented papers on religion, prevention, and promotion? Admittedly, this is a new area of thought, research, and practice. Nevertheless, early as it is in its development, we feel the literature suggests several important guiding principles. We conclude with these principles, the "ten commandments" for prevention and promotion in the religious realm. Keep in mind, however, that *these* commandments are not written in stone, and will likely evolve over time.

First Commandment: Know the Phenomena

The more distant and removed we are from phenomena, the more simple and uniform they appear to be. This aphorism holds true for the phenomena of religion and prevention. From a distance they seem to be straightforward processes, but when they are examined more closely, as they have been here, it becomes clear that each is quite diverse and complex. An appreciation for the rich, variegated nature of religion and prevention is critical to effective action in this arena.

Second Commandment: Know the Local Setting

The settings in which preventive and promotive activities occur have their own distinctive traditions, goals, and norms for behavior. Religious settings are no exception to this rule. They too have their own unique histories, ideologies, and structures for accomplishing their missions and maintaining themselves as systems. Learning something about the special character of any particular setting is another prerequisite to successful prevention and promotion.

Third Commandment: Know the Level of Analysis

In these chapters, religion has been described as a multi-level phenomenon, one which is expressed through individuals, groups, congregations, denominations, religious communities, and society more generally. Similarly, as the papers taken together show, efforts to prevent problems and promote well-being can take place in any of these strata. In the relatively unchartered landscape of religious prevention and promotion, it is particularly important to simultaneously consider levels of problem-definition and of problem-solution, for solutions are not likely to be effective unless they are targeted to the appropriate level of analysis.

Fourth Commandment: Know Oneself

The notion of the human service professional as objective and detached, with only the well-being of those he or she serves in mind, is particularly hard to sustain when it comes to the religious realm. Like others, we carry along our own world view and attitudes toward religion, shaped from childhood to adulthood through our families, schools, religious systems, professions, and society. Few of us emerge from this process without biases towards religion of one sort or another. The challenging, but important task is to become aware of these biases, positive or negative, and to become sensitive to how they can affect preventive or promotive work in the religious domain.

Fifth Commandment: Do Not Worship False Gods

The traditional ideals of science (e.g., definitive experiments; universal theories) and of psychological intervention (e.g., professional control; value-free involvement) may impede, and disrupt, research and action in the domain of religion and prevention. Alternative ideals are necessary, and may include the valuing of simultaneous-divergent explanations of phenomena, local as opposed to universal theory, sharing of control with those being studied or helped, and acknowledging the centrality of values in science and application.

Sixth Commandment: Do Not Disempower

Our goal is to enhance the psychological and material resources available to groups in society, not to diminish them. Above all, we need to avoid doing harm by diminishing various sources of psychological and material power for individuals and groups, including those sources we may not understand or personally value. In the domain of religion and prevention, respect for the spiritual dimension of life of those we work with and have impact upon is particularly important.

Seventh Commandment: Seek Out New Forms and Means of Collaboration and Partnership

To learn about and work with religion and religious personnel, new forms and means of collaboration may be necessary. These may include, though not be limited to, creating shared narratives, reciprocal ministry, participant-research or participant-action roles in our own religious settings, and mutual empowerment.

Eighth Commandment: Be Humble

The theory and practice of prevention are relatively new historical developments. As recent, and perhaps even more tenuous, has been the relationship between religious and human service communities. When it comes to religion and prevention, then, there are few grounds for arrogance or smugness. There are important limits to what we know about these worlds and how effectively we work within them. Appreciation for what we *do not know* is another essential guide for work with religion as a preventive resource.

Ninth Commandment: Seek Wisdom

We need to learn to ask the most important questions about individuals, communities, health and well-being, and to seek answers through a diversity of means and approaches, both traditional and novel. We have much to learn from, and can create many opportunities to collaborate with and serve the millions of Americans who search for meaning and community in religious settings and spiritual contexts. As we seek wisdom we should, like Moses, seek guidance in high places, looking simultaneously for hard evidence and light.

Tenth Commandment: Celebrate Paradox and Diversity

To facilitate progress in research and action, it is important to understand and appreciate different, even contradictory forms of spirituality, religious coping, personal meaning, community, status, and power—in the lives of individuals and communities. In so doing, we will avoid the temptation to remake religion and religious settings into our image.

For human service workers to date, it has not been clear where or how the quest for the promised land concerning prevention and promotion should proceed. We hope this book on religion, prevention, and well-being will provide insight, enhance motivation, and serve as a resource for those interested in broadening the quest to encompass the domain of religion and religious settings.

REFERENCES

Beit-Hallahmi, B. (1974). Psychology of religion 1880-1930: The rise and fall of a psychological movement. *Journal of the History of the Behavioral Sciences, 10,* 84-90.

Carson, R. J. (1976). *Mental health centers and local clergy: A source book of sample projects.* Washington, DC: Community Mental Health Institute.

Crim, K., Bullard, R. A., & Shinn, L.D. (Eds.). (1989). *The perennial dictionary of world religions.* San Francisco: Harper and Row.

Edelstein, B. A., & Michelson, L. (Eds.). (1986). *Handbook of prevention.* New York: Plenum Press.

Frazier, E. F. (1964). *The Negro church in America.* New York: Schocken.

Gallup, G., Jr., & Castelli, J. (1989). *The people's religion: American faith in the 90's.* New York: Macmillan Publishing Company.

The Holy Bible. Authorized King James Version, Victoria, Australia: World Bible Publishers.

Jacquet, C. (Ed.). (1989). *The yearbook of American and Canadian churches 1989.* Nashville: Abingdon.

Maton, K. I., & Pargament, K. I. (1987). The roles of religion in prevention and promotion. *Prevention in Human Services. 5*(2), 161-205.

Princeton Religion Research Center. (1984). *Religion in America.*

Rosten, L. (1975). *Religions of America: Ferment and faith in an age of crisis.* New York: Simon and Schuster.

Smart, N. (1989). *The world's religions.* Englewood Cliffs: Prentice-Hall.

Whitlock, G. E. (1973). *Preventive psychology and the church.* Philadelphia: Westminster Press.

PART ONE:
RELIGION AS A RESOURCE FOR PREVENTIVE ACTION: CONCEPTUAL AND EMPIRICAL FOUNDATIONS

Religious Perspectives on Prevention: The Role of Theology

Bernard Spilka

University of Denver

Robert A. Bridges

University of Colorado at Denver

SUMMARY. Both conceptually and in actual practice, the Judeo-Christian heritage has always been involved in the prevention of individual and social problems. Focusing on American Protestant Christianity, two main theological trends, traditional and modernist, are delineated and explored with respect to their positions concerning prevention. Beginning with the premise that theology performs as cultural ideology, and acts to legitimate social, economic, and political power, in the main, traditional theology is shown to support conservative individualistic preventive views and actions. There are notable exceptions to this position, but they have not been culturally influential. In contrast, modernist theology challenges the status quo by adopting a collective social orientation to prevention that stresses the significance of transaction and context on all levels from the situational to the societal. Relative to the development and utilization of prevention ideas and practices, these variant theological positions are likely to find expression in competing political agendas.

In its over 2000 year history, the western religious heritage has always been a party to psychosocial distress and disorder. Paradoxically, religion sometimes supports conditions that exacerbate human misfortune while concurrently working to alleviate suffering (Moberg, 1962; Tawney, 1926). Still, as Maton and Pargament (1987) poignantly note, "Religion

---

Reprints may be obtained from Bernard Spilka, University of Denver, Colorado Seminary, Department of Psychology, University Park, Denver, CO 80208.

19

represents an important resource for efforts to prevent significant personal and social problems" (p. 161).

This historical record of religious ambivalence attests to the difficulty within Christianity of attaining theological accord regarding social issues and remedial methods. In terms of preventing social problems, the most pertinent theological categories involve human nature, sin and evil, the nature of God, and the means of salvation. These are most relevant to prevention precisely because they directly address such concerns as health and disease, individual and social responsibility, and questions of ultimate meaning.

Though there has been increasing recognition that the problems of men and women often relate to their place in the social order, religious bodies have had great difficulty addressing social issues in collective terms. Historically, Christian churches and their supporting theologies view human problems as products of individual action (sin). The accompanying suffering has been seen as "one's cross to bear" upon the road to salvation. Moral instruction has likewise aimed at inculcating righteousness in the individual. Only recently has such education attempted to broaden personal morality to include the cultural milieu.

Where once Christianity defined a more or less single religious direction for all humanity, in today's world, this focus has become more complex and fragmented. Secularization and the increasing significance of social science has stimulated a wide range of both theological accommodation and resistance to these new religious views. Generally speaking, the contemporary task is one of making choices between individualism and community, and supernaturalism versus naturalism. Broadly defined, the issue is religion in or out of the world. Classical theological doctrines that denote the nature of God, humanity, evil, sin, salvation, sanctification, justification, the Bible, and so forth, have been modified. When these modern tenets are compared with their traditional counterparts, the sociocultural significance of religious institutions and their ideologies is made explicit. Their import for the broad realm of prevention is, of course part of this picture.[1]

Since theology, for example, has always had much to say about marital relations, it is relevant to the issue of domestic violence. Typically, in such situations, the woman is psychologically victimized and socially ostracized. Preventive measures may be variously understood depending on one's theological perspective. For example, a traditional perspective is likely to adopt an almost exclusively personalistic orientation to this problem. Marital discord is regarded a manifestation of sin, as neither the husband nor wife is living in accordance with God's will. The woman's sin may be defined as failure to submit herself to the divinely ordained role proper for a wife. This is often viewed as the sin of pride. Conversely, the man's sin may be a refusal to properly exercise his authority and husbandly responsibilities as spiritual leader and shepherd of the family.

In contrast, a modernist theological orientation looks at the issue of domestic violence in inclusive terms. Sin now considers the individual, society, and culture. The sociocultural milieu, by perpetuating dualistic standards for men and women, supports the attitude that women are "second class citizens." This patriarchal outlook implicitly abets male aggression toward females. The modernist perspective therefore indicts individuals and institutions alike. Both are culpable and sinful to the degree they maintain psychosocial support for what is fundamentally "systemic sin" that fosters injustice. In specific, a modernist-feminist viewpoint sees sexism and its cultural backing as "the original sin" (Daly, 1973). Personal sin lies in the victim's refusal to leave the abusive situation as well as in the perpetrator's continued violent acts. Preventive action now includes removal of the victim from the situation, therapeutic intervention for the abuser, and sociocultural correction of sexual inequities.

Previous research (Bridges, 1989) indicates that modernist-traditional theological understandings of male-female relationships, and the presumed roles of each sex to God, are sharply polarized. These differences also relate to variant images of God, human nature, and salvation, leading to contrasting views of what preventive measures should be employed. Workers in this area would then utilize different methods with traditionalists than with modernists.

We are suggesting that the core elements relating religion and prevention emanate from the ideological (theological) bases of the Judeo-Christian tradition. Our focus is upon (1) the dominant historical form of Christianity that prevails in the American milieu, i.e., those views that underscore the American value of "individualism;" and (2) the more modern emphasis of Christianity upon the values of relationship and communal cooperation. We must also recognize that both of these perspectives have been influenced by what Cogley (1968) calls our "secular age." As Niebuhr (1957) observed "theological opinions have their roots in the relationship of the religious life to the cultural and political conditions prevailing in any group of Christians" (p. 16).

Although this issue goes well beyond the present paper as it concerns the legitimation and transformation of religious themes into sociocultural norms (see below), it does affect our ideas about prevention. For example, Rotenberg's (1978) demonstration of the influence of Calvinist ideas on modern secular conceptions of deviance on both personal and societal levels supports not only abnormal forms of self-blame and possibly depressive and suicidal reactions, but also individualistic punishment-treatment approaches to personal and social disorder.

THEOLOGY IN THE CONTEXT OF WESTERN CULTURE

Theologies function as world-views for many people, and have been subtly integrated into the basic values of society. Thus they make claims not only about God, but also the nature of the cosmos, the natural world, social reality, and humanity. Theology further offers interpretations of personal and social life-situations through metaphysical assumptions that provide "a coherent set of categories for the interpretation of all experience" (Whitehead, 1929, p. 7). These assumptions are often couched in a theological terminology that connects life experience to an "ultimate reality." As Novak (1968) observed:

> . . . the astute reader of theological discourse will soon discover that every sentence in such discourse, however, obliquely, refers to human actions, or dispositions, or programs. . . . The "Kingdom of God" . . . has an other worldly, apocalyptic concomitant; yet in its own right, it is a concrete this-worldly ideal. Theology studies ultimate visions of communal relationships and personal identity, insofar as these affect actual human experience. (p. 52)

Theology as legitimation. In previous work, the authors suggested that "theologies . . . represent ideas which become legitimated by being religiously attached and interpreted so that they influence the world-views of large groups of people" (Bridges & Spilka, 1988, p. 2). The term "legitimation" is used by Berger (1967) to denote "socially objectivated 'knowledge' that serves to explain and justify the social order" (p. 29). Basically, legitimations define realities. Berger and Luckmann (1967) further assert that "legitimations explain the institutional order by ascribing cognitive validity to its meanings . . . and justif(y) the order by giving normative dignity to its practical imperatives" (p. 93). Finally, Berger (1967) notes religion "has been historically the most widespread and effective instrumentality of legitimation" (p. 32). This "instrumentality" is initially formed in the theologies that both justify the spiritual order and its sociocultural context by giving the latter divine (ontological) status.

Among other emphases, some of these theologies are highly individualistic, others social. With regard to prevention, the personal or collective implications of various programs may determine whether religionists and churches offer a particular program support or criticism.

THE NATURE AND CONTENT OF THEOLOGY

Even though theology has been defined as "an undistorted hearing of God's word with a view to salvation" (Rahner & Vorgrimler, 1965, p. 456), historically and contemporaneously, the message has not been clear. There are not only theologies for every religious group that has ever been formed, but within such bodies, agreement comes hard. All we can say is that theologians have attempted to apply scripture and theology to every aspect of life, and in the process, as already noted, theologies have become "world views" for many people. These are basically interpretations of scripture, the religious writings of past thinkers, and current experience.

To illustrate the kind of problem that has implications for prevention, we may examine that most central issue in theology, the religious path to salvation. This has been a major source of conflict in religious quarters. Conservatives of a Calvinist bent argue that the "attempt to reform individuals, primarily by improving their income and living conditions ignores Christ's method of bettering society by remaking individuals" (Berkhof quoted in Smith, 1985, p. 145). This choice continues the classical tradition of effecting social change by inculcating morality (righteousness) in the individual. In contrast, religious modernists locate the sin in the individual and the social order. To illustrate, the traditionalist would support self-monitoring by an industry in order to maintain ethical standards; the modernist would sponsor legislation to punish wrong-doers while attempting to strengthen individual moral codes. Theologically, the issue is whether each person pursues salvation as a single, separate entity in prime relationship to God, or gains salvation through a "consciousness that human existence . . . is the process by which men and women make themselves by making their own cultures and societies" (Ogden, 1979, p. 12). This latter view sponsors community action, whether it be political, economic, or social.

This individual-social dichotomy is further exacerbated by the difficulties of transformations that have taken place in theological concepts over time. If scripture is to be the ultimate reference, the issue becomes which scripture and for what purpose is it to be used. For example, Schoenfeld (1989) points out the significance of justice in the Old Testament, and its replacement by love (agape) in the New Testament. Of import to the social role of prevention, he notes the association of justice with power, and observes that

> . . . an emphasis on agape and minimization of justice has important consequences for political views supported by the Christian church. The most important ones are a conservative political orientation coupled with an opposition to social change. It is for this reason that liberal theologians are seeking to give new meaning to the New Testament's ideal of love so that it can be used in their quest for social justice. (p. 243)

In other words, emphasizing love constitutes a politically conservative agenda that takes religion out of the cultural sphere, and places responsibility fully on the individual.

We have been speaking of Christian theology rather broadly, when each of the 200 plus Christian religious organizations in the United States claims uniqueness, though their theologies greatly overlap. Moving to a level above the many specific points that distinguish among these groups, a manageable number of theological perspectives may be abstracted. These are usually identified as fundamentalist, pentecostal, evangelical, process, feminist, and liberation. Theoretical distinctions among these empirically reduce to two broad patterns (Bridges, 1989). Basically, these may be denoted as *traditional* and *modernist*. The former includes the first three forms noted above, while the latter contains the last three ideologies. In brief, traditional theology emphasizes Scripture as the revealed "truth" about the world, regardless of the teachings of modern secular knowledge. It seeks to maintain pre-modern views of (1) God as omnipotent, omniscient, and omnipresent, and (2) of human nature as "fallen" and totally dependent on God. Modernist theology uses human experience (1) as the basis of scriptural interpretation, and (2) to reconcile traditional concepts with current knowledge. Relative to prevention, the traditionalist treats sickness and disorder, both personal and social, as acts of God. The modernist views such problems as primarily the result of ignorance and systemic sin.

Although we use the terms traditional and modernist more or less as pure types, these are not unitary, invariant positions. Differences exist among those so labeled, not only on an individual level, but also between the groups these designations cover. For example, evangelicals are likely to differ from pentecostals and fundamentalists on many issues, even though there is much overlap. Similarly, there is often variation between process and liberation theologians. The implications of theology for prevention will, however, center about these two theological positions.

THE NATURE OF PREVENTION

Nearly 60 years ago, Adolph Meyer wrote:

> Communities have to learn what they produce in the way of mental problems and waste of human opportunities, and with such knowledge they will rise from mere charity and mere mending, or hasty propaganda to well balanced early care, prevention and general gain of health. (cited in Bloom, 1977, p. 69)

Adopting this premise, public health and welfare services and the helping professions began to focus on strategies of prevention which decrease the likelihood of disorder and disease. Typically, such strategies not only recognize various forms of prevention, but also determine populations in need of preventive care plus the types of delivery systems best suited to such groups. Caplan's (1964) model of prevention processes denotes *primary* prevention as concerned with forestalling the disordered state of affairs before it gets started. *Secondary* prevention is comprised of efforts to interfere with the process once it has started, and *tertiary* prevention attempts to contain the effects of the problem process after it is over.

THEOLOGICAL IMPLICATIONS FOR PREVENTION

At some level, theology is always buttressed by Scripture, and rather than resolving disagreement, such reference can exacerbate conflict. For example, Bloom (1977) shows how disease and prevention may involve the physical environment (e.g., pollution, psychological fit, modifiability, etc.), and theological controversy involving scripture is evident in a current debate on the issue of environmental preservation versus exploitation (Eckberg & Blocker, 1989). In Genesis 1:28 humanity is told that it should both subdue and replenish the earth. Some religionists emphasize the first instruction, i.e., humanity's dominion over nature; others stress both concerns and espouse a stewardship role. Religion and theology can thus legitimate either the abuse of the environment or favor its conservation.

The relationship of theology to prevention is not simply abstract meat for debate among theologians, or between religionists and those engaged in prevention efforts. Such viewpoints often translate into political, economic, and social conflicts that may involve violence and destructive behavior. A self proclaimed "moral majority" expresses itself by taking action against an opposition, "secular humanists," which is usually identified with liberal causes. Those supporting progressive prevention efforts may find themselves engaging in similar activity. For example, witness the extreme actions of those favoring or opposing abortion and animal rights. From a liberation perspective, Assmann (1976) notes that "against systems which perpetuate violent oppression of the poor, violent actions may be necessary countermeasures" (p. 121). One side of this struggle denies the validity of a collective agenda, while their antagonists see social reform as the essence of their faith.

In like manner, to claim that AIDS is God's punishment for homosexuality, is unlikely to support medical and social efforts at AIDS prevention. The development of the New Christian Right and religio-political movements such as the Moral Majority represent theologies that oppose efforts to solve/prevent problems by human means in many cases since the difficulties are assumed to be ordained by God. For example, here one finds opposition to the provision of birth control information, the use of public funds for abortion, and the Equal Rights Amendment among other social concerns (Wilcox, 1989).

THEOLOGY AND THE CONCEPTUAL MODEL OF PRIMARY PREVENTION

Sin and the Impossibility of Primary Prevention

While the aforementioned definitions of primary, secondary, and tertiary levels of prevention are useful, their distinguishing characteristics may become blurred in theological conception and practice. For example, primary prevention attempts to intervene in the problem-process before it can be manifested as a social problem. From a theological viewpoint, irrespective of doctrinal differences between traditional and modern orientations, the disordered state of affairs is regarded as an existential given. In other words, the pre-conditions for disease and disorder (e.g., original sin) are always present.

Strictly speaking, primary prevention is therefore a theological impossibility because the world and all humanity exist within a state of "sin." Invariably formulated in terms of the "Fall" — the fall of both nature and humankind, sin is defined by traditionalist groups as "rebellion against God's righteousness" (Fundamentalist view); "rebellion against God's authority, manifest in hate and human pride" (Pentecostal view); or as "an excess of self-love and egocentricity" (Evangelical view). In short, these views hold that "sin is more than missing the mark, it is also a fatal sickness" (Bloesch, 1982, p. 93). We should not overlook the use of "sickness," for this occurs to people as single, separate entities. Corrective possibility, must then rely exclusively on the individual who is paradoxically, totally dependent on the supernatural grace of a transcendent God. A millennial hope can be theorized, but short-term amelioration of social problems must be ruled out. The theological impossibility of primary prevention can thus eliminate all social action while one prays for the end-time in which individual perfection will be attained and Christ will return to earth.

Sin may also be interpreted in historical, social, and cultural terms as modernist theology espouses. Evil can be viewed as "oppressive structures, i.e., social, cultural, political, and economic, sexual, racial, and so forth, that aid the exploitation of humanity" (Liberationist view). Sin therefore symbolizes a pre-existing state of disorder into which we are born, and in which we live our lives. The best we can do is engage in measures of damage control. Though assessment of this "damage" and the methods of "control" (intervention) vary as a function of different theological perspectives, the only theological resource people have is to overcome sin via efforts at salvation. We thus return to this individual-collective issue which is clearly basic to understanding how churches and their theologies may aid or hinder efforts at prevention.

Social Factors and Individual Fate in Traditional Theology

Caplan's (1964) psychiatric orientation treats primary prevention as a community concept. "It does not seek to prevent a specific person from becoming sick. Instead, it seeks to reduce the risk of a whole population, so that, although some may become ill, their number will be reduced" (p. 26). Here primary prevention emphasizes both the "causes of illness and the reasons for health" (p. 12). Caplan further claims that certain "host factors" i.e., age, sex, socioeconomic status, and ethnicity may be termed "factors of individual fate . . . which cannot be manipulated" (p. 27). If Caplan means that individuals possessing these host factors are not targets for prevention efforts, he has adopted the classic individualism of conservative theology.

Traditional theology perceives "host factors" as expressions of "God's will," omniscience, and plan for individuals. With regard to gender, this position avers that "every entity from greatest to least (has) its status and purpose in the graded hierarchy of reality" (Barbour, 1966, p. 18). Within this "chain of being," the lines of power are clearly drawn. "Females are naturally subject to the male's guidance and domination because that is the . . . order of creation" (Bridges, 1989, p. 282).

In like manner, race becomes an inconsequential factor in which biblically, "there is neither male or female, slave or master (black, brown, yellow, or white) in the body of Christ. All are slaves in Christ" (Acts 17: 24-28). Issues of "racism" cannot be collectively defined, but are variously understood as "an extension of personal sin" (Fundamentalist view); "our natural rebellion against God's law" (Pentecostal view); or "man's egocentricity which leads him to defy God and use his neighbor in a way that is contrary to God's will" (Evangelical view).

With respect to socioeconomic class, one need go no further than Calvin's doctrine of "pre-election," in which economic status is regarded as a mark of God's grace and favor towards the elect. Simply put, the poor are poor because God has so ordained them. A socially well-ingrained variant of this theme is the widespread belief in a "just world" (Rubin & Peplau, 1975). "God's in his heaven — All's right with the world" becomes a theological statement which justifies the status quo, and informs believers that one's place in society may be predestined from on high — "You always have the poor with you." Traditional theology places these "ascribed matters of individual fate" beyond the potential of human alteration.

Social Factors and Individual Fate in Modernist Theology

Modernist theologies do not see the foregoing issues as predetermined structural "accidents" of nature and destiny that cannot be manipulated. Viewing them as "matters of individual fate" constitutes part of an ideology that can inculcate helplessness in those who are oppressed, while simultaneously legitimating the status quo and its supportive power structures. In contrast, modernist theology holds that "while all may be sinners, not all are oppressors; while oppressed and oppressors are both victims [of the status quo], they are not victims in the same way: (Graham, 1987, p. 8). "Oppression refers to the social and cultural experience of being exploited and negated psychologically, economically, culturally, and politically by virtue of one's identification with a gender, race, or class" (Graham, 1987, p. 7). Because these referents have an impersonal character, those with power can easily deny that they personally contribute to states of injustice. Such an attitude may be rationalized by maintaining that the "underclass must bear the blame" for its disadvantaged situation (Bridges, 1989), or that there is nothing illegal about one's behaviors that create or perpetuate injustice for others.

In keeping with Schoenfeld's (1989) views on justice, modernist theologies attempt to reestablish the primacy of morality over strict legality by calling for renewed emphasis upon the messages of the Old Testament in general, and on prophetic scripture in particular. The latter calls for reform of sociocultural systems which maintain structures of injustice. According to Gutierrez (1973), "the God of Exodus is the God of history and of political liberation . . . The struggle for justice is also the struggle for the Kingdom of God" (pp. 157-168). These and other writings based on the Old Testament stress collective social responsibility.

The problem is therefore not sex, race, or class, but how these factors are regarded individually and culturally. Self-serving sociopolitical beliefs can support a sinful state of affairs, and practices that sustain oppressive forces. The traditionalist faithful should not question this "natural order."

Theology and Avenues to Action

A prime goal of Caplan's (1964) model of psychiatric primary prevention is to move "toward improving nonspecific helping resources in the community and in reducing those conditions which we have some reason to believe . . . are conducive to some particular mental disorder" (p. 30). These resources are metaphorically denoted as "provision of supplies." They are defined on three levels: physical, psychosocial, and sociocultural, and are addressed differently by theological traditionalists and modernists.

Because of the individualistic focus of traditional theology, primary preventive measures would emphasize psychosocial resources, particularly the psychological, and minimize the role of physical and sociocultural supports. The psychosocial level permits personal salvation to enter the picture by allowing sin and the fundamental bond between the individual and God to be the crucial factors. This perspective assumes that social problems can only be alleviated through individual religious devices, i.e., faith, prayer, conversion.

Defining the psychosocial level further, Caplan (1964) lists three main components: (1) needs for exchange of love and affection, (2) the need for limitation and control (patterns of self assertion or submission to authority), and (3) needs for participation in [meaningful] joint activity. Disorder at the psychosocial level occurs "if significant others do not perceive, respect, and attempt to satisfy these needs . . . or if satisfactory relationships are interrupted through illness, death, or disillusionment" (Caplan, 1964, p. 32). If these psychosocial requirements are taken literally, they support the individualism of traditional theology. Love is exclusively interpersonal; control refers to self-control and obedience; and joint activity is circumscribed by "Golden rule" notions. The ideal for human relationships is individual commitment to a God that promises eternal life in exchange for personal obedience and devotion. As a program for either the prevention or correction of mental disorders, this is extremely limited and limiting.

The modernist theological perspective teaches a different orientation towards the various "supply provision" levels. All three are interrelated, and cannot be considered separately. Preventive intervention on any one level necessarily impacts the others. The search is for underlying connections among these levels. People and institutions are conceptualized in transactional and dialectical rather than interactional relationships, and individually and collectively they are held morally responsible as being "part of the problem, *and* part of the solution." To speak of primary, secondary, and tertiary prevention as if they were independent, is simply to stress, somewhat expediently, certain aspects of the total prevention process.

THEOLOGY AND SECONDARY AND TERTIARY PREVENTION

In practice, distinctions between primary, secondary, and tertiary forms of prevention often overlap and can become confusing. Bloom (1978) speculates that "it might prove better to return to the older terms of *prevention, treatment, and rehabilitation*" (p. 75). This language reflects more clearly the preventive goals of Judeo-Christian theology whether it be traditional or modernist. From the former perspective, treatment is analogous to "atonement-salvation," and implies individual responsibility. Treatment for the sins and disorders of the human condition is dependent upon a conviction that the sufferings of this world are "tests and tribulations upon the pilgrim's path to glory" (Bridges, 1989, p. 230).

Rehabilitation, from a traditionalist perspective, is fundamentally sanctification — becoming holy and morally pure. In such a view, marital discord may be seen as a "test" from God to both parties to strengthen their souls. Conversion and intense religious experiences are often taken as signs of necessary spiritual growth; however even depression can be regarded as a deepening of one's soul. In this framework, rehabilitation is not a contextual or situational concern. Theoretically, secondary and tertiary preventions do consider these latter issues, but the individual is most likely to be the object of action.

Modernist theologies, as already noted, emphasize sociocultural factors via the theme of salvation by liberation. This allows cultural, political, and economic factors to come into play. The problem is understanding how such forces are manifested in everyday life and personal disorder. The idea that theology is essentially political and "fundamentally committed to the individual's salvation of the whole world" (Solle, 1971, p. 60) is difficult to translate into strategic terms. Still, efforts are being made along such lines. Feminist theology stresses how women's troubles relate to their lack of equal rights and personal control in life. One form of secondary intervention might insist upon language revision in both the secular and religious domains so that male pronouns no longer include women. A tertiary focus might be the opening of more positions of power and authority for women. The recent development of Feminist therapies also constitutes another current expression of the modernist version of secondary and tertiary prevention.

The modernist emphasis on God's immanence, as morally and ontologically involved in the world, unites the deity and humanity; they become co-creators of both present and future realities. Individuals and social structures are to be simultaneously treated and rehabilitated. There is a potential for such work in today's spiritual therapies for alcohol and drug addiction. Many, however, lean more toward the traditional theological view of a passive person relating to an active God. This is also true of pastoral counseling and therapy which has generally identified with a phenomenological methodology (Stern, 1985; Stern & Marino, 1970). There is, however, some recognition that pastoral therapies should be considered in relation to historical, community, and ideological referents (Graham, 1987; Ramsden, 1970; Strunk, 1985; Vande Kemp, 1985).

THEOLOGY IN ACTION

To date, Maton and Pargament (1987) have provided the definitive action statement on religion and prevention. It "covers the waterfront" on the level of practice by looking at both churches and their supporters relative to inreach and outreach activities. Inreach refers to preventive actions which focus on the individual and/or the church body itself. Outreach emphasizes preventive actions that enter the larger sociocultural milieu. Even though we have stressed the role of traditional theology as sponsoring *inreach*, modernist theologies and institutions perform similar functions. The emphasis is on how the religious world view influences individual thinking and action. With respect to *outreach*, traditional religion generally identifies with sociocultural forces that oppose social change, yet is sometimes associated with a surprising liberalism on domestic welfare issues (Lipset & Raab, 1970).

With regard to inreach, all religious systems are involved in prevention at one level or another, but as Maton and Pargament (1987) point out, there are a variety of *inreach pathways*. Institutional religion may open a number of preventive avenues. For example, in certain traditional churches, deviance may be focused into acceptable expressions or suppressed as the disturbed person is socialized by the religious group. Distressed people may also find a haven from the trials of life within a religious community that emphasizes spiritual defenses against psychosocial pressures. Religious activities may also be therapeutic as prayer, conversion, and religious experience can alleviate anxiety and stress (Spilka, Hood, & Gorsuch, 1985). Maton and Pargament (1987) further detail the role of religious ideas and actions in accomplishing such beneficial ends. Such preventive and corrective potential may, however, be counterbalanced by the exacerbation of mental problems by some theologies and religious systems. These can act as sources of abnormal motivation and ideas, and may demand compliance in thinking and behavior that strain certain people beyond their capacities. Prevention and promotion sometimes go hand in hand.

With respect to *outreach pathways*, as already stated, traditional theology is often a socially conservative force (Marty, 1970). There have, however, been significant departures from this stance as some of these religious bodies have been in the forefront of liberal action (Yinger, 1946). Early in the 20th century the pentecostal movement along with a number of evangelical churches viewed specific forms of social action as harbingers of the millennial age. Outreach prevention measures involved missionary and witnessing activities designed to treat and rehabilitate the "wayward sinner," "heathen pagan," or "immoral society." These ventures almost always stressed the morality of volunteerism — an avenue for individuals to take.

The last half-century has witnessed increasing use of what Maton and Pargament (1987) term a "Social Action pathway." In the early 1940s, religious publications such as *Christian Century* and *Christianity and Crisis* spoke in favor of national and international collective programs to foster peace, and alleviate poverty and social problems (Yinger, 1946). Support for these efforts rapidly faded because of the lack of culturally legitimating mechanisms. Radical recommendations such as "modification of the profit motive" (p. 171) may have contributed to the development of modernist theologies which see political and economic solutions as the only avenues to real social change and prevention. Outreach from the modernist perspective means empowerment "to influence social policies which contribute to racial discrimination, economic injustice, and political oppression," and by these means "reduce environmental stress and enhance psychological well-being" (Maton & Pargament, 1987, p. 181).

A CONCLUDING PERSPECTIVE

The preceding discussion has focused on the implications of theology for prevention, and has alluded in a few places to the flexibility with which religionists interpret scripture. Different emphases may result in either a conservative or liberal stance. Such tendencies clearly demonstrate that theology is a human enterprise. When sacred doctrines are encountered that seem to support or oppose certain approaches to prevention, religionists, in practice, find ways of selecting scripture and theology so that what appears as anathema finds acceptance. The implications of theology are always shaped by human needs and cognitions.

If there is a basic premise that must be recognized relative to the development of prevention programs, it is that these must, in the last analysis, involve a political agenda. Theology itself is inherently political (Cobb, 1982), and American history has often demonstrated that religious bodies frequently use the mandates of their theology as political imperatives. These force religionists into the political arena, either to support or oppose prevention programs based upon their underlying theological import. Currently, the Equal Rights Amendment, abortion rights, research on AIDS, homosexual rights, and domestic violence are examples of such politically toned issues. They represent areas of conflicting theological legitimation, with implications for prevention and promotion, that are likely to be with us for a very long time.

NOTE

1. Although we use the designations of traditional and modernist here as they are generally understood, they are more fully explained later.

REFERENCES

Assmann, H. A. (1976). *A theology for a nomad church*. Maryknoll, NY: Orbis.

Berger, P. L. (1967). *The sacred canopy*. Garden City, NY: Doubleday.

Berger, P. L., & Luckmann, T. (1967). *The social construction of reality*. Garden City, NY: Doubleday (Anchor).

Bloesch, D. (1878). *Essentials of evangelical theology* (Vols. 1 and 2). San Francisco: Harper & Row.

Bloom, B. (1977). *Community mental health: A general introduction*. Monterey, CA: Brooks/Cole.

Bridges, R. A. (1989). *Preliminary steps towards the construction of a theologically-based questionnaire*. Unpublished Ph.D. dissertation, Joint program Iliff School of Theology and University of Denver.

Bridges, R. A., & Spilka, B. (1988, October). *Steps towards the construction of a systematic theological questionnaire*. Paper presented at the Convention of the Religious Research Association. Chicago, IL.

Caplan, G. (1964). *Principles of preventive psychiatry*. New York: Basic.

Cobb, J. B., Jr. (1982). *Process theology as political theology*. Philadelphia: Westminster.

Cogley, J. (1968). *Religion in a secular age*. New York: Frederick A. Praeger.

Daly, M. (1973). *Beyond God the father*. Boston: Beacon.

Graham, L. K. (1987). A pastoral theological appropriation of family therapy. *Journal of Pastoral Psychotherapy*, *1*, 3-17.

Gutierrez, G. (1987). *On Job: God-talk and the suffering of the innocent*. Maryknoll, NY: Orbis.

Lipset, S. M., & Raab, E. (1970). *The politics of unreason*. New York: Harper & Row.

Marty, M. E. (1070). *Righteous empire: The Protestant experience in America*. New York: Dial.

Maton, K. I., & Pargament, K. I. (1987). Roles of religion in prevention and promotion. In L. A. Jason, R. E. Hess, R. D. Felner, & J. M. Mortisugu (Eds.), *Prevention: Toward a multidisciplinary approach*. New York: The Haworth Press, Inc.

Moberg, D. O. (1962). *The church as a social institution*. Englewood Cliffs, NJ: Prentice-Hall.

Niebuhr, H. R. (1957). *The social sources of denominationalism*. New York: Meridian.

Novak, M. (1968). Secular saints. *The Center Magazine*. *1*(4), 51-59.

Ogden, S. M. (1979). *Faith and freedom: Toward a theology of liberation*. Nashville: Abingdon.

Rahner, K., & Vorgrimler, H. (1965). *Theological dictionary*. New York: Seabury.

Ramsden, W. E. (1973). Community involvement as ministry. In O. Strunk Jr.

(Ed.), *Dynamic interpersonalism for ministry: Essays in honor of Paul E. Johnson.* Nashville: Abingdon.

Rotenberg, M. (1978). *Damnation and deviance.* New York: The Free Press.

Rubin, Z., & Peplau, A. (1973). Belief in a just world and reactions to another's lot: A study of participants in the national draft lottery. *Journal of Social Issues,* 73-93.

Schoenfeld, E. (1989). Justice: An illusive concept in Christianity. *Review of Religious Research, 30,* 236-245.

Smith, G. S. (1985). *The seeds of secularization: Calvinism, culture, and pluralism in America, 1870-1915.* Grand Rapids, MI: Eerdmans.

Solle, D. (1971). *Political theology.* Philadelphia: Fortress.

Spilka, B., Hood, R. W., Jr., & Gorsuch, R. L. (1985). *The psychology of religion: An empirical approach.* Englewood Cliffs, NJ: Prentice-Hall.

Stern, E. M. (1985). *The psychotherapy patient.* New York: The Haworth Press, Inc.

Stern, E. M., & Marino, B. G. (1970). *Psychotheology.* New York: Newman.

Strunk, O., Jr. (1985). Dealing with proceptive countertransference-like issues: The factor of psychotherapeutic ideology. In E. M. Stern (Ed.), *The psychotherapy patient.* New York: The Haworth Press, Inc.

Tawney, R. H. (1926). *Religion and the rise of capitalism.* New York: Harcourt, Brace.

Vande Kemp, H. (1985). Psychotherapy as a religious process: A historical heritage. In E. M. Stern (Ed.), *The psychotherapy patient.* New York: The Haworth Press, Inc.

Whitehead, A. N. (1929). *Process and reality.* New York: Macmillan.

Wilcox, C. (1989). Evangelicals and the moral majority. *Journal for the Scientific Study of Religion, 28,* 400-414.

Yinger, J. M. (1946). *Religion in the struggle for power.* Durham, NC: Duke University Press.

A Sociological Overview: Mental Health Implications of Religio-Cultural Megatrends in the United States

Keith A. Roberts

Fireland College
Bowling Green State University

SUMMARY. Several long-term religio-cultural trends in America, especially those associated with the radical individualism of the culture, may have a significant impact on the environment in which human service professionals work. These trends may contribute to increased anomie and alienation, factors which tend to work counter to prevention in human services. Nonetheless, probably at no time in history have local clergy been as well trained or as critically positioned to work in league with helping professionals.

The purpose of this article is to spell out large scale religio-cultural trends in the United States and to reflect on the meaning of these trends for mental health and for the provision of mental health services. Such a task is risky and speculative, for one must paint with a very broad brush. A wide diversity of religious groups and movements exists in North America, each with its own agenda. There are also countervailing forces within the society, and there are contradictory elements even within each religious group or movement (Roberts, 1990). Discernment of an overriding trend is therefore fraught with peril. Nonetheless, there are some long term trends which sociologists and historians have identified which affect the religious and cultural climate in which human service professionals work. It is this macro perspective which I seek to elucidate. As such, this

Reprints may be obtained from Keith A. Roberts, Fireland College, Bowling Green State University, 901 Rye Beach Road, Huron, OH 44839-9791.

37

is a socio-historical essay rather than a summary of findings from an empirical study. Since I am trying to identify dominant trends in the U.S., most of my generalizations will refer to conventional denominational religion rather than to religious or ethnic subcultures.

FUNCTIONS OF RELIGION
WHICH RELATE TO MENTAL HEALTH

Before launching into an overview, we need to clarify some of the social functions of religion, especially those which impact the mental health of citizens. Perhaps the most obvious function of religion is to provide a sense of meaning and purpose in life — a sense that suffering, pain, and death have a larger meaning, and that justice and goodness *will* ultimately be rewarded. As a number of scholars (Batson & Ventis, 1982; Frankl, 1962; Yinger, 1970) have pointed out, having a sense of meaning or purpose in life can be a vital component in one's mental health. Anthropologists Clifford Geertz (1966) and E. E. Evans Prichard (1972) report with interest that their informants in nonindustrial societies were quite willing to give up their theodicy, their explanation of the meaning of events, in favor of a better one. What they adamantly refused to do was to give up their explanation for none at all, i.e., to leave events to themselves and attribute them with no meaning. The chaos of such a world was intolerable.

A second function is that religion provides individuals with feelings of belonging and enhances their sense of identity. Research on commitment to religious groups shows that a sense of belonging is typically prior to belief in the ideological system (Greeley, 1972; Roberts, 1980). Not only are friendship networks and group solidarity important to an individual's sense of self, but religious groups sacralize (make sacred and distinctive) important status changes in the lives of individuals. Reaching adulthood, getting married, becoming a parent, and facing death are all commemorated with rites of passage that give public sanction and acknowledgement to personal transformations.

A third function of religion is that it can enhance social solidarity and stability for the society as a whole. It can provide social "glue" in the form of common beliefs and common commitments; it can legitimize society's norms and structures; and it can sacralize cultural values and definitions of morality. Anthropologist Clifford Geertz (1973) comments on this latter process when he reflects on his cross-cultural studies of religion:

The need for a metaphysical grounding for values seems to vary quite widely in intensity from culture to culture and from individual to individual, but the tendency to desire some sort of factual basis for one's commitments seems practically universal; mere conventionalism satisfies few people in any culture. However its role may differ in various cultures, religion gives to a set of social values what they perhaps most need to be coercive: An appearance of objectivity. In sacred rituals and myths, values are portrayed not as subjective human preferences, but as the imposed conditions for life. (p. 131)

Religion can give power and imperative to societal values by giving them supernatural sanction. But we might add that religious groups can also sacralize reform or revolutionary movements as well. Religion does not always play a conservative role, and its ability to sanction change may itself be constructive when the social structures have become oppressive. As we shall see, weakening of the ability of religion to fulfill these functions may have important consequences for the society and for the health of individual members.

SOCIAL STRUCTURE
AND PERSONALITY ADJUSTMENT

The social structure of a society can have important consequences for individual personality adjustment by fostering either of two conditions: alienation or anomie. Those who do not feel a part of a group, who feel adrift and isolated, experience alienation. Alienation often happens in societies which are highly integrated and harmonious. The alienated person is one who is excluded or who does not identify with the stable and integrated group. In more complex societies, one may be alienated from the larger social order, but may gain solace in a religious or ethnic subgroup. Likewise, one may be alienated from a religious group in a complex culture, but find support in identification with the larger culture or with a voluntary association, such as a veterans or civic group. The most distressing alienation in modern societies, however, is experienced by those alienated persons who never find a group with which to identify.

Anomie often feels much the same as alienation, but in reality its cause is usually the opposite. Anomie is a feeling of normlessness and disorientation — a lack of connectedness — which occurs because the society itself is not well integrated and the norms do not seem compelling.

Both processes can be destructive to mental health, as has been well documented. Durkheim (1964), for example, pointed out that the likelihood of a person committing suicide can be increased by alienation (egoistic suicide) or by disintegration of social solidarity (anomic suicide). And Kai Erikson (1976) has documented some of the devastating mental health consequences of loss of community, for the very existence of a supportive community plays a vital role in the stability of individuals and relationships.

In all fairness, we should also recognize that in some circumstances, alienation or marginality may also be growth producing and thus in some ways conducive to personality adjustment. Some scholars have argued that alienation from groups inhibiting personal growth or from unhealthy societal value-orientations may be beneficial to individuals. Such alienation may, for example, stimulate an individual's coping skills and sense of individual uniqueness (Maton & Pargament, 1987). However, it is important to recognize that any social phenomenon may be simultaneously functional and dysfunctional, affecting different dimensions of mental health at the same time. Further, it may well be that for alienation to be growth producing, the person may need to have an alternative source of group support and identification.

While different types of social conditions tend to cause anomie or alienation, complex post-industrial societies, like the United States, sometimes generate both. The mass bureaucratic structure can lead to alienation, while the existence of pluralism may foster anomie (Berger, 1967). Religion is capable of combating both alienation and anomie, but changes in religion in modern American society have made it more difficult for religion to serve as a counterforce to these conditions.

In this paper we will explore two large-scale or "macro" trends in religion in the modern world: secularization and the radical individualization of religion and of cultural values. We shall then discuss the possible mental health implications of these trends.

MACRO-TREND #1: SECULARIZATION

No discussion of macro trends in religion and culture would be complete without mention of secularization, for it is one of the most widely used explanations of the cultural transformation of the western world. Yet there has been considerable disagreement about how to define secularization and how to assess it (Roberts, 1990; Stark & Bainbridge, 1985). Secularization has often been defined as the decline of religion, with drops in church membership statistics and church attendance rates since World War II cited as evidence of this decline. The difficulty with these statistics is that the decade of the 1950s was an atypical decade and hardly one to serve as a baseline for comparisons (Roberts, 1990).

If one instead takes a long-term view, one finds a very different pattern. Recent analysis of historical records suggests that in 1776 — the "good old days" of American colonialism — church membership was about 10% (Stark & Finke, 1988), and church attendance was probably less than 20% of the population (Hudson, 1973). Church membership and attendance have gradually and rather steadily *increased* since that time, until the relatively small downturn of the past three decades. Even now, religious affiliation and participation run far ahead of the norm for any period in American history prior to 1840.

Additionally, we have recently witnessed the revival of religious fervor in evangelical churches, suggesting a renewal of religion in America (Warner, 1988). A Gallup Poll (1987) revealed that in 1986, 45% of Protestants and one-third of all Americans identified themselves as born-again. The claims of a severe decline of religion in North America grossly misrepresent reality. If secularization means long term and pervasive decline in religious involvement, secularization has simply not been happening.

This new perspective has forced some social scientists to redefine secularization as a decline of supernaturalism — in the culture at large and in religious systems (Johnson, 1979; Stark & Bainbridge, 1985). Our society is most likely to look to empirically tested answers to problems, be they medical, psychological, technological, or environmental. We no longer believe, for example, that lightning is an expression of the wrath of God, although our ancestors believed that only a little more than two hundred years ago (Stark & Bainbridge, 1985).

Other evidence, including opinion and attitude surveys of the American public, also suggests a decline in supernatural beliefs. This includes drops in the number of people who believe in God, the number who pray daily, and the number who believe in heaven or hell (Gallup Poll, 1987; Greeley, 1969, 1972).

But Stark and Bainbridge argue rather convincingly that secularization within a society is "self-limiting." They point out that most persons who indicated "no religious preference" in surveys are not secular empiricists. Instead, such respondents tend to believe in astrology, Transcendental Meditation, yoga, or some other form of supernaturalism. Indeed, in the regions of the country where traditional forms of religion are weakest, secular humanism does not abound; cults do. Stark and Bainbridge maintain that cults arise precisely to fill a vacuum — a need for supernatural compensators when this-worldly resources are insufficient to address problems.

As the central cultural values of our society have become less supernatural in orientation, conventional religious groups have coped by lowering tension with the larger society—including adoption of theologies that are consistent with scientific empiricism and are themselves more naturalistic or secular. Stark and Bainbridge (1985) assert that in the 17th century European scientists (like Galileo) were forced by the church to recant their findings, but "in this century it has been the religious intellectuals, not the scientists, who have done the recanting" (p. 434). They report that as mainline religion has secularized, cults and evangelical movements have blossomed to fill the void. They believe that the overall amount of supernaturalism in the society has not really declined. It has simply appeared in new forms and under the auspices of new organizations.

Later in this paper I will suggest that this transformation of religion has implications for both the "meaning" function of religion and the "sacralization of social norms." The loss of utter sacredness and certainty of religious and cultural norms is a contributing factor in the growth of anomie.

MACRO-TREND #2: INDIVIDUALIZATION OF CULTURE AND RELIGION

Perhaps the most important macro-trend in American meaning systems and values has been that toward ever greater individualization. We will look at three dimensions of this issue: a long-term decline in commitment to the community and to the "general good" in our culture, the "privatization" of religion, and the trend to the "marketing" of religion. Radical Individualism and Loss of Commitment to the Community

The first dimension of individualization which we explore here is the long term transformation of American culture toward ever greater emphasis on individualism. Bellah, Madsen, Sullivan, Swindler, and Tipton (1985) have conducted an analysis of American culture which is relevant to our concern. Their research explores changes in American culture since early colonial days.

Individualism has long been a central or core value in American life, the very term having been coined in America and popularized by Benjamin Franklin (Bellah, 1985). The ideas of individual freedom extended to many arenas, not the least of which was a free market economy in which each individual was free to pursue his or her individual or familial self-interests. But Bellah and his associates point out that there was another cultural value orientation which served as a countervailing force or counterbalance to extreme individualism. This counterbalance was a profound commitment to the Common Good. The Common Good was itself a product of two separate traditions: the republican tradition of service to the society and the Biblical tradition of the covenant community.

The republican tradition was the secular version of the common good, and was expressed in the public speeches and writings of such figures as Thomas Jefferson, George Washington, James Madison, John Adams, and Alexander Hamilton. While they defended the right of individuals to pursue their own course of action without interference from government and while they established legal protection for that right, these leaders also felt that the idea of people doing whatever they pleased—such as pursuing money for its own sake—was utterly unpalatable (Bellah et al., 1985, p. 31). All behavior of the citizenry was to be guided by moral commitment to the public good. While John Adams and other founders of the country defended the legal right of individuals to pursue their individual self-interests, they devoted their own lives and resources to serving the public, sometimes to the detriment of their own economic well-being. They were also convinced that most citizens were committed to the public good or "principles of virtue." Extreme individualism was counterbalanced by civic loyalty and responsibility. Indeed, Thomas Jefferson maintained that if the citizenry became too obsessed with individual concerns, such as "the sole faculty of making money," the future of the republic would be bleak and tyranny not far away (Bellah et al., 1985, p. 31).

The other strain of thought in Colonial America which served as a countervailing force to unfettered pursuit of individual self-interest was Biblically-based covenant theology—the idea that humans exist in a covenant relationship with God. Freedom, as defined by ministers such as John Winthrop, was liberation from tyrannical control by government officials, but it was "moral freedom" to pursue that which is "good, true and honest" without interference. And it was to be guided at all times by God's commandments and by the charge to create a Covenanted Community—a society ultimately loyal to God and to the will of God. Pursuit of self-interest for its own sake was antithetical to this perspective.

Bellah and his colleagues cite a number of types of data which suggest that the cultural values emphasizing community (and serving as a counterweight to individualism) have been substantially weakened over the past two centuries. They do not claim that this was a sudden process, for the expansion of individualism as a more dominant American value-orientation has been gradual. But in depth interviews with a sample of contemporary Americans suggest that the old republican vision and the original Biblical emphasis on community have waned significantly. The central commitment of Americans has become much more narrowly defined; individual or immediate family wants and needs not only are primary, but are not complemented with a larger vision of self-in-community. In some cases this is reflected in definitions of "pursuit of happiness" that are psychotherapeutic. For others the central commitment is to economic self interests — a commitment that ignores societal needs unless those social needs impact directly on the individual.

Warren Bennis (1989) suggests that the very idea of the "American Dream" has been transformed in this individualizing trend. The American Dream originally was a collective dream for a free and democratic society. The first step toward attainment of this dream was providing responsible, educated citizens. Now the idea of the American Dream has become one of individual affluence and family consumption of material goods. With the introduction of television, VCRs, Nintendos, and other technological consumer novelties in our homes, the American family has started to engage in what Bennis calls "cocooning." Yet because the change in the meaning of the "American Dream" has been gradual, most Americans are not aware of the transformation. They believe the idea of the American Dream has always focused on economic success.

According to Bellah and his colleagues (1985), this profound individualism transforms the very idea of commitment. "It enables the individual to think of commitments . . . as enhancements of the sense of individual well-being rather than as moral imperatives" (p. 47). All moral values, then, become relative to the definitions of the individual rather than being moral absolutes. Even the marriage relationship may be affected — made more fragile — by this conceptualization of commitment.

This "radical individualism," as Bellah calls it, also leaves individuals feeling that they face the world alone, without a larger supportive community. He concludes that contemporary American culture "defines personality, achievement, and the purpose of human life in ways that leave the individual suspended in glorious, but terrifying, isolation" (1985, p. 6). A feeling of isolation is, of course, the essence of alienation.

The transformation toward greater individualism is a transformation not only of American culture, but may well be manifested in a gradual shift in the value orientation of religion in America. The Biblical idea that salvation is corporate, that the entire community will be saved or damned together, began eroding with the Protestant Reformation. A core part of Max Weber's (1947, 1958) argument about the affinity of Protestantism and capitalism was that Calvin placed the individual utterly alone before God — to be blessed or cursed. Part of the reason that capitalism and Calvinism were so compatible was that in both cases, the individual was on his or her own. Increased individualism in American religion represents an extension of this orientation.

The trend has not been without reversals. The theologies of American colonial preachers were in some ways less individualistic than Calvin's, and as late as the early 1900s a Social Gospel theology was being preached from many pulpits. Contemporary American religion, whether Christian, Jewish, or even cultic, is certainly not without its social conscience. But few of the great pulpiteers of our day, and certainly none of the televangelists, place the same emphasis on the collective good as did the early puritans.

The profound emphasis on the individual is not a phenomenon of one particular political or theological orientation. It is celebrated — with somewhat different applications and emphases — by both liberals and conservatives. The Libertarians on the right and the Civil Liberties Union on the left are similar in celebrating the autonomy of the individual.

Bellah and his colleagues argue that individualism has long been an American value and that it is important for the legal structures to continue to protect individual freedoms. However, they also assert that the dysfunctions of radical individualism were guarded against through a moral climate that called persons to sacrifice individual self-interest in favor of the common good. The moral climate, reinforced through a republican vision for some intellectuals, and through a sacred Biblical calling for many others, served as a corrective to selfish individualism and corroding of public spirit. The loss of the sacralization of the Common Good may well be a contributing factor in the mental health climate of the country and in our inability to mobilize the public to prevent or to correct social problems (Sarason 1986).

Privatization of Faith

A second dimension of the individualization process of religion is the tendency of individuals to construct their own religious world-view, somewhat independently of religious groups or organizations. These religious or quasi-religious systems of belief are alternatively called "invisible religions," "privatized religion," or "do-it-yourself religion." Due to the great pluralism of religion in the United States and the wide range of popular philosophies, citizens are able to pick and choose and to formulate their own philosophy of life. Many people piece together their own meaning system, drawing eclecticly from such diverse sources as popular religious tracts, Playboy magazine, "pop psychology" theories, "pop religion" as presented by televangelists, and popular television programs.

Various organizations, political philosophies, and social movements compete to shape the philosophy of life of American citizens. Even business enterprises like Amway Corporation seek to motivate workers by stressing certain value orientations and establishing mechanisms which enhance the plausibility of the philosophy of life they advocate. From such sources, individuals construct their own individual meaning system—their own private religion.

The impact of this trend toward privatized religion may be important both for the religious climate of the U.S. generally and for traditional religious organizations in particular. In their study of mainline religion, Roof and McKinney (1987) conclude that "the enemy of church life in this country is not so much 'secularity' as 'do-it-yourself' religiosity" (p. 56). Reginald Bibby (1987) suggests a similar process in Canada and spells out the implications for conventional religious groups. He writes that religion in Canada is becoming "religion a la carte." He elaborates the metaphor: "Canadians are still eating in the restaurants (i.e., mainline denominations). But their menu choices have changed . . . . (Many) are opting only for appetizers, salads, or deserts (funerals, weddings, and baptisms), rather than full course meals" (pp. 133-134). He believes religious commitment in Canada is becoming more casual and more privatized.

The consequences of privatized meaning systems are mixed. Some scholars see a positive trend in that each person is forced to think through his or her own system of values. One can no longer simply adopt the traditions of the past without reflecting on those values and meaning systems (Bellah, 1970; Parsons, 1963). On the other hand, not everyone is prepared to construct and maintain their own independent value system. Without a group, a set of rituals and mythologies, a system of symbols, and other components of a plausibility structure, the beliefs and values do not seem compelling. They become arbitrary choices rather than eternal imperatives (Berger, 1967, 1979; Roberts, 1990).

Because many privatized meaning systems exalt the autonomy of the individual (including self-realization and "finding oneself"), the locus of meaning is often in the individual's biography (Luckmann, 1967). Thus, the system of meaning may be relevant only to the individual—ignoring the larger community or the larger social structure. Not only do privatized systems tend to ignore the community, but they often provide no community of support. Bellah and his colleagues (1985) reported that one of their informants even named her religion after herself; she believed in her own idiosyncratic "Sheilaism." While other subjects did not name their faith in such a manner, the effect was similar. Such privatized faith systems are unlikely to provide the sacralization of social norms and social values which is normally one of the functions of religion. Without the sacralization of cultural norms and values, the conditions giving rise to the confusion and disorientation of anomie are present.

Marketing of Religion

The marketing of religion is an outcome of this competitive environment. Religious systems and "philosophy of life entrepreneurs" begin to compete for members, and as they do, they begin to look for those ideas and those services which "sell" well with the public. Nowhere is this more evident than in televangelism. As recently as the 1960s, television ministry was controlled almost entirely by mainline conventional denominations. The fact that it is now dominated by evangelicals is in large part a result of the history of urban revivalism. Charles Finney, Dwight Moody, and Billy Sunday each contributed to the reshaping of revivalism into a rational corporative enterprise that would have been unrecognizable to such Great Awakening preachers as Jonathan Edwards (Frankl, 1987; Hadden & Shupe, 1988). Billy Sunday's strategy, for example, involved working out the efficiency of his organization by determining the "cost per convert." He refined revivalism as a business to a point that his model could be called "scientific management in the pulpit." The urban revivalists created a method which continues to shape strategy and programming among televangelists today: entertainment appeal, image management, professional organization, definitions of ministerial success based on business models, and constant modification of the "product" to meet market appeal.

Razelle Frankl (1987) has documented the extent to which religious broadcasters deliberately market their product. They assess audience characteristics and use that information to shape the content of programming. The result is that the message itself is eventually transformed. Frankl found from her content analyses of programming that virtually all televangelists preach some variety of "the Gospel of Prosperity." And the incredible need for ever more cash to maintain the televangelism empires means that pressure continues on the electronic preachers to deliver whatever "sells."

While televangelism is the most obvious expression of the marketing of religion in contemporary America, the need for church growth and maintenance of local congregations means that the temptation to modify the message — the product — to appeal to the "market" is ever-present. But such modification of the message itself contributes to cynicism about the ultimate truth of the theology being preached. Such cynicism is the antithesis of sacralized norms and values. Ultimately such marketing of the faith in order to build numbers may contribute to anomie.

IMPLICATIONS
OF RELIGIO-CULTURAL TRENDS
FOR MENTAL HEALTH

It would be a gross oversimplification to suggest that the macro-trends described in this paper have had only one sort of effect on mental health. If we have learned anything in recent years, it is that changes in an institution or a society always have a diversity of influences, sometimes quite contradictory.

Seminary professors, clergy, and other mainline denominational leaders have become more sensitive in recent decades to the mental health consequences of religion. The quality of pastoral care training has improved, ministers are more likely to give credence to empirical research regarding mental health than were the clerics in earlier periods of American history, they are more likely to recognize the limits of pastoral training in providing care in dealing with the mentally ill and to refer persons to appropriate agencies, and clergy are even likely to be sensitive to the mental health effects of the worship experience (Clinebell, 1965). Unlike Jonathan Edwards and many other preachers of his day and before, most mainline clergy do not intentionally try to foster feelings of guilt and shame in worshippers (Kelley, 1972). The overall increase in awareness among religious leaders of nonsupernatural causes of social and personality dysfunctions has to be constructive to a preventative climate.

Likewise, the increased value given to the importance and uniqueness of each individual and the reduction of rigid requirements of conformity and conventionalism must certainly have had positive mental health consequences. The historical practice of ejecting persons from church membership for violation of church norms — unconventional theological beliefs, or consumption of alcohol, or other sins — must have been less than constructive to the self-esteem and personality adjustment of those charged (Clinebell, 1965). But as we look at the transformations which have occurred, there have been some dysfunctions as well. A number of scholars feel that the loss of supernaturalism in religious systems has made those beliefs and values more susceptible to disconfirmation (Berger,

1967; O'Dea, 1966; Stark & Bainbridge 1985). Stark and Bainbridge, for example, suggest that by modifying theological ideas to be compatible with scientific findings, mainline theologians have reduced one of the factors which provide sacredness and unquestioned believability for their system. If, indeed, the plausibility of beliefs has been weakened, that in turn may contribute to increased anomie or normlessness. For those who are able to cope with ambiguity, this anomie is not so devastating. But for many people who are less self directing, it can be a torturous experience — one which does not necessarily lead to growth.

Stark and Bainbridge also believe that some human needs cannot be met in the natural world or satisfied with empirical proofs. Such nonempirical compensators would include the comfort of believing that there is an existence after death or the hope which one gains in believing that goodness and justice will ultimately be rewarded. Needs for such supernatural compensators vary from person to person, but where they are strong, the comfort and hope which religious systems provide can be beneficial. The decline of supernaturalism may, therefore, have some negative consequences for personality adjustment.

The trend toward radical individualism may have even more important consequences. The trend toward privatization of systems of meaning and the growing awareness by the public of the marketing of religious systems mean that plausibility structures are likely to be further weakened and the chances of anomie increased. The apparent trend toward religion "a la carte" suggests that religion does not call forth the same level of commitment as it has previously elicited. This does not mean that religion is without an important function. Those "crisis" services of providing rites of passage (weddings, baptisms, and funerals) may be important to the people who use them. But the traditional religious meaning systems are not compelling for many people. People may still be attending church in large numbers, but their values and sense of purpose in life are not necessarily based on church dogma (Luckmann, 1967; Roof & McKinney, 1987; Wood, 1981).

If the norms and beliefs are not compelling, religion is not likely to be able to sacralize norms and values of the larger society. Marriage, for example, does not have the same sacredness it once had in our society. In so far as social values are not sacralized, the entire society may be more subject to "cultural wobble" and anomie.

Of all of the trends described in this paper, the one which may be most troubling for the provision of social services is the long-term cultural trend involving a decrease in commitment to the larger community. This loss of a sense of community may increase alienation, for if Bellah and his associates are correct, citizens may find less meaning in social bonds and may therefore be less likely to feel integrated into the society. The lack of experience of support from one's community or one's church can only be deleterious to prevention and amelioration of problems.

Radical individualism may finally have one other consequence. Insofar as citizens conceive of individuals as autonomous "self-made" men and women, and insofar as citizens fail to recognize the role of the community and social conditions in contributing to dysfunctions of individuals, there may be a greater chance of those same citizens blaming the victims for their plight. When victims are blamed for their circumstances and when problems are defined in private terms, resources are less likely to be provided for prevention or amelioration (Hills, 1980).

Indeed, the victims may also accept that definition of the situation and blame themselves. Sarason (1986) argues that the agony of dealing with disabled or malfunctioning family members is magnified by the lack of perceived community support, the tendency for people to view problems as personal or family issues which do not involve the community, and the inclination for persons therefore to blame themselves for the stresses they experience.

Despite these large scale trends, contemporary religious groups do sometimes enhance the overall "prevention environment" of a local community. Some congregations do still provide a theology which stresses a sense of community—thereby providing an ideology which countervails some of the radical individualism of the culture. They also provide a support network which can be an invaluable resource for prevention. And the clergy in local congregations are in an excellent position to provide a "case management" role. If constructive relationships exist between human services agencies and clergy, ministers can not only be involved in referral, but can—and often do—provide the ongoing pastoral role of trusted confidant who coordinates the delivery of services.

WHAT CAN BE DONE
ABOUT THE MACRO TRENDS?

When one is dealing with macro trends, the solutions are complex, at best. Cultural trends are shaped by many contributing variables. We dare not be sanguine about our ability to stem the tide of a trend when scores of factors are at work and when changing only one or two of those variables may well prove futile. Furthermore, some of the antidotes may be more unpalatable than the ailment we presently face.

One remedy to anomie is already at work in our society. Religious groups with absolutistic orientations, whether they be in the form of charismatic cults or in the form of fundamentalist groups, clearly reduce anomie for their members. The answers are certain and ambiguity is removed (Ammerman, 1987; Bromley & Shupe, 1979; Downton, 1979; Lofland, 1977; Warner, 1988). While most of these absolutistic groups are alienated from the larger society, they do tend to have intense networks within themselves. But intense identification with a subgroup which is alienated from the larger society is not likely to result in commitment to the larger Common Good. Indeed, many such groups foster intense out-group antipathy. Further, there are other mental health costs to this type of rigid solution (Clinebell, 1965; Maton & Pargament, 1987), and many of us will find this remedy of extreme dogmatism less than appealing.

Peter Berger (1979) has proposed that we need to return to a sense of sacredness and to a profound supernaturalism in our religion. Supernatural systems tend to have stronger "plausibility structures" and are, therefore, more likely to be effective in combating anomie. Even if we do grant that this is an appropriate remedy, it is not clear how we achieve it. Simply calling for more supernatural belief is not likely to do the trick, especially when it is advocated on the grounds that it might have certain social benefits. A this-worldly reason for believing in an other-worldly realm is not apt to be compelling.

Another solution to the anomie problem is for persons to learn to live with ambiguity, and to discover that commitment can be made in the midst of relativity and pluralism. But if cognitive developmentalists in the Piagetian tradition are correct, this requires a rather advanced level of cognitive development, one which most college students and much of the general public have not achieved (Kitchener, 1986; Kohlberg & Gilligan, 1971; McKinnon & Renner, 1971; Perry 1970; Wilcox, 1979). It may well be that the price we must pay for pluralism is that we must put up with a significant number of legalistic and absolutistic religious groups that help people cope with anomie.

Solutions to alienation are also being offered by a number of churches and by various civic and self-help groups. The fastest growing religious groups are those which have a variety of mechanisms to enhance a feeling of belonging (Roberts, 1990). Further, many churches—liberal and conservative—have established small groups within their churches to enhance intimacy and sharing. When one develops an interpersonal bond with any one group within an organization, one's commitment to the larger organization tends to be enhanced—unless, of course, the smaller group is itself alienated from the larger collectivity and has developed high boundaries (Roberts, 1980).

Self help groups, such as Alcoholics Anonymous and Parents Anonymous, also foster rather intense self-disclosure and interpersonal sharing. This often leads to high levels of intimacy and identification. However, all of these church and therapeutic groups may fail to reach the mass of Americans. Further, this solution is often limited in that it does not necessarily address the cultural trend toward radical individualism. Self-help therapy groups often have rather individualistic solutions to the problems they gather to address. Still, religious special interest groups (peace groups, anti-abortion task forces, mission groups, and self-help associations) are growing so fast and becoming so important that Robert Wuthnow (1988) reports that they are as important to the structure of American religion as denominationalism. Their consequences and their potential deserve our attention.

Ameliorating the trend toward extreme individualism will require a number of modifications in cultural values. The church is one institution which is well-suited to address such values. It is one major institution in society in which the cultural value system emphasizes a nurturing, caring community and in which part of the job description of its chief officer (the pastor) is care of persons and cultivation of community.

The church also has an important ideological resource—the Biblical emphasis on covenant theology. My own familiarity with seminaries and with theologians around the country convinces me that the theological education of our clergy is not lacking in emphasis on commitment to community. It is important to recognize, however, that the theological orientation of a local congregation is shaped by many factors, and the theology of the pastor is only one of many variables. Indeed, the very trend toward the marketing of religion in America creates an environment in which external elements can become important in shaping the ideology of a church. Traditional theology is clearly not the sole force at work (Hadden, 1969; Roof and McKinney, 1987; Wood, 1981). Because the laity play an important part in shaping the subculture of a local congregation, helping professionals who are church members can assist their pastors in giving center stage to covenantal theology.

Human services professionals who are not active in traditional religious organizations may also consider utilizing local ministers as resources and allies in combatting alienation and anomie. Clergy often have a unique relationship to members of their congregations and have access to valuable ideological and community resources. While some mental health professionals are personally alienated from the ideology of Bible study and prayer groups, these groups can often be enormously supportive to participants. Intimate sharing commonly occurs, mutual support develops, and the tone is much more supportive and much less judgmental than many outsiders believe.

It may also be possible to rally the historic republican spirit of the Common Good. John F. Kennedy was able to stimulate a good deal of idealism in this country, and another dynamic and idealistic President might well do the same. A major thrust toward civic education in our public schools might also help, though it would need to involve more than the narrow chauvinism that has sometimes passed for civic education. A key element would need to be instilling in young people a sense of service to the community.

An even more powerful factor in shaping cultural values might lie in television. A number of scholars studying television have noted its role in shaping the culture. Cross cultural studies of nations such as Brazil are especially impressive in suggesting the power of television programming in setting the values and the agenda of a nation (Kottak, 1990). Media scholar George Gerbner has even suggested that in the modern world, television serves much of the function of religion in an earlier era, uniting a population in a common set of images and symbols (Kottak, 1990).

Some scholars believe that television and VCRs have significantly contributed to the individualization and loss of public spirit. This is not just because of the content of programming, but because television viewing has consumed hours that used to be spent in more public and interpersonal activity (Bennis, 1989). Television, many believe, is intrinsically isolating. However, Kottak's cross-cultural research demonstrates that in the right cultural environment, television can actually contribute to social interaction and can enhance commitment to the larger society. If the heros and heroines of televisionland in the U.S. were to demonstrate a high degree of commitment to the Common Good—in word and in deed—their example might serve a powerful moral force similar to that of covenantal theology in an earlier era. Until the cultural heros of our younger generation are those who are concerned for the quality of the community, we will probably not see dramatic changes in the trend toward radical individualism.

CONCLUSION

While anomie and alienation are normally created by different types of structural conditions, complex modern societies such as our own are capable of producing both phenomena. While religious institutions are capable of functioning to combat anomie and alienation, large scale religious and cultural trends may have reduced the capacity of religion to play these roles. The capacity of religion to sacralize social norms and values and to provide ultimate meaning to individuals appears to have been reduced because of weakened plausibility structures. Meanwhile, the long-term increase in radical individualism and the subsequent decline in commitment to the community and the common good may increase the feeling of alienation and the tendency to blame victims.

It would be easy to overstate the negative and to fail to recognize that all social changes involve countervailing forces and contradictory affects. Religion is a complex phenomenon. It involves many different kinds of institutions, many subcommunities with diverse sets of norms, and many different theologies. I have been asked to paint with a broad brush in looking at megatrends. My sobering conclusions should not be read to suggest that religion is no longer capable of contributing to mental health in a variety of ways. I only suggest that the role of religion in the larger culture and certain changes of values in the larger culture have in some ways been less than ideal if one's criterion for evaluation is conduciveness to mental health.

Despite these religio-cultural megatrends, probably at no other time in history have local clergy been as well trained or as critically positioned to work in league with helping professionals. The church or synagogue still provides one of the most humane and nurturing linkages to society for many people. And in many ways human services professionals are currently providing services that have traditionally been provided by religious groups. Clergy and helping professionals often continue to provide collateral and complementary services by providing linkages to the community and its resources.

REFERENCES

Ammerman, N. (1987). *Bible believers: Fundamentalists in the modern world*. New Brunswick, NJ: Rutgers University Press.

Batson, D. C., & Ventis, W. L. (1982). *The religious experience*. New York: Oxford University Press.

Bellah, R. N. (1970). Religious evolution. In R. N. Bellah, *Beyond belief*. New York: Harper and Row.

Bellah, R. N., Madsen, R., Sullivan, W. M., Swindler, A., & Tipton, S. M. (1985). *Habits of the heart: Individualism and commitment in American life*. Berkeley: University of California Press.

Bennis, W. (1989). *Why leaders can't lead*. San Francisco: Jossey Bass.

Berger, P. L. (1967). *The sacred canopy*. Garden City, NY: Doubleday.

Berger, P. (1979). *The heretical imperative*. Garden City, NY: Anchor.

Bibby, R. (1987). *Fragmented gods: The poverty and potential of religion in Canada*. Toronto: Irwin.

Bromley, D. G., & Shupe, A. D. (1979). *Moonies in America*. Beverly Hills: Sage.

Clinebell, H. J. (1965). *Mental health through Christian community*. Nashville: Abingdon

Downton, J. V. (1979). *Sacred journeys: The conversion of young Americans to Divine Light Mission*. New York: Columbia University Press.

Durkheim, E. (1964). *Suicide*. Glencoe, IL: Free Press

Erikson, K. (1976). *Everything in its path*. New York: Simon and Schuster.

Evans-Prichard, E. E. (1937). *Witchcraft, oracles, and the Azande*. Oxford: Clarendon.

Frankl, V. E. (1962). *Man's search for meaning* (Rev. ed.). New York: Simon and Schuster.

Frankl, R. (1987). *Televangelism: The marketing of popular religion*. Carbondale: Southern Illinois University Press.

Gallup Poll. (1987). *The Gallup report: Religion in America*. Princeton, NJ: The Gallup Poll.

Geertz, C. (1966). Religion as a cultural system. In M. Banton (Ed.), *Anthropological approaches to the study of religion*. London: Tavistock.

Geertz, C. (1973). Ethos, world view, and the analysis of sacred symbols. In C. Geertz, *The interpretation of culture*. New York: Basic Books.

Greeley, A. (1969). *Religion in the year 2000*. New York: Sheed and Ward.

Greeley, A. (1972). *The denominational society*. Glenview, IL: Scott Foresman.

Hadden, J. K. (1969). *The gathering storm in the churches*. Garden City, NY: Doubleday.

Hadden, J. K., & Shupe, A. (1988). *Televangelism*. New York: Henry Holt.

Hills, S. (1980). *Demystifying social deviance*. New York: McGraw-Hill.

Hudson, W. S. (1973). *Religion in America* (2nd ed.). New York: Charles Scribner's Sons.

Johnson, B. (1979, August). *A fresh look at theories of secularization*. Paper presented at the meeting of the American Sociological Association, Boston, MA.

Kelley, D. M. (1972). *Why conservative churches are growing*. New York: Harper and Row.

Kitchener, K. S. (1988). The reflective judgement model: Characteristics, evidence, and measurement. In R. A. Mines & K. S. Kitchener (Eds.), *Adult cognitive development*. New York: Praeger.

Kohlberg, L., & Gilligan, C. (1971). The adolescent as a moral philosopher: The discovery of the self in a post-conventional world. *Daedalus, 100*, 1051-1086.

Kottak, P. K. (1990). *Prime-time society: An anthropological analysis of television and culture*. Belmont, CA: Wadsworth

Lofland, J. (1977). *Doomsday cult* (enlarged ed.). New York: Irvington.

Luckmann, T. (1967). *The invisible religion*. New York: Macmillan.

Maton, K. I., & Pargament, K. I. (1987). The roles of religion in prevention and promotion. *Prevention in Human Services, 5*(2), 161-205.

McKinnon, J. W., & Renner, J. W. (1971). Are colleges concerned with intellectual development. *American Journal of Physics, 39*, 1047-1082.

Niebuhr, H. R. (1960). "Faith in god and in gods." In H. R. Neibuhr, *Radical monotheism and western culture*. New York: Harper and Row.

O'Dea, T. F. (1966). *The sociology of religion*. Englewood Cliffs, NJ: Prentice-Hall.

Parsons, T. (1964). Christianity in modern industrial society. In E. Tiryakian (Ed.), *Sociological theory, values, and sociocultural change*. Glencoe, IL: Free Press.

Perry, W. G. (1970). *Forms of intellectual and ethical development in the college years*. New York: Holt, Rinehart, and Winston.

Roberts, K. A. (1990). *Religion in sociological perspective* (2nd ed.). Belmont, CA: Wadsworth.

Roof, W. C., & McKinney, W. (1987). *American mainline religion*. New Brunswick, NJ: Rutgers University Press.

Sarason, S. B. (1986). And what is the public interest? *American Psychologist*, *41*, 899-905.

Stark, R., & Bainbridge, W. S. (1985). *The future of religion: Secularization, revival, and cult formation*. Berkeley: University of California Press.

Stark, R., & Finke, R. (1988). American religion in 1778: A statistical portrait. *Sociological Analysis*, *49*, 38-51.

Warner, R. S. (1988). *New wine in old wineskins*. Berkeley: University of California Press.

Weber, M. (1947). *The theory of social and economic organization*. (A. M. Henderson and T. Parsons, Trans.). New York: Oxford University Press.

Weber, M. (1958). *The protestant ethic and the spirit of capitalism*. (T. Parsons, Trans.). New York: Scribner.

Wood, J. R. (1981). *Leadership in voluntary organizations: The controversy over social action in the protestant churches*. New Brunswick, NJ: Rutgers University Press.

Wuthnow, R. (1988). *The restructuring of American religion*. Princeton, NJ.: Princeton University Press.

Review of Religion and Mental Health: Prevention and the Enhancement of Psychosocial Functioning

I. Reed Payne
Allen E. Bergin
Kimberly A. Bielema
Paul H. Jenkins

Brigham Young University

SUMMARY. After reviewing a representative sample of the better studies exploring how religion relates to mental disorders, we have discovered several domains of positive association between the two. These include family variables, well-being and self-esteem, personal adjustment, social conduct, alcohol and drug abuse, sexual permissiveness, and suicide. On the other hand, we found little evidence supporting religious influence in the prevention of serious clinical diagnoses like bipolar disorders, major depression, schizophrenia, obsessions, and panic disorders. The role of religion in these, however, has not been sufficiently studied.

Contrary to some opinions, religious affiliation is not damaging to mental health, nor is it entirely predictive of better mental health. The more useful question to ask is *how* a person is religious rather

---

The authors are grateful to David Greaves for many helpful suggestions and acknowledge support from the Dean's Research Fund, College of Family, Home and Social Sciences, Brigham Young University. Portions of this article were presented by Allen E. Bergin in the William James Award address of Division 36, American Psychological Association during its Boston convention, August, 1990.

Reprints may be obtained from I. Reed Payne, Department of Psychology, Clinical Psychology, and School Psychology, 284 TLRB, Brigham Young University, Provo, UT 84602.

than *whether* a person is religious. Specific measures of religiosity such as intrinsic and extrinsic orientation, level of commitment, and activity level provide more informative findings than rougher estimates like affiliation.

The potential influence of religion on positive mental health and psychosocial functioning is considerable. Caplan (1972) states that next to families, religious institutions are the most universal of all groups that provide support. Reynolds (1982) notes that there is a religious group in nearly every community in the United States, with a total membership in excess of 127,000,000. There are at least 250,000 clergy who can serve as resource persons. Clinebell (1970) describes religious institutions as "a sleeping giant, a huge potential of barely tapped resources for fostering positive mental health."

Primary prevention of mental illness and promotion of mental health are regarded as worthwhile objectives by almost all professionals; yet, most mental health efforts in our time have centered on treatment or involvement after the individual has become mentally disabled or emotionally ill. Secondary prevention calls for prompt treatment to reduce disruption and prevent chronic problems from developing. Tertiary prevention attempts to further minimize long-term consequences. In a sense, primary, secondary and tertiary preventions can be seen as covering the range of conditions that cause, contribute, maintain, or continue the harmful effects of mental disorders. We should be concerned about establishing conditions that foster positive mental health and prevent mental illness; and that is what this article is about. Our synthesis is divided into three naturally occurring domains in the research literature:

1. *Psychological Adjustment.* This concerns inner personality dynamics and adaptive aspects of normal and mildly disturbed persons.
2. *Social Conduct.* This concerns overt patterns of social pathology as manifested in conduct and interpersonal relationships (e.g., drug use, sexual conduct), as opposed to internal conflicts, moods, and so forth.
3. *Mental Illness.* This concerns moderate and severe disorders, such as those traditionally classified as neuroses, psychoses, and personality disorders.

PSYCHOLOGICAL ADJUSTMENT

Religiosity and Well-Being

Well-being is the general focus of several studies attempting to relate religiosity to mental health. Measures of well-being are extremely varied as are the measures of religiosity, making generalization difficult. Nevertheless, the trend is primarily positive across diverse studies. While this implies a robust phenomenon over a variety of situations, the dimensions connecting well-being with religiosity are often elusive.

In their longitudinal study of religion and well-being among 1,650 men and women in their early 50s, Willits and Crider (1988) found that "religious attitudes positively related to overall well-being and community and marital satisfaction of both men and women and to the job satisfaction of men. Present church attendance was positively associated with overall and community satisfaction but not with other dependent variables" (p. 281). They concluded that religiosity is associated with feelings of enhanced overall well-being, and "adherence to traditional religious beliefs was the most consistent positive correlate of well-being" (p. 291).

In a study of 836 older adults, mean age 73.4 years, positive correlations were found between morale and three religious measures (Koenig, Kvale, & Ferrel, 1988). The religious measures were "organized religious activities," "non-organized religious activity" (e.g., private prayer), and "intrinsic religiosity." In general, only physical health accounted for more variance than did religious variables. Among the three religiosity variables, intrinsic religiosity and organizational religious activity showed the strongest positive correlations with morale and coping.

Roth (1988) studied spiritual well-being and marital adjustment in a sample of 147 married individuals from churches in Southern California. He found that spiritual well-being correlated significantly with marital adjustment. The existential well-being component of the spiritual well-being scale correlated highly with marital adjustment scores at most marital stages.

An article by Carson, Soeken, and Grimm (1988) related hope to spiritual well-being, existential well-being, and religious well-being. "Responses showed that both trait and state hope are positively related to spiritual well-being, existential well-being, and religious well-being." It is argued, in turn, that hope is critical to physical and psychosocial well-being and plays an important role in coping with illness and suffering.

Relationships between religiosity, life meaning, and well-being were explored by Chamberlain and Zika (1988) using a sample of women. The religion and well-being relationship was variable. The findings essentially support earlier results which demonstrate that the religiosity/well-being relationship, where it does occur, is "positive but small." This may be due to the possibility that well-being is the result of a number of weak factors rather than a consequence of a limited number of potent factors.

Five religiosity variables were included in a study of well-being by Petersen and Roy (1985). Well-being in this study was defined by the variables of anxiety and meaning and purpose. Only religious salience had a significant positive relationship with meaning and purpose, and only church attendance had a significant negative relationship with anxiety. Thus, aspects of religious commitment which affect one dimension of well-being may not necessarily affect another.

A meta-analysis found religion to be significantly and positively related to subjective well-being (Witter, Stock, Okun, & Haring, 1985). Religiosity was found to do well in predicting the well-being of black men and women (St. George & McNamara, 1984).

The trend of positive relationships between religiosity and a subjective sense of well-being is enhanced by the heterogeneity of the populations that have been studied. However, definitive conclusions are hampered by the variability of definitions and measures of religiosity and well-being. We await a programmatic approach where replications across populations and the use of more standard measures yield results that can serve as mental health markers.

Religion and Self-Esteem

Self-esteem is a core concept in mental health and psychological well-being. The implications of research on religiosity and self-esteem are often represented as equivocal since negative, positive and nonsignificant results have all been reported (Aycock & Noaker, 1985; Bahr & Martin, 1983). In the Aycock and Noaker (1985) article, Christian subgroups (N = 351) were compared with general volunteers (N = 1,115) with resulting nonsignificant differences on self-esteem. It was also noted that the eldest Evangelical groups in this study evidenced the lowest self-esteem levels. Bahr and Martin (1983) also found little relationship between religiosity and self-esteem among 500 high school students.

Critics of the measures used in self-esteem research point to biases against orthodox subjects (Cartner, 1983; Moberg, 1983). Further, ideological conflicts appear in some studies between secular or humanistic assumptions and traditional religious values (e.g., Gartner, 1985; Hood, Morris, & Watson, 1986; Strunk, 1985; Van Leeuwen, 1985). In a significant study, Watson, Hood, Morris, and Hall (1985) stated, "It was found that a sensitivity to the humanistic language of self measures and to the guilt dimensions of orthodox views was in fact useful in demonstrating positive associations between self-esteem and a number of religiosity measures including those related to sin" (p. 116). In essence, the orthodox language of sin and the humanistic language of self-esteem are at least partially incompatible and may account at times for divergent or negative findings. In a later study, Watson, Morris, and Hood (1987) again showed humanistic values to be antithetical to an orthodox commitment. Controlling for these value biases and for the guilt language of sin produced positive relationships between self-functioning and religiosity (intrinsic).

Particularly noteworthy is the five part programmatic empirical research of Watson, Morris, and Hood (1988a, 1988b, 1988c, 1989a, 1989b). Their subjects included both male and female undergraduates at a state university. In their initial study, Watson, Morris, and Hood (1988a) found support for the idea that orthodox conceptualization of sin can promote adaptiveness to self and others. Intrinsicness and beliefs relating to grace tended to predict an internal state of awareness and less depression. In part two of their series (1988b), the authors concluded that "Grace and an intrinsic religious orientation were generally consistent with healthy psychological characteristics. . . ." (p. 270). In contrast, extrinsicness and orthodox beliefs related to guilt were associated with maladjustment. Thus, we get a hint of some of the healthy and unhealthy components of religion. Again, in part three (1988c), extrinsic attitudes and beliefs regarding guilt were related to problematic self-functioning. Intrinsicness and grace beliefs showed complex linkages with irrational thinking and less depression.

In part four of the series, Watson, Morris, and Hood (1989a) found intrinsicness and belief in grace related to emotional empathy. Grace was predictive of less distress and depression. Earlier relationships of these variables with lack of assertiveness were not found. "Overall, intrinsicness, grace, and self guilt seemed to operate within a more-or-less integrated matrix of orthodox perspectives that produced beneficial psychological effects" (p. 44). The final study in the series (1989b) found that belief in grace, alone or in combination with intrinsic religiosity, was congruent with a belief in authority and equalitarianism while negatively related to narcissistic exploitiveness, machiavellianism and excessive individualism.

Wickstrom and Fleck (1983), in a study of 130 students from 12 Christian colleges, found that "consensual" religious (extrinsic) people have negative self-esteem, feelings of powerlessness, and feel a lack of control in their lives. The "committed" (intrinsic) religious orientation was found to be the most significant variable, having a negative correlation with dysfunctional attention-seeking. The authors noted that these findings are consistent with previous research showing that consensual people have feelings of greater interpersonal distance, move away from people (Spilka & Mullin, 1974), perceive others as less trustworthy (Maddock & Kenny, 1972), and evaluate others on the basis of social position and other materialistic concerns (Spilka & Minton, 1975).

Research suggesting possible interactions between self-esteem and other variables is offered by Falbo and Shepperd (1986). This study examined the association of religiosity with self-esteem and self-righteousness. Four typologies were created by pairing high and low self-righteousness with high and low self-esteem: broad-minded (low in self-righteousness/ high in self-esteem), insecure (high in self-righteousness/low in self-esteem), arrogant (high in self-righteousness/high in self-esteem), and meek (low in self-righteousness/low in self-esteem). The broad-minded had high scores on intrinsic and quest orientation to religion while the insecure had high scores on extrinsic religious orientation. The other two types were less differentiated with arrogant most like the insecure and the meek most like the broad-minded. The complexity of the relation between self-righteousness and mental health is made clearer by these relationships. The broad-minded would seem to reflect mental health more than the insecure typology.

Recent directions in self-esteem and religiosity research show more positive relationships as long as religion is defined as "intrinsic." Previous findings of negative relationships between self-esteem and religiosity may have been a function of humanistic language and of orthodox religious language biases. When proper controls are exercised, there is little relation between a belief in sin and poor self-functioning. Self-esteem seems to be a component of a healthy religious orientation.

Developmental Aspects of Religion and Mental Health

A developmental perspective on religion and mental health is beginning to empirically unfold, as illustrated in Worthington's recent article on faith across the life span (1989). Identifying developmental factors that are linked with psychological growth and adaptiveness may be the most important aspect of research on prevention. Attempts to integrate religion with other features of development have borrowed extensively from Piaget, Kohlberg, and Erikson, such as in Fowler's "Stages of Faith" theory (1981) which explains changes in religious growth as paralleling cognitive and moral development. A "transitional theory" has also been proposed to account for the development of religious faith. Transition can refer to crises (Hall, 1986), identity issues (Spero, 1987), or coping strategies (Pargament, 1987). Cognitive attribution theory is also seen as relevant to the life-transitions model of religious development. All of these themes — moral development, cognitive growth, and personality and mental functioning under stress — have been related to religious variables.

A variety of studies contribute to the picture of preventive possibilities in development across the life span. An examination of children who had cancer revealed that religion was helpful to the family in coping with the threat of death (Spilka, Zwartjes, Zwartjes, Heidman, & Cilli, 1987). Children regarded as religious responded differently than those who were nonreligious or came from nonreligious homes. Religious children had immediate questioning and even depression in reaction to the diagnosis. Nonreligious children showed immediate anger, fear and denial to the diagnosis. Religious children seemed to understand their illness more than nonreligious children. There was more familial closeness, especially with mother and child, in families with high religious involvement. Olson, McCubbin, Barnes, Larsen, Muxen, and Wilson (1983) discovered that religious families in the childbearing and rearing years perceived themselves to have lower stress than nonreligious families. Such was not true of families in the earlier or later years of the family life cycle.

In a longitudinal study at Duke (Blazer & Palmore, 1976), religious attitudes and behaviors were positively correlated with adjustment to aging. It is pointed out by Worthington (1989) that several studies which controlled for health status, financial status, sex, and social support discovered religious beliefs and religious participation were still related to feelings of well-being among the elderly, and only health status accounted for more variance than religion.

Spilka, Hood, and Gorsuch (1985) reviewed 36 empirical investigations of death and religious involvement. A conclusion was "Of these (36 studies), the great majority, 24, reported that stronger faith or afterlife views are affiliated with less death concern and fear" (p. 131). Another finding was that intrinsic religiosity, in contrast to extrinsic religiosity, was associated with less fear of death. And finally, older religious individuals showed little or no fear of death (p. 139).

In a longitudinal study of Mormon college students, Bergin and his associates (1990) found religious and personality development to be intertwined. Different pathways to mental health and pathology occurred. The most common developmental pattern consisted of benevolent child rearing, smooth or continuous religious development, and mild religious experiences. These people were rated by interviewers as conforming to the parental faith without the common adolescent turbulence, and their reported religious feelings were real but not dramatic. For these subjects, institutionalized religion provided stimuli for growth that reinforced positive aspects of family life and helped them prevent pitfalls. These subjects became normal, resilient adults. This appears to be consistent with *primary prevention*. Those whose child-rearing was more conflict-laden experienced diverse consequences from religious influence. They were also assessed by the same interview coding scheme. Several manifested discontinuities in religious commitment over time that were part of a troubled life in that they became inactive or deviated from norms of the religious subculture. Troubled personal development and troubled religiosity seemed to go together, but a number of these subjects later found healing in intense religious experiences that compensated for deficiencies in their personalities. These people then showed significant improvement in mental health and thus experienced *secondary prevention* due to religious influences. In a few cases, the structure of religious belief and activity provided temporary relief from emotional conflict but did not resolve the deeper problems. The religious involvement seemed to strengthen unadaptive defenses that later gave way, yielding an increase of disturbance. It appears that, for many, religious influences were therapeutic, while for some, the religious factor was part of a self-defeating pattern.

At all stages of life, then, we find evidence of religion interacting with personality variables in a manner that might promote mental health. Still, the positive aspects of religion are not always separated from negative effects. Intrinsic and extrinsic religiosity offer a promising way to specify what amounts to healthy versus unhealthy religion.

Intrinsic/Extrinsic Religiosity

Allport and Ross's (1967) concept of intrinsic and extrinsic religiosity has withstood the test of time. While some criticisms exist, the differences between intrinsicness and extrinsicness seem to hold up across a variety of conditions (Donahue, 1985). These scales are an excellent example of operationalizing a concept of religiosity. Definitions of intrinsic versus extrinsic religiosity typically refer to ends versus means, unselfish versus selfish, and committed versus utilitarian. Intrinsic people internalize their beliefs and live them regardless of consequences, while extrinsic people use religion as a means of obtaining status, security, self-justification and sociability.

Wiebe and Fleck (1980) compared intrinsically and extrinsically religious and nonreligious subjects consisting of 158 male and female Canadian university freshmen. Intrinsics "tended to have a greater concern for moral standards, conscientiousness, discipline, responsibility and consistency than those who were extrinsically religious or nonreligious." In addition, intrinsics were more sensitive, dependent, empathic, and open to their emotions, and reflected more conservative and traditional attitudes. In contrast, extrinsically religious and nonreligious subjects seemed to reflect greater self-indulgence, indolence and lack of dependability. They also showed themselves to be more flexible, self-reliant, skeptical, and pragmatic and less sentimental. The extrinsics and nonreligious were also described as more innovative, analytical, and free thinking.

Sevensky (1984) makes a penetrating observation regarding the danger of a biased and narrow view of mental health. He states, "Perhaps such highly praised characteristics as tolerance of ambiguity, flexibility, openness, and searching are — at least beyond a certain point — contributory to neither mental health or spiritual maturity." Definitions are critical to conclusions!

Baker and Gorsuch (1982) noted that anxiety has correlated both positively and negatively with religion in past research. The reason suggested is that global undifferentiated measures were used. Their research demonstrates the validity of this idea by correlating "trait anxiety" with the intrinsic and extrinsic scales. Intrinsics showed less and extrinsics showed more anxiety on most, though not all, of the trait anxiety components. Intrinsicness appeared to be associated with higher ego strength, more integrated social behavior, less paranoia or insecurity, and less anxiety, while extrinsicness was associated in the opposite direction. It was suggested that if research samples contain more extrinsics than intrinsics, the positive correlation of religiosity and anxiety will be found with general measures of religiousness but the correlation will be negative if more intrinsics are found in the population.

Bergin, Masters, and Richards (1987) studied Mormon students in psychology classes at Brigham Young University. They found that intrinsic religiosity is negatively correlated with anxiety and positively correlated with self-control and better personality functioning as measured by the California Psychological Inventory. The opposite was true of extrinsic religiosity. In general these findings are consistent with Allport's (1968) statement, "I feel equally sure that mental health is facilitated by an intrinsic, but not by an extrinsic, religious orientation" (p. 150).

Psychological adjustment as defined by well-being, self-esteem, adaptive age-related variables and numerous other characteristics, such as consistency, openness, ego strength, and sensitivity, has been shown to correlate with various measures of *religiosity*, particularly intrinsicness. These positive relationships at least raise the plausibility of prevention of mental health problems. Although causal connections are best estimated by longitudinal studies, repeated correlations of the kind described above also strengthen the likelihood that religiosity makes a difference in adjustment. Child development guidelines and religious education that emphasize inward religious conviction as opposed to creating a "righteous" social image may lead to better psychological adjustment.

SOCIAL CONDUCT

Religion and the Family

Much research deals with the way people live rather than how they feel. The social influence of religion concerns how the functioning of individuals, families and religious groups effects society.

Studies indicate that religious families differ from non-religious families and that religion plays an important role in the organization of the family. Students report that parents are similar to themselves in religious commitment. Generally, religious students come from religious homes and non-religious students from non-religious homes. Also, religious students tend to perceive their families as more happy, warm, and accepting than non-religious students (Johnson, 1973). A trend across the literature reveals that religiously homogamous (spouses of the same faith) marriages are characterized by greater marital happiness than are heterogamous marriages (Heaton, 1984; Ortega, Whitt, & William, 1988).

Another positive relationship exists between religiosity and marital adjustment. A study by Hunt and King (1978), involving 64 married couples, utilized 17 religiosity measures to measure religion, where six dimensions were clearly related to the quality of marriage. The six religious variables were organized activity in church, extrinsic (conventional — pro-religious) religious motivation, tolerance of others, creedal assent, orientation to growth and striving, and religious agreement. Marital adjustment was measured by the Locke-Wallace marital adjustment scale. Religion was found to be positively related to better marital adjustment, happiness, and satisfaction.

Church attendance correlates positively with duration of marriage, satisfaction with family life, and commitment to the institution of marriage (Larson & Goltz, 1989). According to a review by Jernigan and Nock (1983), the most important predictor of marital stability is church attendance. Several other studies have documented a positive relationship between religiosity and marital stability and happiness (Kunz & Albrecht, 1977; Schumm, Bollman, & Jurich, 1982; Shrum, 1980). Williams (1983) showed that, on the dimension of subjective marital satisfaction, religiosity emerged as the factor explaining most of the variance for both women and men.

Religion also operates as a deterrent to divorce (Hunt & King, 1978; Shrum, 1980). It has been argued that the religiously active are less likely to divorce because of values, and that this does not mean that they have happier marriages; but Kunz and Albrecht (1977) found religious activity (church attendance) to be strongly related to such variables as absence of disagreement over marital roles and willingness to marry the same spouse again, as well as to the absence of divorce. The willingness to marry the same person was designed to expose the unhappy, yet intact, marriages.

Many people, particularly the nonreligious, believe that religion has a negative effect on the sexual fulfillment of married couples. Considering the commonly hypothesized repressive role of religion relative to sex, the results of Tavris and Sadd (1977) are surprising. They found that very religious women report greater happiness and satisfaction with marital sex than either moderately religious or nonreligious women. Higher proportions of the religious group also claim to be orgasmic more often and more satisfied with the frequency of their sexual activity than their nonreligious counterparts.

Another study asked if a relatively low level of sexual gratification would influence a woman's overall satisfaction with her marriage (Bell, 1974). The conclusion was that, among women, religious commitment counters the impact of low sexual gratification in their marriages. Although the findings did not generalize to men, it was clear that a relatively low level of sexual gratification has a more negative impact on less religious women than those who are religious. Religious women are also predictably more conservative in their sexual behavior than are women who are not religious, in reference to extramarital sex and fellatio (Bell, 1974; Hong, 1983).

It appears from the above data that religion does not have the predicted stereotypically negative effect on marital sex. In fact, Tavris and Sadd (1977) indicated that religiosity is advantageous for the sexual aspect of marriage and may help prevent sexual problems. To the extent that religion also mitigates marital conflict and divorce, and enhances family cohesion, it may be considered a benevolent societal influence.

Religion and Premarital Sex

There is a trend of positive correlations between religion and the inhibition of premarital sexual behavior and permissive sexual attitudes (Hong, 1983; Miller & Olson, 1988; Rohrbaugh & Jessor, 1975; Sack, Keller, & Hinkle, 1984; Werebe, 1983). Faulkner and DeJong's (1966) 5-D scale was used in several of these studies. The results showed that the ritualistic dimension (attendance, prayers, reading the Bible) is not as important a correlate of sexual control as the intellectual (miracles and religious truth), ideological (idea about the deity and view of the Bible), consequential (business on the sabbath), and experiential (interpretation of existence) dimensions (Cardwell, 1969; Ruppel, 1970). A related finding was that men differed from women in their orientations in that, even within the religious groups, the sexual liberalism of males was higher than that of females (Davids, 1982).

Religious denomination also has an influence upon premarital sexual permissiveness. While most of the literature relates premarital sex to religion in general, some studies have looked at several of the major denominations (Bell & Blumberg, 1959; Clayton, 1968). Catholics, both males and females, were found to have a significantly higher rate of premarital coitus than their Protestant or Jewish counterparts. According to Heltsley and Broderick (1969), this may be a function of how a religion advances non-permissiveness (abstinence). They theorized that the effect of an inhibitory value is substantial only if it is expressed as a clear and unambiguous prohibition rather than mere discouragement of a behavior.

The potential inhibiting influence of religion as a preventive factor has fostered many prevention programs in churches around the United States. One such program, entitled OCTOPUS (Open Communication regarding Teens Or Parents Understanding Sexuality), which started in Illinois, is expanding to different areas of the country. It is a church based sexuality-education program for adolescents and their parents. The primary goal of the program is to confirm religious values and to prevent unplanned teen pregnancy. Several churches have tried the program, with a high success rate in lowering the incidence of premarital sexual intercourse among the members of the group and minimizing the number of teenage pregnancies (Isberner & Wright, 1990). The Search institute (Strommen, 1980) also offers many programs and insights for prevention. Although many prevention programs are conducted in the church itself, it seems that through the instilling of religious values in other settings, such as the home, might produce similar results.

Mahoney (1980) found that religiosity is negatively related to premarital sexual intercourse, but, in the case of highly religious males, he found a higher incidence of fellatio, even higher than that of the nonreligious males. This study indicates that the motivation behind conservative premarital sexual behavior and attitudes is often not as lofty as one might believe. Although their beliefs may emphasize the prohibition of coitus outside marriage, these religious males can experience sexual satisfaction without losing their technical virginity.

The potential of religion for the prevention of premarital intercourse and pregnancy is readily seen. Special efforts within religious groups may be needed however. Membership alone may not always have the desired impact.

Religion and Alcohol Abuse

A relationship between religiosity and the non-usage or moderate usage of alcohol has been extensively documented (Amoateng & Bahr, 1986; Cochran, Beeghley, & Bock, 1988). Amoateng and Bahr (1986) claim that whether or not the religion specifically teaches against alcohol use, those who are active in a religious group consumed substantially less than those who were not active. As expected, denominations do differ in their use of alcohol, and they differ from the nonreligious groups. Bock, Cochran, and Beeghley (1987) found that the impact of religiosity on alcohol use is greatest among denominations taking a strong stand against its consumption, because religious groups serve as a significant reference group.

The least drinking and negative consequences, when comparing Catholics, Jews, and Protestants, appeared among Jews. The most drinking and negative consequences were among Catholics. Alcohol restraint is instilled by Jewish norms, and even amid peer influences the college students remain committed to their strong Judaic tradition (Perkins, 1985).

Mormons, in all the studies in which they were examined, used alcohol much less frequently than other religious groups (Amoateng & Bahr, 1986). In fact, Utah, which is 70% Mormon, ranks 50th nationally in per capita alcohol consumption but 35th in the rate of alcoholism (Martin, Heaton, & Bahr, 1986). Mormonism holds very negative attitudes toward drinking. However, while a smaller proportion of Mormon college men and women drink than any other religious group studied, "of the Mormons who drink, 88% had been tight, 74% drunk, and 40% had passed out" (Strauss & Bacon, 1953). Perhaps because of the strictness of the doctrine concerning alcohol use, those who broke the religious "law" took their transgression to the limit. As far as prevention is concerned, strict religion may be a two-edged sword, deterring alcoholism and alcohol abuse, but resulting in greater abuse when the "rules" have been broken.

Even after inebriety has become established, religion is often a powerful force in achieving abstinence. One organization that consistently uses religion, or at least a dependence on a higher power, to overcome and prevent problems is Alcoholics Anonymous (AA). When reviewing the religious background of alcoholics, a strong intrinsic religiosity is rarely the case (Dickman, 1977; Walters, 1957). Dickman (1977) went so far as to say that spirituality, besides having a positive effect on the recovering alcoholic, may also prevent alcoholism by reinforcing a lifestyle of sobriety. The culture itself may also have a preventive program embedded in its mores, as with the Indian Shaker Church (Slagle & Weibel-Orlando, 1986). This church has a culture-based alcoholism intervention program that uses spirituality, as well as other aids, to help intervene before a serious alcoholism problem develops. Since alcohol abuse may be strongly inhibited by religiosity, further investigation of all its preventive potential would seem worthwhile.

Religion and Drug Abuse

As expected from the previously mentioned results, drug abuse is related to the absence of religion in a person's life. This trend has been attested to by several researchers (Adlaf & Smart, 1985; Avtar, 1979; Davids, 1982; Jessor, Jessor, & Finney, 1973). The predominant measure of religiosity in this research has been church attendance. In a study done in Britain (Adlaf & Smart, 1985) the findings indicated that church attendance was more strongly related to drug use than was the intensity of people's religious feelings.

Lorch and Hughes (1985) surveyed nearly 14,000 youths and found that conservative religious groups have lower percentages of substance abuse in general, while the more liberal religious groups have slightly lower percentages of *heavy* substance abuse. Correlations between six measures of religion and eight measures of substance abuse were consistently negative but rather small. The most significant findings was that the "importance of religion" to the person was the best single predictor of substance abuse. The authors state that, "This implies that the controls operating here are deeply internalized values and norms rather than . . . fear . . . or peer pressure" (p. 207).

Denominations do not differ very much, independent of the above findings, with the exception of Mormons. Of the ten denominational groups studied by Lorch and Hughes (1985), the most proscriptive religion (Mormonism) was the greatest deterrent for both alcohol and drugs. The lowest percentage of the Mormon young people had ever tried any of the substances listed, and they had the lowest percentage of heavy users (Amoateng & Bahr, 1986).

Gorsuch and Butler (1976) conclude that religion influences the rate of drug abuse. However, they note that religion is a form of cultural tradition and socialization; therefore, the whole connection is open to further evaluation. That relationship needs to be researched to determine the elements associated with the subcultural membership which influence drug use. Of course, it is difficult to disentangle religion from socialization and cultural influences in theorizing about causes or cures.

Despite debate over the exact nature of the religious dimension, the socialization that religion provides can be interpreted as a preventive measure toward drug abuse. As shown consistently in statistical studies, religion is associated with non-experimentation with drugs and, of those who do try, few become heavy users as compared to the nonreligious (with the exception of a few strict religions). The preventive implications of religion on drug abuse appear comparable to the implications for alcohol abuse.

Religion and Suicide

Another behavior of concern is suicide. Overall, religious people commit suicide less often than do the nonreligious (Bibby, 1979; Lester, 1988; Mandle, 1984; Stack, 1983a; Stack, 1983b). As expected, those who exhibit high levels of religiosity also have negative opinions concerning suicide. It is far less acceptable as an alternative in problem-solving by religious people than it is by those who are lower in religiosity (Hoelter, 1979).

Although the acceptability of suicide is very low, is it possible that religious people may have the idea to commit suicide, even the desire, and still refrain? Salmons and Harrington (1984) studied suicidal ideation in university students and other groups and obtained significant results to the effect that a lower percentage of religious people admit to suicide ideation on questionnaires.

A classic study by Emile Durkheim (1966) showed that where a society has been closely organized, whether on a religious, family, or national basis, suicide has been correspondingly rare. He claimed that individualism was replaced by collectivism through religion, and that religious people cling to life because of their subordination to the religious institution. Durkheim felt that the quality of one's relationships with others and with social and cultural groups determines one's vulnerability to suicide. The church and the family are reserves of strength in times of need and discouragement, and the community helps the individual solve or cope with his or her problem (Stack, 1983b).

Stack (1983b) offered the possibility that other aspects of religion might help prevent suicide:

1. The commitment that some individuals feel toward religion helps to give them a sense of self-esteem that they would not experience otherwise. "Religion assuages all manner of human disappointments" (p. 370).
2. Religion offers an alternative stratification system. In religious organizations, unlike society, people are given a high rank if they follow moral principles. Given that low self-esteem is part of a suicidal personality, the self-esteem offered by religion may serve as a deterrent to suicide.
3. Most Western religions believe in Satan and in a responsive God. These beliefs in justice, an afterlife, and the possibility of Hell reduce self-destructive behaviors.

In summary, we have found a consistent pattern of positive correlations between religious affiliation and involvement and a variety of prosocial forms of conduct. Religious lifestyles seem, on the whole, to be socially integrative. We hold to this general conclusion while acknowledging several limitations to it such as:

1. Nearly all studies have been done on mainstream religious groups that are representative of primary socialization processes that have been dominant in the culture. We have little evidence in other groups, and these groups may be growing, proportionately, in the populations.
2. Though they are small in number, some studies did not yield results consistent with our conclusions.
3. The results that do support the overall findings are not always robust.

MENTAL ILLNESS

"Mental health" is a positive term. "Mental illness" is negative. We promote "mental health" (i.e., positive traits such as resilience under stress) and by doing so we prevent "mental illness" (i.e., psychiatric disturbances). While the findings reported above concerning adjustment and mood states show a relationship between religion and *positive mental health*, (healthy traits), unfortunately, we do not have definitive findings that link positive religious development with the prevention of *mental illness*. Such a link must be inferred because the longitudinal studies needed to show the long-term effects of religious factors have not been done. Currently, we are limited to mostly short-term studies that correlate religious measures with measures of pathology.

The literature in the area of religion and mental health and illness has grown to the point that the National Institute of Mental Health (1980) printed a separate bibliography on the topic. Because of so many contradictory results and ambiguous findings, several authors have published reviews of the literature. These reviews consolidate a mass of information and serve as a reference base.

Bergin (1983) focused on mental illness in his meta-analysis of 24 studies and 30 outcomes between the years 1951 and 1979. Twenty-three percent of the effects tabulated showed religion measures associated with poorer mental health. In contrast, 47% showed religion associated with better mental health and 30% reported no significant relationship. Bergin reported an overall meta-analytic correlation across all of the religion measures and pathology measures of only $-.09$. This type of finding lends little support to either side of the debate concerning mental illness. It also suggests that the research results are based upon divergent samples and unstandardized measures of religiousness which makes consistent findings difficult to obtain.

A more comprehensive review of the religion and mental health literature was conducted by Judd (1985). He examined 116 studies that were not included in the Bergin review and another review by Lea (1982), and he extended the time span to include studies from 1918 to 1985. Comparable to the findings of Bergin, Judd found that approximately one-third of the results showed a positive relationship between religion and mental health, one third a negative relationship, and one third manifested a null relationship. When lumped together, the positive results canceled out the negative results to accentuate the null relationship. However, the process of simply combining all outcomes arithmetically can be questioned.

Unfortunately, the major reviews of the religion and mental health literature reveal a number of deficiencies in our knowledge. Although studies and reviews frequently have the term "mental health" in the title, the actual phenomenon studied often has nothing directly to do with mental functioning. For instance, Judd's review of 116 studies contains numerous reports on religion and social attitudes, like prejudice, but only 20 studies used pathology measures and only 10 dealt with clinical populations. The vast majority of studies were done with normal college students.

The same criticisms hold true for the Lea review. Although all 24 of the studies Bergin subjected to meta-analysis included a pathology measure, none of the studies sampled psychiatric populations and 18 of them were done with college students.

While some mental illness may be assessed in relation to religiosity at the extreme end of the sample distributions in these studies, the findings cannot be generalized to the mentally ill. Typical of the studies reviewed is one by Wilson and Miller (1968) that reported a modest correlation of .20 between Manifest Anxiety and religiosity among 100 students at the University of Alabama. But these results were contradicted by Bohrnstedt, Borgatta, and Evans (1968), who compared 3,700 religious and non-religious University of Wisconsin students on the *MMPI*. They found only a few differences, and these favored the religious subjects (cf. Bergin, 1983, p. 173).

The few studies done on truly disturbed populations tend to divide into two subgroups—those that show no relation between religion and disturbance and those showing less disturbance among the more religious. An example of the former is the Midtown Manhattan Study in which population samples were assessed clinically. It showed more mental impairment among the non-religious and some religious subgroups but less impairment in some other religious subgroupings (Srole, Larger, Michael, Opler, & Rennie, 1962). An example of the latter is Stark's (1971) comparison of religious involvement among 100 mentally ill persons and 100 matched controls, wherein the mentally ill proved to be distinctly less religious on several measures. A number of studies have done a variation on Stark, showing that the more religiously active are less disturbed; however, causality is open to question. It is entirely possible that persons who become mentally dysfunctional simply drop out of religious activities as well as other activities, and this could account for the finding that religiously active subgroups often show less disturbance on pathology scales. In sum, studies of pathological populations provide about the same information as studies of normal populations: The relation between undifferentiated religion and mental illness is ambiguous. Careful delineation of *types* of religiousness, such as intrinsic, has not been done in the mental illness studies.

It is also difficult to infer prevention from the data that is available in the religion and mental illness literature because of the lack of studies which deal with prevention head-on. Generally, positive effects of religion are found with variables that are more indirectly related to mental health such as well-being, marital stability, personal adjustment, and social conduct. It is safe to say that religion is positively correlated with adjustment, but the relationship with mental illness is more elusive. Specific measures of religiosity such as intrinsic/extrinsic orientation, level of commitment, or activity level provide more informative ideas than rougher estimates of religion, like denominational affiliation, which explain little about a person's way of being religious.

It appears that active, committed, intrinsically religious persons have better personal adjustment. It is a small theoretical step to conclude that since those with positive mental health are freer of mental illness and pathology, intrinsic religiousness may well contribute to prevention. Along these lines of reasoning, it seems plausible that religious organizations which foster the development of an intrinsic orientation would contribute to the mental well-being of their adherents. But, even here, we cannot show a direct effect of this religious factor on the prevention of major mental illnesses. Such may prove to be possible, but the positive possibilities are yet to be fully tested. In the meantime, we cannot draw any definite conclusions regarding mental illness and religiosity. It is quite possible that the etiology of mental illness may include familial and biological factors that sometimes override psychosocial factors such as religiosity.

CONCLUSION AND SPECULATIONS

"Religion as prevention" is a concept based on an illusion—*the uniformity myth*. The myth would state that one religion is as good as another, or that one set of religious practices, beliefs, and commitments has the same impact as another. The work with intrinsic and extrinsic religiosity contradicts this notion and supports the assertion that some ways of being religious are healthier than other ways.

The type of religion most closely tied with good mental health is an internalized religion. "Intrinsic" best defines healthy religion at this point. This means higher commitment, seeing religion as an end in itself, unselfishly lived with less regard for consequence than principle. Such is concomitant with greater concern for moral standards, discipline, consistency, conscientiousness and resistance to external pressure to deviate.

A benevolent transference of intrinsic religious values in the context of child rearing may be associated with emotional security and cognitive structures for effectively coping with life events in ways that enhance meaning, growth, and adjustment across the life span. Awareness of extrinsic religiosity and associated negative correlates should serve as a warning that some forms of religion are not benign but may accompany, if not encourage, maladjustment. Religious behaviors, practices, level of commitment and involvement, and intention or motivation may result in important differences in whether or not psychological problems are prevented and mental health is promoted. Further, it would seem that healthy religious involvement is better than no religious involvement as far as adjustment and well-being are concerned.

Further speculations regarding the positive trends would include these points:

1. Strong religious values may correlate positively with mental health in part because both reflect the optimum socialized behaviors of the culture.
2. Mental health values might overlap with religious values. (Even so, we must be careful not to equate viable religion with mental health.)
3. Some forms of religiosity are likely congruent with personal growth, achievement, stability, avoidance of a harmful lifestyle, family cohesion and self-actualization.
4. There may be religiously encouraged developmental patterns that are basically prosocial and extend over the life span.
5. A sense of direction, destiny, purpose and transcendent meaning can be helpful in providing consistency and guidance across time and situations.
6. The survival of religion may say something about its utility and adaptability.

Some healthy aspects of religion have been identified and seem to be robust. Religion is positively implicated in a sense of well-being, self-esteem and personal adjustment. Other areas showing a relationship with religion are family lifestyles, drug and alcohol abuse, sexual behavior, and suicide. The correlates between religiosity and mental health suggest the potential for prevention of problems is a reality. While serious mental disorders are not so affected by religiosity, the broad scope of positive mental health, as reflected by psychological adjustment, correlates with some aspects of religiosity (e.g., intrinsic) to confirm a positive trend in virtually every area examined.

Mental health workers need to be aware of the positive potential of religious involvement. Theories of pathology and psychotherapy are secular and do not lead naturally to thinking of religion as a health promoting agent. In fact, early research and theory portrayed religion as anti-health. Although it is true that certain religious orientations (e.g., extrinsic) are often associated with counterproductive aspects of life, religiosity that is internalized, committed, mature, and unselfish will generally be found on the side of mental health. Even so, the picture is more complex than a summary can indicate.

It remains for researchers studying religion and mental health to further explicate the dimensions of religiosity and their interaction across populations and across situations. Specificity, careful sampling, control of variables, appropriate designs and replications, building on the extensive work already done, will undoubtedly yield interesting and useful results. Religious beliefs and practices are powerful forces in our society, as yet only partially understood.

REFERENCES

Adlaf, E. M., & Smart, R. G. (1985). Drug use and religious affiliation, feelings, and behaviour. *British Journal of Addiction, 80,* 163-171.

Allport, G. W., & Ross, J. M. (1967). Personal religious orientation and prejudice. *Journal of Personality and Social Psychology, 5,* 432-443.

Allport, G. W. (1968). *The person in psychology, selected essays.* Boston: Beacon.

Amoateng, A. Y., & Bahr, S. J. (1986). Religion, family and adolescent drug use. *Sociological Perspectives, 29,* 53-76.

Avtar, S. (1979). Religious involvement and anti-social behavior. *Perceptual and Motor Skills, 48,* 1157-1158.

Aycock, D. W., & Noaker, S. (1985). A comparison of the self-esteem levels in evangelical Christian and general populations. *Journal of Psychology and Theology, 13*(3), 199-208.

Bahr, H. M., & Martin, T. K. (1983). "And thy neighbor as thyself": Self-esteem and faith in people as correlates of religiosity and family solidarity among Middletown high school students. *Journal for the Scientific Study of Religion, 22*(2), 132-144.

Baker, M., & Gorsuch, R. (1982). Trait anxiety and intrinsic-extrinsic religiousness. *Journal for the Scientific Study of Religion, 21*(2), 119-122.

Bell, R. R., & Blumberg, L. (1959). Courtship intimacy and religious background. *Marriage and Family Living, 21,* 356-360.

Bell, R. R. (1974). Religious involvement and marital sex in Australia and the United States. *Journal of Comparative Family Studies, 5*(2), 109-116.

Bergin, A. E., Masters, K. S., Stinchfield, R. D., Caskin, T. A., Sullivan, C. E., Reynolds, E. M., & Greaves, D. W. (1990). Religious life-styles and mental health. In L. B. Brown & H. N. Malony (Eds.), *Religion, personality, and mental health.* New York: Springer.

Bergin, A. E. (1983). Religiosity and mental health: a critical reevaluation and meta-analysis. *Professional Psychology: Research and Practice, 14*(2), 170-184.

Bergin, A. E., Masters, K. S., & Richards, P. (1987). Religiousness and mental health reconsidered: A study of an intrinsically religious sample. *Journal of Counseling Psychology, 34*(2), 197-204.

Bibby, R. W. (1979). *Consequences of religious commitment: The Canadian case*. Presented at the annual meeting of the society for the Scientific Study of Religion, Antonio, Texas.

Blazer, D., & Palmore, E. (1976). Religion and aging in a longitudinal panel. *The Gerontologist, 16*(1), 82-85.

Bock, E. W., Cochran, J. K., & Beeghley, L. (1987). Moral messages: the relative influence of denomination on the religiosity-alcohol relationship. *The Sociological Quarterly, 28*, 89-103.

Bohrnstedt, G. W., Borgatta, E. G., & Evans, R. R. (1968). Religious affiliation, religiosity, and *MMPI* scores. *Journal for the Scientific Study of Religion, 7*, 255-258.

Caplan, G. (1972). *Support systems and community mental health: Lectures on concept development*. New York: Behavioral Publications.

Cardwell, J. D. (1969). The relationship between religious commitment and premarital sexual permissiveness: A five dimensional analysis. *Sociological Analysis, 30*(2), 72-80.

Carson, V., Soeken, K. L., & Grimm, P. M. (1988). Hope and its relationship to spiritual well-being. *Journal of Psychology and Theology, 16*(2), 159-167.

Chamberlain, K., & Zika, S. (1988). Religiosity, life meaning and well-being: Some relationships in a sample of women. *Journal for the Scientific Study of Religion, 27*(3), 411-420.

Clayton, R. R. (1968). Religious orthodoxy and premarital sex. *Social Forces, 47*, 471-474.

Clinebell, H. J. (1970). The local church's contribution to positive mental health. In H. J. Clinebell (Ed.), *Community mental health: The role of church and temple*. Nashville: Abington Press.

Cochran, J. K., Beeghley, L., & Bock, E. W. (1988). Religiosity and alcohol behavior: An exploration of reference group theory. *Sociological Forum, 3*(2), 256-276.

Davids, L. (1982). Ethnic identity, religiosity, and youthful deviance: The Toronto computer dating project – 1979. *Adolescence, 17*(67), 673-684.

Dickman, C. H. (1977). *Therapeutic effects of spirituality on alcoholism*. Unpublished master's thesis, University of Utah, Salt Lake City.

Donahue, M. J. (1985). Intrinsic and extrinsic religiousness: review and meta analysis. *Journal of Personality and Social Psychology, 48*, 400-419.

Durkheim, E. (1966). *Suicide*. New York: Free Press.

Falbo, T., & Shepperd, J. A. (1986). Self-righteousness: Cognitive, power, and religious characteristics. *Journal of Research in Personality, 20*, 145-157.

Faulkner, J. E., & DeJong, G. F. (1966). Religiosity in 5-D: An empirical analysis. *Social Forces, 45*(2), 246-254.

Fowler, J. W. (1981). *Stages of faith*. New York: Harper and Row.

Gartner, J. (1983). Self-esteem tests: A Christian critique. In C. W. Ellison (Ed.),

Your better self: Christianity, psychology, and self-esteem. New York: Harper and Row.

Gartner, J. (1985). Religious prejudice in psychology: Theories of its cause and cure. *Journal of Psychology and Christianity, 4*(1), 16-23.

Gorsuch, R. L., & Butler, M. C. (1976). Initial drug abuse: A review of predisposing social psychological factors. *Psychological Bulletin, 83*(1), 120-137.

Hall, C. M. (1986). Crisis as an opportunity for spiritual growth. *Journal of Religion and Health, 25,* 8-17.

Heaton, T. B. (1984). Religious homogamy and marital satisfaction reconsidered. *Journal of Marriage and the Family,* 729-733.

Heltsley, M. E., & Broderick, C. (1969). Religiosity and premarital sexual permissiveness: Reexamination of Reiss's traditionalism proposition. *Journal of Marriage and the Family, 31,* 441-443.

Hoelter, J. W. (1979). Religiosity; fear of death and suicide acceptability. *Suicide and Life-Threatening Behavior, 9*(3), 163-172.

Hong, S. M. (1983). Gender, religion, and sexual permissiveness: Some recent Australian data. *The Journal of Psychology, 115,* 17-22.

Hood, R. W., Jr., Morris, R. J., & Watson, P. J. (1986). Maintenance of religious fundamentalism. *Psychological Reports, 59,* 547-559.

Hunt, R. A., & King, M. B. (1978). Religiosity and marriage. *Journal for the Scientific Study of Religion, 17*(4), 399-406.

Isberner, F. R., & Wright, W. R. (1990). Sex education in Illinois churches: The octopus program. *Journal of Sex Education and Therapy,* 29-33.

Jernigan, J. D., & Nock, S. L. (1983, November). *Religiosity and family stability: Do families that pray together stay together?* Paper presented at the annual meetings of the Scientific Study of Religion, Knoxville, Tennessee.

Jessor, R., Jessor, S. L., & Finney, J. (1973). A social psychology of marijuana use: Longitudinal studies of high school and college youth. *Journal of Personality and Social Psychology, 26*(1), 1-15.

Johnson, M. A. (1973). Family life and religious commitment. *Review of Religious Research, 14,* 144-150.

Judd, D. K. (1985). *Religiosity and mental health: A literature review—1928-1985.* Unpublished master's thesis, Brigham Young University, Provo, Utah.

Koenig, H. G., Kvale, J. N., & Ferrel, C. (1988). Religion and well-being in later life. *The Gerontologist, 28*(1), 18-29.

Kunz, P. R., & Albrecht, S. L. (1977). Religion, marital happiness, and divorce. *International Journal of Sociology of the Family, 7,* 227-232.

Larson, L. E., & Goltz, J. W. (1989). Religious participation and marital commitment. *Review of Religious Research, 30*(4), 387-400.

Lea, G. (1982). Religion, mental health, and clinical issues. *Journal of Religion and Health, 21*(4), 336-351.

Lester, D. (1988). Religion and personal violence (homicide and suicide) in the U.S.A. *Psychological Reports, 62,* 618.

Lorch, B. R., & Hughes, R. H. (1985). Religion and youth substance use. *Journal of Religion and Health, 24*(3), 197-208.

Maddock, R., & Kenny, C. (1972). Philosophies of human nature and personal religious orientation. *Journal for the Scientific Study of Religion, 11*, 271-227.

Mahoney, E. R. (1980). Religiosity and sexual behavior among heterosexual college students. *The Journal of Sex Research, 16*, 97-113.

Mandle, C. L. (1984). Suicide: A human problem. *Educational Horizons, 62*(4), 119-123.

Martin, T. K., Heaton, T. B., & Bahr, S. J. (Eds.). (1986). *Utah in demographic perspective*. Salt Lake City: Signature Books.

Miller, B. C., & Olson, T. D. (1988). Sexual attitudes and behavior of high school students in relation to background and contextual factors. *The Journal of Sex Research, 24*, 194-200.

Moberg, D. O. (1983). The nature of the social self. In C. W. Ellison (Ed.), *Your better self*. San Francisco: Harper and Row.

National Institute of Mental Health (1980). *Religion and Mental Health: A Bibliography*. (DHHS Publication No. ADM 80-964). Washington, DC: U. S. Government Printing Office.

Olson, D. H., McCubbin, H. I., Barnes, H., Larsen, A., Muxen, M., & Wilson, M. (1983). *Families: What makes them work*. Beverly Hills: Sage.

Ortega, S. T., Whitt, H. P., & William, J. A., Jr. (1988). Religious homogamy and marital happiness. *Journal of Family Issues, 9*(2), 224-239.

Pargament, K. I. (1987, August). *God help me: Towards a theoretical framework of coping for the psychology of religion*. Paper presented at the meeting of the American Psychological Association, New York City.

Perkins, W. H. (1985). Religious traditions, parents, and peers as determinants of alcohol and drug use among college students. *Review of Religious Research, 27*, 15-31.

Petersen, L. R., & Roy, A. (1985). Religiosity, anxiety, and meaning and purpose: Religion's consequences for psychological well-being. *Review of Religious Research, 27*(1), 49-62.

Reynolds, M. M. (1982). Religious institutions and the prevention of mental illness. *Journal of Religion and Health, 21*(3), 245-253.

Rohrbaugh, J., & Jessor, R. (1975). Religiosity in youth: A personal control against deviant behavior. *Journal of Personality, 43*(1), 136-155.

Roth, P. D. (1988). Spiritual well-being and marital adjustment. *Journal of Psychology and Theology, 16*(2), 153-158.

Ruppel, H. J. (1970). Religiosity and premarital sexual permissiveness: A response to the Reiss-Heltsley and Broderick debate. *Journal of Marriage and the Family, 32*, 647-655.

Sack, A. R., Keller, J. F., & Hinkle, D. E. (1984). Premarital sexual intercourse: A test of the effects of peer group, religiosity, and sexual guilt. *The Journal of Sex Research, 20*, 168-185.

Salmons, P. H., & Harrington, R. (1984). Suicidal ideation in university students and other groups. *International Journal of Psychiatry, 30*(3), 201-205.

Schumm, W. R., Bollman, S. R., & Jurich, A. P. (1982). The "marital conventionalization" argument: Implications for the study of religiosity and marital satisfaction. *Journal of Psychology and Theology, 10,* 236-241.

Sevensky, R. L. (1984). Religion, psychology, and mental health. *American Journal of Psychotherapy, 38*(1), 73-86.

Shrum, W. (1980). Religious and marital instability: Change in the 1970s? *Review of Religious Research, 21,* 135-147.

Slagle, A. L., & Weibel-Orlando, J. (1986). The Indian Shaker church and alcoholics anonymous: Revitalistic curing cults. *Human Organization, 45,* 310-319.

Spero, M. H. (1987). Identity and individuality in the nouveau-religious patient: Theoretical and clinical aspects. *Psychiatry, 50,* 55-71.

Spilka, B., Hood, R. W., & Gorsuch, R. (1985). *The psychology of religion.* Englewood Cliffs: Prentice Hall.

Spilka, B., & Minton, B. (1975, October). *Defining personal religion: Psychometric, cognitive, and instrumental dimensions.* Paper presented at the 1975 convention of the Society for the Scientific Study of Religion, Washington, DC.

Spilka, B., & Mullin, M. (1974, October). *Personal religion and psychosocial schemata: A research approach to a theoretical psychology of religion.* Paper presented at the 1974 convention of the Society for the Scientific Study of Religion, Washington, DC.

Spilka, B., Zwartjes, W. J., Zwartjes, G. M., Heideman, D., & Cilli, K. A. (1987). *The role of religion in coping with cancer.* Unpublished manuscript, University of Denver.

Srole, L., Larger, T., Michael, S. T., Opler, M. K., & Rennie, T. A. (1962). *Mental health in the metropolis* (Vol. 1). New York: McGraw-Hill.

St. George, A., & McNamara, P. H. (1984). Religion, race and psychological well-being. *Journal for the Scientific Study of Religion, 23*(4), 351-363.

Stack, S. (1983a). A comparative analysis of suicide and religiosity. *The Journal of Social Psychology, 119,* 285-286.

Stack, S. (1983b). The effect of the decline in institutionalized religion on suicide, 1954-1978. *Journal for the Scientific Study of Religion, 22*(3), 239-252.

Stark, R. (1971). Psychopathology and religious commitment. *Review of Religious Research, 12,* 165-175.

Strauss, R., & Bacon, S. D. (1953). *Drinking in College.* New Haven: Yale University Press.

Strommen, M. P. (1980). Religious beliefs: Powerful predictors of actions and behavior.

Strunk, O., Jr. (1985). Dealing with proceptive countertransference-like issues: The factor of psychotherapeutic ideology. In E. M. Stern (Ed.), *Psychotherapy and the religiously committed patient.* New York: The Haworth Press, Inc.

Tavris, C., & Sadd, S. (1977). *The Redbook report on female sexuality.* New York: Delacorte Press.

Van Leeuwen, M. S. (1985). *The person in psychology: A contemporary Christian appraisal.* Grand Rapids: Eerdmans.

Walters, O. S. (1957). The religious background of fifty alcoholics. *Quarterly Journal of Studies on Alcohol, 18,* 405-413.

Watson, P. J., Hood, R. W., Jr., Morris, R. J., & Hall, J. R. (1985). Religiosity, sin, and self-esteem. *Journal of Psychology and Theology, 13*(2), 116-128.

Watson, P. J., Morris, R. J., & Hood, R. W., Jr. (1987). Antireligious humanistic values, guilt, and self-esteem. *Journal for the Scientific Study of Religion, 26*(4), 535-546.

Watson, P. J., Morris, R. J., & Hood, R. W., Jr. (1988a). Sin and self-functioning, part 1: Grace, guilt, and self-consciousness. *Journal of Psychology and Theology, 16*(3), 254-269.

Watson, P. J., Morris, R. J., & Hood, R. W., Jr. (1988b). Sin and self-functioning, part 2: Grace, guilt, and psychological adjustment. *Journal of Psychology and Theology, 16*(3), 270-281.

Watson, P. J., Morris, R. J., & Hood, R. W., Jr. (1988c). Sin and self-functioning, part 3: The psychology and ideology of irrational beliefs. *Journal of Psychology and Theology, 16*(4), 348-361.

Watson, P. J., Morris, R. J., & Hood, R. W., Jr. (1989a). Sin and self-functioning, part 4: Depression, assertiveness, and religious commitments. *Journal of Psychology and Theology, 17*(1), 44-58.

Watson, P. J., Morris, R. J., & Hood, R. W., Jr. (1989b). Sin and self-functioning, part 5: Antireligious humanistic values, individualism, and the community. *Journal of Psychology and Theology, 17*(2), 157-172.

Werebe, M. J. G. (1983). Attitudes of French adolescents toward sexuality. *Journal of Adolescence, 6,* 145-159.

Wickstrom, D. L., & Fleck, J. R. (1983). Missionary children: Correlates of self-esteem and dependency. *Journal of Psychology and Theology, 11*(3), 226-235.

Wiebe, K. F., & Fleck, J. R. (1980). Personality correlates of intrinsic, extrinsic, and nonreligious orientations. *The Journal of Psychology, 105,* 181-187.

Williams, C. M. (1983). *Marital satisfaction and religiosity.* Unpublished master's thesis, University of Utah, Salt Lake City.

Willits, F. K., & Crider, D. M. (1988). Religion and well-being: Men and women in the middle years. *Review of Religious Research, 29*(3), 281-294.

Wilson, W., & Miller, H. L. (1968). Fear, anxiety and religiousness. *Journal for the Scientific Study of Religion, 7,* 111.

Witter, R. A., Stock, W. A., Okun, M. A., & Haring, M. J. (1985). Religion and subjective well-being in adulthood: A quantitative synthesis. *Review of Religious Research, 26*(4), 332-342.

Worthington, E. L., Jr. (1989). Religious faith across the life span: Implications for counseling and research. *The Counseling Psychologist, 17*(4), 555-612.

Religious Factors in Physical Health and the Prevention of Illness

Jeffrey S. Levin

Eastern Virginia Medical School

Harold Y. Vanderpool

The University of Texas Medical Branch

SUMMARY. Many scientists often assume that religious preference and involvement have little effect on physical health, or that, if such effects exist, few studies have addressed this issue. In actuality, there is a long tradition of empirical research on the interconnections of religion and physical health. Theoretical speculation as to the reasons for such a salutary effect of religious belief or involvement has been prominent in the writings of distinguished scholars and physicians past and present. Furthermore, the existence of such religion-health connections is a nearly universal feature within the cosmologies of religious traditions and is supported by empirical evidence from various scientific disciplines. This essay surveys religious factors in physical health, discussing why religious indicators should be significantly related to health status, critically reviewing key empirical evidence, offering explanations for such findings, and noting their implications for the prevention of illness.

Despite the widespread assumption that the effects of religious involvement or of particular religious beliefs represent an underinvestigated topic of medical research or do not merit the attention of scientists, the empirical study of religious factors in physical health and illness has been a major research endeavor for nearly two centuries. Over 300 studies have appeared in the fields of epidemiology (Jarvis & Northcutt, 1987; Levin &

Reprints may be obtained from Jeffrey S. Levin, Department of Family and Community Medicine, Eastern Virginia Medical School, Post Office Box 1980, Norfolk, VA 23501.

83

Schiller, 1987), gerontology (Levin, 1988; Witter, Stock, Okun & Haring, 1985), and the behavioral sciences and health behavior. Recent theoretical papers have suggested reasons for positive findings linking religious involvement or belief with physical health (e.g., Idler, 1987; Levin & Vanderpool, 1989; Vaux, 1976), while historical and theological essays have outlined the broader interconnections of religion and medicine (Vanderpool, 1977, 1980; Vanderpool & Levin, 1990). Until very recently, however, this gold mine of information was largely overlooked, unreviewed, and unsynthesized. Indeed, many researchers may still be unaware that this wealth of data exists, as exemplified by such statements as, "[T]here has been a paucity of studies examining the epidemiological effects of religion on health" (Byrne & Price, 1979, p. 7).

Recent review articles have begun to synthesize data linking religious variables and physical health and to elaborate frameworks for explanation and further study (Jarvis & Northcutt, 1987; Levin & Vanderpool, 1989; Schiller & Levin, 1988). By identifying social, psychological, biological, and behavioral pathways or mechanisms by which religious preference and involvement influence health, such frameworks are valuable in that they help to identify opportunities for preventive health interventions. Paradoxically, while many researchers continue to produce empirical evidence for salutary religious effects, the emergence of this field of inquiry has suffered from a sort of collective amnesia on the part of social scientists, epidemiologists, and biomedical professionals whose tacit professional knowledge tends to downplay the role of religious belief and involvement as salient influences upon health. As a result, only in recent years have linkages between religion and health begun to be exploited for purposes of health promotion and disease prevention (e.g., Department of Health and Human Services, 1987).

This paradox is especially troubling, because the need for empirical research on the role of religiosity or religiousness in health and healing has long been advocated by leading figures in medicine. From Billings (1891) and Osler (1910) to contemporaries such as Frank (1973), many clinicians have argued that religion, generally defined, represents a rich source of social, cultural, ideological, intrapsychic, and familial influences on physical health and well-being. Yet, despite the support of these influential figures, the idea that one's religious background or experiences might determine or predict one's physical health status or, at the population level, rates of disease or death has remained a marginal issue for allopathic medicine, where it represents "part of the folklore of discussion on the fringes of the research community" (Levin & Schiller, 1987, p. 10). By all appearances, this marginal issue seems to be, at best, an insignificant area of research. Appearances, however, are often misleading.

In the past century, hundreds of scientific publications have identified significant religious differences in rates of health, disease, and death and have pointed to indicators of religious belief and involvement as having significant effects on various physical health outcomes. The earliest work in this area consisted of anecdotal reports, descriptive epidemiology, and simple demographic breakouts, but was scattershot because it neither built upon a particular research tradition nor lay the groundwork for programmatic studies. This early research is exemplified by reports that noted the apparent absence of penile cancer in Jews (Travers, 1837) and of uterine cancer in nuns (Rigoni-Stern, 1842), and the differential rates of morbidity and mortality across various religious groups (Billings, 1891). A more sophisticated example is Durkheim's classic *La Suicide* (1897), perhaps the first systematic work of social epidemiology.

By the turn of the century, more programmatic work began focusing on the relative risk (or protection) among Jews of certain patterns and sources of morbidity and mortality, mostly related to heart disease and uterine cancer. Through the 1940s, dozens of studies detailed the advantages manifested by Jews relative to Gentiles with respect to cervical cancer (see Levin & Schiller, 1987), with the favorable role of male circumcision usually singled out as responsible for this finding. For many years, these studies were cited as evidence of the preventive health benefits of circumcision. This research was reviewed in Kennaway's "The Racial and Social Incidence of Cancer of the Uterus" (1948)—perhaps the finest epidemiologic literature review ever written. This comprehensive summary of studies detailed racial, ethnic, religious, and national differences in the incidence of uterine cancer. Subjects included Hindu, Muslim, Parsi, Christian, Chinese, and Jewish women from over a dozen sites around the world. Social-class differences were also explored, and a wide-ranging set of alternative hypotheses was proposed to explain identified differences in incidence. These included factors related to economic conditions, childbearing, early marriage, genetics, circumcision, douching, and ritual observances associated with menstruation and childbirth within Judaism, Islam, Hinduism, and the Parsi faith. While this excellent review was never adequately followed up, it exemplifies the value for health educators and others of examining alternative explanations for ostensibly religious effects on health.

By the 1950s, epidemiologists had begun to extend their consideration beyond Jews to other cohesive, behaviorally strict groups such as Seventh-Day Adventists (Stanton, 1989), Mormons (e.g., West, Lyon & Gardner, 1980), the Amish (e.g., Hamman, Barancik & Lilienfeld, 1981), Hutterites (e.g., Morgan, Holmes, Grace, Kemel & Robson, 1983), Parsis (e.g., Jussawalla, Yeole & Natekar, 1981), and members of the clergy (e.g., King & Locke, 1980). By the 1960s, continuous measures of religious beliefs, attitudes, and behaviors began to be utilized — no longer just categorical religious affiliation variables — indicating a willingness to move beyond descriptive studies and investigate religious effects more directly. The most seminal research in this vein were Scotch's studies of hypertension in Zulus (Scotch, 1960, 1963) and the many studies by Comstock and associates using data from the Washington County, Maryland, epidemiologic census (e.g., Comstock & Tonascia, 1977). At the same time, Moberg (1953a, 1953b) pioneered a similar program of research within gerontology, where the study of religious factors in health has since grown quite rapidly. These studies in aging tend to focus on the effects of religious involvement on subjective indicators of physical health, such as self-report measures of global and functional health status, disability, and somatic symptomatology (see Levin, 1988).

In the last several years, more systematic research programs have begun to be developed, such as the work of Koenig and associates on the effects of religiosity, variously defined, on the health of geriatric patients (e.g., Koenig, Smiley & Gonzales, 1988). Ongoing research on the effects of religious involvement within allied fields such as health services research, psychiatry, and family studies has reached new levels of sophistication. In addition to this rediscovery and synthesis of earlier work and a general upgrading of methodological and analytical approaches, recent studies have benefited from thoughtful exploration of "classical" statements on the intersections of religion and health by many of the 20th Century's most respected philosophers and scientists. Two recent books on religion and health (Clements, 1989; Koenig et al., 1988) pay tribute to the long legacy of thought on the roles of religious preference, belief, and involvement in health within Western philosophy, psychiatry, and Judaeo-Christian theological traditions, a legacy also present within Eastern (Rama, 1978), esoteric (Gerber, 1988), and folk (Sempebwa, 1983) traditions. Far from representing marginal issues, as they are for many physicians and scientists, these legacies propose the existence of symbiotic relationships between religion, physical health, and illness.

RELIGION AS A MULITFACETED
HEALTH-RELATED PHENOMENON

Despite secular pronouncements that it has, or soon will, decay and die, religion continues to exist as a stubborn, ever-present feature and force in society. Desirous of ending vicious rivalry and warfare, Enlightenment thinkers in the 17th and 18th Centuries prophesied religion's replacement by reason and science. Viewing religion as an entrenched capitalist tool fueling social inequity, Marx predicted that religion would fade away with the emergence of classless societies (Green, 1990). Finding it a source of infantile dependency and social repression, Freud viewed religion as fading away when humans, aided by psychoanalytic insight, attain psychological maturity (Wallwork, 1990). Informed by these criticisms, struck by religion's seemingly nonsensical claims, and often escaping from or growing beyond the religious orientations of their childhoods, many researchers and medical professionals may feel that since religion means little to them personally, it must not be a very salient force generally.

As a beginning point, researchers interested in investigating the roles of religion in physical health and illness should distinguish their personal beliefs and/or involvement from the beliefs and involvement of those in the populations they investigate. This stance constitutes no plea for or disguised defense of "religion," but, rather, entails a curiosity about or an openness to religion as a possible factor of force in health. While outright opposition to or advocacy of religion is readily recognized as an impediment to such research (Ellis, 1980), assumptions about religion that diverge dramatically from those of populations under study may keep investigators from discovering the influence of religion in such populations. For example, given the legacy of opposition to religion in the history of medicine (White, 1960) and the fact that only 16 percent of scientists report belief in life after death, it is no wonder that little credibility might be given to the 67 percent of American adults who profess this belief (Gallup & Proctor, 1982), or to the 42 percent of Americans who attend church or synagogue at least weekly (a constant figure for decades), the 77 percent who believe in heaven, the 58 percent who believe in hell, or the 24 percent who believe in reincarnation (Gallup & Gallup, 1988, 1989).

"Religion," however, constitutes much more than what persons say they believe. As such, its influence exceeds an avowal of dogma. As a human phenomenon, religion is multifaceted; it includes and interrelates at least these "religion-making characteristics": (1) the affirming of a world-view that includes faith in some superempirical, usually supernatural being(s) or powers; (2) rituals and ceremonious behaviors such as prayer, meditation, recitations, and rites; (3) moral codes; (4) distinctions between sacred and profane actions and objects; (5) characteristic motivations and emotions; and (6) ongoing social organizations that are usually long-lived and ethnically or regionally specific, such as Irish Catholics, Scotch-Irish Presbyterians, Ashkenazi Jews, Southern Baptists, Japanese Buddhists (Alston, 1967; Levin & Vanderpool, 1987).

Although religion's comprehensiveness connotes power beyond simplistic equations of religion with belief, its greater, lasting, and stubbornly-persisting influence resides in the functions it fulfills. Linked to various ethnic heritages, religion provides meaning, memory, systems of support, mutual aid, and a means of coping and comfort in the face of difficulty, disaster, and triumph (Vanderpool & Levin, 1990) — provisions which social epidemiologists have found to strongly benefit health (see Insel & Moos, 1974). Furthermore, through teachers and prophets, religious traditions provide avenues of change, reform, and protest; and through rites of passage, religion serves to guide individuals from birth, through cycles of growth and maturity, to separation and death (Abramson, 1980; Vanderpool & Levin, 1990). Finally, by relating groups or peoples to that which is defined as absolute and supremely powerful, religious groups are elevated beyond a sense of helplessness, confusion, and insignificance to levels of social control, empowerment, and mastery — affects which are believed to positively influence health (Levin & Vanderpool, 1989).

So, are there grounds for suspecting that religion has contributed, for better or worse, to the prevention of illness and the fostering of health? The grounds for this expectation are great (Vanderpool, 1988) because the powers and functions of religion just noted have been for centuries specifically targeted at physical health and illness. Tradition after tradition has prescribed and proscribed norms and rules for everything from eating and drinking, to expressions of human sexuality, hygiene, and respective displays of human emotion, to the care and treatment of the sick, diseased, dying, and dead, and the ways in which the human body may be altered or mutilated. Without doubt, many religious traditions do seek to influence or control various health-related beliefs, attitudes, and behaviors. The questions that remain pertain not to whether this has been and is being done, but to issues such as: What measurable effects (for good or ill) does religious involvement have on patterns of health status, morbidity, and mortality? Do such respective patterns differentially manifest across particular religious traditions? How are these patterns of influence related to or mediated by such factors as social class, secularization, and levels of religious commitment or subjective religiosity (Levin & Vanderpool, 1987)? Although the multifaceted, inclusive nature of religion gives credence to its influence on physical health and illness, this same multifaceted character gives rise to the following caution: since religion is a multidimensional phenomenon or "meta-construct," explanations for its influence may be varied.

In a recent review essay, Levin and Vanderpool (1989) enumerated a multifactorial set of hypotheses which focus on the different structural and functional components of religion discussed above. These hypotheses can be operationally tested as alternative or additive explanations for significant associations between religious and health indicators. Each explanation accounts for significant findings on the basis of mechanisms or pathways well-established through social-epidemiologic research. These explanations include:

1. religiously dictated health-promotive regimens for *behaviors* governing cigarettes, alcohol, drugs, diet, exercise, sex, and hygiene;
2. *psychological effects* of religious involvement resulting from fellowship, cohesiveness, participation, social support, and a general sense of belonging;
3. *psychodynamics of religious belief systems* which foster peacefulness, self-confidence, autonomy, and a sense of purpose on the one hand, and guilt, depression, self-doubt, and co-dependency on the other;
4. *psychodynamics of religious rites* which buffer stress and are conducive to easing of grief, dread, anxiety, or entrapment, or that provide for escape, catharsis, or empowerment;
5. *psychodynamics of religious faith* as a source of assurance or expectation of deliverance, healing, or better health; and
6. *superempirical or supernatural influences* which could account for measurably significant improvements in health status among the religious — changes unaccountable for by all presently known and testable variables (Byrd, 1988).

In addition, given the degrees to which religious traditions preserve patterns of interfamilial and ethnic identity, *hereditary factors* associated with religious identification may also be associated with longevity, physical health, or disease yet independently of religious belief and ritual. A case in point is Tay-Sachs, a metabolic disease of infancy and early childhood which strikes Jews of Ashkenazi (or European) descent at a rate of ten times that of children of other religio-ethnic groups (Krupp, Schroeder

& Tierney, 1987, p. 1048). This elevated risk is clearly a function of a genetic predisposition and is not an outcome of any psychosocial or behavioral phenomenon concomitant to Jewish belief or worship.

Another explanation for significant findings linking religious indicators and health outcomes is the presence of *methodological flaws*. That is, for various reasons related to faulty study design and execution, particular significant findings are spurious, or not real. Typical reasons for spurious findings include errors in (a) *conceptualizing* or defining religion or religiosity, (b) *operationalizing* or measuring aspects of religiosity in the populations and religious groups under consideration, and (c) *designing* research studies and *analyzing* data (e.g., not controlling for relevant background or mediating variables, such as the constructs mentioned in the above description of alternative explanations).

Finally, these explanations may interact symbiotically with one another, giving rise to *multifactorial explanations* (Levin & Vanderpool, 1989). The word "multifactorial" thus serves as a critical concept in three respects: first, *theoretically* (as a basis for assessing religion's force and impact on physical health); second, *conceptually* (as a foundation for identifying and measuring religious variables pertinent to health); and, third, *operationally* (as a reminder that these variables may act in concert with one another to measurably impact on health and illness).

EVIDENCE OF A SALUTARY
RELIGIOUS EFFECT

Empirical findings are largely supportive of a salutary effect for religious involvement. Unlike the literature on religion and mental health (see Larson, Pattison, Blazer, Omran & Kaplan, 1986), findings relating religious variables to physical health outcomes have been surprisingly consistent. While existing studies nonetheless suffer collectively from various limitations that prevent conclusive *proof* of such an effect (e.g., inconsistent measurement of religiosity across studies, lack of multi-wave designs needed to assess causality), this summary conclusion is suggestive and provocative for several reasons.

First, religious involvement has been found to be positively associated with health status regardless of how such involvement is defined or measured. Constructs such as organizational religious behavior (e.g., church or synagogue membership or attendance), nonorganizational behavior (e.g., prayer, listening to religious TV/radio/music), and subjective religiosity or other attitudinal measures (e.g., the importance of religion) each have been related significantly to physical health.

Second, such associations have been found for a variety of both subjective and clinical health outcomes, including global self-ratings of physical health; summary scores of symptomatology; incidence, prevalence, and mortality rates for various conditions; psychosocial and behavioral indices closely tied to health (e.g., Type A, stress, locus of control, contraceptive use); and even the somatic subscales or dimensions of various indices of mental health, depression, and psychological well-being.

Third, these findings have continued to appear over the past century in the literatures of several disciplines or research traditions, including epidemiology, gerontology, and the behavioral sciences and health behavior. Some of these notable findings will now be reviewed and, through reference to the multifactorial framework of Levin and Vanderpool (1989), their preventive implications discussed.

Epidemiologic Evidence

Epidemiology is typically defined as the study of the distribution and determinants of health, illness, disease, and death. Social and psychosocial epidemiology focus, respectively, on the effects of social and social-psychological constructs on these indices. One of the most popular and, until recently, unrecognized classes of social-epidemiologic constructs has been religion. In fact, such an extensive body of published research exists on the physical health effects of religious involvement and on religious differences in health that the term "epidemiology of religion" has been proposed to designate this area of study as a distinct subdiscipline (Levin & Vanderpool, 1987).

Over fifty studies which include religious indicators have examined *cardiovascular disease* (see Levin & Schiller, 1987), and it appears that while certain expressions of religiosity seem to exert a generally protective effect, particular religious groups are at greater risk than others. For example, religious attendance (Comstock, 1971) and belief in the importance of religion (Marmot & Syme, 1976) are inversely related to heart disease incidence and mortality rates. However, numerous studies have found higher such rates among Jews than among various comparison populations of Catholics and/or Protestants (see Levin & Schiller, 1987). In a review of this literature, Kaplan (1976) suggests a number of social and psychodynamic explanations for such findings, including the convergence of the Type A or coronary-prone personality or behavioral pattern with the so-called Protestant work ethic. Recent empirical evidence supports the notion that religious involvement, Type A, and cardiovascular disease are indeed significantly, if confusingly, interrelated in certain religious groups but not in others (Levin, Jenkins & Rose, 1988).

Several studies of *gastrointestinal diseases* point to an elevated risk of colitis and enteritis in Jews relative to non-Jewish comparison groups. Notable among these are studies by Monk and associates which found that this Jewish disadvantage persists despite controlling for the effects of numerous social and psychological factors, including social class, marital status, residence, and life stress (Monk, Mendeloff, Siegel & Lilienfeld, 1969, 1970). By ruling out various psychosocial explanations, the likelihood of a behavioral (e.g., dietary) or hereditary explanation is strengthened. This is not to deemphasize the influence of psychological factors in this area; it just suggests that a psychosocial explanation does not completely account for the elevated risk among Jews. A hereditary explanation is further supported by studies which reveal Ashkenazi Jews to be at much greater risk than Jews of Sephardic heritage (e.g., Birnbaum, Groen & Kallner, 1960), groups in which dietary habits of the devout would likely be similar.

With respect to *uterine cancer*, dozens of studies have highlighted the advantage exhibited by Jewish women relative to Protestant and Catholics in both morbidity and mortality (see Levin & Schiller, 1987). A similar advantage has also been documented in varying degrees among Mormons, Seventh-Day Adventists, Hutterites, the Amish, Muslims, and Parsis, each in contrast to "all others" comparison groups. Studies such as those reviewed decades ago by Kennaway (1948) suggest that the explanation for this finding derives from the influence of religiously sanctioned behaviors in regard to hygiene and sexuality. For example, each of these religiously defined groups prescribes certain ritual observances (e.g., circumcision, *mikveh*) and normative practices (e.g., monogamy, intramarriage) which constitute a life style conducive to cervical health.

For *other cancers*, while there is some variation in religious findings depending upon the site or type of cancer, a salutary religious effect generally seems to operate. Most typically, studies report the lowest rates of incidence and mortality among behaviorally strict religious groups such as Mormons, Seventh-Day Adventists, Hutterites, and the Amish (Troyer, 1988). However, even within such groups, a significant gradient may exist such that highly religiously involved Mormons, for example, experience lower cancer rates than less active Mormons (Enstrom, 1975; Gardner & Lyon, 1982). Possible explanations include the salutary effects of adherence to a religiously sanctioned life style (e.g., in re: diet), the stress-buffering effects of regular religious fellowship, the beneficial psychodynamic effects of religious faith and active participation, or, most likely, some combination of all of these. Furthermore, in holistic health and new age circles, it has long been tacitly asserted that certain personality types engendered by particular religious or spiritual world-views render one more or less vulnerable to getting and succumbing to cancer (e.g., Hay, 1982).

Studies of the effect of religious involvement on *mortality* are more difficult to interpret. The religiously active (such as the clergy) seem to live longer, healthier lives, perhaps for reasons related to life style, fellowship, and psychodynamics. For example, in a comprehensive series of studies, King and colleagues found that the clergy, regardless of denomination, were at considerably lower risk than laypeople for most causes of mortality (e.g., King & Locke, 1980). Nevertheless, great care needs to be taken in interpreting such findings. For example, clergy active in missions work have long been known to have *elevated* mortality rates. Yet rather than point to an explanation based, say, on the deleterious psychosocial consequences of intense religious involvement or on the loneliness or stresses of being a missionary, this finding might simply be due to the heightened exposure of Western missionaries to infectious diseases in nonindustrialized nations. The determination of the correct underlying explanation is obviously critical to the development of appropriate preventive health programs for this group of religious. For example, psychological counseling, stress-reduction, and behavior-change interventions might all be well-intentioned, but of little immediate use to people whose primary need is effective immunization.

The relationship between religion and *hypertension* has been subjected to considerably more direct study and greater scrutiny than any other physical health outcome. Furthermore, there has been a greater trend toward analyses of religious involvement as opposed to intergroup comparisons (e.g., Jews versus Gentiles). A recent review (Levin & Vanderpool, 1989) identified about two dozen studies of the blood-pressure effects of behavioral and attitudinal measures of religious commitment or preference. The authors concluded that religious commitment exerts a strong, protective effect on blood pressure and that highly devout, behaviorally strict religious groups (e.g., Mormons, Seventh-Day Adventists, Buddhists, Orthodox Jews, the clergy) have significantly lower rates of hypertension morbidity and mortality than comparison populations. The explanation for this finding would seem to be considerably more multifactorial than for other health outcomes. A comprehensive accounting for such a religious effect on blood pressure would have to include religiously sanctioned health-related behaviors, the stress-buffering effects of worship, and the beneficial psychodynamics of fellowship, as well as a hereditary component. Each of these mechanisms has been used to justify and encourage Church-based efforts in blood pressure screening, client referral, compliance tracking, patient education, and the establishment of support groups (DHHS, 1987).

In summary, epidemiologic studies of religious factors point to a protective role for religious involvement with regard to a wide range of physical health outcomes. In addition, lower levels of risk, across the board, are found among adherents to certain well-defined religions or religious sects which make strict life-style demands. As of yet, no studies have *explicitly* tested multilevel mechanisms integrating social, psychological, and biological pathways which might help to explain these results. The sheer volume and general consistency of findings nevertheless strongly encourage additional research and challenge the popular notion among many clinicians and scientists that no religion-health association exists or merits further scrutiny.

Gerontological Evidence

Recent reviews (Koenig et al., 1988; Levin, 1988; Witter et al., 1985) have identified scores of empirical studies investigating religion and aging. Over twenty of these studies have focused specifically on the effects of religious measures either on physical health or on psychological well-being controlling for the effects of physical health (see Levin, 1988; Witter et al., 1985). In reviewing these studies, Levin (1988) found several consistent trends. First, among older people, indicators of organizational religious involvement (e.g., religious attendance, church membership) are positively associated with self-ratings and other indicators of physical health. Second, measures of nonorganizational religious involvement (e.g., listening to religious TV or radio, reading the Bible, praying) seem to be inversely related to physical health. These summary conclusions suggest the operation of what researchers have termed the "proxy effect"—that is, an explanation for significant associations between religiosity and physical health in older people grounded in the likelihood that organizational religious indicators actually measure functional health. This proxy effect exemplifies what was referred to in the multifactorial framework as a methodological explanation.

The proxy effect was first noted by Comstock and Tonascia (1977) and later was partly supported by the empirical findings of Steinitz (1980). Levin and Vanderpool (1987, p. 593) describe the proxy effect as follows:

. . . among older subjects, the frequency of religious attendance may be a proxy for disability or functional health rather than an indicator of some influence of religion *per se.* . . . In other words, correlations between health and religious attendance may, in reality, represent correlations between health and functional health (i.e., the capability to get out of bed and go to services). Not surprisingly, such associations between churchgoing activities and health tend to be highly significant in a positive direction.

In addition, disabled older persons who curtail their religious attendance for health-related reasons may tend to compensate for this by increasing their nonorganizational religious involvement (Mindel & Vaughan, 1978). Therefore, as a sequela of the proxy effect, inverse associations between nonorganizational religious indicators and health status also may be spurious.

A recent series of analyses by Levin and Markides has confirmed the presence and salience of the proxy effect (Levin & Markides, 1985, 1986, 1988; Markides, Levin & Ray, 1987). In one study (Levin & Markides, 1986), the authors alternatively controlled for social class, subjective religiosity, social support, and disability in an effort to explain the effect of religious attendance on subjective health. They found that controlling for the effects of the first three factors failed to explain away this finding, but that controlling for the effect of disability reduced the association to insignificance. This underscores the differential salience of religious involvement to health at different stages of the life cycle. While religious participation may serve as a source of healthful social support for the young, for the elderly it may serve more as an *indicator* or manifestation of continued activity and good health.

Behavioral-Science Evidence

Unlike studies in epidemiology and gerontology, research relating religious indicators to health-related psychosocial or behavioral measures is not confined to a particular field or discipline. As a result, no single literature review has yet assessed the scope of published research. It is anybody's guess as to how many studies exist; a few are well known, but, depending upon how loosely the term health behavior is defined, hundreds of studies of discrete health behaviors (e.g., alcohol consumption, cigarette smoking, adolescent sexual behavior) may have included measures of religiosity.

Studies in this area fall into three broad categories. First, there are those which have examined religious indicators in relation to specific health-related *social-psychological constructs*. These include Type A behavior (e.g., Levin et al., 1988), locus of control (Jenkins & Pargament, 1988; Levin & Schiller, 1986; Pargament, Brannick, Adamkos, Ensing, Kelemen, Warren, Falgout, Cook & Myers, 1987), and life change and stress (Jenkins, 1979). Findings have tended to be significant both statistically and substantively. Notable examples include the Type A results discussed earlier (Levin et al., 1988); a significant interaction between religious behavior and life stress on certain outcomes, such as impulse control problems (Jenkins, 1979), but not on others, such as self-esteem and mastery (Krause & Tran, 1989); and a complex interplay of health locus of control and denominational theology on the success of a self-care health-education intervention (Levin & Schiller, 1986). In this latter study, higher internal locus of control scores were more common in members of denominations whose theology emphasizes free will and makes strict behavioral demands (e.g., Catholicism, Mormonism), while higher external scores were more typical of individuals who belonged to historically Calvinist denominations (e.g., Presbyterians) in which the prevailing theological perspective is more deterministic.

Second, a number of older studies have examined religion in relation to particular *medical-sociological constructs*. These include classic papers by Zborowski (1952) and Mechanic (1963) on religion and illness behavior, by Suchman (1964) on religion and preventive behavior, and the less frequent investigation of religion and sick-role behavior (e.g., O'Brien, 1982). Once again, significant findings have emerged from these studies, but interpreting them is difficult because the conceptualization of and motivations for these behaviors present certain problems. In particular, these behaviors capture and are motivated by a wide variety of attitudes and situations divergently related to physical health. For example, preventive behavior, such as routine prenatal care visits and attendance at wellness classes, reflects a health-promotive outlook and is common in already healthy individuals. On the other hand, illness and sick-role behavior are most likely to occur in response to acute and more chronic health problems, respectively, and thus reflect poor physical health.

Third, countless studies have reported significant findings relating indicators of religious belief or involvement to many *health behaviors*, such as smoking, drinking, dietary habits, and the use of contraceptives. For example, in a study of adolescent females, Studer and Thornton (1987) found an inverse association between attendance at religious services and the use of an effective, medical method of contraception. Like many studies of religion and health behavior, this study's findings have important implications at several levels: for the development of meaningful predictive models of contraception; for the content of programs designed to teach adolescents about birth control; and, ultimately, for efforts both to prevent teenage pregnancies and to lower the incidence of concomitant, preventable disease outcomes such as cervical cancer.

FURTHER IMPLICATIONS
FOR THE PREVENTION OF ILLNESS

To summarize, empirical evidence points to a significant, salutary effect of religious involvement on physical health. In light of these findings, and in conjunction with the pathways and mechanisms identified in the multifactorial framework (Levin & Vanderpool, 1989), several additional recommendations can be made for the planning and implementation of preventive health interventions.

First, the *epidemiologic* findings outlined earlier suggest a range of intervention targets (Eng, Hatch & Callan, 1985), each one addressing a particular linkage or explanation as suggested by Levin and Vanderpool (1989). For example, in those instances in which important associations between religion and physical health are explained by *behavior or life style*, health promotion efforts targeting behavioral changes and directed to both individuals and groups can be developed. In their homiletic and other roles, pastors can be especially valuable agents of health-directed behavioral change (Levin, 1986), both actively and by supporting and sanctioning congregational activities (Wu & Hatch, 1989). For *hereditary linkages* associated with religio-ethnic traditions, genetic counseling directed to the populations especially at risk may be warranted, such as synagogue-based programs to detect Tay-Sachs disease in Jews of European heritage (Krupp et al., 1987). Insofar as salutary *psychosocial effects* of religion are ascertained, programs entailing communal social activities can be developed, such as programs in religiously-operated nursing homes, or outreach efforts and self-help groups can be established within naturally occurring social networks, such as inner-city church-based perinatal care programs. The latter may be especially valuable in communities where reductions in public resources have created gaps in services (Olson, Reis, Murphy & Gehm, 1988). Finally, identifying the beneficial *psychodynamic effects* of religious participation within synagogues and churches can foster additional forms of self-actualization and fellowship, from Pentecostal healing groups (McGuire, 1988) to new age classes on kundalini yoga, astral projection, and healing past lives (see Levin & Coreil, 1986).

Second, findings from *gerontology* point to similar types of interventions. A case in point would be the continued establishment of church-based clinics (see Westberg, 1984) catering especially to geriatric populations whose declines in functional health limit their access to primary care and other services. Such programs may include the provision of personal care, social services, and emotional support (Sheehan et al., 1988), along with other activities promoting the health of congregants. These types of interventions may be especially valuable for underserved populations, such as rural blacks, for whom the Church may itself represent a "therapeutic community" (Gilkes, 1980). Even more to the point would be the provision of services facilitating independence and ambulation among elderly adults and access to organized forms of religious worship among the homebound. As discussed earlier, considerable research has identified the barriers imposed by age-related disability on public religious participation, as well as the importance of religious attendance for the health of older adults.

Third, research in the *behavioral sciences* has identified religious belief systems as salient influences on physical health both through health-related attitudes and experiences and through social and health behavior. Vaux (1976) outlines three dozen health-related behaviors from discrete personal regimens (e.g., exercise, vaccination, sexual habits, handling stress) to more interpersonal actions (e.g., hospital volunteering, parenting skills, ecological consciousness, respecting physically challenged individuals), each of which is shaped or determined by religious beliefs. Furthermore, the effects and salience of religious beliefs on health behavior vary widely across religions and even across denominations and sects within given religions (Spector, 1979).

Information linking religious beliefs and involvement to health beliefs, attitudes, and behaviors, and to health status, especially in older or underserved populations, can be of inestimable value to community health educators, caseworkers, and health planners in formulating needs assessments, planning interventions, and evaluating existing programs. It must be kept in mind, however, that deleterious health-related behaviors, attitudes, and beliefs oftentimes are imbedded within a religious world-view which considers physical concerns such as health status and functional capability to be base and material in comparison to transempirical "reality." At the same time, other religious world-views and their respective communities of adherents view God as immanent in the world, and thus ultimately concerned for the physical well-being of humanity. Indeed, the delivery of what we now call human services was at one time the sole province of churches and synagogues. Once secular educators, planners, and policymakers approach religious phenomena with greater objectivity and circumspection, they may discover new means and sources of power for fostering salutary health-related beliefs, attitudes, and behaviors and, eventually, for promoting and improving health.

REFERENCES

Abramson, H. J. (1980). Religion. In S. Thernstrom et al. (Eds.), *Harvard encyclopedia of American ethnic groups* (pp. 869-875). Cambridge, MA: The Belknap Press.

Alston, W. P. (1967). Religion: General definitions and characteristics. In P. Edwards (Ed.), *Encyclopedia of Philosophy* (Vol. 7, pp. 141-144). New York: Macmillan.

Billings, J. S. (1891). Vital statistics of the Jews. *North American Review, 153*, 70-84.

Birnbaum, D., Groen, J. J., & Kallner, G. (1960). Ulcerative colitis among the ethnic groups in Israel. *A.M.A. Archives of Internal Medicine, 65*, 843-848.

Byrd, R. C. (1988). Positive therapeutic effects of intercessory prayer in a coronary care unit population. *Southern Medical Journal, 81*, 826-829.

Byrne, J. T., & Price, J. H. (1979). In sickness and in health: The effects of religion. *Health Education, 10*, 6-10.

Clements, W. M. (Ed.). (1989). *Religion, aging and health: A global perspective*. Compiled by the World Health Organization. New York: The Haworth Press, Inc.

Comstock, G. W. (1971). Fatal arteriosclerotic heart disease, water hardness, and socio-economic characteristics. *American Journal of Epidemiology, 94*, 1-10.

Comstock, G. W., & Tonascia, J. A. (1977). Education and mortality in Washington County, Maryland. *Journal of Health and Social Behavior, 18*, 54-61.

Department of Health and Human Services. (1987). *Churches as an avenue to high blood pressure control*. NIH Pub. No. 87-2725. Washington, DC: U.S. Government Printing Office.

Durkheim, E. (1897). *La suicide*. Paris: Alcan.

Ellis, A. (1980). Psychotherapy and atheistic values: A response to A. E. Bergin's psychotherapy and religious values. *Journal of Consulting and Clinical Psychology, 48*, 635.

Eng, E., Hatch, J., & Callan, A. (1986). Institutionalizing social support through the church and into the community. *Health Education Quarterly, 12*, 81-92.

Enstrom, J. E. (1975). Cancer mortality among Mormons. *Cancer, 36*, 825-841.

Frank, J. D. (1973). *Persuasion and healing: A comparative study of psychotherapy* (rev. ed.). Baltimore: The Johns Hopkins University Press.

Gallup, G. (1989). 68% believe in life after death. *The Houston Post*, April 22, A-29.

Gallup, G., & Gallup, A. (1988). Church attendance, membership still important in U.S., poll says. *The Houston Post*, December 18, A-30.

Gallup, G., & Proctor, W. (1984). *Adventures in immortality*. New York: Mc-Graw-Hill Book Company.

Gardner, J. W., & Lyon, J. L. (1982). Cancer in Utah Mormon women by church activity level. *American Journal of Epidemiology, 116*, 258-265.

Gerber, R. (1988). *Vibrational medicine*. Santa Fe, NM: Bear and Company.

Gilkes, C. T. (1980). The black church as a therapeutic community: Suggested areas for research into the black religious experience. *The Journal of the Inter-denominational Theological Center, 8*, 29-44.

Green C. (1990). Karl Marx: Religion as a social narcotic and reactionary ideology. In R. A. Johnson (Ed.), *Critical issues in modern religion* (2nd ed., pp. 213-240). Englewood Cliffs, NJ: Prentice-Hall, Inc.

Hamman, R. F., Barancik, J. I., & Lilienfeld, A. M. (1981). Patterns of mortality in the Old Order Amish: I. Background and major causes of death. *American Journal of Epidemiology, 114*, 845-861.

Hay, L. L. (1982). *Health your body: The mental causes for physical illness and the metaphysical way to overcome them* (new rev. ed.). Santa Monica, CA: Hay House.

Idler, E. L. (1987). Religious involvement and the health of the elderly: Some hypotheses and an initial test. *Social Forces, 66*, 226-238.

Insel, P. M., & Moos, R. H. (1974). *Health and the social environment*. Lexington, MA: D.C. Heath and Company.

Jarvis, G. K., & Northcutt, H. C. (1987). Religion and differences in morbidity and mortality. *Social Science and Medicine, 25*, 813-824.

Jenkins, C. D. (1979). Psychosocial modifiers in response to stress. In J. E. Barett et al. (Eds.), *Stress and mental disorder*. New York: Raven Press.

Jenkins, R. A., & Pargament, K. I. (1988). Cognitive appraisals in cancer patients. *Social Science and Medicine, 26*, 625-633.

Jussawalla, D. J., Yeole, B. B., & Natekar, M. V. (1981). Histological and epidemiological features of breast cancer in different religious groups in Greater Bombay. *Journal of Surgical Oncology, 18*, 269-279.

Kaplan, B. H. (1976). A note on religious beliefs and coronary heart disease. *Journal of the South Carolina Medical Association, 15* (5), supplement, 60-64.

Kennaway, E. L. (1948). The racial and social incidence of cancer of the uterus. *British Journal of Cancer, II*, 177-212.

King, H., & Locke, F. B. (1980). American White Protestant clergy as a low-risk population for mortality research. *JNCI, 65*, 1115-1124.

Koenig, H. G., Smiley, M., & Gonzales, J. P. (1988). *Religion, health, and aging: A review and theoretical integration*. New York: Greenwood Press.

Krause, N., & Tran, T. V. (1989). Stress and religious involvement among older blacks. *Journal of Gerontology: Social Sciences, 44*, S4-S13.

Krupp, M. A., Schroeder, S. A., & Tierney, L. M., Jr. (1987). *Current medical diagnosis & treatment 1987*. Norwalk, CT: Appleton & Lange.

Larson, D. B., Pattison, E. M, Blazer, D. G., Omran, A. R., & Kaplan, B. H. (1986). Systematic analysis of research on religious variables in four major psychiatric journals, 1978-1982. *American Journal of Psychiatry, 143,* 329-334.

Levin, J. S. (1986). Roles for the black pastor in preventive medicine. *Pastoral Psychology, 35,* 94-103.

Levin, J. S. (1988). Religious factors in aging, adjustment, and health: A theoretical overview. *Journal of Religion and Aging, 4,* (3/4), 133-146.

Levin, J. S., & Coreil, J. (1986). "New age" healing in the U.S. *Social Science and Medicine, 23,* 889-897.

Levin, J. S., Jenkins, C. D., & Rose, R. M. (1988). Religion, Type A behavior, and health. *Journal of Religion and Health, 27,* 267-278.

Levin, J. S., & Markides, K. S. (1985). Religion and health in Mexican Americans. *Journal of Religion and Health, 24,* 60-69.

Levin, J. S., & Markides, K. S. (1986). Religious attendance and subjective health. *Journal for the Scientific Study of Religion, 25,* 31-40.

Levin, J. S., & Markides, K. S. (1988). Religious attendance and psychological well-being in middle-aged and older Mexican Americans. *Sociological Analysis, 49,* 66-72.

Levin, J. S., & Schiller, P. L. (1986). Religion and the Multidimensional Health Locus of Control scales. *Psychological Reports, 59,* 26.

Levin, J. S., & Schiller, P. L. (1987). Is there a religious factor in health? *Journal of Religion and Health, 26,* 9-36.

Levin, J. S., & Vanderpool, H. Y. (1987). Is frequent religious attendance *really* conducive to better health?: Toward an epidemiology of religion. *Social Science and Medicine, 24,* 589-600.

Levin, J. S., & Vanderpool, H. Y. (1989). Is religion therapeutically significant for hypertension? *Social Science and Medicine, 29,* 69-78.

Markides, K. S., Levin, J. S., & Ray, L. A. (1987). Religion, aging, and life satisfaction: An eight-year, three-wave longitudinal study. *The Gerontologist, 27,* 660-665.

Marmot, M. G., & Syme, S. L. (1976). Acculturation and coronary heart disease in Japanese-Americans. *American Journal of Epidemiology, 104,* 225-247.

McGuire, M. B. (1988). *Ritual healing in suburban America* (pp. 38-78). New Brunswick, NJ: Rutgers University Press.

Mechanic, D. (1963). Religion, religiosity, and illness behavior. *Human Organization, 22,* 202-208.

Mindel, C. H., & Vaughan, C. E. (1978). A multidimensional approach to religiosity and disengagement. *Journal of Gerontology, 33,* 103-108.

Moberg, D. O. (1953a). The Christian religion and personal adjustment in old age. *American Sociological Review, 18,* 87-90.

Moberg, D. O. (1953b). Church membership and personal adjustment in old age. *Journal of Gerontology, 8,* 207-211.

Monk, M., Mendeloff, A. I., Siegel, C. I., & Lilienfeld, A. (1969). An epidemiological study of ulcerative colitis and regional enteritis among adults in Baltimore—II. *Gastroenterology, 56,* 847-857.

Monk, M., Mendeloff, A. I., Siegel, C. I., & Lilienfeld, A. (1969). An epidemiological study of ulcerative colitis and regional enteritis among adults in Baltimore — III. *Journal of Chronic Diseases, 22,* 565-578.

Morgan, K., Holmes, T. M., Grace, M., Kemel, S., & Robson, D. (1983). Patterns of cancer in geographical endogamous subdivisions of the Hutterite Brethren of Canada. *American Journal of Physical Anthropology, 62,* 3-10.

O'Brien, M. E. (1982). Religious faith and adjustment to long-term hemodialysis. *Journal of Religion and Health, 21,* 68-80.

Olson, L. M., Reis, J., Murphy, L., & Gehm, J. H. (1988). The religious community as a partner in health care. *Journal of Community Health, 13,* 249-257.

Osler, W. (1910). The faith that heals. *British Medical Journal,* June 18, 1470-1472.

Pargament, K. I., Brannick, M. T., Adamkos, H., Ensing, D. S., Kelemen, M. L., Warren, R. K., Falgout, K., Cook, P., & Myers, J. (1987). Indiscriminate proreligiousness: Conceptualization and measurement. *Journal for the Scientific Study of Religion, 26,* 182-200.

Rama, S. (1978). *A practical guide to holistic health.* Honesdale, PA: The Himalayan International Institute.

Rigoni-Stern. (1842). Fatti statistici relativi alle malattie cancerose che servirono di base alle pocho cose dette dal dott. *G Servire Prog Path e Terap, 2,* 507-517.

Schiller, P. L., & Levin, J. S. (1988). Is there a religious factor in health care utilization?: A review. *Social Science and Medicine, 27,* 1369-1379.

Scotch, N. A. (1960). A preliminary report on the relation of sociocultural factors to hypertension among the Zulu. *Annals of the New York Academy of Science, 84,* 1000-1009.

Scotch, N. A. (1963). Sociocultural factors in Zulu hypertension. *American Journal of Public Health, 53,* 1205-1213.

Sempebwa, J. W. (1983). Religiosity and health behaviour in Africa. *Social Science and Medicine, 17,* 2033-2036.

Sheehan, N. W., Wilson, R., & Marella, L. M. (1988). The role of the Church in providing services for the aging. *The Journal of Applied Gerontology, 7,* 231-241.

Spector, R. E. (1979). *Cultural diversity in health and illness* (pp. 114-123). New York: Appleton-Century-Crofts.

Stanton, H. (1989). *Bibliography of health research on Seventh-Day Adventists.* Wahroonga, NSW, Australia: Adventist Health Department.

Steinitz, L. Y. (1980). Religiosity, well-being, and *Weltanschauung* among the elderly. *Journal for the Scientific Study of Religion, 19,* 60-67.

Studer, M., & Thornton, A. (1987). Adolescent religiosity and contraceptive usage. *Journal of Marriage and the Family, 49,* 117-128.

Suchman, E. (1964). Sociomedical variations among ethnic groups. *American Journal of Sociology, 70,* 319-331.

Travers, B. (1837). Observations on the local diseases termed malignant. *Medical Chirurgical Transactions, 17,* 337.

Troyer, H. (1988). Review of cancer among 4 religious sects: Evidence that lifestyles are distinctive sets of risk factors. *Social Science and Medicine, 26,* 1007-1017.

Vanderpool, H. Y. (1977). Is religion therapeutically significant? *Journal of Religion and Health, 16,* 255-259.

Vanderpool, H. Y. (1980). Religion and medicine: A theoretical overview. *Journal of Religion and Health, 19,* 7-17.

Vanderpool, H. Y. (1988). Medicine and medical ethics. In C. H. Lippy & P. W. Williams (Eds.), *Encyclopedia of the American religious experience* (Vol. 3, pp. 1253-1265). New York: Charles Scribner Publishing Company.

Vanderpool, H. Y., & Levin, J. S. (1990). Religion and medicine: How are they related? *Journal of Religion and Health, 29,* 9-20.

Vaux, K. (1976). Religion and health. *Preventive Medicine, 5,* 522-536.

Wallwork, E. (1990). Sigmund Freud: The psychoanalytic diagnosis — infantile illusion. In R. A. Johnson (Ed.), *Critical issues in modern religion,* 2nd ed. (pp. 118-145). Englewood Cliffs, NJ: Prentice-Hall, Inc.

West, D. W., Lyon, J. L., & Gardner, J. W. (1980). Cancer risk factors: An analysis of Utah Mormons and non-Mormons. *JNCI, 65,* 1083-1095.

Westberg, G. F. (1984). Churches are joining the health care team. *Urban Health, 13* (9), 34-36.

White, A. D. (1960). *A history of the warfare of science with theology in Christendom* (Vols. I and II, 1898). New York: Dover Publications.

Witter, R. A., Stock, W. A., Okun, M. A., & Haring, M. J. (1985). Religion and subjective well-being in adulthood: A quantitative synthesis. *Review of Religious Research, 26,* 332-342.

Wu, D., & Hatch, J. (1989). The rural minister's role in health promotion. *The Journal of Religious Thought, 46,* 69-77.

Zborowski, M. (1952). Cultural components in responses to pain. *Journal of Social Issues, 8,* 16-30.

Religion and Prevention of Illness in Later Life

Harold G. Koenig

Duke University Medical Center

SUMMARY. Research findings indicate that traditional Judeo-Christian beliefs and behaviors may be related to adjustment and well-being in later life. This has prompted some investigators to hypothesize that such effects on mental health might further influence both physical health and healthcare utilization. This paper reviews research that has examined the relationship between religion and health in later life, synthesizes the results from a wide range of studies, and discusses the preventive implications of this work.

Religion beliefs and behaviors are common among older adults. This is true for the elderly in the community (Princeton Religion Research Center, 1982) and those in medical outpatient settings (Koenig, Moberg, & Kvale 1988). This high prevalence of religious behaviors has intrigued medical and social scientists, who have sought to understand their psychological origin and their function in later life. Traditional Judeo-Christian teachings frequently involve suggestions and admonitions concerning physical and mental health, and belief in supernatural healing is a major component of fundamentalist and evangelical teachings and rituals. Freud believed that religion originated out of man's insecurity and helplessness against the powerful forces of nature that surrounded and threatened to overcome him. In *Future of an Illusion* (1927), he characterized religion as a universal neurosis and likened it to obsessive-compulsive disorder found in the mentally disturbed. While Freud believed that adherence to the universal neurosis might spare some individuals from constructing a personal one, he also felt that religion led to an unhealthy repression of

Reprints may be obtained from Harold G. Koenig, Geriatric Medicine, Center for Aging and Human Development, Duke University Medical Center, Durham, NC 27706.

natural instincts. Because religion was only partially successful in controlling such impulses, psychological instability would follow. Freud called for the replacement of religious belief and ritual by the rational operation of the intellect, which would lead to more effective and durable control over these drives and fears.

Not all mental health specialists, however, shared Freud's view. Contemporaries such as Carl Jung and Oskar Pfister believed that religious behaviors and beliefs might serve a positive function in maintaining mental and physical health. Since then, a number of recent investigations have sought to clarify this controversial subject by examining the relationship between religion and a variety of health parameters in systematically selected psychiatric and non-psychiatric populations. Because of the stresses on both physical and mental health in later life, and the high prevalence of religious beliefs and behaviors at this time, the elderly have been a prime target for such studies. In this paper, the results of past and recent studies will be reviewed. The emphasis will be on how religious beliefs or behaviors might buffer against or lead to ill health in later life.

RELIGION AND MENTAL HEALTH

A number of studies have examined the relationship between religion and adjustment or well-being in elderly populations. Blazer and Palmore (1976), studying 272 elderly volunteers in the First Duke Longitudinal Study, found that religious attitudes and activities were positively related to feelings of usefulness and adjustment; however, correlations were stronger with religious activity than with attitude. During eighteen years of follow-up, religious attitudes remained stable while church attendance declined. Correlations between adjustment and religious behaviors/attitudes increased in strength over time, suggesting that as health, financial and social resources declined with aging, religion became an increasingly important factor in maintaining well-being. Likewise, a Canadian study of Hunsberger (1985) found significant correlations between religious belief, personal adjustment, happiness, and subjective health in a sample of 85 elderly volunteers. In a community study of 836 older persons of widely-varying religious affiliation and commitment, Koenig, Kvale, and Ferrel (1988) found moderately strong relationships between intrinsic religiosity (reflecting beliefs and attitudes associated with a deep commitment to one's faith), religious social activity, and well-being. These correlations remained significant after controlling for health, social support, and financial status. Correlations were strongest among women and subjects age 75 or older, among whom religious variables contributed more of the explained variance in well-being (25%) than any other variable except for health.

On the other hand, Barron (1958) found no difference in adjustment between religious and non-religious men in New York City (New York College Study); most participants, however, were less than 65 years of age. Covalt (1960), reporting on her experience with geriatric patients in private medical practice, seldom found patients seeking spiritual help or asking for a minister; in fact, when a patient brought a Bible to the hospital with them, it was often a sign of an insecure, troubled individual. This study, however, was based on anecdotal reports rather than empirical data. Markides, Levin, and Ray (1987) reported results from an eight-year longitudinal study of life satisfaction, religious attendance, religiosity, and prayer in a sample of predominantly Mexican-American Catholics aged 60 and over. They found only weak correlations between these variables which lost significance altogether once other factors such as functional status, sex, and age were controlled; unlike Blazer and Palmore, they found no increase in the strength of the correlations between religious variables and life-satisfaction over time. Hence, while most studies indicate a positive relationship between religion and adjustment in later life, there remains controversy on the strength of this association and whether it remains stable or increases with aging. No empirical study conducted in elderly populations has yet reported a significant inverse relationship between religious behaviors and mental health (Koenig, Smiley, & Gonzales, 1988).

RELIGIOUS COPING

Religious coping is the reliance on religious belief or activity to help manage emotional stress or physical discomfort. In the elderly, there is commonly an emphasis on trust or faith in God, prayer, or Scripture reading; less commonly on religious social activity (Koenig, George, & Siegler, 1988). Religious coping is common among older adults dwelling in the community. Coping behaviors were examined in a stratified, random sample of 100 participants in the Second Duke Longitudinal Study (Koenig et al., 1988). Participants were not prompted to give a religious response; rather, they were asked open-ended questions about how they handled or got through stressful situations. Religious coping was spontaneously noted as a coping behavior by 45% of respondents in at least one of three stressful life periods. Seven percent repeatedly gave religion as the primary factor enabling them to cope with each of the three worst events/experiences in their life; when compared with non-religious copers or occasional religious copers, these consistent religious copers scored highest on 9 out of 12 standardized psychological measures of adjustment (Koenig, Siegler, & George, 1989). This method of measuring religious coping (by spontaneous response to open-ended coping questions) has now been validated in a sample of over 800 older adults (unpublished data).

In an attempt to better understand the personality of older religious copers, 16 personality factors (Cattell 16-PF) were compared between religious and non-religious copers; both cross-sectional and longitudinal (6 year) comparisons were available (Koenig, Siegler, Meador, & George, 1990). Religious copers were less likely to be dominant or aggressive and more likely to be sensitive or tender-minded; the latter association disappeared once sex was controlled (women were both more likely to be tender-minded and more likely to be religious copers). There was no difference between religious and non-religious copers on guilt-proneness or likelihood of having psychosomatic symptoms. Thus, no evidence was found that religious coping results in an unhealthy repression of lower impulses, prevents the resolution of intrapsychic conflicts or predisposes to neurotic personality traits. In fact, longitudinal analysis demonstrated that women religious copers became less tense or frustrated and more relaxed or tranquil over the six year study period.

RELIGIOUS COPING AND DEPRESSION

The relationship between religious coping and more serious mental disturbances such as depression or anxiety is another dimension of significance for the prevention of illness. Depression is particularly common among elderly persons with medical illness; compared with rates in the community-dwelling elderly, major depression is over 10 times as common in medically-ill hospitalized patients (Koenig, Meador, Cohen, & Blazer, 1988; Weissman, Leaf, Tischler, Blazer, Karno, Bruce, & Florio, 1988). Depression has been shown to impair recovery from hip fracture (Mosey 1988) and impair function in patients with severe lung disease (Light, Merrill, Despairs, Gordon, & Mutalipassi, 1986). Hospital stay of depressed patients is double that of non-depressed patients, even after controlling for severity of physical illness, age, and functional status; likewise, inhospital mortality is significantly higher among depressed patients, particularly those with cancer (Koenig, Shelp, Goli, Cohen, & Blazer, 1989). Unfortunately, the treatment of depression in medically-ill older patients is fraught with difficulty. Antidepressants commonly have serious side-effects that interact with the physical illness and medical regimen of patients; furthermore, their efficacy in the treatment of depression in this setting has not been established (Koenig & Breitner, 1990; Koenig, Goli, Shelp, Kudler, Cohen, & Meador, 1989).

Given this situation, there is a need to identify factors that help bolster the coping ability of patients. The evidence is mounting that religion — at least that based on the Judeo-Christian belief system — may be such a factor. In a three-year longitudinal study, O'Brien (1982) examined the role of religion in the adjustment of patients on chronic hemodialysis; she found that 74% of patients noted that religious or ethical beliefs were to some degree associated with adjustment to their disease. After three years of follow up, 27% of reinterviewed patients in the overall sample noted their reliance on religion had significantly increased. Those reporting the most positive attitudes toward religion also reported the highest degree of interactional behavior, the highest compliance with the therapy, and the least amount of alienation (O'Brien 1981). Religious coping may also include unconventional activity such as taking a religious pilgrimage. Morris (1982) examined the impact of a religious pilgrimage to Lourdes on depression and anxiety in 24 medically ill older persons. Using standardized measures of depression and anxiety, she found a significant decrease in symptoms following the pilgrimage that persisted for at least 10 months after returning home. In an early study of religion in psychiatric inpatients, Wolff (1959) found that religious beliefs helped disorganized elderly state hospital patients overcome grief and depression over their condition. In a more recent study, Kroll and Sheehan (1989) reported that religious beliefs were less common among patients with major depression than in those with other disorders; two-thirds of their sample, however, were under age 35. Based on high prevalence of religious beliefs among patients, they concluded that religion played an important and often central role in the lives of many patients, and noted that religion may have a positive value in filling a void and supplying strength and meaning in life. How might traditional Judeo-Christian religious behaviors and belief patterns buffer against depression? Behaviors such as prayer, trust or faith in God, or reading religious literature such as the Bible may confer an inner peace through building up hope, encouraging positive attitudes towards the situation, and distracting the individual from senseless ruminations concerning problems over which they have little control. Believing that there is a God in control of the situation who cares about them personally, has their best interests in mind, and is responsive to their prayers, may ease the anxiety associated with their condition or situation. Individuals often describe their relationship to God as if he were a person or a friend, and it was through that relationship that strength was obtained, (Koenig, George, & Siegler, 1988). "Putting it in the hands of the Lord" may displace the burden of uncontrollable stressful situations away from the individual and thus obtain at least temporary psychological relief. Furthermore, religious organizations are important sources of informal social support for many older persons, both blacks (Taylor & Chatters 1988) and whites (Koenig, Moberg, & Kvale, 1988). In a study of elderly adults attending a geriatric assessment clinic in central Illinois, patients were asked how many of their five closest friends were members of their church congregation; over half noted that either four or five of their five closest friends were from this source. Social support may be a critical variable affecting both the genesis and outcome of depression. George, Blazer, Hughes, and Fowler (1989) recently reported that perceived adequacy of social support (measured by the Duke Social Support Index) was a strong predictor of recovery from major depressive disorder in a 6-32 month follow up of 150 middle-aged and elderly depressed inpatients.

Geographical factors have been purported to influence the religion-mental health relationship. Many of the studies that have demonstrated a positive relationship between adjustment or well-being and religion have been conducted in the Southern United States where religious beliefs and practices are particularly common. This has caused some investigators to attribute these findings to cultural or economic factors. However, Kroll and Sheehan (Minnesota), O'Brien (Washington, DC) and Idler (Connecticut) have reported a similar relationship between religion and mental health in more northern climates. Thus, it is clear that the association between religion and well-being also occurs in geographical areas distant from the Bible-belt South. It is also unlikely that religious coping is a behavior only of the poor and uneducated. Participants in the Second Duke Longitudinal Study were predominantly middle-class whites (Koenig, George, & Siegler, 1988).

RELIGION AND PHYSICAL HEALTH

To what extent might positive effects of religion on mental health transfer over to positive effects on physical health? As noted before, depression may exert a negative impact on recovery from illness, mortality, and health care utilization. A number of studies have examined the relationship between religion and self-reported health, functional status, specific illnesses such as hypertension and cancer, mortality, and self-destructive behaviors such as cigarette smoking, drug and alcohol use.

Overall Health and Functional Status

While church attendance has been linked to various indicators of overall health in a number of studies, this relationship is likely confounded by functional status or extent of physical disability (Levin & Markides, 1985). Because persons who are sick or disabled are less able to get to church, it may appear that church attendance is related to better health; when functional status is controlled, however, the relationship weakens considerably (although does not entirely disappear). The extent to which functional status confounds this relationship has not been settled, since other factors may be operative. Idler (1987), in a report from the Yale Health and Aging Project, noted that the *perception* of disability may be affected by religious coping. For men at any given level of chronic medical illness, those who said they receive a great deal of strength from religion were less likely to see themselves as disabled.

Hence, simply controlling for perceived disability may not be adequate when studying the complex relationship between church attendance and health status. The more religious elderly may cope better with a given level of objective physical disability and consequently perceive themselves as less disabled. Hence, when level of disability is measured by self-report scales (rather than by objective measurement) in the religious elderly, they may paint an unduly optimistic picture of their health status. When this perceived disability is then controlled for in regression models, it does not take into account the positive effects that religious attitudes may have had on the elders' view of their illness and the degree to which they allow any given level of illness to disable them. Hence, in order to truly test whether the inverse relationship between physical illness and church attendance can be explained by the inability of disabled persons to attend church, physical disability must be determined by objective (not subjective) measures.

Blood Pressure

A number of studies have demonstrated an inverse relationship between blood pressure and church attendance (Armstrong, Merwyck, & Coates, 1977; Graham, Kaplan, Cornoni-Huntly, James, Becker, Hames, & Hayden, 1978; Walsh, 1980). Larson, Koenig, Kaplan, Greenberg, Logue, and Tyroler (1989) found that "importance of religion" has an even greater association with lower diastolic blood pressures than church attendance. They report that high importance of religion and frequent church attendance interacted in such a way that diastolic pressures in this group were significantly lower than in men of the low importance, low attendance group. This relationship was particularly strong among men aged 55 or over and among smokers. In a study of geriatric medical outpatients, Koenig, Moberg, and Kvale (1988) found no relationship between church attendance and hypertension; however, there was a trend towards higher pressure in men with low intrinsic religiosity.

On the other hand, one study has found higher prevalence of hypertension among older Mexican Americans who rated themselves "highly religious" (43%) compared with those "less than very religious" (30%) (Levin & Markides, 1985). The authors explained that higher levels of guilt arising from pressures to conform to high behavioral standards might give rise to stress-related health problems such as hypertension. Recall, however, that in the Koenig, Siegler, Meador, and George (1990) study of personality and religious coping in later life, there was no evidence that religious copers were more guilt-prone than non-religious copers. Racial and denominational differences between samples (Mexican Catholics versus white Protestants) may have accounted for these different findings.

It is not clear how religion, particularly cognitive measures such as "importance of religion" or "intrinsic religious motivation," might exert a positive effect on blood pressure. Neuropsychological mechanisms, however, may explain these effects. Anxiety may play a role in the etiology of hypertension, and relaxation techniques have been successfully used to lower blood pressure (Blanchard & Miller, 1977; Jacob, Kramer, & Agras, 1977). By relieving anxiety, religious cognitions may help to decrease blood pressure. Koenig, Moberg, and Kvale (1988) found that intrinsic religiosity was significantly lower among older women patients with anxiety disorders. In the longitudinal analysis of the personality and religious coping study mentioned earlier, women religious copers became less tense or frustrated and more relaxed or tranquil over time (Koenig, Siegler, Meador, & George, 1990). Likewise, an inverse relationship between death anxiety and religious behaviors in elderly women has been reported (Koenig 1988). Hence, both organizational and private religious activity and belief may protect against anxiety that adversely affects blood pressure.

Cancer

Some investigators have found lower rates of cancer in certain religious groups; these differences have been explained by dietary and health practices (Armstrong et al., 1977; Gardner & Lyon 1982a; Gardner & Lyon 1982b; Mayberry 1982). Koenig, Moberg, and Kvale (1988) and Acklin, Brown, and Mauger (1983) also found cancer somewhat less common among medical patients with high intrinsic religiosity. Nevertheless, a clear relationship between religiosity and cancer rates has not been established.

RELIGION AND MORTALITY

As with overall health, differences in mortality reported between frequent and infrequent church attenders may be confounded by functional status. Those persons who are too disabled to attend church are more likely to be sicker and have a higher mortality rate. Some investigators, however, have found lower mortality rates among religious older adults whose religiosity was assessed using cognitive measures rather than church attendance. Zuckerman, Kasl, and Ostfeld (1984) found that "strength derived from religion" was the strongest inverse predictor of 2-year mortality among the three variables (including church attendance) in their religiosity index. They report a mortality rate of 42% among older adults in poor health scoring low on the religiosity index, compared with a rate of 19% for high scorers. Reynolds and Nelson (1981) have reported similar findings for a sample of 193 male veterans residing in a nursing home; patients with lower religiosity were more likely to die during the follow up period. Whether or not religious attitudes prolong survival in late life is unclear, as is the mechanism by which such effects might be affected. However, given the inverse relationship been depression and survival among older individuals (particularly those in ill health), the association between religious attitudes and survival might be mediated through a similar mechanism.

RELIGION, DRUG AND ALCOHOL USE

Drug abuse in chronically ill older persons has received little systematic study, particularly its interaction with religious factors. Khavari and Harmon (1982) found a strong inverse correlation between the degree of professed religious belief and the use of drugs. In a sample of 4,853 subjects, those who claimed that they were "not religious at all" were significantly more likely to use psychotropic medications than very religious subjects. While individuals up to age 85 were included in this study, most were younger adults. Koenig, Moberg, and Kvale (1988) also reported that smoking was less common in older medical patients with higher intrinsic religiosity. More studies are clearly needed on this subject.

There is fortunately more data on alcohol consumption than for drug use. Koenig, Moberg, and Kvale (1988) reported significantly less alcohol use in older medical patients who scored high on intrinsic religiosity.

Other investigators have likewise reported lower rates of alcohol use among more religiously oriented subjects (Khavari & Harmon, 1982; Parfrey, 1976; Zimberg, 1977). For some older individuals, cessation of problem drinking has occurred following a positive change in their feelings about religion (Koenig, Smiley, & Gonzales, 1988). Prior to Alcoholics Anonymous, the prognosis for alcoholics was dismal: 28% died prematurely, 51% drank the for the rest of their lives, and 21% recovered. Of those who recovered, a significant proportion (33%) did so as a consequence of religious experience (Lamere, 1953). Alcoholics Anonymous has made a major impact on the recovery of alcoholics, and much of its success has been attributed to the spiritual dimension that is central to its 12 steps of recovery (Wilson, 1968). Hence, religion may have an important effect on health through prohibitions against behaviors such as drug and alcohol abuse. Its greatest impact, however, is that it provides a viable alternative to alcohol or drug abuse for individuals with feelings of discouragement and depression that underlie these self-destructive behaviors.

HEALTHCARE UTILIZATION

To what extent does religion influence the utilization of healthcare resources among older adults? Again, the data are sparse. Among studies that have been reported, most operationalize the religious variable as religious affiliation (Schiller & Levin 1988); in a few reports, frequency of church attendance has been examined. Levin and Markides (1985) examined the impact of frequency of religious attendance and self-rated religiosity on days spent in bed and physician visits per year (measured by retrospective self-report). The sample was composed of 1125 predominantly Mexican-American Catholics, one-third of whom were men. In men age 65-80, they found a non-significant trend towards fewer disability days and physician visits among more frequent church attenders. Schiller and Levin (1988) examined the effects of religious attendance, holding a church office, and other religious variables on physician visits, time since hospitalization, and length of hospital stay. The sample consisted of 909 adults residing in the Appalachian area of West Virginia. Neither religious affiliation nor attendance were related to health care utilization. Holding a church office, however, was positively related to shorter length of hospital stay and longer time since last hospitalization (even after controlling for age and health variables). Clearly, more work is needed to obtain better estimates of the impact of religious and non-religious coping behaviors on health care utilization before conclusions can be drawn.

NEGATIVE INFLUENCES OF RELIGION ON HEALTH

Thus far, the reader may have perceived this section as a "positive" review of the literature on the impact of religion on health. To a certain extent, this is true. Studies that demonstrate a lack of association seldom find their way into the literature. What is remarkable however, is that so few reports of a negative relationship between religious variables and health outcomes have appeared in studies of older adults.

While not yet studied in a systematic fashion, a number of reports have appeared of adverse outcomes following "faith healing" where patients with serious illness either failed to seek appropriate medical attention or did not comply with medical recommendations (Coakley & McKenna, 1986; Smith, 1986). The subject of faith healing has been discussed in greater depth elsewhere (Editorial 1985; Koenig, Smiley, & Gonzales, 1988, pp. 46-48, 83-91). Overzealous religious practices that involve activities counter to health or medical practice, however, are not common even among Fundamentalist and Evangelical religious traditions which most strongly advocate the supernatural aspects of physical healing. Francis MacNutt (1974) provides a balanced approach in his book Healing which emphasizes the strengths and limitations of this method. In fact, Judeo-Christian scriptures are quite clear about the role that medicine should play in people's lives:

> Honor a physician. . . . for the uses which ye have of him, for the Lord hath created him. For from the Most High cometh healing . . . The Lord hath created medicine for the good of the earth . . . He hath given men skill, that He might be honored in His marvellous works. (Book of Ecclesiasticus, 190 BC)

Of greater concern are religious beliefs and practices associated with sects and cults at the fringe of mainline religious traditions. Galanter (1982) discusses psychopathology among members of religious sects such as Divine Light Mission, Hare Krishna, Unification Church, Soka Gakkai, Devotees of Baba, the Subud, and Erhard Seminars Training (EST) groups. Involvements in a sect or cult can be dysfunctional to the older adult who becomes isolated from his or her peers and develops rigid, fixed beliefs which interfere with his relationships and emotional well-being. On the other hand, there is little evidence to suggest that devout, even fervent, adherence to traditional Judeo-Christian belief and practice as espoused by stable religious groups (to whom the vast majority of elderly are affiliated), has adverse health effects. Expression of extreme or inappropriate guilt, grandiose behaviors, or obsessive-compulsive activities in mentally ill elders may be associated with religious ideation. While a religious focus occurs in many patients with psychosis, this seldom indicates that religion is etiologically related to the psychosis. This point is obvious from the very large number of perfectly rational older adults who are devoutly religious.

Studies have demonstrated that a person's concept of God may be integrally related to the relationship between belief and mental health. Individuals who see God as angry and punishing may not cope as well as those who perceive God as loving, rewarding, and protecting (Pargament, Ensing, Falgout, Olsen, Reilly, Van Haitsma, & Warren, in press). A person's view of God as a loving and protecting figure may reflect how one perceived his/her own parent while growing up. If that parent was punitive and distant, then one's image of God may similarly reflect these characteristics. Because of the close association between mental health and early parental-child relationships, individuals with mental disturbance may have a misconception of God that prevents them from turning to this source of comfort when the need arises.

Similarly, different religious coping styles may have positive or negative implications for mental health. "Self-directing" or "collaborative" styles that emphasize the individual's responsibility in problem solving appear to be positively related to competence. In contrast, the "deferral" style of coping that places all the responsibility for problem resolution on God is negatively related to measures of successful coping (Pargament, Kennell, Hathaway, Grevengoed, Newman, & Jones, 1988).

CONCLUSIONS AND IMPLICATIONS FOR PREVENTION

Religious beliefs and activities are common among older adults today. Many individuals rely heavily upon religious behaviors to cope with emotional and physical distress that occur later in life. Research has shown that traditional Judeo-Christian beliefs and activities may buffer against the stresses that accompany ill-health and protect against depression; these effects may further impact on health care utilization and physical health outcomes.

The research outlined in this section has important implications for preventive action in the elderly. First is that religion may assist in the maintenance of mental health and well-being. For instance, a woman in her 70s whose husband dies may suddenly find herself alone and without a confidant. Perhaps she does not have any children or the children are actively engaged in raising their own families and struggling with their own problems; many of her friends may have died or have health problems themselves that make them unavailable. Not only must she often bear the grief of bereavement but also the burden of managing the affairs of her household alone. Starting over and breaking into a new circle of friends, may be quite difficult at this time in life. If coping attempts fail, she may seek help from her physician or other health professional. One referral option available to clinicians is that of the church. Religious activities such as church attendance and other involvement in the religious community helps to cultivate close relationships with age-matched peers. These relationships are strengthened by a shared world-view, value system, and a common hope both in life and in death. Thus, the support system provided by church members in later life is of particular importance because of the constriction of social support that occurs as a consequence of sickness and death of family members and other friends.

Ezra Griffith, a Yale psychiatrist, has studied the psychological effects of church participation among Blacks. His reports indicate a plethora of positive mental health effects from such involvement, and that for all intents and purposes, the Black church may actually be serving as a community-based mental health system for this segment of the population that cannot afford nor will seek formal psychiatric care (Griffith, 1983; Griffith, English, & Mayfield, 1980; Griffith & Mahy, 1984; Griffith, Young, & Smith, 1984). Should serious mental health problems arise, other church members may help to identify such problems and direct the elder to appropriate professional services. Hence, the need for collaboration between the healthcare system and religious communities.

In addition to providing a source of peers, religious communities provide reinforcement of beliefs that relieve anxiety and attitudes of relating to others that help maintain social relationships. Health-destructive coping behaviors such as drug or alcohol use are discouraged, whereas mental health enhancing behaviors such as service to others are encouraged. Much conventional wisdom concerning mental illness prevention is distilled in religious precepts that discourage self-preoccupation, worry, and dwelling on one's own plight, and encourage self-sacrifice, changing things that can be changed and accepting those that cannot, and meditation on good things: "whatever is true, whatever is honorable, whatever is pure, whatever is lovely, whatever is of good repute, if there is any excellence and if anything worthy of praise, let your mind dwell on these things" (Philippians 4:8). This is precisely the concept underlying cognitive therapy for depression, which holds that dysfunctional thoughts or unhealthy preoccupations lead to and maintain depressive states (Beck, 1976).

Much mental illness, whatever age it occurs, has at its roots unresolved feelings of guilt over things done to others or anger and resentment over what others have done to self. Christian religious tradition provides a cognitive framework that allows for the resolution of guilt through forgiveness of self and the release from resentment or hatred through forgiveness of others. The great emphasis on forgiveness in this religion, and the clear prohibitions against judging others and self-pride, at the very least provide the principles by which mental health may be maintained and quality of individual and social life maximized.

The potential effects of religious belief and community involvement on prevention of mental illness may also have similar effects on maintaining physical health in later life. Again, Judeo-Christian beliefs emphasize the need to care for the physical body—both in terms of proper nutrition (through dietary practices), protection against disease (hand cleaning, food preparation, avoidance of sexual promiscuity), and avoidance of excesses that would be inimical to health (gluttony or alcoholism). Hence, there may be direct positive effects of religious belief and practice on physical health. Secondary effects on health, though prevention of stress-related physical disorder, may be accomplished through maintenance of psychological well-being and relief from anxiety. Cardiovascular disorders, particularly myocardial infarction and stroke, are the most common causes of death in later life. Several studies as noted earlier have demonstrated an inverse relationship between hypertension and religious beliefs and activities. Redford Williams (1989) in his book The Trusting Heart summarizes research from a wide range of disciplines that demonstrates the devastating effects that anger, aggression, distrust, and other "negative" emotions can have on the cardiovascular system. Religion again provides a cognitive framework for dealing with anger and aggression directed at self and others, and allows emotional release through rituals such as confession and activities such as singing and dancing. Aggressive drives which might otherwise be expressed in physically destructive ways, through religious belief and ritual, may be sublimated into altruistic social involvements.

An essential aspect of maintaining health and preventing disease, is a quick recovery from illness and prevention of secondary complications. Successful psychological coping enables the older person to effectively participate in the treatment of his/her illness. For instance, a 75 year old man falls because of a cardiac arrythmia and experiences a hip fracture and has surgery; in order for full recovery, he must be motivated to participate actively in physical therapy as he exercises to strengthen the muscles around his affected leg and to comply with medical therapy for his heart after discharge. An 82 year old woman suffers a stroke that affects her ability to get about independently. Recovery is again heavily dependent upon her motivation in therapy to adapt to losses in function by learning new ways to cope with the disability. Depression, anxiety, discouragement or hopelessness can severely affect the rate of recovery in these two cases by impairing motivation and leading to non-compliance. Complications may then ensue that prolong convalescence or lead to new illness. Again, religious beliefs and private activities such as prayer or Bible reading may help the older person to have hope, find meaning in their suffering, and relieve anxiety from being out of control. The religious community — both clergy and church members — may provide support by visiting, listening, and realistically encouraging, as well as meeting spiritual needs through prayer and other rituals (providing of sacraments, for instance). A visit from another elder in the congregation who has experienced a similar illness and has recovered, may provide encouragement for the hospitalized person and enhance well-being of the visitor. Thus religion may assist with illness prevention in both sick and well elderly.

Religious education programs, outreach activities based upon a cooperative effort between churches and social service agencies, and social interactional programs could be targeted towards the elderly — particularly those who are disabled and housebound. The Shepherd's Center approach (Koenig, 1986a; Koenig, 1987) is a model in this regard. Based in church facilities and supported almost entirely by private funding and donations from local businesses, this approach utilizes the skills and abilities of the healthy elderly to help the less fortunate elderly in the community to maintain independence. It also enhances a sense of purpose for the well elderly and provides an avenue for them to carry out in real life their Judeo-Christian principles, which in this religious tradition are primarily centered around service to others. Initiating such programs, however, takes a great deal of commitment and administrative planning by both church and lay leadership.

FINAL COMMENT

There is little direct evidence to indicate that religious coping has any less of an impact on mental and physical health in younger individuals than in the elderly; however, like many other behaviors, religious coping may take time to develop, stabilize, and reach its maximum utility as a coping behavior. Because later life can be a time of both physical and emotional stress, it may be at this time that coping behaviors are truly tested. In earlier years, when individuals are actively engaged in their occupation or family and have a great deal of control over their environment and life course, religion may appear to have little relevance. Old age, however, can bring with it a future that is less certain, a life over which the individual has less control, and a physical body which is less responsive to their needs. At this time, when other coping behaviors dependent on health, wealth, and social support are less available, religious coping may be particularly helpful. Clearly, however, additional empirical studies are needed to examine the relationship between religious coping, depression and other mental disorder in younger and older populations, in and outside of the medical setting.

Over the past several decades, there has been an increasing rate of depression in individuals born after World War II (Klerman & Weissman 1989). This trend is real, and has resisted efforts by epidemiologists to explain it by artifacts of sampling, changes in diagnostic criteria, reporting bias, or limitations of recall. This increasing rate of depression parallels trends for alcoholism, drug abuse, and suicide over the past four decades. In a recent longitudinal study of drug use in over 1000 adolescents in New York City, Kandel and Davies (1986) reported high rates of drug abuse; they also found that depressive symptoms usually preceded the onset of drug use. Likewise, there has been a dramatic increase in suicide and homicide among 15 to 24 year olds in the past three decades (Holinger, Offer, & Zola, 1989), with suicide reaching a rate of 13.6/100,000 that is the highest ever recorded for this birth cohort (1953-1962). Homicide rates have also increased, especially among young black males (Klerman, 1980). These trends are concerning and have occurred simultaneously with a decline in the importance of the family and religious values.

Perhaps there are lessons that we can learn from our elders. Depression, while common in all age groups, is lowest among individuals age 65 or over (Koenig, 1986b). Alcohol consumption and illicit drug use also is less among older persons. Conversely, church attendance, importance of religion, and religious coping are more common in this cohort. It is difficult to sort out the selection factors responsible for these differences, be it age, cohort, or period effects. Data are mounting, however, to suggest that religious coping—based on Judeo-Christian religious beliefs, attitudes, and activities—may be an important buffer for some individuals against the stresses that accompany physical illness, acute hospitalization, and perhaps other stresses as well. There is preliminary evidence to suggest that through a positive impact on mental health and an inverse relationship with self-destructive activities such as alcohol, cigarette, and drug abuse, religious behaviors and attitudes may also have a positive influence on survival and health care utilization. For persons in later life, then, religious beliefs and behaviors appear to be important factors in illness prevention.

Given the widespread use of religion as a coping behavior among older adults, health professionals may choose to incorporate this perspective into work. Miller and Martin (1988) outline how religion can be integrated in behavioral efforts to promote mental health. Professionals should not be reluctant to discuss religious issues with their older patients, given their relevance and potential impact on health. Norms for addressing religious issues with patients are not well established and further research is needed to determine when, where, and what behaviors are appropriate for health care providers (Koenig, Bearon, & Dayringer 1989). In any case, healthcare professionals should maintain respect for the religious beliefs and behaviors of patients and grant them the opportunity to practice these behaviors, particularly when serious illness occurs or death approaches.

REFERENCES

Acklin M. W., Brown E. C., & Mauger P. A. (1983). The role of religious values in coping with cancer. *Journal of Religion and Health, 22*, 322-333.

Armstrong, B, Merwyck, A., & Coates, H. (1977). Blood pressure in Seventh Day Adventist vegetarians. *American Journal of Epidemiology, 105*, 444-449.

Barron, M. L. (1958). The role of religion and religious institutions in creating the milieu of older people. In D. L. Scudder (Ed.), *Organized religion and the older person*. Gainsville: University of Florida Press.

Beck, A. T. (1976). *Cognitive therapy and emotional disorders*. NY: International University Press.

Blanchard, E. B, & Miller, S. T. (1977). Psychological treatment of cardiovascular disease. *Archives of General Psychiatry, 34*, 1402-1416.

Blazer, D. G, & Palmore E. (1976). Religion and aging in a longitudinal panel. *The Gerontologist, 16*, 82-85.

Coakley, D. V., & McKenna, G. W. (1986). Safety of faith healing. *Lancet, i*, 444.

Covalt, N. (1960). The meaning of religion to older people. *Geriatrics, 15*, 658-664.

Editorial (1985). Exploring the effectiveness of healing. *Lancet, ii*, 1177-1178.

Freud S. (1927). Future of an Illusion. In J. Strachey (Ed.), *The standard edition of the complete psychological works of Sigmund Freud* (1962). (Vol. 21). London: The Hogarth Press.

Galanter, M. (1982). Charismatic religious sects and psychiatry: an overview. *American Journal of Psychiatry, 139*, 1539-1548.

Gardner, J. W., & Lyon, J. L. (1982a). Cancer in Utah Mormon women by church activity level. *American Journal of Epidemiology, 116,* 258.

Gardner, J. W., & Lyon, J. L. (1982b). Cancer in Utah Mormon men by lay priesthood level. *American Journal of Epidemiology, 116,* 243-257.

George, L. K., Blazer, D. G., Hughes, D. C., & Fowler, N. (1989). Social support and the outcome of major depression. *British Journal of Psychiatry, 154,* 478-485.

Graham, T. W., Kaplan, B. H., Cornoni-Huntley, J. C., James, S. A., Becker, C., Hames, C. G., & Hayden, S. (1978). Frequency of church attendance and blood pressure elevation. *Journal of Behavioral Medicine, 1,* 37-43.

Griffith, E. (1983). The impact of sociocultural factors on a church-based healing model. *American Journal of Orthopsychiatry, 53,* 291-302.

Griffith, E., English, T., & Mayfield, V. (1980). Possession, prayer, and testimony: therapeutic aspects of the Wednesday night meeting in a black church. *Psychiatry, 43,* 120-128.

Griffith, E., & Mahy, G. E. (1984). Psychological benefits of spiritual Baptist mourning. *American Journal of Psychiatry, 141,* 769-773.

Griffith, E., Young, J. L., & Smith, D. L. (1984). An analysis of the therapeutic elements in a black church service. *Hospital and Community Psychiatry, 35,* 464-469.

Holinger, P. C., Offer D., & Zola, M. A. (1989). A prediction model of suicide among youth. *Science,* in press.

Hunsberger, B. (1985). Religion, age, life satisfaction, and perceived sources of religiousness: A study of older persons. *Journal of Gerontology, 40,* 615-620.

Idler, E. L. (1987). Religious involvement and the health of the elderly: Some hypotheses and an initial test. *Social Forces, 66,* 226-238.

Jacob, R. G., Kramer, H. C., & Agras, W. S. (1977). Relaxation therapy in the treatment of hypertension. *Archives of General Psychiatry, 34,* 1417-1427.

Kandel, D. B., & Davies, M. (1986). Adult sequelae of adolescent depressive symptoms. *Archives of General Psychiatry, 43,* 255-264.

Khavari, K. A., & Harmon, T. M. (1982). The relationship between the degree of professed religious belief and use of drugs. *International Journal of Addictions, 17,* 847-857.

Klerman, G. L. (1980). Homicide among black males. *Public Health Report, 95,* 549-550.

Klerman, G. L., & Weissman, M. M. (1989). Increasing rates of depression. *Journal of the American Medical Association, 261,* 2229-2234.

Koenig, H. G. (1986a). Shepherds' Centers: Elderly people helping themselves. *Journal of American Geriatric Society, 34,* 73.

Koenig, H. G. (1986b). Depression and dysphoria among the elderly: Dispelling a myth. *Journal of Family Practice, 23,* 383.

Koenig, H. G. (1987). Shepherds' Centers: Role of the physician. *Geriatric Consultant.* (May/June).

Koenig, H. G. (1988). Religion and death anxiety in later life. *Hospice Journal, 4*(1), 3-24.

Koenig, H. G., Moberg, D. O., & Kvale, J. N. (1988). Religious and health characteristics of patients attending a geriatric assessment clinic. *Journal of the American Geriatric Society, 36,* 362-374.

Koenig, H. G., Kvale, J. N., & Ferrel, C. (1988). Religion and well-being in later life. *The Gerontologist, 28,* 18-28.

Koenig, H. G., Smiley, M., & Gonzales, J. (1988). *Religion, health and aging.* Westport, CT: Greenwood Press.

Koenig, H. G., George, L. K., & Siegler, I. C. (1988). The use of religion and other emotion-regulating coping strategies among older adults. *The Gerontologist, 28,* 303-310.

Koenig, H. G., Meador, K., Cohen, H. J., & Blazer, D. (1988). Depression in elderly men hospitalized with medical illness. *Archives of Internal Medicine, 148,* 1929-1936.

Koenig, H. G., & Breitner, J. (1990). Use of antidepressants in medically ill older patients: A review and commentary. *Psychosomatics, 31,* 22-32.

Koenig, H. G., Siegler, I. C., & Meador, K. G., & George, L. K. (1990). Religious coping and personality in later life. *International Journal of Geriatric Psychiatry, 5,* 123-131.

Koenig, H. G., Siegler, I. C., & George, L. K. (1989). Religious and non-religious coping: Impact on adaptation in later life. *Journal of Religion and Aging, 5*(4), 73-94.

Koenig, H. G., Shelp, F., Goli, V., Cohen, H. J., & Blazer, D. G. (1989). Survival and healthcare utilization in elderly medical inpatients with major depression. *Journal of American Geriatric Society, 37,* 599-606.

Koenig, H. G., Goli, V., Shelp, F., Kudler, H. S., Cohen, H. J., Meador, K. G., & Blazer, D. G. (1989). Antidepressant use in older medically ill inpatients: Lessons from an attempted clinical trial. *Journal of General Internal Medicine, 4,* 498-505.

Koenig, H. G., Bearon, L., & Dayringer, R. (1989). Physician perspectives on the role of religion in the physician-older patient relationship. *Journal of Family Practice, 28,* 441-448.

Kroll, J., & Sheehan, W. (1989). Religious beliefs and practices among 52 psychiatric inpatients in Minnesota. *American Journal of Psychiatry, 146,* 67-72.

Lamere, F. (1953). What happens to alcoholics? *American Journal of Psychiatry, 109,* 673.

Larson, D. B., Koenig, H. G., Kaplan, B. H., Greenberg, R. F., Logue, E., & Tyroler, H. A. (1989). The impact of religion on blood pressure status in men. *Journal of Religion and Health, 28,* 265-278.

Levin, J. S., & Markides, K. S. (1985). Religion and health in Mexican Americans. *Journal of Religion and Health, 24,* 60-69.

Levin, J. S., & Markides, K. S. (1986). Religious attendance and subjective health. *Journal for the Scientific Study of Religion, 25,* 31-40.

Light, R. W., Merrill, E. J., Despairs, J., Gordon, G. H., & Mutalipassi, L. R. (1986). Doxepin treatment of depressed patients with chronic obstructive pulmonary disease. *Archives of Internal Medicine, 146,* 1377-1380.

MacNutt, F. (1974). *Healing*. Notre Dame: Ave Maria Press.

Markides, K. S., Levin, J. S., & Ray, L. A. (1987). Religion, aging, and life satisfaction: An eight-year three-way longitudinal study. *The Gerontologist, 27*, 660-665.

Mayberry, J. F. (1982). Epidemiological studies of gastrointestinal cancer in Christian sects. *Journal of Clinical Gastroenterology, 4*, 115-121.

Miller, W. R., & Martin, J. E. (1988). *Behavior therapy and religion: Integrating spiritual and behavioral approaches to change*. Newbury Park: Sage Publications.

Morris, P. A. (1982). The effect of pilgrimage on anxiety, depression and religious attitude. *Psychological Medicine, 12*, 291-294.

Mosey, J. M. (1988). Depressive symptomatology in older females following hip fracture. *Gerontologist, 28*, 284A.

O'Brien, M. E. (1981). Effective social environment and hemodialysis adaptation—a panel analysis. *Journal of Health and Social Behavior, 21*, 360-370.

O'Brien, M. E. (1982). Religious faith and adjustment to long-term hemodialysis. *Journal of Religion and Health, 21*, 68-80.

Parfrey, P. S. (1976). The effect of religious factors on intoxicant use. *Scandinavian Journal of Social Medicine, 3*, 135-140.

Pargament, K. I., Kennell, J., Hathaway, W., Grevengoed, N., Newman, J., & Jones, W. (1988). Religion and problem-solving process: Three styles of coping. *Journal for the Scientific Study of Religion, 27*, 90-104.

Pargament, K. I., Ensing, D. S., Falgout, K., Olsen, H., Reilly, B., Van Haitsma, K., & Warren, R. (in press). God help me (I): Religious coping efforts as predictors of the outcomes to significant negative life events. *American Journal of Community Psychology*.

Princeton Religion Research Center (1982). *Religion in America*. Princeton, NJ: The Gallup Poll.

Reynolds, D. K., & Nelson, F. L. (1981). Personality, life situation, and life expectancy. *Suicide and Life-Threatening Behavior, 11*, 99-110.

Schiller, P. L., & Levin, J. S. (1988). Is there a religious factor in health care utilization?: A review. *Social Science and Medicine, 27*, 1369-1379.

Smith, D. M. (1986). Safety of faith healing. *Lancet, i*, 621.

Taylor, R. J., & Chatters, L. M. (1988). Church members as a source of informal social support. *Review of Religious Research, 30*, 193-203.

Walsh, A. (1980). The prophylactic effect of religion on blood pressure levels among a sample of immigrants. *Social Science and Medicine, 14B*, 59-63.

Weissman, M. M., Leaf, P. J., Tischler, G. L., Blazer, D. G., Karno, M., Bruce, M. L., & Florio, L. P. (1988). Affective disorders in five US communities. *Psychological Medicine, 18*, 141-154.

Williams, R. (1989). *The trusting heart*. NY: Random House (Times Books).

Wilson, B. (1968). The fellowship of alcoholics anonymous. In E. Cantanzaro (Ed.), *Alcoholism*. Springfield, IL: Charles C Thomas.

Wolff, K. (1959). Group psychotherapy with geriatric patients in a state hospital setting: Results of a three year study. *Group Psychotherapy, 12*, 218-222.

Zimberg, S. (1977). Sociopsychiatric perspectives on Jewish alcohol abuse: Implications for the prevention of alcoholism. *American Journal for Drug and Alcohol Prevention, 4*, 571-579.

Zuckerman, D. M., Kasl, S. V., & Ostfeld, A. M. (1984). Psychosocial predictors of mortality among the elderly poor: The role of religion, well-being, and social contacts. *American Journal of Epidemiology, 119*, 410-423.

PART TWO:
RELIGION AS A RESOURCE FOR PREVENTIVE ACTION: TOWARD THE PROMISED LAND

THE PSYCHOLOGICAL PERSPECTIVE

The Religious Dimensions of Coping: Implications for Prevention and Promotion

William L. Hathaway
Kenneth I. Pargament

Bowling Green State University

SUMMARY. In this article, the role of religion in the coping process is examined. The authors conceptualize the coping process as a dynamic, interaction between several different elements of coping: situations, appraisals, activities, functions, psychosocial resources and constraints, and outcomes. The research on the relationship between religion and each of these elements is reviewed in order to address two general questions: "when is religion involved in coping," and "how is religion involved in coping?" Based on this review, the authors discuss the value of religion for prevention and promotion work in a number of areas including: preventing negative events, cognitive stress inoculation, competency building, and resource provision. Finally, some special challenges posed by prevention work in a religious context are briefly examined.

Reprints may be obtained from William L. Hathaway, Department of Psychology, Bowling Green State University, Bowling Green, OH 43402.

129

Religion has often been held to be a central factor in the way people cope with life's demands. There are numerous psychological (Ellis, 1970; Freud, 1961), theological (Lewis, 1962), and philosophical (Peterson, 1982) treatments of the role of religion in dealing with various coping tasks. Frequently, writers have assumed simplistic models of religious coping. Recall, for instance, Freud's (1961) well known conceptualization of religion as a neurotic wish-fulfillment. Yet consider the complexity in the relationship between religion and psychosocial functioning suggested by the following case example:

> Mrs. B., a middle-aged housewife, experienced considerable difficulty adjusting to a move across the country for her husband's new job. She felt loss over leaving behind a close fellowship at her old church and viewed the task of searching for a new church as a burden. After finding a new church, she had problems developing new friendships, and became discontented. Mrs. B. had been actively involved in lay ministry in the past but was having difficulty getting started in the new church. Since she viewed her ministry work as an important part of her identity, she started to have feelings of low self-worth and became depressed. Mrs. B. found some consolation in her faith that God would help her adjust. But when her discontent continued, she sought help from a minister who referred her to a mental health professional. She had some difficulty following through on this initially, because she did not want to go to a counselor who might be hostile to her faith. She eventually discovered a therapist who shared her religious background and entered counseling.

Personal religiousness may operate in a variety of ways for any given individual. Mrs. B.'s religion provided her with coping tasks (finding a new church home), strategies (trusting God, seeking congregational support, performing religious duties), resources (pastoral counseling), and constraints (she only sought help compatible with her religious beliefs).

The role of religion in the coping process appears to be complex. This example points to some of the ways religion may be utilized to deal with problem situations. Yet religion may be utilized in a proactive manner in coping as well. For instance, some religious organizations help their members adjust to a relocation by performing various networking functions such as enlisting the help of a new congregation in welcoming the member to the community. Such services can facilitate adjustment to a relocation and help prevent some of the difficulties present in the case of Mrs. B.

This article will review what is currently known about religious coping and consider its implications for prevention and promotion. However, before this discussion a brief overview of the coping framework adopted by the authors will be provided.

THE COPING PROCESS

Coping can be defined as a process through which individuals try to understand and deal with significant personal or situational demands in their lives (Folkman & Lazarus, 1984). Several complex, active and continually evolving elements in the coping process can be identified (Cohen, 1987; Lazarus & Folkman, 1984). These include situations, appraisals, coping activities, psychosocial resources and constraints, and coping functions. A model of the coping process which specifies these elements is depicted in Figure 1 (Pargament, 1990).

It is important to note that the various elements in the coping process are closely interconnected. None of the elements act in isolation from each other; they are part of a dynamic process in which change in any element has ramifications for the whole process. Thus, the coping process is transactional.

Situations. The model begins with "situations" that people encounter, such as major events, chronic problems, daily tasks, or other problems. While this is a convenient starting place, it is important to note that people are actively involved in constructing their situations as well as responding to them (Tyler, Gatz, & Keenan, 1979). For instance, people decide to get married and in the process create a new situation with which to cope.

Most coping theorists stress that events by themselves are not very strong predictors of *how* an individual will behave. There are, after all, numerous examples of people coping very differently with the same situations (Bulman & Wortman, 1977; Frankl, 1963; Glick, Weiss, & Parkes, 1974). Furthermore, only modest correlations have been found between the total number of major life events and subsequent well-being (Rabkin & Struening, 1976).

Appraisals. How people construe or "appraise" a situation is an important determinant of how they will respond (Litt, 1988). Lazarus and Folkman (1984) distinguish between two related aspects of this appraisal process: evaluations of the situation's implications for the person (primary appraisal) and evaluation of the resources and options for handling the situation (secondary appraisal). McCrae (1984) has also pointed out that different kinds of events pose different types of coping demands. Situa-

Figure 1. The Coping Process

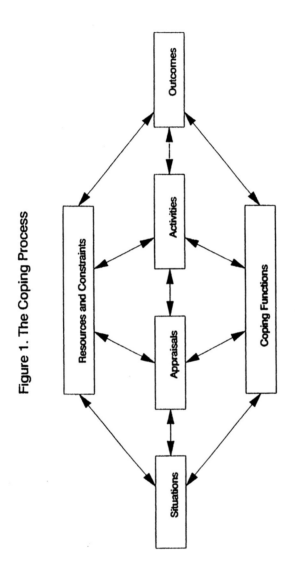

tions may be viewed as more or less threatening, challenging, taxing, or opportune.

Coping Activities. Coping has a behavioral component as well as a cognitive one: depending, in part, on how the situation is appraised, individuals can use any of a variety of activities to cope. Examples of such activities include information-seeking, direct action, inhibition of action, problem redefinition, emotional maintenance, and seeking support from others (Cohen, 1987; Lazarus & Folkman, 1984; McCrae, 1984).

Outcomes. Coping can impact people at a variety of levels including psychological, social, and physical (Cohen, 1987). For instance, coping may result in an altered sense of self-esteem thereby affecting the individual at a psychological level. A person's coping efforts may tend to either alienate others or enlist their support, thereby influencing social outcomes. Coping can contribute to numerous physical outcomes such as a reduction or increase in headache pain.

It should also be noted that the outcomes of coping may be mixed: a particular coping activity may have both positive and negative outcomes. Consider the common observation that "Type A" personalities may be "high achievers" in their careers but are at increased risk for a variety of health problems. Therefore, it is often more appropriate to ask "effective for what" rather than merely "how effective is it" when assessing the outcomes of coping.

Resources and Constraints. A number of personal and social factors serve as resources and constraints which shape the coping process. These factors include a person's generalized psychosocial competence, attitudes and beliefs, physical health, financial status, social networks, and social norms (Collins, 1986; Heller & Swindle, 1983; Tyler, 1978). For instance, social networks may provide members with advice, guidance, and models for dealing with certain kinds of circumstances. On the other hand, poverty, moral taboos, or psychological difficulties place important limitations on the ways people can cope.

Coping Functions. Finally, people engage in coping for diverse reasons. While the functions of coping may be broadly classified as problem-solving or emotional self-maintenance (Lazarus & Folkman, 1984), a variety of more specific functions can be identified: desires for greater self-esteem, a sense of power or control in life, a sense of meaning in life, personal growth, a sense of hope, feelings of intimacy, expression of feelings, a sense of personal identity, restraints on undesirable impulses and feelings, and comfort-seeking (Pargament, 1990).

RELIGION AND THE PROCESS OF COPING

Many people claim to be at least somewhat religious. In a Gallup poll, nine out of ten Americans report they have never doubted the existence of God; further, most Americans belong to a religious congregation (Gallup & Castelli, 1989). There is also evidence that religion is a prevalent factor in the coping process. The Religion and Coping Project conducted by Pargament and his associates (1989) explored religious coping through survey research of approximately 600 members of 10 midwestern congregations with diverse religious and socioeconomic backgrounds. Thirty-nine percent of the respondents said religion was considerably involved in coping with a significant negative life event, another 39% said it was somewhat involved, and only 22% said that religion was not involved in their coping at all. Koenig, George, and Siegler (1988) reported that almost half of their older adult sample spontaneously mentioned the use of religion in coping during interviews. They note that "religious attitudes and activities were found to be the predominant coping behaviors reported by older adults in this series of studies and others . . . regardless of research method employed" (p. 309).

Of course not everyone turns to religion for help in coping. Prior to his death, columnist Steward Alsop wrote:

> I wish I could say that this strange experience with leukemia has given me profound spiritual insights. But it hasn't. The big bearded reality of my childhood is no longer a reality to me. . . . I have been an agnostic since I was about eighteen. I am an agnostic still. (cited in Fichter, 1981, p. 56)

This quotation (and other evidence as well) belies the old adage that "there are no atheists in the foxholes." But clearly some times, places, and people call for more religious involvement in coping than others.

When Do People Turn to Religion in the Coping Process?

Two general conditions appear to increase the likelihood of religious involvement in coping. First, religion must be *available* to people. Numerous studies have shown that children are likely to adopt the religious orientations of their parents; religious parents tend to have children who become religious, and parents who are not religious tend to have children who do not become religious (e.g., Hunsberger & Brown, 1984). It only makes sense that without a background in this realm of experience, religious approaches become less available as sources of interpretation and solution to problems. Conversely, greater involvement in, experience with, and commitment to a religious way of life, increases the availability of religious coping options. For example, in the Religion and Coping Project, religious involvement in coping was associated with more frequent prayer and church attendance, a more intrinsic religious orientation, and a greater number of personal religious experiences with God.

However, availability, in itself, is not the full story. Many people have strong backgrounds in religion, yet turn away from it during crucial moments in life. Religious involvement in coping is also dependent upon the degree to which it offers a *compelling* way of dealing with problems. Wrapped up in the association of religion with critical times and transitions in life is the perception that religion offers a more plausible response to the questions raised by these times and changes than other frameworks of belief and practice. Birth, death, injustice, tragedy, mysterious events — these are some of the events of life not as easily explained by secular perspectives, and these are some of the events so often tied to religion.

On the other hand, the individual is less likely to look to religion when other approaches to the world are more convincing. For example, Kroll-Smith and Couch (1987) describe the lack of religious involvement by residents coping with an underground mine fire which eventually destroyed the life of a Pennsylvanian town. Although the residents of the town were religious, they viewed the fire as "manmade" in nature. The solutions they pursued were, in turn, political and secular, rather than religious.

How Is Religion Involved in the Coping Process?

As was noted earlier, some theorists have tended to suggest simplistic relationships between religion and coping. For example, Ellis (1970) has argued that religion can be reduced to irrational supernaturalism, while Freud (1961) saw it simply as neurotic wish fulfillment. Others have attempted to define a less negative role for religion in coping but still advance simplistic relationships. For instance, Rothbaum, Weisz and Snyder (1982) suggest that, when a situation is viewed as uncontrollable, religion may be used as a means of gaining "secondary control": "understanding and thereby accepting the event" rather than focusing on ways to change it (p. 25).

An increasing body of research has attempted to address the issue empirically. These studies have reported mixed results: sometimes religiousness is related to good coping adjustment (e.g., O'Brien, 1982), sometimes a negative relationship is noted (e.g., Rosenstiel & Keefe, 1983),

and sometimes religiousness seems to make little difference for the outcomes of coping (e.g., Barbarin & Chesler, 1986). The ambiguity in the
available data about the relationship between general religiousness and the
coping process should not be surprising for a number of reasons. Much of
the research uses overly simplistic measures of religion such as frequency
of church attendance or prayer (Ventura & Boss, 1985; Yates, Chalmer,
St. James, Follansbee, & McKegney 1987; Zuckerman, Kasl, & Ostfeld,
1984). Although this type of research can be useful in suggesting that
religion is a significant factor, it provides very little information about
exactly what it is in religion that makes a difference in the coping process.
   Another reason for the ambiguous findings may be that both religion
and coping are complex areas of human functioning. There are varieties of
ways of being religious and varieties of ways of coping. For instance, a
particular type of religious coping may lead to positive outcomes in some
situations but have negative or little impact in other situations. Also consider that some religious interpretations of a situation may be health enhancing while others might be health hindering. Thus, it is important to
look at the role of religious coping in a more differentiated manner. The
following discussion will focus on some of the specific contributions religion might make to each of the elements of the coping process and, in
turn, their relationships to the outcomes of coping.

Situations

   Many situations that people face are, in themselves, religious in nature.
Some of the most significant life events are marked by "rites of passage"
which are distinctly religious such as Bar Mitzvot, baptisms, and conver-
sions. Furthermore, religions often prescribe daily religious tasks which
can be sources of ongoing stress or uplifts for their adherents such as
witnessing or daily devotionals (Foster, 1978). Swihart and Richardson
(1987) note that "spiritual problems can create stress within the individual
to the point that crisis takes place" (p. 119). They enumerate a number of
spiritual situations that can lead to crises including conversion, disap-
pointment in spiritual leaders, doctrinal conflicts, church separation and
rejection, and disrupted spiritual life arising from doubt, anger at God, or
guilt. Consider the following comments of an adolescent experiencing
religious doubt:

> I wonder if God really loves us like people say he does. Then why
> does he let people hurt so much, why are people homeless, why are
> people murdered, and why is the world so screwed up. . . . I have
> been everywhere from suicidal to happy to drug-related high. And
> the only time that I felt that I've experienced God was when I was

suicidal. How can a true God desert me through most of my life and only intervene when I want nothing more than to be side by side with him. I don't believe that this world is what God had in mind. Where did he go? (Kooistra, 1990, pp. 88-89)

Religion may also increase or decrease the likelihood of the occurrence of key situations. For example, some researchers have pointed out the compatibility between many religious proscriptions and "healthy life-styles" that reduce the chance of certain emotional problems and physical conditions such as coronary heart disease and hypertension (Benson & Proctor, 1984; Martin & Carlson, 1988). Numerous studies have shown that religiousness is related to lower frequency or intensity of various health problems (Levin & Schiller, 1987), drug and alcohol abuse, and non-marital sexual involvement (Spilka, Hood, & Gorsuch, 1985).

There is some evidence that religion is particularly helpful in coping with high stress situations such as major life events. A number of studies suggest that various dimensions of religion can buffer the influence of stress on outcomes ranging from depression to mortality (Maton, 1989; Park, Cohen, & Herb, in press; Williams, Larson, Buckler, Heckman, & Pyle, 1989; Zuckerman, Kasl, & Ostfeld, 1984). For example, Maton (1989) studied 91 college bound high school students through their first semester of college. He found that self-reported spiritual support substantially predicted emotional adjustment for those under high stress but not for those under low stress.

Because much of the research has assumed that religion is most relevant for coping with major life events, studies have typically restricted their focus to individuals facing high stress situations such as cancer (Acklin, Brown & Mauger, 1983; Jenkins & Pargament, 1988), the death of a child (Cook & Wimberley, 1983), severe accidents (Bulman & Wortman, 1977), or poverty (Rosen, 1982). Yet it should also be noted that, in addition to its potential relevance for coping with major life events, religion may be used to handle minor situations such as daily hassles (Compas, Forsythe, & Wagner, 1988).

Appraisals

Individuals make a variety of attributions about situations from a religious framework. For instance, differing views of God can lead to different appraisals of situations. Life events can be viewed as a reward from a loving God, punishment from an angry God, unintended by a kind, non-intervening God, as the will of a mysterious God, and as an opportunity or challenge for growth (Pargament & Hahn, 1986; Spilka, Shaver, &

Kirkpatrick, 1985). Consider these diverse religious appraisals by women facing infertility problems (cited in Greil, Leitko, & Porter, 1986):

> But it was like if there is this God who's this wonderful person, why is he doing this to us? We've been good people, we've played by the rules and we've done what we should have done all of our lives. "Why is He punishing us?" was how I felt. (p. 4)
>
> I don't really blame God, but sometimes I wonder. God knows how much I love children. . . . I just can't figure out why he doesn't let me have some . . . maybe . . . there's a child overseas that just absolutely really needs us, and this is the only way he could make that come out. . . . (p. 7)

Religious appraisals may be especially common in coming to terms with tragic life events such as sudden, terminal illness or the death of a young child (Bulman & Wortman, 1977; Cook & Wimberley, 1983; Peteet, 1985). Cook and Wimberly (1983) found three common religious appraisals in parents of children who died because of medical problems: blaming God, self-blame, and finding a purpose in the death.

In these types of tragic situations religious attributions may impact the individual's evaluation of threat involved. O'Brien (1982) cites the following statement of a chronic dialysis patient who had experienced three cardiac arrests and numerous surgeries: "Each time I knew everything would be all right because I asked God to carry me through—I know that He's got His arms around me" (p. 76).

Religion may also contribute to the way people appraise daily hassles. For instance, a belief that God is directing one's life towards some special goal may help make a tedious job more tolerable.

In addition to these influences on primary appraisals of threat, challenge or loss, religion may contribute to the person's secondary appraisals about what can be done to handle the situation. For instance, a person may believe that he/she can turn to others in their congregation for advice and support if needed, or may feel that otherwise uncontrollable situations, such as terminal illness, may be dealt with by spiritual practices such as prayer. Accordingly, exhortations such as, "God will never give more than we can handle or endure with His help," are common in the popular religious culture.

Religion can also restrict the range of coping options a person is willing to consider. Tunks describes a 40 year-old widow who had remained with her abusive husband because she felt her faith demanded that she suffer his beatings (cited in Conwell, 1986). Some individuals appraise their religious communities as discouraging support seeking or sharing of problems. For instance, a domestic violence victim stated: "The feeling I got from our church was that I was to suffer in silence" (Bowker, 1988; p. 233). The existing research suggests that there are some differences in the efficacy of various religious appraisals. For instance, attributing a situation to either a loving, benevolent God or to a mysterious God's will is associated with more positive adjustment (Cook & Wimberly, 1983; Grevengoed & Pargament, 1987; Jenkins & Pargament, 1988). Viewing a situation as a punishment from an angry God is related to poorer adjustment (Grevengoed & Pargament, 1987; Pargament, 1989).

Coping Activities

Religion can affect coping activity by providing people with a repertoire of coping strategies. People draw on social, interpersonal, cognitive, spiritual, and behavioral aspects of their faith to cope with problems. Consider the following statements by Bill Wilson, the founder of Alcoholics Anonymous:

> At the hospital I was separated from alcohol for the last time. Treatment seemed wise, for I showed signs of delirium tremens.
> There I humbly offered myself to God, as I understood Him, to do with me as He would, I placed myself unreservedly under His care and direction. I admitted for the first time that of myself I was nothing; that without Him I was lost. I ruthlessly faced my sins and became willing to have my new-found Friend take them away, root and branch. I have not had a drink since. (cited in Van Cleave, Byrd, & Revell, 1987; p. 102-103)

Wilson reported yielding "control" of certain unmanageable behaviors to God, while at the same time taking active responsibility for other parts of the recovery process. This pattern of "accepting powerlessness, surrender, and spirituality" is expressed in the "twelve steps" of Alcoholics Anonymous and related groups. Recognizing one's powerlessness in uncontrollable situations and deferring to a "higher power" has become an important part of recovery programs and support groups for many addictions (Baugh, 1988; Van Cleave et al., 1987).

There may be a number of such religious coping styles adopted by individuals. Pargament and his associates (Hathaway & Pargament, 1989; Pargament, Grevengoed, Hathaway, Kennell, Newman & Jones, 1988) have reported empirical support for three religious coping styles. Collaborative religious copers report actively working together with God to deal with problems. Deferring religious copers acknowledge a passive posture in which they defer responsibility for coping entirely to God. Self-directing religious copers take an active role in coping but view God as being uninvolved. Although the coping styles are related to each other, they have distinct implications for adjustment. The collaborative and self-directing styles relate positively but deferring relates negatively to competence.

Other research has shifted the focus from such dispositional styles to situation-specific or episodic coping strategies (Horton, Wilkins, & Wright, 1988; Koenig, George, & Siegler, 1988; Koenig, Siegler, & George, 1988; Pargament, 1990). As part of the Religion and Coping Project, Pargament (1989) used factor analysis to place 31 different strategies within six categories of religious coping: spiritually-based, good deeds, religious support, discontent, pleading, and religious avoidance. Table 1 presents some examples of each of these strategies and their relationship with the three measures of adjustment used in the Religion and Coping Project: a measure of change in religiousness, an index of the resolution of the event, and a measure of recent mental health status. Note the complexity indicated by the findings: some of the strategies related positively to outcome, others related negatively, and some had mixed relationships with outcome.

Pargament et al. (1989) found that the religious coping strategies were associated in differing ways with non-religious coping strategies. For example, spiritually-based coping activities were associated with a focus on the positive, active problem-solving, and social support. Religious discontent, on the other hand, related to less focus on the positive and more avoidance of problems. However, they go on to note that the religious coping strategies made a significant contribution to outcomes independent of both non-religious coping and general religious dispositions. Thus, the religious strategies provide additional but related avenues of coping from non-religious coping efforts and general religious styles.

Religion may also influence the selection of non-religious coping activities (Ebaugh, Richman, & Chafetz, 1984; Mechanic, 1974). Ebaugh and her colleagues (1984) found sectarian difference in the way religion was used to respond to crisis. Charismatics tended to rely on their groups for social support, Bahai's utilized intellectual coping strategies such as interpreting writings, and Christian Scientists were more involved in positive thinking.

Psychosocial Resources and Constraints

Religion brings a range of social and psychological resources and constraints to the coping process. At a social level, religion can provide such resources as financial assistance, social support, and prescriptions for how to deal with problems. However, it can also limit a person's available

Table 1

Some Different Religious Coping Activities and Their Outcomes

Coping Activity	Examples	Outcomes		
		Religious	Event-Specific	Mental Health
Spiritually-based	trusting God for protection turning to God for guidance	+++	++	+
Good Deeds	confessing sins being more loving	++	+	+
Religious Support	receiving support from clergy receiving support from the church	++	+	+
Discontent	feeling angry with God questioning one's faith	-	-	-
Pleading	asking for a miracle asking God why it happened	+	-	-
Religious Avoidance	letting God solve the problem focusing on the world-to-come instead of the problem	++	+	+

<u>Size of Relationship</u>

+ or -   modest $(r < .4)$
++   moderate $(.4 < r < .7)$
+++   large $(r > .7)$

resources by proscribing against certain courses of actions. Consider the following advice given to domestic violence victims by clergy:

> Stay and work things out. God expects that.
> Hope for the best. God will change him. Pray.
> He is hopeless and cruel but you are married to him.
> Try harder not to provoke him. (Horton, Wilkins, & Wright, 1988; p. 242)

Religion may influence the coping process at an individual level as well. People vary in their religious beliefs, commitments, practices, and orientations in ways that have implications for coping. Religious beliefs can encourage continued coping through the hope that either circumstances will change or all will be made right in an afterlife (Kahoe, 1982). Religious practices, such as devotional meditation, have been reported to reduce anger and anxiety (Carlson, Bacaseta, & Simanton, 1988). Finally, religious coping differences have been noted between individuals who have different orientations to their faith. For instance, while intrinsically oriented individuals view religion as a master motive, having value in itself, extrinsically oriented individuals are religious in order to obtain some other, non-religious goal (Allport & Ross, 1967). Reilly and Falgout (1988) reported the following in the Religion and Coping Project sample:

> For the intrinsically-oriented, religious coping centers around the use of faith and the desire for closeness with God in situations which may threaten the person spiritually but offer opportunities for growth. For the extrinsically-oriented, religious coping is tied not to faith, but to works. Religion is called on in situations which severely test the individual's ability to cope. Here the individual looks to religion for personal aid—self-esteem, control, self-actualization. (p. 9)

Differences in religiousness may also be associated with differences in the efficacy of coping. For example, comparing more religious women with less religious women who had experienced a loss in pregnancy, Lasker, Lohmann, and Toedter (1989) found stronger correlations between religious coping and perinatal grief among the more religious.

Coping Functions

Religion can be used to achieve a number of different ends. For example, in the following case example a teenager used his religion to enhance self-esteem and intimacy.

> Tom was a socially marginal teenager who grew up in a medium-sized community. He felt "invisible" in most social situations. At school he was neither rejected nor popular. Tom became more involved at church and several people made comments such as, " . . . it is very good to see a young person interested in serving God." Tom began to develop a sense of self-worth and decided to dedicate himself to religious service since this is where he felt he could make a contribution.

Five different purposes of religion were identified through factor analysis in the Religion and Coping Project study: self-development, spiritual, resolve, sharing and restraint. Most of the religious functions had at least a modest relationship to religious outcomes such as "feeling closer to God" (Pargament et al., 1989). Although the observed relationship was small, the spiritual function was the only religious function related to mental health. This function is aimed at fostering closeness with God, finding meaning in life, and developing hope about the future. It is also important to stress that different people may look to religion for different purposes.

SUMMARY

When one approaches the issue of religious coping from a more differentiated perspective, the rich and complex role of religion in coping becomes apparent. Various uses of religion in coping have a significant, and sometimes substantial, association with adjustment. However, religion does not always work in the same way: while some forms of religious coping facilitate adjustment, others seem to hinder it. In western culture, approaches to religious coping which emphasize faith in a God who is appraised as loving and providential, involve that faith in coping strategies, and yet encourage the individual to engage in realistic problem-solving, appear to contribute to positive outcomes. Religious coping approaches that view God as punishing and place the individual in passive dependence on that God for problem-solving relate to negative outcomes.

The initial evidence suggests that religious coping adds something to the coping process beyond what we know from more, general forms of coping and from dispositional forms of religiousness, such as religious orientation. Specific uses of religion in the coping process can be identified which account for outcomes of coping independently of these other factors.

However, the religious coping research is young and many questions still need to be examined. It is likely that an even more intricate picture of the role of religion in coping will emerge as the field gets more refined. For example, we might expect more comprehensive and differentiated systems of religious belief and practice to be more compelling and more helpful to people faced with situations that challenge their world-view (e.g., McIntosh & Wortman, 1989). We might also expect that different strategies will work better in different situations or in different cultures. Perhaps a deferring approach in which the individual relies on God to solve a problem may prove more helpful as the situation becomes more uncontrollable (Pargament, Grevengoed, Hathaway, Kennell, Newman, & Jones, 1988). Park, Cohen, and Herb (in press) conducted a promising study in this direction. Among several interesting and complex findings, they report that an intrinsic religious orientation buffered the effects of uncontrollable life stress on subsequent levels of depression for Protestant but not Catholic college students.

RELIGIOUS COPING AND PREVENTION

Although the relationship between religion and the coping process appears to be complex, it is evident that many people turn to their faith in order to cope with life's demands. As a significant force for many people in society, religion likely serves an important role in preventing and/or promoting various psycho-emotional problems. The available data suggest that there may be more and less effective religious involvements. Thus, preventive interventions may attempt to foster the health enhancing, and reduce the health-hindering, aspects of religious coping (Collins, 1986).

The general coping model described earlier suggests at least four potential points of such preventive interventions; preventing negative events, fostering "stress inoculating" religious appraisals, helping religious communities build competencies in their members, and developing resources for coping.

Preventing Negative Events

The religious community can be an important force in preventing situations which tax peoples' coping resources. For instance, religious groups often prescribe "healthy lifestyles" which reduce the risk of negative physical and emotional events (Martin & Carlson, 1988). Religious advocacy of certain lifestyles sometimes makes use of formal education programs. For instance, Lorch (1987) surveyed all of the churches in a large, Western city to find what churches had conducted youth drug or alcohol education programs within the last three years. About half of the churches reported having a program in this time span. The churches were motivated to provide these programs on religious grounds: approximately 98% felt that it was their duty to try to prevent substance abuse among their members. Lorch found that " . . . these substance use programs generally consisted of at least one or two sessions a year with most using both church and outside speakers for these sessions" (p. 113).

The religious community could be encouraged to promote specialized ministries, education programs, or other institutional activities that help prevent negative events. A broad spectrum of potentially stressful life situations may also be mitigated against by the religious community including divorce, homelessness, social isolation, or financial problems. For instance, in recent years there has been an increasing emphasis in Christian media on money management issues. A number of Christian professional financial consultants have developed active ministries aimed at helping Christians from a broad range of financial backgrounds learn how to become "financially free." The work is typically justified on spiritual grounds: "in order for Christians to be responsive to God's direction for their lives they need to be 'free' of crippling financial circumstances." Yet the financial counseling ministries also have potential mental health benefits by reducing the likelihood of financial stress.

Cognitive Stress Inoculation

To the extent that more adaptive religious appraisals can be adopted in place of less adaptive ones, cognitive stress inoculation training may mitigate the effects of potentially stressful situations (Meichenbaum & Jaremko, 1983). One important facet of this training is to help individuals become aware of their underlying appraisal process and develop more functional appraisals.

This process could be carried out through religious education programs or religious services. For instance, religious educators could be encouraged to teach about diverse ways of conceptualizing situations within their faith traditions. This increase in the available religious options for appraising situations would likely mitigate against stress invoking cognitions such as "polarization" (e.g., the situation must be either "all bad" or "all good"). For example, a common "stress invoking" religious attribution is the belief that bad events signify "punishment from God." In contrast to this view, a variety of alternative attributions could be pointed out such as bad events signifying an opportunity for growth, the result of "natural process," or an opportunity for God's power to be demonstrated as the following vignette from the New Testament suggests:

> As he went along, he saw a man blind from birth. His disciples asked him, Rabbi, who sinned, this man or his parents, that he was born blind? Neither this man nor his parents sinned, said Jesus, but this happened so that the work of God might be displayed in his life. (John 9:1-3, New International Version)

Competency-Building

Religious communities can also provide a context for building competencies in their members. Congregations currently provide mental health related education through activities such as marriage enrichment programs, parenting skill training, communication training, and job skill training (Maton & Pargament, 1987). The Stephen Series provides an example of a church based program that integrates mental health education with lay ministry (Haugk, 1985). The program was developed by an ordained minister/clinical psychologist and is designed to promote one-on-one caring skills in lay ministers. Although the program has a theological mission, psychological principles of skilled helping are incorporated such as assertiveness training, listening skills, dealing with affect, crisis intervention, and principles of confidentiality. Nearly 40,000 Stephen ministers have already been trained. Such training programs increase the likelihood that religious adherents will receive constructive assistance when dealing with routine coping tasks that might otherwise become more problematic.

A number of studies have shown that many people who are not affiliated with formal religious groups identify themselves as religious (Princeton Religion Research Center, 1986). Furthermore, secular professionals often encounter clients who relate legal, medical, psychological or other problems to religious issues (Fichter, 1981; Peteet, 1985). A number of secular professionals have developed programs which explicitly includes a religious dimension in their service provision. For instance, the Granger-Westberg Holistic Health Centers has a religious professional on the staff, assesses spiritual development with clinical scales, and incorporates a spiritual growth plan into its health care model. McSherry's (1983) research suggests that such holistic approaches may lead to better health outcomes than traditional monodisciplinary ones. Such programs emphasize the proactive role of religious value systems in motivating individuals to pursue more health enhancing lifestyles.

It is also possible to enhance competency by encouraging the religious community to make use of natural religious pathways such as sermons, Bible study, and religious education materials. One way that religious groups attempt to "build-up" or "edify" their members is by providing relevant instruction. Sermons, topical Bible studies, and other religious instruction modes often discuss such things as marital communication skills, ways of dealing with interpersonal conflict, or how to maintain oneself while going through a difficult problem. For example, a well-known religious music series for children devoted an album to instruction in problem-solving skills within a religious framework (Rettino & Rettino, 1985).

It is not uncommon for religious adherents to complain that their congregations seem out of touch with life and irrelevant to the demands of day-to-day existence (Schroeder & Obenhaus, 1964). However, numerous religious education materials explicitly focus on coping issues. For instance, Educational Ministries, Inc. publishes a series of teaching aides for religious educators aimed at helping children "cope with death," "cope with divorce," or deal with "feelings" (Ward, 1981; 1983; 1984). These publications make numerous references to mental health literature on the subjects. Prevention workers could target and disseminate this type of information to those religious communities voicing a need for coping skills information.

Resource Provision

The clergy are often among the first places people turn for help (Bell, Morris, Holzer, & Warheit, 1976). Furthermore, the clergy operate within a tradition in which they have a "right of access" to reach out to members. It is generally viewed as appropriate for ministers to visit a parishioner at home, work or in other settings and discuss personal matters. Thus the clergy are in an advantageous position for prevention work. Yet there is a great deal of variability in how prepared ministers are to reach out to help people cope with life's demands.

Programs which help ministers function better in their people-helping roles would translate into better pastoral resources for the laity in the coping process. For instance, a number of professionals who work with domestic violence treatment have outlined preventive intervention programs to help the clergy detect the abuse problem earlier, deal with it more appropriately, and empower the congregation to become actively anti-abuse (Horton & Williams, 1988). Other programs have been developed which foster general helping skills in church leaders: The Stephen Series, mentioned earlier, increases the available pool of skilled helpers who can identify problems at an early stage.

Since congregations naturally provide coping resources and constraints for individuals, programs can be directed at facilitating this process. For instance, the Church and Community Project developed at McCormick seminary, uses public funds to help churches develop various self-perpetuating social service programs such as job training for the unemployed or prepared meal delivery for shut-ins. The Congregation Development Program, created by Pargament, Ensing, Falgout, and Warren (1988), uses needs assessment methods to identify strengths and weaknesses in congregations and provide them with feedback about ways to pursue their goals more effectively.

Many denominations and interdenominational groups support various social outreach programs with money, personnel, political advocacy, and other resources. When denominations "catch a vision" for the importance of a particular social program, they can be primary facilitators. For instance, the Campaign for Human Development, which spends millions of dollars on various social action, community development, and self-help projects, receives substantial support from the religious community. Denominational groups also make major contributions to many regional social development programs. The Communities Organized for Public Service (COPS) provides a good example. COPS spends millions of dollars on community improvement in low-income Mexican-American areas of San Antonio (Maton & Pargament, 1987). The local Roman Catholic churches have supported COPS from its inception with many vital resources. Thus, enlisting denominational support for programs aimed at resource provision can be an important strategy for prevention work.

Special Challenges

Although these few examples suggest the feasibility of religious coping based prevention programs, a number of challenges remain. In particular, both a pragmatic and an ethical obstacle arise for programs aimed at promoting some forms of religious coping over others: religious communities may view such change efforts as an infringement on their creedal or ritual traditions and actively oppose such prevention efforts. Thus prevention programs must be sensitive to the range of religious coping options present in a particular group, and argue for change in terms meaningful to the religious community. In this direction, it is important to remember that mental health and religious communities may see the functions of the coping process differently. The former will typically advocate coping for the purposes of problem-solving, social, or psychological well-being. While the religious community may not exclude these functions of religious coping, it will be more likely to emphasize the *spiritual* purposes of coping.

Perhaps the greater challenge, however, is to overcome stereotypes and misconceptions about religious life, including the belief that religious institutions are simply quasi-mental health centers, that religion is simply "all-good" or "all-bad," or that religion is no longer a very important part of people's lives. On the contrary, the evidence shows: religious systems are, in fact, religious; religion is a complex multi-dimensional phenomenon with a variety of psychological and social implications; and religion remains an important force in the lives of many people. With these fundamental "facts of religious life" in mind, the mental health professional is likely to find new doors opened for preventive and promotive activities within religious communities.

REFERENCES

Acklin, M., Brown, E., & Mauger, P. (1983). The role of religious values in coping with cancer. *Journal of Religion and Health, 22,* 322-333.

Allport, G. W., & Ross, J. M. (1967). Personal religious orientation and prejudice. *Journal of Personality and Social Psychology, 5,* 432-443.

Barbarin, O. A., & Chesler, M. (1986). The medical context of parental coping with childhood cancer. *American Journal of Community Psychology, 14,* 221-235.

Baugh, J. R. (1988). Gaining control by giving up control: Strategies for coping with powerlessness. In W. R. Miller & J. E. Martin (Eds.), *Behavior therapy and religion: Integrating spiritual and behavioral approaches to change* (pp. 125-38). Newbury Park: Sage.

Bell, R. A., Morris, R. R., Holzer, C. E., & Warheit, G. J. (1976). The clergy as a mental health resource: Parts I and II. *The Journal of Pastoral Care, 30,* 103-115.

Benson, H., & Proctor, W. (1984). *Beyond the relaxation response*. New York: New York Times Books.

Bowker, L. H. (1988). Religious victims and their religious leaders: Services delivered to one thousand battered women by the clergy. In A. L. Horton & D. Williams (Eds.), *Abuse and religion: When praying isn't enough* (pp. 229-234). Lexington, MA: Lexington.

Bulman, R. J., & Wortman, C. B. (1977). Attributions of blame and coping in the "real world": Severe accident victims react to their lot. *Journal of Personality and Social Psychology, 35,* 351-363.

Carlson, C. R., Bacaseta, P. E., & Simanton, D. A. (1988). A controlled evaluation of devotional meditation and progressive relaxation. *Journal of Psychology and Theology, 16,* 362-368.

Cohen, L. (1987). Measurement of coping. In S. V. Kasl & C. L. Cooper (Eds.), *Stress and health: Issues in research methodology* (pp. 283-305). New York: John Wiley.

Collins, G. R. (1986). *Innovative approaches to counseling*. Waco: Word.

Compas, B. E., Forsythe, C. J., & Wagner, B. M. (1988). Consistency and variability in causal attributions and coping with stress. *Cognitive Therapy and Research, 12,* 305-320.

Conwell, W. L. (1986). Chronic pain conceptualization and religious interpretation. *Journal of Religion and Health, 25,* 46-50.

Cook, J., & Wimberly, D. (1983). If I should die before I wake: Religious commitment and adjustment to death of a child. *Journal for the Scientific Study of Religion, 22,* 222-238.

Ebaugh, H., Richman, K., & Chafetz, J. (1984). Life crises among the religiously committed: Do sectarian differences matter? *Journal for the Scientific Study of Religion, 23,* 19-31.

Ellis, A. E. (1970). The case against religion. *Mensa Journal, 132,* 5-6.

Fichter, J. (1981). *Religion and pain: The spiritual dimensions of health care*. New York: Crossroad.

Folkman, S., & Lazarus, R. (1980). An analysis of coping in a middle-aged community sample. *Journal of Health and Social Behavior, 21,* 219-239.

Foster, R. J. (1978). *A celebration of discipline: The path to spiritual growth*. New York: Harper and Row.

Freud, S. (1961). *The future of an illusion*. (J. Strachey, Trans.) New York: W. W. Norton. (Original work published 1928.)

Frankl, V. (1963). *Man's search for meaning*. New York: Washington Square.

Gallup, G. Jr., & Castelli, J. (1989). *The people's religion: American faith in the 90s*. New York: MacMillan.

Glick, I. O., Weiss, R. S., & Parkes, C. M. (1974). *The first year of bereavement*. New York: Wiley.

Greil, A. L., Leitko, T. A., & Porter, K. L. (1986). *Theodicy and religious involvement among infertile couples*. Paper presented at the Society for the Scientific Study of Religion, Washington, DC.

Grevengoed, N., & Pargament, K. (1987). *Attributions for death: An examination* of the role of religion and the relationship between attributions and mental health. Paper presented at the Society for the Scientific Study of Religion, Louisville, KY.

Hathaway, W., & Pargament, K. (in press). Intrinsic religiousness and competence: Inconsistent mediation by different religious coping styles. *Journal for the Scientific Study of Religion*.

Haugk, K. (1985). *Christian caregiving—a way of life*. Minneapolis: Augsburg.

Heller, K., & Swindle, R. (1983). Social networks, perceived social support, and coping with stress. In R. D. Felner, L. Jason, J. Mortisugu, & S. Farber (Eds.), *Preventive psychology: Theory, research and practice*. New York: Pergamon.

Horton, A. L., Wilkins, M. M., & Wright, W. (1988). Women who ended abuse: What religious leaders and religion did for them. In A. L. Horton & D. Williams (Eds.), *Abuse and religion: When praying isn't enough* (pp. 235-246). Lexington, MA: Lexington.

Horton, A. L., & Williams, D. (1988). What incest perpetrators need (but are not getting) from the clergy and treatment community. *Abuse and religion: When praying isn't enough* (pp. 259-266). Lexington, MA: Lexington.

Hunsberger, B., & Brown, L. B. (1984). Religious socialization, apostasy, and the impact of family background. *Journal for the Scientific Study of Religion, 23*, 239-251.

Jenkins, R., & Pargament, K. (1988). Cognitive appraisals in cancer patients. *Social Science and Medicine, 26*, 625-633.

Kahoe, R. (1982). *The power of religious hope*. Paper presented at the annual meeting of the American Psychological Association, Washington, DC.

Koenig, H. G., George, L. K., & Siegler, I. C. (1988). The use of religion and other emotion-regulating coping strategies among older adults. *The Gerontologist, 28*, 303-310.

Koenig, H. G., Siegler, I. C., & George, L. K. (1989). Religious and nonreligious coping: Impact on adaptation in later life. *Journal of Religion and Aging, 5*, 73-94.

Kooistra, W. P. (1990). *The process of religious doubting in adolescents raised in religious environments*. Unpublished doctoral dissertation, Bowling Green State University.

Kroll-Smith, J., & Couch, S. (1987). A chronic technical disaster and the irrelevance of religious meaning: The case of Centralia Pennsylvania. *Journal for the Scientific Study of Religion, 26*, 25-37.

Lasker, J. W., Lohmann, J., & Toedter, L. (1989). *The role of religion in bereavement: The case of pregnancy loss*. Paper presented at the Society for the Scientific Study of Religion, Salt Lake City.

Lazarus, R., & Folkman, S. (1984). *Stress, appraisal, and coping*. New York: Springer.

Levin, J., & Schiller, P. (1987). Is there a religious factor in health? *Journal of Religion and Health, 26*, 9-36.

Lewis, C. S. (1962). *The problem of pain*. New York: MacMillan.

Litt, M. D. (1988). Cognitive mediators of stressful experience: Self-efficacy and personal control. *Cognitive Therapy and Research, 12,* 241-260.

Lorch, B. R. (1987). Church youth alcohol and drug education programs. *Journal of Religion and Health, 26*(2), 106-114.

Martin, J. E., & Carlson, C. R. (1988). Spiritual dimensions of health psychology. In W. R. Miller & J. E. Martin (Eds.), *Behavior therapy and religion* (pp. 57-110). Nebury Park: Sage.

Maton, K. I., & Pargament, K. I. (1987). Roles of religion in prevention and promotion: The challenge for community psychology. In L. Jason, R. Felner, R. Hess, & J. Mortisugu (Eds.), *Communities: Contributions from allied disciplines* (pp. 161-205). New York: The Haworth Press, Inc.

Maton, K. (1989). The stress-buffering role of spiritual support: Cross-sectional and prospective investigations. *Journal for the Scientific Study of Religion, 28,* 310-323.

McCrae, R. (1984). Situational determinants of coping responses: Loss, threat, and challenge. *Journal of Personality and Social Psychology, 37,* 919-928.

McIntosh, D. W., & Wortman, C. B. (1989). *Parental religious change in response to their child's death.* Paper presented at the Society for the Scientific Study of Religion, Salt Lake City, Utah.

McSherry, E. (1983). The scientific basis of whole person medicine. *Journal of the American Scientific Affiliation, 35*(4), 217-224.

Mechanic, D. (1974). Social structure and personal adaptation: Some neglected dimensions. In G. V. Coehlho, D. A. Hamburg, & J. E. Adams (Eds.), *Coping and adaptation* (pp. 32-44). New York: Basic Books.

Meichenbaum, D., & Jaremko, M. E. (1983). *Stress reduction and prevention.* New York: Plenum.

O'Brien, M. (1982). Religious faith and adjustment to long-term hemodialysis. *Journal of Religion and Health, 21,* 68-80.

Pargament, K. I. (1990). God help me: Towards a theoretical framework for the psychology of religion. *Research in the Social Scientific Study of Religion, 2,* 195-224.

Pargament, K. I., Ensing, D. S., Falgout, K., Olson, H., Reilly, B., Vander-Meulen, K., & Warren, R. (1989). *Religious coping efforts as predictors of the outcomes to significant negative life events.* Paper presented at Society of the Scientific Study of Religion, Salt Lake City, Utah.

Pargament, K., Ensing, D. S., Falgout, K., & Warren, R. K. (1988). Consultation with churches and synagogue. In P. A. Keller & S. R. Heyman (Eds.), *Innovations in clinical practice: A source book* (Vol. 7, pp. 393-406). Sarasota: Professional Resource Exchange.

Pargament, K., Grevengoed, N., Hathaway, W., Kennell, J., Newman, J., & Jones, W. (1988). Religion and problem-solving: Three styles of coping. *Journal for the Scientific Study of Religion, 27,* 90-104.

Pargament, K., & Hahn, J. (1986). God and the just world: Causal and coping attributions to God in health situations. *Journal for the Scientific Study of Religion, 25,* 193-207.

Park, C., Cohen, L. H., & Herb, L. (In press). Intrinsic religiousness and religious coping as life stress moderators for Catholics versus Protestants. *Journal of Personality and Social Psychology.*

Park, C., & Cohen, L. H. (In Press). Religious beliefs and practices and the coping process. In B. Carpenter (Ed.), *Personal coping: Theory, research, and application.* New York: Praeger.

Peteet, J. R. (1985). Religious issues presented by cancer patients seen in psychiatric consultation. *Journal of Psychosocial Oncology, 3,* 53-66.

Peterson, M. L. (1982). *Evil and the Christian god.* Grand Rapids: Baker.

Princeton Religious Research Center. (1986). *Faith development and your ministry.* Princeton, NJ: Author.

Rabkin, J., & Struening, E. (1976). Life events, stress and illness. *Science, 194,* 1013-1020.

Reilly, B., & Falgout, K. (1988). *The ecology of religious coping.* Paper presented at the annual meeting of the American Psychological Association, Atlanta, GA.

Rettino, E., & Rettino, D. (1985). *Kid's praise 5: Psalty's camping adventure* (Album). Costa Mesa, CA: Maranatha! Music.

Rosen, C. C. (1982). Ethnic differences among rural impoverished elderly in use of religion as a coping mechanism. *Journal of Rural Community Psychology, 3,* 27-34.

Rosenstiel, A. K., & Keefe, F. J. (1983). The use of coping strategies in chronic low back pain patients: Relationship to patient characteristics and current adjustment. *Pain, 17,* 33-44.

Rothbaum, F., Weisz, J. R., & Snyder, S. S. (1982). Changing the world and changing the self: A two-process model of perceived control. *Journal of Personality and Social Psychology, 42,* 5-37.

Schroeder, W. W., & Obenhaus, V. (1964). *Religion in American culture.* New York: The Free Press.

Spilka, B., Hood, R., & Gorsuch, R. (1985). *The psychology of religion: An empirical approach.* Englewood Cliffs, NJ: Prentice-Hall.

Spilka, B., Shaver, P., & Kirkpatrick, L. (1985). A general attribution theory for the psychology of religion. *Journal for the Scientific Study of Religion, 24,* 1-20.

Swihart, J. J., & Richardson, G. C. (1987). *Counseling in times of crisis.* Waco, Texas: Word.

Tyler, F. B. (1978). Individual psychosocial competence: A personality configuration. *Educational and psychological measurement, 38,* 309-323.

Tyler, F. B., Gatz, M., & Keenan, K. (1979). A constructivist analysis of the Rotter I-E scale. *Journal of Personality, 47,* 11-35.

Van Cleave, S., Byrd, W., & Revell, K. (1987). *Counseling for substance abuse and addiction.* Waco, Texas: Word.

Ventura, J. N., & Boss, P. G. (1983). The family coping inventory applied to parents with new babies. *Journal of Marriage and the Family, 45,* 867-875.

Ward, E. M. (1981). *Feelings grow too!* Brea, CA: Educational Ministries.

Ward, E. M. (1983). *Helping children understand death*. Brea, CA: Educational Ministries.

Ward, E. M. (1984). *Helping children cope with divorce*. Brea, CA: Educational Ministries.

Williams, D. R., Larson, D. R., Buckler, R. E., Heckman, R. C., & Pyle, C. M. (1989). *Religion and psychological distress in a community sample*. Paper presented at the Annual meeting of the American Psychological Association, New Orleans.

Yates, J., Chalmer, B., St. James, P., Follansbee, M., & McKegney, F. (1981). Religion in patients with advanced cancer. *Medical and Pediatric Oncology*, *9*, 121-128.

Zuckerman, D., Kasl, S., & Ostfeld, A. (1984). Psychological predictors of mortality among the elderly poor: The role of religion, well-being, and social contacts. *American Journal of Epidemiology*, *119*, 410-423.

Religious Aspects
in the Resolution of Parental Grief:
Solace and Social Support

Dennis Klass

Webster University

SUMMARY. The chapter examines religious aspects of the resolution of parents' grief after the death of a child. The experience of solace or consolation is identified as the central religious experience in resolution. Solace is seen rooted in the internalization of the inner representation of the dead child. Examples of several kinds of solace are given. Social support is identified as the most important determinant of the quality of the resolution of grief. The interactions within a local chapter of the Compassionate Friends, a self-help group of bereaved parents, are shown to facilitate and support the experience of solace. The relationship of solace to larger issues of faith and doubt and the implications for research and action in prevention are explored.

The dreams of lifetimes die when children die. The hurt is often nearly unbearable. But if we allow ourselves the freedom of grief and sorrow we also open the paths of new happiness and new hopes and new dreams.

And the child who was a part of us will live in our memories and our hearts.

—from a Compassionate Friends newsletter

The death of a child in the late twentieth century is a catastrophic loss for which we have little readily available comfort or explanation. Yet we find that parents do achieve resolution to their grief that offers them new

---

Reprints may be obtained from Dennis Klass, Webster University, 470 East Lockwood, St. Louis, MO 63119.

155

and health-giving ways of being in the world. The processes and interactions by which bereaved parents achieve resolution are complex because
the bonds we have with our children are complex. Those bonds reach back
into our experience of being parented and reach forward to the potential
for fulfillment which our children represent (Benedek, 1959, 1970,
1975). The obligations to which parents commit themselves are grounded
in the defining ideals of the society. Parenting and the attendant social
roles provide the primary means of self definition in a time when the
public spheres of job and citizenry are routinized in the mass culture. It is
hard to know if or how parenting and parental grief in the modern developed world are different from parenting and parental grief in other times
and places. But clearly the death of a child in contemporary America
presents parents with spiritual and psychological issues for which the society has not prepared them. Death defines the limits of human existence.
Scholars of comparative religion have often defined religion as the means
by which humans transcend those limits (Chidester, 1990). In most religious discussion, the death of the self is the key death. But parental grief
is unique, for it is the death of the parent's self that was invested in the
child. As bereaved parents often remind themselves, when our parents die
we lose our past, when our children die, we lose our future. Most scholar-
ship in religion focuses on analysis of the historically given symbols in
religions. But "transcend" is a verb. It is what people do. This is a study
of bereaved parents transcending the human limitations they find in the
death of their child.

METHOD

This paper emerges from an ethnographic study (Becker, 1970; Geertz,
1973; Glaser & Strauss, 1967; Powdermaker, 1966; Wax, 1971; Whyte,
1973) with a local chapter of The Compassionate Friends (TCF), a self-
help group of parents whose children have died. Observation at TCF
meetings, interviews with bereaved parents, and TCF chapter newsletters
over a ten year period are the data base of this study. Ethnography is an
appropriate method for both psychology of religion and self-help research. Brown notes in his review of methodology that the psychology of
religion, "should probably consider using procedures and methods of assessment that are more directly observational than the verbally-based
methods of self-report that have become standard in the psychology of
religion" (1987, p. 35). Levy says that given the difficulty in self-help
research, ethnography provides the most appropriate method of research
(1984, p. 161). I wanted to understand the range and depth of parental

grief and to understand the psychic changes and social interactions which are the resolution of that grief. Ethnography captures the meaning of bereavement from the perspective of those who have experienced it. Using ethnography we can get inside what Ninian Smart terms the experiential and social dimensions of religion. The method also allows us to trace interactions within Smart's mythic, doctrinal, ritual, ethical, and material dimensions (Smart 1983, 1989).

SOCIAL EQUILIBRIUM/INNER EQUILIBRIUM

The resolution of parental grief is the achievement of a new social equilibrium and a new intrapsychic equilibrium (Klass, 1988). The bereaved find new orientation in the social environment around which to build a new set of social interactions which define the social self (Bowlby, 1980; Parkes, 1972; Parkes & Weiss, 1983; Raphael, 1983; Worden, 1982). The second equilibrium, which is the focus of this study, is a new psychological equilibrium as the inner representation of the dead child finds a place within the ongoing life of the bereaved parent. As George Vaillant says, "Grief work is remembering, not forgetting; it is a process of internalizing, not extruding. Attachment, if properly treated, provides us strength forever" (1985, p. 63). The inner representation of the child provides *solace* within a world made forever poorer by the death of the child.

SOLACE

The defining characteristic of solace is the sense of soothing. The word means to comfort, to alleviate sorrow or distress. It is that which brings pleasure, enjoyment, or delight in the face of hopelessness and despair. Paul Horton (1981) finds that the majority of people have a history of solace that they nurture. He finds that the earliest solace is what D. W. Winnicott (1953, 1971) calls the transitional object. That is, an object in a psychic space that mediates between the experience of the inner world and the external world. A familiar child's transitional object is Linus's security blanket in the Peanuts comic strip. The security such an object provides helps children explore new situations and adjust to unfamiliar environments (Passman, 1976; Passman & Weisberg, 1975). Winnicott finds an explanation of religious experience in the origin and development of the transitional object:

> The task of reality-acceptance is never completed; . . . no human being is free from the strain of relating inner and outer reality, and

. . . relief from this strain is provided by an intermediate area of experience which is not challenged (arts, religion, etc.). This intermediate area is in direct continuity with the play area of the small child who is "lost" in play. (1971, p. 13)

Solace has three characteristics:

1. It is experienced as blended inner and outer reality; that is, it feels as if it is both inside the self and outside the self,
2. It is derived from, but not reducible to, the earliest experience of the mother, and
3. The comfort is not challengeable, for the experience of solace is self-validating (Horton, 1981, p. 26).

Solace is quite different than what Helfaer calls the core religious experience: the appropriation of cultural symbols and synthesis of the ego which we call faith. Faith functions as ego identity and cultural role identity by which the individual locates him/herself as an individual self in the world (Helfaer, 1972, pp. 310-313). While we will show that solace interacts with cultural symbols, we will see that individuals do not usually change cultural symbol systems after the death of their child.

The majority of people find their way in the world by adopting a map of invisible reality given to them within religious institutions and cultural affiliations. But the death of the child often takes these parents into religious territory that is less well mapped. The maps they find in their resolution are often beyond the scope of the conventional religion, beyond the scope of, as Erwin Goodenough calls it, the "blueprint" (1986) provided by the institutional and theological cultural symbols which individuals bring to the death of their child. When we enter the lives of bereaved parents we often find ourselves at that level of analysis that Thomas Luckmann (1967) calls the invisible religion. As David Chidester says, "There is a sense in which the shared symbolization of death within a community reveals an essentially religious response to human limits that may not register explicitly in the organized institutions of religion" (1988, p. 14).

SOLACE IN BEREAVED PARENTS

The solace bereaved parents find in the *internalized inner representation* of their dead child can take many forms. A rough typology of those forms can be drawn from Volkan's study of internalization. For most parents, we find what Volkan calls *introjection*, that is the inner representation of the child is held as a frozen entity in the psyche in a way that the sense of the presence of the child can be evoked. The inner representation feels largely outside the self representation and thus has an objective character even as it feels very much inside the self. Some parents move to another kind of internalization, *identification*. The inner representation of the child is merged with the self representation in a way that the two become indistinguishable. While this is not the forum for a full discussion of the vicissitudes of the inner representations of dead children, we can present enough examples to show the range of possibilities.

Introjection

Some examples of introjection are *linking objects, religious devotion,* and *memory*.

Linking objects. Linking objects are objects connected with the child's life that link the bereaved to the dead; in so doing, they evoke the presence of the dead. We find that many parents use linking objects that are physical artifacts for extended periods after the death of their child. We can see how linking objects function in a simple way in a letter written to a dead child at the end of the day the family brought out Christmas decorations.

> The nice thing about today was that in getting everything unpacked, I got a part of you back for a while. It was comforting to get all those things out that family and friends had given you. All those ornaments to put on the tree with your name on them. There's also that blonde little boy on the rocking horse figurine that will always be with me. And last, but not least, your stocking. . . . As I sit here writing this and looking at the tree and stockings, it hurts to know you are gone. I miss you more than I could ever say, but you'll be with us in spirit this Christmas, just as you are every other day of the year.

We find a development in the use of linking objects through the early months and years of grief from close and immediate physical contact with the object, then having the object in close proximity, and finally having the object out of view, but taking solace knowing the object is safely stored. We can see that movement in a newsletter report on a stuffed orange dog:

> When he died . . . that orange dog became a special symbol to me. When I looked at it I remembered how D.'s face brightened so when he saw it. . . . It even smelled like D to me. . . .
> That dog was like a crutch for me. I felt that as long as it was near

me as I went to sleep each night, so I could reach out and touch it or smell it, that D.'s death was not so final. . . . One day as I cleaned, I put the dog in another room and found I didn't miss it. By then the memories of D. were ingrained into my mind so well I didn't need to look at a symbol of his life to remember him by. . . .

Now the orange dog sits on my dresser in a rather inconspicuous spot. It will never be just another stuffed toy to me, but it has served its purpose and now sits as a friendly reminder of its past owner.

If the linking object is rich enough in its symbolism, it can serve as an enduring, communally-shared sign to the parent. For this to happen, the object must have a cultural meaning by which the parent can connect her or his personal solace to that provided within the social reality. The grave site is a linking object for many families and in our study, where the grave is far away, several families use trees planted in the child's memory as linking objects. One couple we interviewed shared a linking object that has cultural symbolism. When we asked the mother, "Do you ever sense that C. is still around?" she answered:

Every time I see a mourning dove. Mourning doves are magnificent. The day after C. died, Cliff and I were sitting in the den looking out the window and there was a mourning dove on the porch. I didn't know what it was at the time, so I got out my bird book and looked it up. It is m-o-u-r-n-i-n-g dove, not m-o-r-n-i-n-g. It was so ironic because here I'd just lost a daughter and I'm getting out my bird book to look for mourning doves. It was phenomenal that we would see a mourning dove when we were mourning. It's got to mean something, right? So the two of us took this as, "This is C. C. is with the dove. . . ." It's really fascinating because I'll find myself thinking about her and I'll look around and see the mourning dove. That has become a symbol of C.

Religious devotion. After the death of the child, some of the thematic memories of the child and the emotional states connected with the memories may be integrated into the parent's previous religious devotion. Religious devotion can be simple habitual repetition or a socially expected activity done by rote. But devotion also can engage the devotee's life in a way which overcomes the distinction between inner and outer experience. To the extent religious devotion occurs within the psychic space that is both inner and outer reality, it has the character of a transitional object (Bollas, 1978; Eigen, 1981; Gay, 1983). As religious devotion has that character, it has a sense of security similar to that first experienced with the mother, and has truths that are self-validating to the believer.

For those parents with a well-developed sense of the sacred within a stable religious tradition, the dead child can be integrated into the ritual experience of the sacred. One woman in our study lost two children in the same auto accident. The ritual of the Catholic Mass, which makes the presence of the Son of God real, makes the presence of her children real. Yet the solace she has within the religious tradition is not shared by her other children, and she feels uncomfortable speaking of her experience in front of them. She wrote a letter to her dead daughters:

> When I think of you in Heaven I feel peaceful. I think of all the angels and saints and even relatives you are with. . . . Every time I attend the sacrifice of the Mass, at the part where our Blessed Lord comes into our hearts, I feel so close to your angelic presence. What a divine experience! The only problem is that it doesn't last long enough. If only the others could share these feelings. I am afraid to say much about these feelings to your brothers and sisters-in-law. I don't want to widen their hurt. Please try to send some peace from God to them and all of us who miss you so much.

For parents with less well-developed histories of ritual devotion in a well-defined tradition, there are doctrines and myths within the wider culture which, although somewhat more vague, channel the religious sense. Almost all the parents in our study felt that the child is in heaven. A mother reflected in a newsletter, "A. will always be my six-year-old "baby boy. . . ." Silly as it may sound, I have this mental picture of A., free now to run and play and be happy in heaven."

The sense that the child is in heaven is widely shared even by those for whom heaven is not part of their theology or for whom other aspects of their former faith have been unhelpful. Knapp (1986) found that his interviewees could not sustain a belief that there is no afterlife. Several people in the study felt the child to be with another significant person who had died. One woman whose father died four years before her child reported:

> It was hard after my father died because I always had this sense that I didn't know where he was. . . . After L. died I was really bothered that I didn't know where she was and that somehow that meant that I didn't know she was safe. That lasted two years. One day I started crying and I realized I wasn't just crying for L. I was missing my father. And suddenly I just thought, "Daddy is taking care of L. She is OK because she is with him and that's where he is.

It is like they are together.'' That sounds so simple-minded. I don't believe in heaven or afterlife. I think we just live on in memory. But it just feels like I don't have that worry about either of them any more. I know they are together.

Though it is very difficult to know how often it occurs, and it is difficult to separate the parent's memory from the actual happenings, in a significant number of cases where the child has had a long illness, the child often has nonordinary experiences that help the parent with the belief that the child is in heaven. One mother reported that her eight-year-old, in a partial coma his last morning, talked to an unseen figure, and said, "No, I don't want to go with you. I want to stay with my mama." The social worker on the case said she called the house to see how things were going that day and heard the child saying it in the background. On the social worker's advice, the mother lay with the child, and hugged him and said that it was all right to go, that she and his father would miss him very much and that they would remember and love him always. About half an hour later the child awoke from the coma, looked at his mother and said, "I love you, mama." Then he fell asleep in her arms. He did not awake. Though the mother is not actively religious, that experience is for her a self-validating proof that her child is in heaven and that she will see him again.

The natural order. Naturalistic mystical experience (Hood, 1977) is common. Parents feel the presence of the child within that experience. One mother reported that on her daily walks she could quietly feel a sense of communion with her son who had been dead for ten years.

> I'm a walker. I remember I used to take long walks with T. We would go at any time of the year. In the winter he would roll in the snow and make angels. In the fall he would gather leaves. In spring and summer he would watch birds and pick wildflowers. Sometimes I remember those times when I walk, but sometimes it is just the beauty. Like the other day, I was out early and as the sun rose, I was at peace and T. was a part of that.

Memories. Bereaved parents can find the space that is between the self and the other in memory that is cherished and nurtured in the bereaved parent's aloneness. Unconflicted and peaceful memory is often at the end-point of a difficult process of separating self representation from the inner representation of the child. Memories are at first very painful. A common phenomenon among bereaved parents is guilt when they discover they no longer feel sad all the time. As one person said, "All I have left of my child is my sadness. If I give that up, then I really have to let go of my child." One mother reflected on the discovery that letting go of the pain did not also mean letting go of the child.

> You know, I remember being afraid that someday I would wake up and my feeling of being bonded to K. wouldn't be there. I thought that when the pain left, she would be gone too. But now I find that I hope the memories will come. . . . Sometimes I just look at her pictures and remember when we took them. I never know when I will look at the pictures, but I feel better afterwards.

For some parents, the ability to remember the child in dreams in a pleasurable way is a dramatic breakthrough in the grieving process. One parent reported in a newsletter article on dreams:

> Just when it seemed as though I could no longer hold on to my sanity, I had a sequence of dreams that gave me back some of my strength. I had a night of beautiful dreams of my son. They were the kind of dreams that seemed so real that each time I woke, it was with tears of happiness and not of sadness. The dream that was the most vivid, and that I derived the most comfort from, was the first one. He was laughing and playing and when he saw me, he walked up to me and we both were so happy to see each other that we burst out laughing. I knew that I couldn't touch him, and I also knew he couldn't come back to me, but to be able to see so plainly in his face and eyes, and to see the love and happiness that was there just for me was all I needed. The day following the dreams was a very happy day for me. I have since had my ups and downs, but when things are bad, I try to recall the happiness I saw on his face.

The inner representation becomes a memory held in that space in the psyche that is neither completely self nor completely other, which has been developed throughout a lifetime, and its comfort is self-validating.

Identification

Linking objects, religious devotion and ideation, and memory are all introjections for all keep the child as a frozen entity in the psyche. The majority of the solace we find in bereaved parents comes from those introjections. We also find the other kind of internalization, identification (Miller, Pollock, & Bernstein, 1968). In identification, the inner representation of the child is integrated into the self in such a way that it is difficult to distinguish the two. Because the inner representation of the child is maintained less as a separate entity, the resolution has a somewhat different character. Identification has a sense of reinvigorated life, of renewed feelings of competence. Introjection has an "otherness" which reminds us of Otto's *Idea of the Holy* (1958) or Eliade's *The Sacred and The Profane* (1957). Identification does not have a self-other sense, for it is the life lived which has meaning. It is the virtues and gifts of the child that live on, not the concrete sense of the child's presence. Many of the parents in our study regard their new life as religious, for the identification provides them with values and interaction modes in a life which seem rich. If religion is as Nels Ferre says, "our normally necessary whole-reaction to what is considered to be most important and most real" (1946, p. 6), it is the new vigor and meaning brought by the values associated with the child which govern the parents' whole-reaction to life.

Often identification is found in a decision to live fully in spite of the death. One parent wrote about positive ways of remembering the child by supporting public memorials to him, but more importantly by finding fullness and meaning in her own life.

> I came to the decision that I was going to try to use my gift of life to the utmost as J. had used his. . . . There is joy in my life now . . . We have sought positive ways to remember J. Members of our family continue to give books to a memorial shelf of books [at the library] . . . started by friends of J. Members of our family periodically give blood to the Red Cross, hoping to help others who may need that gift in their struggle for life. . . . Life will never be the same. I will always be disappointed that J. did not have a longer life, but I will always be proud of him and love him. I continue to search for ways to bring love, hope and meaning in my life as I try to make use of my one gift of life.

The enriched ego is for living in this world, not for dwelling in the past, and the child is carried symbolically into this new life of meaningfulness that the bereaved parent now lives. The parents search for the right metaphor by which to describe the new relationship the parent now feels with the child, for the culture has few symbols that seem adequate. Poet Marcia Alig found the metaphor of prologue.

> Never to know
> the progress of your tale
> I am suspended in doubt.
> Must you remain forever a prologue
> Or could I write the script,

And through my life
state your meaning?

Yes, I will present your messages.
Love, devotion, joy and knowledge:
These truths will speak
through my pages,
Making your prologue —
forever mine.

RELIGION IN THE SELF-HELP PROCESS

We can ask how, in the late twentieth century developed world, the experience of solace impacts on Smart's ritual, doctrinal, mythic, ethical, social, and material dimensions of religious life. It would be an interesting excursion into modern religion if we explored the mythic, ritual, doctrinal, ethical and material coordinates of the solace bereaved parents find in the internalized inner representation of their dead child.

But if our interest is in solace as a necessary component of mental health, we will do better to limit our inquiry, for the social dimension is central in the resolution of grief. The only consistent finding in studies of the duration and intensity of grief is that the most important factor in the resolution of grief is social support. Where social support is good, other things being equal, symptoms are lower and resolution is faster. Most of the research has been done with widows (Arling, 1976; Bowling & Cartwright, 1982; Lopata, 1973; Maddison & Walker, 1967; Parkes & Weiss, 1983; Silverman, 1986; Vachon, Sheldon, Lancee, Lyall, Rogers, & Freeman, 1982). Studies on bereaved parents have shown similar results (Bourne, 1968; Carr & Knupp, 1985; Kowalski, 1984; Schreimer, Gresham, & Green, 1979). Let us, therefore, focus on the social dimension to find the way it interacts with the experience of solace. We will look at The Compassionate Friends (TCF).

TCF has proven to be an effective aid in the resolution of parental grief. There have been no studies large or sophisticated enough to show how those who participate in TCF are different or the same as those who do not participate, or to show how the resolution of grief of participants is different or the same as non-participants. In a self-help group, however, growth and durability is a good measure of effectiveness. A self-help organization which is not effective for a significant number of those participating would not survive. TCF began in England. The first United States chapter was gathered in 1972. In 1990 there were over 600 chapters in the United

States. TCF maintains a national office which publishes newsletters and a wide variety of pamphlets and books. There are also active regional organizations which sponsor regional conference with two to three hundred bereaved parents attending. Local chapters publish newsletters, hold monthly meetings, maintain phone networks, and provide education for medical and social service professionals. Virtually all the national, regional, and local organization is funded by bereaved parents themselves.

There are a great many aspects of self-help intervention with bereaved parents which are not included in this discussion. I have more fully described the TCF process elsewhere (Klass, 1988). In order to focus on the religious aspects of TCF, this discussion excludes the practical guidance members give each other in the new world of parental bereavement. I have also excluded discussion of the value core of all self-help, that the best way to help one's self is to help others. But the focus is on solace, and solace provides our lens on Smart's social dimension.

The statement which is read at the opening of each meeting is a rather modest claim, and certainly not a "religious" claim:

> The Compassionate Friends offers friendship and understanding to bereaved parents. The purposes are to promote and aid parents in the positive resolution of the grief experience upon the death of their child and to foster the physical and emotional health of bereaved parents and siblings.

TCF is not "religious" in the conventional sense. In a statement of principles which govern the group, TCF specifically removes itself from the doctrinal dimension: "We espouse no specific religious or philosophical ideology," and, "We never suggest that there is a correct way to grieve or that there is a preferred solution to the emotional and spiritual dilemmas raised by the death of our children." Yet if solace is a religious aspect of the resolution of parental grief, TCF is a very religious organization, for it facilitates the transformation of the inner representation of the child and provides a community in which that transformation can be validated. TCF nourishes the experience of solace and, at the same time, the group derives the energy upon which it runs from the shared inner representations of the dead children of the members.

Sharing the Bond

We can see many of the dynamics of TCF in a newsletter article written by the coordinator of the local chapter's annual picnic. She says there will be good food and games, but these are the sidekicks of our picnic. The center, the best, the reason we come back year after year is simply to be together. Whether meeting new people, talking to old friends, playing or just being there, it is the gathering that makes this event so special for so many of us.

If our gathering is the center, our children lost are the heart and soul of our picnic. It is for and because of them that we have come, and it is for them that we have our cherished balloon released, a time set aside in our day to remember and include our special children.

Helium filled balloons are passed out, along with markers, giving us all one more chance to tell our children the things we most long to say—mostly "I Love You." And then, oblivious to the world around us, we stand as one, but each involved in his own thoughts, prayer and emotions as we released hundreds of balloons to the sky and they disappear; to a destiny we are certain they will reach.

The children are the heart and soul of the group, for it is the shared inner representations of the dead children which bond the members to each other. The children are in the midst of the group, not simply within each of the individual parents. Yet the inner representations of the children are also wherever balloon messages are carried. The strain of relating inner and outer reality is relieved. The ritual provides a means by which the parent can both reach out to the dead child and feel the presence of the child within. They "stand as one, but each involved in his own thoughts, prayer and emotion." Because the bond with the child is shared within the group, the parents can be in touch privately with the individual inner representation of their child. Because the group shares in the strong bond with the child, there is tremendous strength within the group. Because there is such strength within the group, the bond with the child feels surer. One balloon sent into the sky would seem a lonely and fragile message. Hundreds of balloons, each addressed to an individual child, are sure to get through.

The shared inner representation of the dead children are identification in two senses of that word. In the sense we used it in the early part of this paper, the inner representation of the dead child and the self representation are merged in such a way that the two are indistinguishable. Identification within the group means that the bereaved parents feel that they are like each other, that because they have lost a child, they have more in common than they have in common with non-bereaved parents. The self they see mirrored in the other members is a self that includes the inner representation of the child.

Pain is shared and in that sharing, the relationship with the child is shared within the supportive relationship. One parent described the self-help process in a Compassionate Friends meeting as a circle of weavers in which the bonds that were with the child now become attached and inter-woven with other bereaved parents in the group. Rather than having the child as a frozen entity in the psyche, the inner representation of the child becomes a part of the ongoing social relationship within the group. The sense of oneness with other bereaved parents and the sense of oneness with the inner representation of the dead child can be seen in the "TCF Credo."

> We reach out to each other with love, with understanding and with hope. Our children have died at all ages and from many different causes, but our love for our children unites us. . . . Whatever pain we bring to this gathering of The Compassionate Friends, it is pain we will share just as we share with each other our love for our children.

This process of finding a place for the solace-giving inner representation of the child is not as unique as it might seem. There are parallels between the social support in TCF and the social support at the beginning of the parent-child bond. The quality and nonambivalance of this early bond depends a great deal upon the quality of the social support the new parent has. Ainsfeld and Lipper (1983) show that the quality of the bond can be raised by compensating for the lack of social support. Although researchers think of bonding enhancement as skin to skin contact and other measures, such procedures also involve more active and positive relationships with hospital personnel who give interest, encouragement, and reassurance. Interpersonal sharing provides the social support lacking in the mother's natural support system, and thereby strengthens her relationship to the child (Rutter, 1981).

The set of relationships by which a baby is introduced into a community such as an office or gathering of neighbors is similar to the sharing of the bond with the inner representation of the child in TCF. Each adult in turn holds the new baby and attempts to elicit an interaction with the baby, thus in a small way bonding to the child. Soon the baby tires from the effort to respond to so many faces and the child is passed back to the parent who is affirmed as the child's primary bond. Parents who do not have this social support have trouble establishing a clear bond with the child (Ainsfeld & Lipper, 1983). So too, bereaved parents who do not have social support have trouble establishing the inner representation of the dead child in a solace giving way.

Ritualizing the Memory

The solace of memory is ritualized in TCF, and in a somewhat different way, allows the bond with the child to become part of the bonds with the community. For their yearly holiday candlelight memorial service, many Compassionate Friends chapters have adopted a liturgy from *Gates of Prayer* (1975), a Reform Jewish prayer book.

> In the rising of the sun and in its going down,
> > WE REMEMBER THEM;
> In the blowing of the wind and in the chill of winter,
> > WE REMEMBER THEM;
> In the opening of buds and in the warmth of summer,
> > WE REMEMBER THEM;
> In the rustling of leaves and the beauty of autumn,
> > WE REMEMBER THEM;
> In the beginning of the year and when it ends,
> > WE REMEMBER THEM;
> When we are weary and in need of strength,
> > WE REMEMBER THEM;
> When we are lost and sick at heart,
> > WE REMEMBER THEM;
> When we have joys we yearn to share,
> > WE REMEMBER THEM;
> So long as we live, they too shall live, for they are now a
> part of us as
> > WE REMEMBER THEM.

The candlelight memorial service is the largest gathering of the local TCF chapter. This year there were 700 people. It has grown each year, and the steering committee is planning for 900 next year. There are talks by bereaved parents who are well along in their journey through grief. The TCF Credo is recited. The music is popular songs which, in this context, seem appropriately about the parents and their dead children. Then as the children's names are read, the parents, often accompanied by siblings, grandparents, and other extended family rise and light a candle. The candles used to be ordinary candles with a paper ring for catching wax, but parents' unsteady hands caused too much wax on the carpet, so now the candle is in a small glass with the TCF logo printed on it. The parents take the candle home and can use it in during the holidays as they wish.

Integrating the Experience

Experience of the presence of the dead child or experiences by which solace is discovered are not easily integrated into the social reality of the modern developed world. The majority of members have had at some time a feeling of presence of the dead child and for many the feeling is an accepted part of their daily reality. Most of the members have linking objects which evoke the presence of their child. But such experiences are difficult to integrate into the everyday reality provided by modernity.

There has been a development within the group over the ten years of our study. Early in the study, one father reported an experience of the child speaking to unseen figures as he was dying. In a small meeting, two parents shared similar experiences, but the other five present said they wished they could have had such an experience. For those who did not have such an experience, the experience of parents who did was not adequate to apply to them or to their child. They could only envy the solace the dying children's nonordinary experience brought.

At first the group did not know what to make of such experiences, and the attempts to share them were often very tentative. One of my first speaking assignments in the group was to be on "ideas of the afterlife." I carefully prepared a talk in which I showed the cultural relativity of such ideas and presented alternatives such as the physical immortality of atoms. The group did not like my talk. One mother said to me, "My child is in heaven and you cannot take that away from me." Several years later I gave a talk in her church in which I incorporated some early ideas about solace. Afterwards she shook my hand and said, "You have grown a lot."

As the study progressed, such experiences were integrated into the shared beliefs of the group. At the same time, there was a steady stream of discussion in the popular culture about near death experiences (see Zaleski, 1987) and about the possibility of the paranormal. Now, ten years later, the experiences are routinely reported and integrated into the group's fund of knowledge about grief. That knowledge is not maintained in a theoretical or systematic way, rather it is held as a collection of the experiences of the members and of other people's reactions as the experience was recounted. At a recent meeting, a newer member reported a strange sensation as she lay napping and wondered if she were going crazy. One man turned to another and said, "Well, if she thinks that is strange, why don't you tell her your story, Charlie?" Charlie's story was then recounted, including the disbelieving responses of his relatives. Other stories followed for several minutes. Then after a short silence, the teaching was summed up by a member of long standing who said, "They come to us when we need them." The group maintains the TCF principle of not holding to any doctrinal position, yet at the same time the group validates the experience by saying that the experiences are real, but are different for different people and that what is learned in the experience is for the parent, not for everyone. Nearly every year, one meeting is devoted to these experiences (though I have never again been asked to lead the discussion).

FAITH, DOUBT, COMFORT, AND EMPTINESS

Solace is one element of religious experience. I have attempted to isolate it so we can examine it as we might attempt to isolate a chemical element so we can examine its properties. But religion is a compound, and in the life of any individual solace mixes with other elements.

The parents in our study had religious backgrounds which they brought to the death of their child. That is, all had been exposed to general cultural symbols which are rooted in historic religious traditions. Many parents had active faiths which were founded in strong affiliation with a religious denomination. Many bereaved parents in our study questioned the cultural symbols which order their lives. This doubt, however, does not seem to move parents toward different cultural symbols. In our study, the resolution of doubt is typically either a development within the pre-existing cultural symbols rather than a change in cultural symbols or it is a splitting off of faith into one part of the psyche.

We can see the development with a cultural symbol in one mother who had been taught in Catholic school that if she were good, God would not let anything bad happen.

> A lot of people come up and tell me it was God's will. I just stop them and say, "Look, maybe you think that, but I don't believe that any more. So just don't say that to me." I mean terrible things happen all the time. Before I protected myself because I knew I was safe. I feel the pain now, like what I see in the news. I talked to the priest that married us. He said my faith was maturing. I mean, Jesus suffered. That was God.

Many parents in the study are persuaded by the limitation of God's omnipotence in Kushner's (1981) popular book on the nature of evil. His explanation seems to provide them with a way to maintain the cultural symbols they previously used. But while such theology prevents further erosion of the symbols, it does not usually provide the positive sense of solace.

When parents cannot grow in or maintain the cultural symbols of their faith, the absence of God is felt in parts of the self which are split from parts of the self which still include God. Often solace provides the connection with the transcendent which is felt in a part of the psyche, but there are other possibilities. One woman who had two babies die said:

> There's lots of people who go around thinking if they are good then bad things can't happen to them. I just tell them, "It has to happen to somebody." I don't pray in church anymore. I go because you are supposed to. How can I tell the children to go to church if I don't? But I don't pray. I just do my grocery list. I think I used to pray and feel close to God. But not anymore. I don't feel anything there.

Thus she does not find the presence of God in her solitude as she once did. But her living children should go to church, for that is a rule and if she is to enforce the rule, she too must follow it. If God be dead for her in her soul, God is not dead in her superego nor in her family system.

For most of the parents in our study, it is the internalized inner representation of their child that connects them to the divine even as they feel cut off in other parts of their psyche. In a meeting a father talked of the months of praying during his daughter's illness.

> Some of the children would get better and some would not. One night as she was going to sleep N. asked me, "Daddy, how does God decide who gets the miracles?" I didn't know what to answer her. I still don't. I guess I still believe in miracles. How else do you account for the kids I saw get better with no explanation. But we didn't get one. So where am I now?

If he and his child were passed over in the distribution of miracles, his child was not passed over for heaven. He feels strongly that his daughter is in heaven with God and that he will rejoin her when he dies.

Thus, when the cultural symbols the parents brought into their bereavement cannot be deepened to include the experience of solace and to include the evil the parents have endured, these parents compartmentalize their religious life. In one part of their lifetime they feel themselves cut off from God. Yet in another part, they feel in touch with a child who is in heaven under the care of a protective God, or they feel soothed by ritualized memories which make the child present to them again and in doing so remove the isolation they feel in their world. In those parts of their life where the cultural symbols still provide a map of the invisible reality, the parents can function in the religious institutions as they did before. The diversity of those institutional and doctrinal affiliations is respected within the bonds between TCF members.

CONCLUSION

It is appropriate that we conclude by looking at some of the implications of our study of solace and social support among bereaved parents for prevention research and action. The research implications are easy to draw. While there are quantitative studies which point to some of the findings of my qualitative study (Cook, 1983; Forrest, Standish, & Baum, 1982; Spinetta, Swarner, & Sheposh, 1981; Videka-Sherman, 1982; Videka-Sherman & Lieberman, 1985), there are no quantitative studies on the nature and function of inner representation of the child in the lives of bereaved parents. A wide range of studies have established that the death of a child is a stressor which puts parents at risk in many physical and psychological areas, but there are no studies which ask how finding solace within the loss affects those risks.

There are no adequate qualitative or quantitative studies on different bereavement outcomes on those who use TCF and those who do not, nor on those who affiliate with TCF in different ways (e.g., only reading newsletter, attending a short time, assuming leadership, etc.). Though it would be a difficult task, research also could be designed to explore the ways bereaved parents get or do not get social support in communities such as church congregations. The qualitative study I have begun could be carried forward to better understand the relationship of the inner representation of the child to cultural symbols and to the transformations of cultural symbols within the resolution of parental bereavement.

There are groups of bereaved parents which are focused differently than TCF. Groups like Mothers Against Drunk Driving seem to have quite different dynamics from those of TCF. I made a preliminary study of one such group, Parents of Murdered Children (Klass, 1988), in which I found that political action helped channel the revenge parents wanted after their child was murdered. But much more research could be done in this area. In practice, facilitating solace is prevention, for unresolved grief puts parents at risk (Osterweis, Solomon, & Green, 1984; Zisook & Lyons, 1990). The issue, therefore, is to find ways by which the healing fostered in TCF can be fostered in other contexts as well. Two areas come to mind. First, clergy could develop solace-supporting liturgy. The invention within TCF of rituals and liturgy for bonding with other bereaved parents and for bonding with the dead child indicates that, for these parents, such rituals were unavailable in their community or religious institutions. It would seem that such liturgy could be developed within religious communities as a way of fostering better social support within the community and as a way of integrating the dead child into the life of the community.

Second, mental health professionals might want to reexamine their models of grief. This study indicates that there is a fund of healing which is not fostered within the models of grief currently in vogue. I have shown elsewhere (Klass, 1987) that the contemporary models of grief, which rely on study of widows for data, label most of the phenomena associated with solace as pathology. In informal professional discussions, sometimes a critique of TCF emerges which claims that TCF encourages parents to hold on to the child and therefore impedes the grief by preventing them from letting go and moving on. Thus, there seems to be a disparity between the way mental health professionals understand the nature of resolution and the way members of TCF are resolving their grief. Any intervention which has as its focus themes of letting go, moving on, withdrawing energy from the dead child, or reinvesting is using the model of grief developed in the study of widows and is not, if my findings are valid, appropriate for bereaved parents. Professional interventions cannot and should not duplicate the interactions within a self-help group. But the themes and interactions within TCF show us what bereaved parents invent when left only with their pain, their needs, and each other. Creative mental health professionals could translate the dynamics developed in self-help into interactions within professional models of care which facilitate solace and which develop social support such as we find within the TCF process.

REFERENCES

Ainsfeld, E., & Lipper, E. (1983). Early contact, social support, and mother-infant bonding. *Pediatrics*, *72*(1), 79-83.

Arling, G. (1976). The elderly widow and her family, neighbors and friends. *Journal of Marriage and the Family*, *38*(4), 757-767.

Becker, H. S. (1970). *Sociological work: Method and substance*. Chicago: Aldine.

Benedek, T. (1959). Parenthood as a developmental phase. *American Psychoanalytic Association Journal*, *7*, 389-417.

Benedek, T. (1970). The family as a psychologic field. In E. J. Anthony & T. Benedek (Eds.), *Parenthood: Its psychology and psychopathology*. Boston: Little, Brown.

Benedek, T. (1975). Discussion of parenthood as a developmental phase. *Journal of the American Psychoanalytic Association*, *23*, 154-165.

Bollas, C. (1978). The transformational object. *International Journal of Psychoanalysis*, *60*, 97-107.

Bourne, S. (1968). The psychological effects of stillbirth on women and their doctors. *Journal of the Royal College of General Practice*, *16*, 103-112.

Bowlby, J. (1969). *Attachment and loss* (Vol. 1): *Attachment*. New York: Basic Books.

Bowlby, J. (1973). *Attachment and loss* (Vol. 2): *Separation: Anxiety and anger*. New York: Basic Books.

Bowlby, J. (1980). *Attachment and loss* (Vol. 3): *Loss: Sadness and depression*. New York: Basic Books.

Bowling, A., & Cartwright, A. (1982). *Life after death: A study of the elderly widowed*. London: Tavistock.

Brown, L. B. (1987). *The psychology of religious belief*. New York: Harcourt Brace Jovanovich.

Carr, D., & Knupp, S. F. (1985). Grief and perinatal loss. *Journal of Obstetric, Gynecologic, and Neonatal Nursing*, *14*(2), 130-139.

Chidester, D. (1988). *Salvation and suicide: An interpretation of Jim Jones, the Peoples Temple, and Jonestown*. Bloomington, IN: Indiana University Press.

Chidester, D. (1990). *Patterns of transcendence: Religion, death, and dying*. Belmont, CA: Wadsworth.

Cook, J. A. (1983). If I should die before I wake: Religious commitment and adjustment to the death of a child. *Journal for the Scientific Study of Religion*, *22*(3), 222-238.

Eigen, M. (1981). The area of faith in Winnicott, Lacan, and Bion. *International Journal of Psychoanalysis*, *62*, 413-433.

Eliade, M. (1957). *The sacred and the profane*. New York: Harcourt, Brace & World.

Ferre, N. F. S. (1946). *Faith and reason*. New York: Harper and Brothers.

Forrest, G. C., Standish, E., & Baum, J. D. (1982). Support after perinatal death: A study of support and counseling after perinatal bereavement. *British Medical Journal*, *285*, 1475-1479.

Gates of prayer: The new union prayer book (1975). New York: Central Conference of American Rabbis.

Gay, V. P. (1983). Winnicott's contribution to religious studies: The resurrection of a cultural hero. *Journal of the American Academy of Religion*, *51*(3), 371-395.

Geertz, C. (1973). *The interpretation of cultures*. New York: Basic Books.

Glaser, B. G., & Strauss, A. L. (1967). *The discovery of grounded theory: Strategies for qualitative research*. Chicago: Aldine.

Goodenough, E. R. (1986). *The psychology of religious experience*. New York: University Press of America.

Helfaer, P. M. (1972). *The psychology of religious doubt*. Boston: Beacon Press.

Hood, R. (1977). Eliciting mystical states of consciousness in semistructured nature experiences. *Journal for the Scientific Study of Religion, 16*(2), 155-163.

Horton, P. C. (1981). *Solace, the missing dimension in psychiatry.* Chicago: University of Chicago Press.

Klass, D. (1987). John Bowlby's model of grief and the problem of identification. *Omega, Journal of Death and Dying, 18*(1), 13-32.

Klass, D. (1988). *Parental grief: Solace and resolution.* New York: Springer.

Knapp, R. (1986). *Beyond endurance: When a child dies.* New York: Schocken.

Kowalski, K. E. M. (1984). *Perinatal death: An ethnomethodological study of factors influencing parental bereavement.* Unpublished doctoral dissertation, University of Colorado at Boulder.

Kushner, H. (1981). *When bad things happen to good people.* New York: Schocken.

Lavoie, F. (1984). Action research: A new model of interaction between the professional and self-help groups. In A. Gartner & F. Riessman (Eds.), *The self-help revolution.* New York: Human Service Press.

Levy, L. H. (1984). Issues in research & evaluation. In A. Gartner & F. Riessman (Eds.), *The self-help revolution.* New York: Human Service Press.

Lopata, H. Z. (1973). *Widowhood in an American city.* Cambridge, MA: Schenkman.

Luckmann, T. (1967). *Invisible religion: The problem of religion in modern society.* London: Macmillan, 1967.

Maddison, D., & Walker, W. L. (1967). Factors affecting the outcome of conjugal bereavement. *British Journal of Psychiatry, 113,* 1057-1067.

Osterweis, M., Solomon, F., & Green, M. (Eds.). (1984). *Bereavement: Reactions, consequences, and care.* Washington, DC: National Academy Press.

Otto, R. (1958). *The idea of the holy.* New York: Oxford University Press.

Parkes, C. M. (1972). *Bereavement: Studies of grief in adult life.* New York: International Universities Press.

Parkes, C. M., & Weiss, R. (1983). *Recovery from bereavement.* New York: Basic Books.

Passman, R. H. (1976). Arousal reducing properties of attachment objects: Testing the functional limits of the security blanket relative to the mother. *Developmental Psychology, 12,* 468-469.

Passman, R. H., & Weisberg, P. (1975). Mothers and blankets as agents for promoting play and exploration by young children in a novel environment: The effects of social and nonsocial attachment objects. *Developmental Psychology, 11,* 170-177.

Powdermaker, H. (1966). *Stranger and friend: The way of an anthropologist.* New York: Norton.

Raphael, B. (1983). *The anatomy of bereavement.* New York: Basic Books.

Rutter, M. (1981). *Maternal deprivation reassessed.* Middlesex, England: Penguin.

Schreimer, R. L., Gresham, E. L., & Green, M. (1979). Physician's responsibility to parents after the death of an infant: Beneficial outcome of a telephone call. *American Journal of Diseases of Children*, *133*(7), 723-726.

Silverman, P. R. (1986). *Widow-to-widow*. New York: Springer.

Smart, N. (1983). *Worldviews: Crosscultural exploration of human beliefs*. New York: Charles Scribner's Sons.

Smart, N. (1989). *The world's religions*. Englewood Cliffs, NJ: Prentice-Hall.

Spinetta, J. J., Swarner, J. A., & Sheposh, J. P. (1981). Effective parent coping following the death of a child from cancer. *Journal of Pediatric Psychology*, *6*(3), 251-263.

Vachon, M. L. S., Sheldon, A. R., Lancee, W. J., Lyall, W. A. L., Rogers, J., & Freeman, S. J. J. (1982). Correlates of enduring distress patterns following bereavement: Social network, life situation and personality. *Psychological Medicine*, *12*, 783-788.

Vaillant, G. E. (1985). Loss as a metaphor for attachment. *American Journal of Psychoanalysis*, *45*(1), 59-67.

Videka-Sherman, L. (1982). Coping with the death of a child: A study over time. *American Journal of Orthopsychiatry*, *52*(4), 688-698.

Videka-Sherman, L., & Lieberman, M. (1985). The effects of self-help and psychotherapy intervention on child loss: The limits of recovery. *American Journal of Orthopsychiatry*, *55*(1), 70-82.

Volkan, V. (1981). *Linking objects and linking phenomena: A study of the forms, symptoms, metapsychology, and therapy of complicated mourning*. New York: International Universities Press.

Wax, R. (1971). *Doing fieldwork: Warnings and advice*. Chicago: University of Chicago Press.

Whyte, W. F. (1973). *Street corner society: The structure of an Italian slum*. Chicago: University of Chicago Press.

Winnicott, D. W. (1953). Transitional objects and transitional phenomena. *International Journal of Psychoanalysis*, *34*, 89-97.

Winnicott, D. W. (1971). *Playing and reality*. New York: Basic Books.

Worden, J. W. (1982). *Grief counseling and grief therapy, a handbook for the mental health practitioner*. New York: Springer.

Zaleski, C. (1987). *Otherworld journeys: Accounts of near-death experiences in medieval and modern times*. New York: Oxford University Press.

Zisook, S., & Lyons, L. (1990). Bereavement and unresolved grief in psychiatric outpatients. *Omega, Journal of Death and Dying*, *20*(4), 307-322.

Toward a Psychosocial Conceptualization of Religion as a Resource in Cancer Care and Prevention

Richard A. Jenkins

Vanderbilt University

SUMMARY. Religion frequently appears as a variable in studies of cancer patients, although frequently at the level of demographic variables, such as church attendance. There has been little systematic attempt to integrate this literature or to provide guidance for research and application. This paper attempts to overcome these limitations by providing a framework for considering the research and practice implications religious phenomena (individual practice, denominational teachings, etc.) have for different levels of cancer care and prevention. Consistent with this framework, examples are offered, such as the use of places of worship as venues for reaching high-risk populations. Organizational concerns, such as role negotiation between health care providers and clergy, are also discussed.

Cancer is one of the most significant public health problems in the United States. Approximately one million people are diagnosed with some type of malignancy each year (Silverberg, Boring, & Squires, 1990). About 50% of these individuals are likely to die within five years of diagnosis, although this death rate represents a great improvement over the kind of prognosis that was possible several decade ago (Holleb, 1986). Much of this improvement in survival can be traced to early detection and

The author wishes to thank Ken Pargament, Rob Hess, and Ken Maton for their editorial feedback on previous drafts of this paper. Reprints may be obtained from Richard A. Jenkins, Henry M. Jackson Foundation, Walter Reed Army Medical Center, Building 1, Ward 11, 6825 16th Street, NW, Washington, DC 20307-5000.

large scale screening programs that have established prevention as an important area of clinical cancer practice.

Despite advancements in early detection, as well as improved treatments and efforts to identify causal factors, cancer remains a threatening and poorly understood category of disease. The ambiguity that surrounds cancer's etiology, response to treatment, and potential for recurrence may lead patients and their families to look outside the medical treatment system for answers. The historic role religion has played with regard to questions of health, mortality, and healing makes it a likely source of aid when one is dealing with the uncertainties of cancer. Further, religious organizations play important roles in cancer care through denominational hospitals and social service agencies. Finally, church teachings often involve specific health behaviors, such as diet or the use of substances such as tobacco and alcohol.

Despite the face valid utility of religion in cancer-related situations, little systematic research has been done on this topic. Instead, most studies have used religion in an ancillary fashion, looking at demographic variables like church attendance or religious affiliation and their relationship to relatively global indices of patient functioning such as mood. Absent from the empirical study of religion in cancer has been a guiding framework. This may reflect tensions between religion and fields such as psychology and medicine, where religious phenomena have not been viewed as legitimate areas of scientific inquiry. Indeed, the literature tends to be divided into philosophical discussions of health by theologians or spiritually-inclined laypeople and a fairly unorganized body of work by empirical researchers, with little integration of the two. Some social scientists have attempted to integrate religious phenomena with mainstream theoretical perspectives (e.g., Gorsuch, 1988; Pargament, 1988; Spilka, Shaver, & Kirkpatrick, 1985), however, these models have received only limited research application.

The absence of frameworks for considering religion in cancer may help explain the relative lack of religion-based interventions for cancer. As Thoits (1986) noted in the context of social support research, successful interventions require a prior theoretical understanding of the processes which link variables of interest to specific outcomes. Not surprisingly, the absence of integrative theory and research make it difficult to develop coherent models of intervention which incorporate religion with prevention, treatment, or palliation.

The purpose of this paper is to present a very general framework for looking at the roles of religion in cancer care. This framework approaches cancer and religion through differing levels of analysis (see Table 1). Cancer is considered in terms of different levels of prevention (primary, secondary, tertiary) while religion is examined in terms of different levels of social organization (macrosocial versus microsocial). This framework will be used to review existing literature and to suggest future directions for service providers and researchers.

Macrosocial Analysis of Religion and Health

Macrosocial here refers to religion as a social institution. It also refers to large, complex religious organizations such as religious denominations and places of worship. Religion may have a variety of health-related impacts at this level. For example, religious teachings may speak directly to

Table 1

Integration of Levels of Analysis for Religion and Cancer Care

Cancer Care	Religion	
	Macrosocial	Microsocial
Primary Prevention	Diet Medical practices Sponsorship of smoking cessation programs Religious participation as health protective	Individual practices and interpretation of dogma and teachings
Secondary Prevention	Religious participation as having non-specific health benefits Sponsorship of screening programs Availability of specific high-risk populations	Members as volunteer paraprofessionals Members as links to other social organizations Members as consumers of screening services
Tertiary Prevention	Sponsorship of clinics and hospitals Teachings with regard to individual versus higher power control over illness and mortality	Counsel from clergy Co-parishioners as sources of support Faith as source of hope, solace, comfort, and understanding

health behaviors, such as the prohibitions against alcohol or tobacco made by some faiths. Religious teachings may also have less obvious effects in terms of delineating those aspects of life which are seen as being guided by a higher power, rather than human endeavor. The emphasis that Christian Scientists place on spiritual healing, along with their shunning of common medical practices provides one example of this. Religious bodies, as social organizations, also have important ties to health. Denominational organizations have long been involved in the delivery of health care through the operation of medical centers, clinics, and nursing homes, Churches have also been active in the promotion of self-help programs such as Compassionate Friends and have often served as centers for holistic health programs.

Places of worship permit systematic access to more people than any other adult-oriented setting, except the workplace. This is an important consideration given that worksite programs often serve relatively healthy, low-risk populations (Love, Rodnick, & McPhee, 1985). Indeed, churches provide access to people who cannot be found in the large scale workplaces that have typically received attention in community-based prevention efforts. Hence, they may allow prevention activities to reach people such as retirees, homemakers, farmers, independent business people and those who work in small businesses. The ability to reach the elderly is particularly important, since the incidence and prevalence of cancer increases with age (Yancik, Kessler, & Yates, 1988). A final access consideration involves the linkages churches offer for the community at-large. Parishioners may serve as a pool of potential volunteers for community programs. They may also hold memberships in other formal organizations (e.g., civic or social action groups) that have interests in prevention.

Ethnic minorities are another significant group reached by churches. Places of worship often function as multi-service community centers for recent immigrants and for those who feel discriminated by mainstream white society. Several articles have noted the role of the black church in the provision of health services (Levin, 1984; Mitchell-Beren, Dodds, Choi, & Waskerwitz, 1989).

Microsocial Analysis of Religion and Health

The influence of religion on health at the level of individuals and their reference groups (i.e., close friends, family, coworkers) has only recently received systematic study. Research suggests that healthy and physically ill populations view religious phenomena as important factors that may influence illness and/or recovery (Jenkins, 1985; Pargament & Sullivan,

1981; Spilka & Schmidt, 1983). Thus, religion may be a part of an individual's effort to understand complex health questions that medical science can answer only with great equivocation, such as cancer-related death. Religion may also be a source of support, as in the cases of individual clergy and fellow parishioners (Eng, Hatch, & Callan, 1985). Religion, as interpreted by the individual may also be a source of comfort and support as in achieving solace through faith (Spilka, Spangler, & Nelson, 1983).

PRIMARY PREVENTION OF CANCER

The specification of particular risk factors for cancer remains an area of great controversy. The most unequivocal risk factor is the use of tobacco, which is a major factor in lung cancer and may also contribute to the incidence of other malignancies such as bladder cancer (Einster, 1988). Research on additional factors such as dietary fat and alcohol consumption has produced more varied and contradictory findings (Byers, 1988), while identification of carcinogenic environmental toxins has often been hampered by the small numbers of people or limited durations of exposures that may occur with any one toxin (Swanson, 1988).

Social/behavioral factors have long been implicated in the etiology of cancer. Personality factors such as neuroticism, introversion (Eysenck, 1987), depression (Shekelle, Raynor, Ostfeld, Garron, Bielauska, Liu, Maliza, & Paul, 1981), disrupted early relationships (Thomas, Duszinski, & Shaffer, 1979), and passivity (Greer, Morris, & Pettingale, 1979) have been implicated as risk factors for tumor development, while an assertive personality style has been suggested as relatively cancer resistant (Derogatis, Abeloff, & Melisaratos, 1979; Greer, Morris, & Pettingale, 1979). However, research of this sort suffers from tremendous methodological and conceptual flaws, as well as many contradictory findings (see Fox, 1978 and Redd & Jacobsen, 1988 for reviews). Animal research suggests that cancer is probably not caused by social/emotional factors, although these may influence cancer spread (Sklar & Anisman, 1981). The equivocal findings for personality variables and the nascent status of psychoneuroimmunology research suggest that psychosocial intervention is most likely to have beneficial impacts in terms of changing health behaviors.

Religion and Primary Prevention of Cancer

Epidemiological research has suggested that religious teachings may have primary prevention impacts. For example, observant members of the Seventh-Day Adventist Church, which discourages the consumption of meat and coffee, have lower death rates from cancers of the large bowel, breast and prostate than the general population (Phillips & Snowden, 1983). Also, sects such as the Amish, which proscribe pre-marital or extra-marital sex, have been found to have relatively low rates of cervical cancer (Troyer, 1988). Hence, it appears that church doctrine may influence cancer mortality.

Epidemiological studies have also suggested that microlevel church participation may also affect cancer risk (e.g., Seeman, Kaplan, Knudsen, Cohen, & Guralnik, 1987), although Levin and Vanderpool's (1987) review of the literature suggests that the beneficial effects of churchgoing may be a proxy for whether or not people are physically active. Religious variables have also emerged as predictors of cancer morbidity and mortality. Schmale and Iker (1971) found religious beliefs to be a discriminator of malignant versus benign cervical tumors, however, this study did not specify the particular beliefs that were assessed.

SECONDARY PREVENTION OF CANCER

Recent years have seen decreases in cancer death rates and increases in patient longevity which are largely attributed to the success of secondary prevention programs. Activities of this type are able to detect cancer at relatively early stages when it is most amenable to curative treatments such as chemotherapy and radiation. Screening programs such as mammograms for breast cancer, pap tests for cervical disease, and stool screening for colorectal cancer have all gained popularity in recent years. Propagation of self-care behaviors such as breast self-examination (BSE) has also served as the focus for many recent prevention efforts. Behavioral scientists have played an increasing role in all of these efforts by finding ways to increase participation in screening activities (e.g., Meyerowitz & Chaiken, 1987).

Religion and Secondary Prevention of Cancer

Integration of religion and secondary prevention has begun to occur in recent years at the macrosocial level through the provision of screening or educational programs by organizations that have worked with churches. Mitchell-Beren, Dodds, Choi, and Waskerwitz (1989) describe a program which involved educational and screening interventions for colorectal cancer. This type of cancer is more prevalent in blacks than whites, hence, targeting the black community has special importance. The intervention was conducted by a medical center in conjunction with an association for black nurses and a black pastors' organization. Thus, the intervention was a collaborative effort which used churches to reach a high risk population.

Diana Bransfield of Vanderbilt University (personal communication, 1990) has done pilot work with another approach to church-centered secondary prevention. Bransfield has worked with Southern Baptist churches to encourage the use of BSE and mammography screening programs. Findings from this work suggested that religious coping style affected BSE use (those who viewed themselves as collaborating with God were more likely to use BSE than those whose coping styles were more deferring toward God or more self-directed). Also, women who were presented with a combination of traditional public education concerning mammograms and related theological messages about maintaining one's health made greater use of screening programs in the community than those who received traditional public health messages alone.

TERTIARY PREVENTION OF CANCER

Cancer may be treated by radiation, hormone therapy, surgery, chemotherapy, or some combination of these treatments, depending on the site and type of the disease involved (Holleb, 1986). While recent decreases in cancer mortality are generally credited to secondary prevention efforts, notable gains have occurred in the treatment of certain cancers such as prostate cancer and pediatric leukemia (Silverberg et al., 1990).

The use of psychosocial means for cancer treatment has emerged as an alternative or supplement to the medical procedures outlined in the preceding paragraph. Treatments such as imagery techniques (Simonton, Mathews-Simonton, & Sparks, 1980) and hypnosis (Margolis, 1982-83) have yielded some positive results, however, they have not been tested in controlled trials or with representative samples of the cancer treatment population. Hence, these treatments are generally viewed as "unproven" and "unconventional" therapies. Popular writers in the area of cancer care have suggested that a positive attitude may also enhance disease outcomes (e.g., Siegel, 1986), however, this, too, has not been subjected to controlled scrutiny and remains "unproven."

One study that does suggest that psychosocial intervention may influence cancer survival has recently emerged from the literature. Spiegel, Bloom, Kraemer, and Gottheil (1989) conducted a ten year follow-up of metastatic breast cancer patients who had participated in a weekly support group for months and found that they had longer intervals of survival than those in a no-treatment control group. This result, however, was obtained from a small sample and it is difficult to determine what differential events among patients may have occurred during intervening years between intervention and follow-up to affect survival.

While available research does not unequivocally support the efficacy of any psychosocial treatment for cancer, there is some evidence from the field of psychoneuroimmunology to suggest that psychological states may influence tumor spread (Levy, Herberman, Maluish, Schlein, & Lippman, 1985). This is thought to be due to the influence of psychological states such as depression or loneliness on immune functioning, with regard to natural killer (NK) cells which monitor the presence of malignant cells and have the capability of destroying such cells. Though promising, this literature has not yet established whether changes in immunocompetence associated with psychosocial functioning are large enough and sustained enough to affect disease state over the long term.

Tertiary prevention of cancer has received the most attention in terms of efforts to enhance patients' quality of life once the disease has been identified. Studies have evaluated factors which may enhance adjustment to the disease (e.g., Andersen, Karlsson, Anderson, & Tewfik, 1984; Weisman & Worden, 1976-77), supportive and psychoeducational interventions (see Telch & Telch, 1985 for a review), and interventions such as relaxation training and hypnosis for the mitigation of noxious side effects of treatment such as chemotherapy-related nausea and vomiting (Carey & Burish, 1988).

Religion and Tertiary Prevention of Cancer

Religion has been most studied in the context of the assessment of adjustment in patients who have already been diagnosed with cancer. However, this has typically occurred at the microsocial level where religion variables are relatively ancillary in nature (e.g., demographic variables like church attendance). There have also been several survey studies which have investigated the prevalence of unmet spiritual or existential needs (Cella & Tross, 1986; Driever & McCorkle, 1984; Houts, Yasko, Kahn, Schlezel, Marconi, 1986; Parsons, 1977; Peteet, 1985-86; Weisman & Worden, 1976-77), however, these have offered little specific information regarding what these needs are or what functions they serve in patients' lives.

Research on coping and adjustment has been somewhat more successful in identifying possible roles for religion in cancer patients' lives. Several studies have noted that large percentages (often one-third or more) of cancer patients view religion as a source of support, with prayer being viewed as a major vehicle of support (Castles & Keith, 1979; Kesselring, Dodd, Lindsey, & Strauss, 1986; Spilka, Spengler, & Nelson, 1983).

A second function of religion appears to be explanatory in nature. God or God's will is sometimes mentioned as a causal or maintaining attribution for cancer (Gotay, 1985; Linn, Linn, & Stein, 1982; Taylor, Lichtman, & Wood, 1984). Anecdotal accounts from a cross-sectional study have suggested that patients do not passively turn to God, but rather engage in a more active search for the existential meaning of their disease and engage in a give and take relationship with God (via prayers and acts of faith; Jenkins & Pargament, 1988).

A third line of research has looked at religion as a correlate of adjustment in cancer patients. Several studies have found strong religious beliefs to be related to decreased levels of pain, anxiety, hostility, social isolation and to higher levels of life satisfaction (Acklin, Brown, & Mauger, 1983; Gibbs & Lawlis-Achterberg, 1978; Yates, Chalmer, St. James, Follansbee, & McKegney, 1981). Like other studies, however, these have offered few specifics regarding the actual beliefs involved.

Some findings have suggested that religious phenomena may have negative as well as positive effects. Weisman (1976) found that church attendance was positively correlated with vulnerability to problems of adjustment. Baider and Sarell (1983) found that Israeli breast cancer patients who held fatalistic religious construals of their disease (typically those from non-European backgrounds) were found to be coping less well than those who had more scientific construct systems (typically those from European backgrounds). This study is one of the few to look at more macrolevel aspects of religion such as differing religious traditions.

Overall, studies of coping and adjustment seem to suggest that religious beliefs and practices may be implicated in the regulation of emotions. The functions of support and cognition may be the intervening links here given the general roles of support and cognition in emotional regulation identified elsewhere (e.g., Maton, 1989; Thoits, 1986). It also seems important to note that religion may have emotional costs as well as benefits for patients and that the specific aspects of religion which are associated with these outcomes needs closer scrutiny.

RELIGION AND PREVENTION IN CANCER: INTEGRATION AND IMPLICATIONS FOR INTERVENTION

Despite the unfocused development of research in this area and the paucity of intervention studies, it can be seen that religion has importance in many cancer patients' lives and that religion may serve beneficial purposes at all levels of prevention.

Lifestyle practices identified with particular religious sects appear to have implications for cancer prevention. Denominations that encourage abstinence from tobacco (e.g., Southern Baptist) or proscribe non-marital sexual relations (e.g., Amish) provide examples of how church teachings may incorporate behaviors that are relevant to cancer risk. These kinds of teachings would seem to create conditions for natural experiments investigating the role of health behaviors as risk factors. Indeed, work of this sort has regularly appeared in the epidemiological literature over the past several decades (Troyer, 1988). Interestingly, however, little research has been done to see if the apparent health consciousness of particular denominations might be used as an impetus for other church-based prevention efforts. Further, it would appear that denominations which foster cancer risk reduction behaviors (e.g., abstinence from tobacco) might be natural collaborators for sponsorship of preventive education and intervention programs. This may raise concerns about proselytizing from community residents; however, one might deal with these through ecumenical sponsorship, as well as through joint secular-sectarian sponsorship.

Consideration of religion would seem to be one way of gaining entree into special populations in the community for all levels of prevention. This has a number of implications at the micro- and macro-social levels. Churches make it possible to reach high-risk groups such as the elderly, as well as members of minority groups. This is important, given the higher incidence of cancer among the elderly (Yancik et al., 1988) and the tendency for some cancers to occur more often among certain ethnic groups (Silverberg et al., 1990). The Mitchell-Beren et al. (1989) project demonstrated how screening measures for colorectal cancer could be introduced to a high-risk minority population through collaboration with pastors.

Community access and the availability of special populations afforded by churches has the additional benefit of fostering grass-roots health activity where it may be needed most. An example of this can be seen from the health management literature. Eng, Hatch, and Callan (1985) describe a program conducted with black churches in North Carolina that included training of congregation members as lay health advisors. The advisors helped organize health fairs and assisted with screening programs. They were also trained to facilitate self-help groups, with emphasis on health concerns such as weight reduction and stress management. Thus, parishioners were given valued roles and empowered as lay "experts" in the community.

Access to clergy, by itself, may be helpful in fostering better use of professional care. Clergy are a remarkably under-identified source of informal assistance for health issues. Survey studies have indicated that as much as 40% of the population may consult clergy about health issues (Levin & Vanderpool, 1987). Some of this advice seeking may come because clergy deal with both individual congregants and the wider community (Eng, Hatch, & Callan, 1985), hence, they are a source of knowledge that may be particularly critical for those who lack familiarity with or sophistication about the organized health care system.

Collaboration with religious organizations at a community level may be also helpful when congregants' attitudes and professional health care practice collide, as in the case of patients who eschew curative treatments because they view healing as "God's will." Here, consultation with clergy might help identify ways in which orthodox medical practice might be brought into harmony with a patient's belief system. While an expensive use of time, this might assist in enlisting clergy as aides in dealing with similar situations in the future and in acquainting professionals with ways to deal sensitively with specific types of religious practice in other patients. The possibilities for this type of collaborative intervention also exist at the macrosocial level where one might want to discuss ethical concerns that prevent adherents to a major faith in the community from using screening or rehabilitative services.

It is apparent that religion has a number of coping functions that moderate individual adjustment. These appear to involve support and various cognitive aspects of coping such as meaning in life, causal attributions and attributions of cure. Thus, religion appears to offer patients opportunities for affiliation and help from others as well as personal solace and a means of cognitively organizing and understanding their experience of cancer. The fragmented nature of the literature concerning religion and quality of life suggests caution in applying these findings in interventions. Clearly, there is a need to more precisely identify the situations and processes by which religion may enhance psychosocial functioning in patients. Some of this work, however, could include collection of data on religious variables in the context of ongoing descriptive or intervention research, as well as small scale exploratory efforts with denominations or places of worship as in the case of Diana Bransfield's work with the Southern Baptists.

Religious phenomena may have more immediate salience at the macrosocial level with greater application in terms of secondary prevention. This reflects the vagaries of primary prevention for cancer generally (beyond smoking cessation), the controversial status of non-medical aspects of tertiary prevention, and the theoretical limitations attached to microsocial functions of religion for patients. Clearly, the discussion here has suggested ways that religious phenomena could be considered outside of macrosocial settings and secondary prevention; however, it may be easier to begin thinking in terms of these levels of analysis.

Religious organizations offer an excellent basis for reaching high-risk populations, for enhancing the health care knowledge and skills of many different segments of the population, and for initiating linkages between the organized health care system and the grassroots public (as individuals and as representatives of formal organizations). Religious bodies also provide bases for examining church doctrine-related health practices that may be associated with cancer risk or the use of health services. Churches, as macrosocial agents, also provide a basis for evaluating the efficacy of different forms of health appeals, as in the case of comparing "objective" health information with that framed in religious teachings.

Taking into account findings from different levels of analysis, it is apparent that various aspects of religion have promise for integration into prevention activities for cancer. Much of this requires renegotiation of the relationship between religion and the organized health care system at the micro- and macrosocial levels. This is a somewhat ironic circumstance given the historic links between religion, medicine, and healing. Nonetheless, it is apparent that people involved in cancer care and prevention need to recognize the competencies and access to populations offered by religious organizations. Also necessary is some integration of psychosocial concepts with those relevant to religious, spiritual, or existential concerns. Toward these ends, a framework such as the one offered here may be helpful, by joining together religious and health care concepts in ways that may guide intervention. One basis for promoting negotiation between religious and health care systems may be through the establishment of common concerns. This seems most evident in projects that have sought to enhance screening activities in minority communities where access to health care services may be limited and certain diseases are more prevalent than in the general population. In this regard attention to health and religion in a larger community context may be the key to joining these two systems.

REFERENCES

Acklin, M. W., Brown, E. C., & Mauger, P. A. (1983). The role of religious values in coping with cancer. *Journal of Health and Religion, 22,* 322-333.

Andersen, B. L., Karlsson, J., Anderson, B., Tewfik, H. H. (1984). Anxiety and cancer treatment: Response to stressful radiotherapy. *Health Psychology, 3,* 535-551.

Baider, L., & Sarell, M. (1983). Perceptions and causal attributions of Israeli women with breast cancer concerning their illness: The effects of ethnicity and religiosity. *Psychotherapy and Psychosomatics, 39,* 136-143.

Bransfield, D. D. (1990). Personal communication.

Byers, T. (1988). Diet and cancer: Any progress in the interim? *Cancer, 62,* 1713-1724.

Castles, M. R., & Keith, P. M. (1979). Patient concerns, emotional resources, and perception of nurse and patient roles. *Omega, 10,* 27-33.

Carey, M. P., & Burish, T. G. (1988). Etiology and treatment of the psychological side effects associated with cancer chemotherapy: A critical review and discussion. *Psychological Bulletin, 104,* 307-325.

Cella, D. F., & Tross, S. (1986). Psychological adjustment to survival from Hodgkin's Disease. *Journal of Consulting and Clinical Psychology, 54,* 616-622.

Derogatis, L. R., Abeloff, M. D., & Melisaratos, N. (1979). Psychological coping mechanisms and survival time in metastatic breast cancer. *Journal of the American Medical Association, 242,* 1504-1508.

Driever, M. J., & McCorkle, R. (1984). Patient concerns at 3 and 6 months post diagnosis. *Cancer Nursing, 7,* 235-141.

Einster, V. L. (1988). Trends in smoking, cancer risk, and cigarette promotion: Current priorities for reducing tobacco exposure. *Cancer, 62,* 1702-1712.

Eng, E., Hatch, J., & Callan, A. (1985). Institutionalizing social support through the church and into the community. *Health Education Quarterly, 12,* 81-92.

Eysenck, H. (1987). Anxiety, helplessness, and cancer: A causal theory. *Journal of Anxiety Disorders, 1,* 87-104.

Fox, B. H. (1978). Premorbid psychological factors as related to cancer prevalence. *Journal of Behavioral Medicine, 1,* 45-134.

Gibbs, H. W., & Achterberg-Lawlis, J. (1978). Spiritual values and death anxiety: Implications for counseling with terminal cancer patients. *Journal of Counseling Psychology, 25,* 563-569.

Gorsuch, R. (1988). Psychology of religion. *Annual Review of Psychology, 39,* 201-222.

Gotay, C. C. (1985). Why me? Attributions and adjustment by cancer patients and their mates at two stages in the disease process. *Social Science and Medicine, 20,* 825-831.

Greer, S., Morris, T., & Pettingale, K. W. (1979). Psychological response to breast cancer: Effect on outcome. *Lancet,* 785-787.

Holleb, A. I. (1986). An overview of cancer today. In A. I. Holleb (Ed.), *The American Cancer Society cancer book: Prevention, detection, diagnosis, treatment, cure.* Garden City, NY: Doubleday.

Houts, P. S., Yasko, J. M., Kahn, S. B., Schlezel, G. W., & Marconi, K. M. (1986). Unmet psychological, social, and economic needs of persons with cancer in Pennsylvania. *Cancer, 58,* 2355-2361.

Jenkins, R. A. (1985). *An investigation of cognitive attributes of coping in medical patients.* Unpublished doctoral dissertation, Bowling Green State University.

Jenkins, R. A., & Pargament, K. I. (1988). Cognitive appraisals and psychological adjustment in cancer patients. *Social Science and Medicine, 23,* 186-196.

Kesselring, A., Dodd, M. J., Lindsey, A. M., & Strauss, A. L. (1986). Attitudes of patients living in Switzerland about cancer and its treatment. *Cancer Nursing, 9*, 77-85.

Levin, J. S. (1984). The role of the black church in community medicine. *Journal of the National Medical Association, 76*, 477-483.

Levin, J. S., & Vanderpool, H. Y. (1987). Is frequent religious attendance really conducive to better health?: Toward an epidemiology of religion. *Social Science and Medicine, 24*, 589-600.

Levy, S. M., Herberman, R. B, Maluish, A. M., Schlein, B., & Lippman, M. (1985). Prognostic risk assessment in primary breast cancer by behavioral and immunological parameters. *Health Psychology, 4*, 99-113.

Love, R. R., Rodnick, J. E., & McPhee, S. J. (1988). Community models for cancer prevention and detection. *Cancer, 62*, 1815-1820.

Margolis, C. G. (1982-83). Hypnotic imagery with cancer patients. *American Journal of Clinical Hypnosis, 25*, 128-134.

Maton, K. I. (1989). The stress-buffering role of spiritual support: Cross-sectional and prospective investigations. *Journal for the Scientific Study of Religion, 29*, 310-323.

Meyerowitz, B. E., & Chaiken, S. (1987). The effect of message framing on breast self-examination attitudes, intentions, and behavior. *Journal of Personality and Social Psychology, 52*, 500-510.

Mitchell-Beren, M. E., Dodds, M. E., Choi, K. L., & Waskerwitz, T. R. (1989). A colorectal cancer prevention, screening, and evaluation program in community black churches. *CA-A Cancer Journal for Clinicians, 39*, 115-118.

Pargament, K. I., & Sullivan, M. S. (1981). *Examining attributions of control across diverse personal situations: A psychosocial perspective.* Paper presentation at the annual meetings of the American Psychological Association, Los Angeles, CA.

Pargament, K. I. (1990). God help me: Toward a theoretical framework of coping for the psychology of religion. *Research in the Social Scientific Study of Religion, 2*, 195-224.

Parsons, J. B. (1977). A descriptive study of intermediate stage terminally ill cancer patients at home. *Nursing Digest, 5*, 1-26.

Peteet, J. R. (1985-86). Religious issues presented by cancer patients seen in psychiatric consultation. *Journal of Psychosocial Oncology, 3*, 53-66.

Phillips, R. L., & Snowden, D. A. (1983). Association of meat and coffee use with cancers of the large bowel, breast, and prostate among Seventh-Day Adventists: Preliminary results. *Cancer Research, 43* (Suppl), 2403-2408.

Redd, W. H., & Jacobsen, P. B. (1988). Emotions and cancer: New perspectives on an old question. *Cancer, 62*, 1871-1879.

Schmale, A. H., & Iker, H. (1971). Hopelessness as a predictor of cervical cancer. *Social Science and Medicine, 5*, 95-100.

Seeman, T. E., Kaplan, G. A., Knudsen, L., Cohen, R., & Guralnik, J. (1987). Social network ties and mortality among the elderly in the Alameda County study. *American Journal of Epidemiology, 126*, 714-723.

Shekelle, R. B., Raynor, W. J., Ostfeld, A. M., Garron, D. C., Bielauskas, L.

A., Liu, S. C., Maliza, C., & Paul, O. (1981). Psychological depression and 17-year risk of death from cancer. *Psychosomatic Medicine, 43*, 117-125.

Siegel, B. S. (1986). *Love, medicine, and miracles*. NY: Harper & Row.

Silverberg, E., Boring, C. C., & Squires, T. S. (1990). Cancer statistics, 1990. *CA – A Cancer Journal for Clinicians, 40*, 9-26.

Simonton, O. C., Mathews-Simonton, S., & Sparks, T. F. (1980). Psychological intervention in the treatment of cancer patients. *Psychosomatics, 21*, 226-233.

Sklar, L. S., & Anisman, H. (1981). Stress and Cancer. *Psychological Bulletin, 89*, 369-406.

Spiegel, D., Bloom, J. R., Kraemer, H. C., & Gottheil, E. (1989). Effect of psychosocial treatment on survival of patients with metastatic breast cancer. *Lancet*, (No. 8668), 888-891.

Spilka, B., & Schmidt, G. (1983). General attribution theory for the psychology of religion: The influence of event-character on attributions to God. *Journal for the Scientific Study of Religion, 22*, 326-329.

Spilka, B., Shaver, P., & Kirkpatrick, L. (1985). A general attribution theory for the psychology of religion. *Journal for the Scientific Study of Religion, 24*, 1-20.

Spilka, B., Spangler, J. D., & Nelson, C. B. (1983). Spiritual support in life threatening illness. *Journal of Religion and Health, 22*, 98-104.

Swanson, G. M. (1988). Cancer prevention in the workplace and natural environment: A review of etiology, research design, and methods of risk reduction. *Cancer, 62*, 1725-1746.

Taylor, S. E., Lichtman, R. R., & Wood, J. V. (1984). Attributions, beliefs about control, and adjustment to breast cancer. *Journal of Personality and Social Psychology, 46*, 489-502.

Telch, C. F., & Telch, M. J. (1985). Psychological approaches for enhancing coping among cancer patients. *Clinical Psychology Review, 5*, 325-344.

Thoits, P. A. (1986). Social support as coping assistance. *Journal of Consulting and Clinical Psychology, 54*, 416-423.

Thomas, C. B, Duszinski, K. R., & Shaffer, J. W. (1979). Family attitudes in youth as potential predictors of cancer. *Psychosomatic Medicine, 41*, 287-302.

Troyer, H. (1988). Review of cancer among four religious sects: Evidence that life-styles are distinctive sets of risk factors. *Social Science and Medicine, 26*, 1007-1017.

Weisman, A. D. (1979). A model for psychosocial phasing in cancer. *General Hospital Psychiatry, 1*, 187-195.

Weisman, A. D., & Worden, J. W. (1976-77). The existential plight in cancer: Significance of the first 100 days. *International Journal of Psychiatry in Medicine, 7*, 1-15.

Yancik, R., Kessler, L., & Yates, J. W. (1988). The elderly population: Opportunities for cancer prevention, and detection. *Cancer, 62*, 1823-1828.

Yates, J., Chalmer, B., St. James, P., Follansbee, M., & McKegney, F. (1981). Religion in patients with advanced cancer. *Medical and Pediatric Oncology, 9*, 121-128.

THE RELIGIOUS PERSPECTIVE

Prevention Theory and Action from the Religious Perspective

Robert W. Anderson, Jr.
Kenneth I. Maton
Barbara E. Ensor

University of Maryland Baltimore County

SUMMARY. Based on interviews with nine individuals actively involved in religiously-affiliated service, we describe and examine their perspectives on prevention and on religion as a preventive influence. As an initial attempt to organize religion's implicit theory of prevention, the discussion is organized under three broad head-

The authors gratefully acknowledge the thoughtful input from The Most Reverend William D. Borders, Archbishop of Baltimore; Father Joseph Muth, and Father Maurice Blackwell, Catholic Archdiocese of Baltimore; Reverend Dr. John Sharp, Govans Presbyterian Church, Baltimore; Ms. Sally Robinson, Director, Episcopal Social Services, Baltimore; Rev. Michael Rokos, Episcopal Gunpowder Hundred, Joppa, MD; Sister Judith Schmelz, PhD, The Learning Bank, Community Organized to Improve Life (COIL), Baltimore; Sister Agnes Hughes, I.H.M., PhD, Immaculata College, Philadelphia; and Richard Parsons, PhD, Neumann College, Aston, PA. Reprints may be obtained from Robert W. Anderson, Jr., Department of Psychology, University of Maryland, Baltimore County Campus, 5401 Wilkens Avenue, Baltimore, MD 21228.

195

ings: (1) the religious world view and understanding of prevention; (2) the religious world view in practice, distinctive aspects of religion as prevention; and (3) issues of religious-human services collaboration in preventive action. Described in the context of religion as a different cultural setting, our major assertion is that prevention in religious contexts stems from a global yet differentiated promotion approach to human welfare. Given our assumption that there are special religious influences which promote the health and well-being of individuals and communities, we challenge religion to better mobilize them, and human services to better appreciate and incorporate them.

The topic of religious influence in prevention and promotion has received surprisingly little attention in the prevention literature (cf. Maton & Pargament, 1987). In part, this may be due to limited understanding by prevention researchers and practitioners about the nature and potential of religious influence in general and of religious social ministry (i.e., religious human services or social action) in particular. A primary goal of this chapter is to contribute to the understanding of the links between religion and prevention by articulating the views of religious personnel concerning these links. Enhanced understanding of the religious perspective appears necessary for productive research and collaboration on the part of human service practitioners and researchers. In addition, prevention and human services stand to gain considerably from explication of religion's approach inasmuch as greater appreciation of religion may help generate new ideas about preventive activities and enhance access to certain populations.

With relatively little research concerning religion and prevention to draw upon, we interviewed a number of individuals involved in religious leadership and/or religious human service roles. In all, nine interviews were conducted, each lasting one to three hours. The interviewees included four pastors (two Catholic, one Episcopal, one Presbyterian), two administrators with diocese-wide responsibilities (one Catholic, one Episcopal), two faculty in Catholic liberal arts colleges, and one director of a city-wide literacy program sponsored by an ecumenical/community agency. These nine individuals were selected in part due to their prominence as religious leaders, and in part because access was facilitated, directly or indirectly, through connections we had. No attempt was made to obtain a broadly representative sample of religious denominations nor of types of religious workers, as we believed it necessary to attempt an initial working formulation of religious views before examining any differences within and among religions. We also recognize that by virtue of their leadership characteristics, the views and experiences of our respondents may differ from those of the average religious worker. For this initial venture into the field of religion and prevention, the primary goal was to learn about the linkages between religion and prevention from articulate and interesting people with potential for providing insight into these linkages.

In an effort such as this, issues regarding the definition of religion, and of prevention, are certainly not to be underestimated (cf. Magee, 1967; Sharpe, 1983). Yet while we acknowledge and respect the complexity of both religion and prevention, our goal here is to lay out some potentially important aspects of their interrelationships, not to explicate either religion or prevention in full detail. We approached the task, therefore, from a rather simple perspective. After a brief, global description of prevention (in which prevention of future problems was explicitly contrasted with treatment of preexisting problems), we essentially asked participants, "As you understand your religion, what is it about what you believe and what you do that contributes to prevention?" We asked this in several different ways and contexts, and followed up initial questions with various probes to enhance our understanding of each individual's perspectives. In the course of our interviews, it became increasingly clear that our respondents' religious perspectives were complex and multifaceted rather than simple and uniform, and as suggested by Maton and Pargament (1987), likely influence individuals "and the social world in a variety of ways" (p. 163).

Our discussion is organized under three broad headings: (1) the religious world view and understanding of prevention; (2) religious world view in practice, distinctive aspects of religion as prevention; and (3) issues of religious-human services collaboration in preventive action. Under each heading, we try to distill the essence of our respondents' views and common themes among them, and to clarify linkages to prevention theory and practice. Although religion does not appear to have an explicit theory of prevention, we have assumed that inherent in the religious world view and its assumptions about persons, problems, and helping, there exist some tacit religious conceptualizations of prevention. We make every effort to retain and be faithful to distinctive religious language, and, where possible, to contrast prevailing human service and religious perspectives in clear and meaningful ways. This work is clearly exploratory; our hope is to provide an initial set of ideas or hypotheses to guide future research and action.

RELIGIOUS WORLD VIEW
AND UNDERSTANDING OF PREVENTION

Consistent with Maton and Pargament (1987), we conceptualize the religious world view as a response to the human need for understanding the world, one's particular circumstances, and our inevitable mortality. Each of the nine respondents we interviewed appeared to have a highly developed, articulated religious world view. Of the various aspects of religious world view which emerged in the interviews, we single out three which appear to characterize the religious understanding of and orientation towards prevention and preventive action. These three aspects are: (1) a promotion-oriented philosophy; (2) a holistic view of life, persons and problems, engendering a global but differentiated intervention strategy; and (3) a strong sense of social responsibility, especially concerning the least fortunate in society.

Promotion-Oriented Philosophy

Interestingly, and significantly, it did not appear that any of the respondents explicitly conceptualized prevention as part of their religious world view, nor as a primary focus of their work — although in our discussions it was generally endorsed as legitimate and important. Rather, the goal of promoting well-being, broadly defined, was central. Indeed, several of our respondents considered the term "prevention" egregious because of its sterility and in its implication that persons are somehow "on the brink." From this perspective, to invite people to participate in programs designed to prevent something is to, perhaps self-defeatingly, require a focus on possible negative outcomes, rather than on the positive, promotion-oriented goals and potentials religion seeks to encourage. One theme in the responses to our inquiries about how religion does prevention, in fact, had to do with religion's efforts to help individuals shift attention from problems and deficits to possibilities and promises, "offering hope and empowering the individual."

Our select sample of mainstream Christian religious workers, then, were not in the habit of conceptualizing their work in terms of prevention. Rather, from their promotion-oriented perspective, they implied that prevention would be achieved by their efforts because individuals they affected were becoming more integrated and whole (see *Holistic View of Persons and Problems* below). This "promotion as prevention" perspective is captured in the words of one of our respondents, who stated in response to our probes about religion's preventive philosophy, "Making an individual stronger is prevention."

Holistic View of Persons and Problems:
Global Philosophy, Differentiated Approach

As reflected in the perspectives of our respondents, religion views people in broad, holistic terms, encompassing multiple needs and dimensions including the material, psychological, social, and spiritual (cf. Duchrow, 1984). Consistent with this, "well-being" is understood as the subjective experience of self-worth which comes in large part from experiencing wholeness, integration and balance among these various aspects. Contrasting this encompassing view of the person and well-being, several respondents discussed what they considered the more often narrow, specialized view of the secular helping professional. In particular, they saw helping professionals as more likely to focus on some limited area, paying insufficient attention, for example, to one or more of the following: basic material needs, underlying spiritual needs, critical social needs (i.e., for belonging and community), and important contextual factors (e.g., ethnicity; socioeconomic status).

Corollary to this view that well-being is based on a sense of self-worth, problems are to be understood to reflect in part some deficit in individuals' (or communities') experience of their wholeness and/or worth to themselves or others. Accordingly, for religious workers, a whole family of differentiated solutions is embodied in the goals of providing opportunities and supporting efforts to broaden perspective and experience, and to integrate them with personal needs and goals in everyday life (see below). One respondent called this a "stewardship of self, an attempt to achieve and maintain what the creator intended." Indeed, what is central and perhaps distinctive to the religious perspective of our respondents in this regard is its inherent invitation to participate in integrative activities and processes — i.e., activities and processes which provide opportunities for learning to appreciate and enhance continuity and balance within the material, psychological, social, and spiritual aspects of life. In addition, such opportunities are understood to draw on and foster people's experience of God.

One additional dimension unique to religion, in contrast to secular perspectives, is its call to reconciliation not only among various aspects of life on earth in the here and now, but also with individual subjective understanding and experiences of transcendence. Although we were unable to pursue this in depth in our interviews, it bears mention here because of its centrality to the religious perspective.

Finally, religion's holistic view extends beyond simply appreciating the presence of multiple dimensions. Specifically, this is reflected in assumptions of: (1) an integrated unity among the "parts" of self and human experience which are often compartmentalized in the secular world, and (2) that this unity extends beyond the individual, to families, communities, and over time. For instance, this perspective suggests that helping oneself helps others, and vice versa, as implied in the aphorism "No man is an island." These two levels of unity are seen as coextensive (having the same limits, boundary, or scope) with the promotion of individual and collective spiritual development. Thus, spiritual development on the one hand, and well-being and development (both individual and community) on the other, are understood to develop reciprocally, each being both the result of and medium for the other. Such an appreciation of the whole person within the community guided the efforts of one pastor as he arranged for safe, appropriate housing for the elderly within his parish. While he saw the project as an opportunity for all concerned to grow, he tried to respect the physical, psychological, and social needs of all parties as he planned it.

Interestingly, the integrated, holistic view of life and persons appears, from our perspective, simultaneously to generate global and differentiated approaches to promotion and prevention work. In the parlance of prevention, the approach of religion is global in that a single, underlying factor is implicated in both the understanding of the variety of individual and social problems (an absence of holism/integration) and the resolution and prevention of these various problems (enhancing holism/integration). In other words, one of the overarching goals of religion appears to be to counteract the absence of holism/integration in individual and community lives by finding means to enhance them.

On the other hand, the complexly integrated view of persons, problems and reality enumerated above provides religious workers with a differentiated perspective—one which provides multiple points of entry, multiple domains of focus, and multiple levels of reality in which promotion and prevention may occur. One respondent observed that this is facilitated by an emphasis on broad outcomes rather than on target problems. Others noted that it implied "freedom to seize the moment" and to respond to persons "here and now." Depending on specific strengths, weaknesses and problems, the context and circumstances, and the nature of the personal ministry relationship, a variety of specific strategies and tactics may emerge in relationship to both individuals and groups of individuals. Because individual and group spiritual development are understood as connected and reciprocal, the distinction between these levels of analysis (common in community and clinical psychology) does not appear to be emphasized by religious workers. Both are targets of religious preventive effort.

Thus, we describe the viewpoint of our respondents as global in philosophy, but differentiated in practice. In the parlance of religion, there is a superordinate goal of stimulating, supporting and enhancing a broader vision, and personal and community integration. Simultaneously, there is the awareness that there are many ways in which people (and thus God) can be served, many different needs, and many ways to stimulate, support and enhance vision, holism, and integration. In summary, prevention is understood to occur naturally along the way to more superordinate spiritual goals (underlying global philosophy) within the context of current needs, relationships, and circumstances (resulting in differentiated practice).

If confirmed by future, systematic research, the idea that the basic religious view on prevention is promotion-based, and global but differentiated, has important and provocative implications for prevention workers (i.e., by providing an alternative view of problems and prevention strategies, and an alternative model of service delivery and organization). Conceptually, it would provide a framework for understanding the prevention activities of religion-based programs, both within congregations and in the larger community. Furthermore, from an action perspective, it would provide guidelines for planning interventions which either incorporate religious elements or are conducted in collaboration with religious personnel, settings, and/or populations.

Strong Sense of Social Responsibility, Especially Concerning the Least Fortunate

Implied in the holistic view, and reflected in the work of every one of our respondents was a compelling responsibility to contribute to the well-being of others and of society in general (cf. Coughlin, 1965). One of the distinct assumptions of religion, in fact, is that faith, community, and individual health and well-being grow synergistically as individuals are pulled into balance by religion's invitations to exercise their talents, participate in community, and reach out to others. Indeed, each of our respondents felt and articulated religion's special responsibility to the least fortunate in society—e.g., the poor, the ill, those discriminated against. This is consistent with everyday evidence that religious ministry efforts are often directed toward major social problems involving the poor and needy. As one respondent noted, "it is not enough just to preach on Sunday;" his church, in fact, was actively involved in staffing, supporting, or administrating a number of programs, including a parenting center for unwed mothers, and a support and legal guardian program for the elderly and for individuals without families.

This sense of mission towards the needy and poor has both advantages and disadvantages in terms of religion as a resource for preventive action. On the one hand, it provides motivation and a sense of responsibility for focusing programs on populations at high risk for developing various problems: the poor, the unempowered, and the underserved. In this regard, poverty and lack of power have been implicated as major risk factors for many personal and social problems (e.g., Albee, 1982), and so in this sense religious work has potential for (and may already be having) important preventive impact. On the other hand, to the extent such populations already manifest diagnosable problems or syndromes, such efforts are too late to have a primary preventive impact vis-a-vis the specifically diagnosed condition. As Cowen (1983) notes, primary prevention efforts aimed at reducing the incidence of new cases of problems should focus on individuals who are currently well. Furthermore, inasmuch as religion tends to focus on providing immediate help to the needy in the form of one-on-one helping, which requires high levels of human resources, it may preclude a focus on systemic or environmental change efforts—and the latter may be critical for many primary prevention efforts. Nonetheless, to the extent that motivation to help the poor and unempowered can be applied early in the life cycle (e.g., for new parents; for children), involve large numbers of volunteer resources or include a systemic focus, then this potential limitation of the religious world view can possibly be transformed into a strength in terms of primary prevention work. Additionally, the commitment of religion to the "broken," "disenfranchised," and "suffering" in society may possibly have a primary preventive effect by introducing new paradigms, priorities, or cultural values into society. For instance, Mother Teresa's radical commitment to the poor, Henri Nouwen's to the retarded, and Mitch Snyder's to the homeless, each emergent from religious perspectives and conviction, appear in part to be attempts to influence the fundamental tenets society holds about the meaning of commitment; of disability, health, and wholeness; and of community.

Summary

Based on our efforts to discern and articulate an implicit theory of prevention from interviews, we hypothesize that mainstream religion operates from a holistic, promotion-based, and global but differentiated orientation to prevention. A primary component of this philosophy of intervention is the belief that one important way of understanding problems is that they reflect a lack of integration in individual lives among aspects of self, others, community, and God. Optimal preventive efforts thus invite individuals into processes which (from the religious perspective, through faith and with divine intervention) support appreciation of self-worth, wholeness, and integration and balance among the material, psychological, social, and spiritual dimensions of life. In general, while our respondents did not conceptualize prevention as an explicit goal, the religious world view nonetheless does seem a valuable resource which naturally generates viable and important preventive activities. However, to the extent activities focus primarily on helping those who already manifest definable clinical or other problems, there is a constraint on primary prevention. In the next section we examine the intervention implications of the religious world view more directly, with an explicit focus on its distinctive aspects compared to traditional human services preventive efforts.

RELIGIOUS WORLD VIEW IN PRACTICE: DISTINCTIVE ASPECTS OF RELIGION AS PREVENTION

As described by our respondents, religious perspectives, goals, and settings have important and distinctive implications for religious intervention programs and activities, including those to which we may ascribe preventive significance. Below we discuss four distinctive aspects of religion as prevention: special access; flexibility and breadth of focus; religious motivation: sanctity and continuity; and faith and religious community.

Special Access

Our respondents provided numerous examples of organized religion's special access to individuals throughout the lifespan. Whereas human service professionals essentially rely on a "passive mode" of helping, in which they wait for individuals to seek their help, or make special arrangements to focus on a group of individuals in a certain setting at a certain point in life (e.g., school-based interventions), religious personnel have a more active, socially-sanctioned access to individuals from birth through death. The religious worker apparently is viewed more as an inherent part of the congregational member's social network than as an outside professional (Heifetz, 1987). Consistent with the holistic view discussed above, religion in general, and helping outreach by religious personnel in particular, are apparently seen as natural elements interwoven into the fabric of life.

In part, the special access of the church is facilitated by its social image as a place of refuge for those in need. In this context, our respondents noted descriptions of the church as a setting which offers "hope and acceptance," "a special place," "a certain attitude," or "a calming effect that people recognize and value." To the extent that this view of the church holds true for individuals, religious workers are especially likely to be granted such special access.

The special access of religious workers also appears facilitated in part by a trusting, respectful attitude toward clergy. Thus, one respondent described his ability to garner the active involvement of a large number of inner-city parents, community, and parishioners in his work with troubled youth. This cooperation he felt was greatly enabled by expectations of the positive role of clergy by these various groups. Of course, it should be noted the special access of religion may not be uniform across all community strata, nor for all members of a given community.

While not explicitly raised as an issue by our respondents, one interesting and potentially important question is the nature and extent of differences in access accorded to religious workers by congregational members as opposed to those outside the congregation (who may or may not be religious). Thus, congregational members may welcome or seek out contact with the religious worker or religious program as part of their congregational life, and be psychologically receptive to input. Furthermore, to the extent a sense of community and fellowship exists within a congregation, members may share common goals with the worker, and perhaps a history of reciprocal and positive involvement, which could obviously enhance the access of the religious worker for prevention-relevant intervention efforts.

In contrast, a common religious world view, and a common history of shared community and contact will less likely be present between religious workers and those in the external, non-congregational community. So, in general, the degree of access will presumably be less than within the congregation. Nonetheless, a distinctive access of religion may likely exist to the extent community members accord religious workers a special respect and status. In urban and ethnic minority neighborhoods, for example, in which religious institutions remain a primary force (Moore, this volume), a special, trusting view of religion and religious personnel will be especially likely. Thus, outreach programs likely retain a measure of special access not accorded to human service professionals who are likely to be viewed as outsiders rather than as an intrinsic part of the community.

Flexibility and Breadth of Focus

Our respondents generally indicated a freedom to develop programs in the community, relatively unimpeded by many of the constraints and policies of the human services system. In particular, as specific needs are targeted, religion appears able in many domains to mount a program relatively quickly. For example, one respondent working in a religiously-sponsored community agency emphasized her freedom to develop a literacy program, based only on her having recognized the need for it and spoken informally with her director about it. Of course, depending on the nature of the religious organization within which the religious worker functions, there may be internal constraints from the religious bureaucracy or officials.

An additional aspect of programmatic flexibility was emphasized by two respondents who independently described a common theme of their work to be the facilitation of "connections" among different components of their church and community. They described a variety of ways in which they attempt to bring together members of the congregation and parts of the community targeted by various outreach programs, e.g., addicts. On the programmatic level, each of these ministers emphasized ecumenical networking of resources and support, and the synergistic processes of people meeting in the real world. Their underlying assumption appeared to be that religion works to the extent it occasions, enhances, and supports contact and relationships among diverse people and groups, with the inherent opportunities for dispelling stereotypes and enhancing empathic understanding. The flexibility inherent in the role of minister seemed to enhance this resource facilitator/linker role.

In addition to programmatic flexibility, respondents described a flexibility at the individual level in terms of their ability to tailor their responses to the varied and changing needs of individuals. Specifically, given the holistic perspective discussed above, several respondents emphasized their ability to respond flexibly to whatever needs are presented by individuals at any given point in time, whether they be material, psychological, or spiritual. For instance, one parish youth center provided tutoring, job training and placement, and psychological counseling for individuals and families, as such needs arose. In contrast, secular organizations more often circumscribe their services on the basis of their domain of specialty or the nature of the targeted population (e.g., type of problem, age, or geographical area).

In general, and consistent with the religious world view described earlier, the religious ministry work of our respondents seemed to be guided by its global, promotion-oriented goals of enhancing integration and well-being, while their specific actions were driven by a number of factors, including congregational and community needs, resources and expertise at their disposal, and the mandates and limitations of their ministry and settings. Despite these latter two sets of limitations (indicative of the constraints inherent in any social setting), religion seems to have some distinctive flexibility. For instance, two pastors described their ability to start non-traditional projects, one in housing and one in substance abuse prevention, on a small scale without lengthy bureaucratic approval processes in order to respond to the needs of a few people—and later secure the backing to expand their projects. Further research is necessary to examine the strengths and limitations of various religion-based models of service delivery and program development, and the implications for various preventive and promotive outcomes.

Religious Motivation: Sanctity and Continuity

Another way in which the religious world view may distinctively affect what and how things are done in religious ministry is by providing a distinct motivation. Our interviews suggested at least two vehicles for such a motivational influence: a belief in the dignity and sanctity of all persons, and the implicit call for a continuity in quality of responsiveness and relating to others across work and personal life.

The first of these goes beyond the traditional concept of "respect," and is based in the religious belief in universal "sanctity." In religious terms, this means that all life, and particularly human life, is God-given, and therefore good and sacred—and so, worthy of being treated as God would be. Thus, there is a special religious dimension which goes beyond basic respect for persons. This motivates workers and may enable some qualitatively distinctive ways of conducting human services. As one respondent noted, this "belief in the dignity of the person" is central to religious values. Another noted that, "the values and life goals of a religious person are keys to their quality of work, commitment and dedication" (see also Borowitz, 1984).

The second aspect of religious motivation focuses on the call for continuity across personal and "work" life. As expressed by our respondents, ministry work offers opportunities for ministry in all daily contacts with others, and not simply in the context of formal job responsibilities. Derived from the spiritually-based, holistic appreciation of life, the religious value system expressed by our respondents implied that religious workers tend to view work and non-work life equally as expressions and extensions of their own spiritual life.

Thus, sanctity and continuity help to comprise a "sense of mission" or "call to service" which may distinguish religious motivation from that of the other human services. At a minimum, such sources of motivation clearly differ from those based on career, material success, or status. To the extent these are active in a given religious worker, it seems quite plausible that ensuing interventions might show discernible differences from nonreligious interventions. For example, our respondents suggested that they tend not to think of their work in detached, superficial terms, and attempt to be fully present "as a person," rather than simply as someone in a professional role. Religious workers, motivated in such a fashion, may be especially caring, sensitive, and respectful to clients, colleagues, and others. The extent to which distinctive interpersonal and other characteristics are indeed present in religiously motivated workers, and have distinctive outcomes, represent important questions for future empirical investigation. Independent of the findings of such research, the articulated motivations of religious workers provide an interesting contrast to those articulated outside the religious context.

Faith and Community

Our discussion thus far of religion's special access, flexibility, and motivation fails to capture one other distinctive and important practical manifestation of the religious world view, namely the importance of efforts to foster faith and religious community. While the role of religious content (e.g., religious beliefs), practices (e.g., prayer), and community (congregational membership, participation, or fellowship) as catalysts to health and well-being remain empirical and perhaps somewhat contentious issues, our respondents implicitly ascribe a degree of importance to them for individual well-being. Moreover, the importance of faith and religious community in prevention/promotion and human services helping appears to be receiving increasing emphasis. For example, an explicit focus on such religious factors (e.g., spirituality, fellowship) is clearly central in the 12-step approach to the treatment of alcoholism and other addictions (Whitfield, 1985). At any rate, to the extent that faith and community (and related phenomena such as religiously inspired optimism, meaning, and spirituality) contribute to coping with life stress, their effective promotion in religious intervention programs represents a unique and potentially important component of religious interventions in contrast to secular ones.

It seems reasonable to assume that explicit focus on faith and community would be more evident in settings in which religious values are consensual, i.e., within congregations. Thus, Sunday sermons, weekly bible study groups, congregation-based family or parenting workshops, spiritual development retreats, youth ministry curricula, and so on are more likely to include language and activities related to faith and religious community. Especially if such activities are appropriately targeted and engaging, continuous over time, and linked to well-being, they would represent a unique contribution of religion to promotion and prevention.

One interesting question is the nature of differences which exist in the actions of religious workers geared within, as opposed to outside religious congregations (i.e., programs targeting members versus non-members). To what extent, for example, are prayer, religious discussion, spiritual texts, and community-building included in intervention programs which target the community outside the congregation (e.g., in pregnancy prevention, youth recreation, job-seeking, and family support programs)? Although we did not ask our respondents specifically about this, it would appear to be an important focus for future research, inasmuch as empirical data may enhance the attainment of goals in either context and/or contribute to mutual understanding and collaborative efforts.

Interestingly, however, even if it is found that an explicit focus on faith, community and related concepts are less likely in programs which target the community outside the congregation, religious workers may still exert an indirect religious influence. For example, if program participants (i.e., service recipients) from the larger community perceive and appreciate that religiously-affiliated persons are providing the service, and they experience comfortable access, flexibility, and respect which they attribute to the religious affiliation, then positive views about religious personnel and religion, leading ultimately to positive religious influence and religious development, may be engendered. Clearly, research is necessary to examine both the role and impact of faith and community building, and differences which may exist in the extent or nature of their "invocation" across settings, such as those targeted within congregations or targeted outside in the larger community.

COLLABORATION BETWEEN RELIGION
AND HUMAN SERVICES

The Need for Collaboration

Our respondents uniformly spoke in favor of greater collaboration between religion and human services, acknowledging that religion could benefit from the accumulated knowledge of psychology and other helping professions. As one respondent noted, with the help of psychology "much of what the church is doing in terms of prevention" could be more explicit and thus be improved. Additionally, given that religious resources are typically limited, churches could benefit from the human services in the form of personnel, time, and tangible resources. A second rationale provided for collaboration was that, from the viewpoint of religion, many of the current efforts in the human services are severely limited. In particular, various respondents perceived that inasmuch as human services can be narrow and technical, they devalue the person in general, and the spiritual realm in particular.

In various ways, our respondents acknowledged the strengths and weaknesses of both religious and secular services in meeting the full spectrum of human needs, noting that better collaboration between them would enable them to capitalize on the strengths, and minimize the weaknesses, of each. One respondent noted that "there are always disagreements" both within and between religion and human services, but that it would be better to cooperate on the plenty we agree on, i.e., that people deserve quality lives, and that they benefit from support, enabling, and external interventions at times. Effective collaboration—i.e., the ability to share resources and expertise to meet common goals—requires emphasizing issues on which there is agreement, such as basic respect for people, their rights, and their welfare—despite other disagreements.

The Nature of Collaboration

Collaborative partnership could be developed by combining the perspectives and approaches of both religion and the human services. The key objective of such a partnership, as voiced by several respondents, would be a synergistic combination of perspectives and approaches, resulting in more than just the addition of one to the other. That is, the benefits would be more than simply replicating secular services in religious settings, or using religious perspectives or symbols in otherwise secular settings. Rather, as one respondent noted, a new, broader perspective on helping and prevention could hopefully emerge from the integration of the two.

Several specific ideas about the nature or form of collaboration were also articulated. One was that, based on mutual respect for both religious and secular services, human services personnel could provide technical assistance and consultation, enabling religion to better define and accomplish its proximal goals. Examples of this include consultation on assessment/diagnostic or intervention issues, or about particular psychological issues. Religious workers attempting to assess needs, or to develop an approach to intervention with an identified group, would obviously profit from the insights of professionals with expertise in assessment, program evaluation, program development, or particular populations. Likewise, human services stand to gain much from greater understanding of both the religious experiences of those people with whom they work, and the methods and philosophies of religion as an alternative, allied helping resource.

Obstacles to Collaboration

The positive attitudes towards collaboration expressed by our respondents notwithstanding, it was also clear that major obstacles exist to collaboration between religious and secular services. Fundamentally, the obstacles may be viewed as stemming from the reality that, in many respects, religion and human services represent distinctly different cultures in our society. One interesting manifestation of such "cultural" differences is the different languages of religion and human services, which reflect their respective interests and value systems. Interestingly, at times religious and human service/prevention workers use different words for the same or similar processes or events, and at times, the same terms may have different meaning, depending on the context (e.g., "community," "mission," and "charity"). While prevention workers are likely to use terms such as "prevention of psychological distress," "contextual factors," "risk factors," and "research findings," religious workers may use terms such as "faith," "hope," "love," "spirituality," and "wholeness." Clearly, collaboration can only proceed to the extent that the two groups can clarify and understand each others' language.

A second manifestation of "cultural" difference is the disparity in ways of conceptualizing problems, goals, and intervention strategies. As noted above, our respondents' view of prevention is a global, promotion-based one, which differs markedly from the more specialized, prevention-oriented approach common among prevention workers. The empirical validity of this disparity notwithstanding, its perception by religious workers may contribute to a fear that seeking consultation from human services would invite them to "come in and take over." Our respondents were clear that in their view this is undesirable because it places the prerogatives and goals of religious personnel in jeopardy. The key point is that, from the religious perspective, consultation needs to support, but not supplant, the objectives and directives of the religious setting. That this may not always be the case, or that expectations run counter to it, are major reasons that collaborative efforts may fall short of potential.

A third possible obstacle, stemming from differences in the conceptions religious and nonreligious workers have of each other is that of stereotypes. Our respondents noted that in religious circles human service workers are often viewed as technical, narrow, and somewhat dogmatic adherents to their own particular theoretical perspective (e.g., behavioral, psychodynamic), often distinctly excluding religious values or spiritual life. The philosophical basis of behavioral psychology in logical positivism, for instance, was understood by one respondent as an essentially "valueless" perspective, inimical to the essence of religion and spiritual values. Interestingly, stereotypes of religious personnel on the part of human services workers were also discussed, for example, that religious personnel are concerned only with church growth and membership, are morally dogmatic, and/or hypocritical. As in the society at large, such stereotypes, to whatever extent they may characterize any given setting, interfere with understanding, tolerance, and cooperation on mutual goals. "Cross-cultural" dialogue is necessary to bridge differences in language, to explore and define common goals, and to correct the misconceptions and stereotypes.

We have attempted to describe religion and human services as representing different cultural contexts, and the real obstacles this poses to collaboration are not to be underestimated. Human services and religion, in many respects, have different networks and different social contacts which make it difficult for each to come to know and understand the other naturally. Constitutional "separation of church and state" and ethical sensitivity to intrusive practices often serve to further alienate the two. Our assertions here are grounded not in attempts to minimize these, but in efforts to recommend that we seek and support mechanisms to facilitate shared activities.

Based on our interviews, we believe there is strong reason for optimism about the prospects of enhancing religion-human services synergistic and collaborative efforts in prevention. For instance, that our respondents were already somewhat conversant in the languages of both religion and psychology (due in part to liberal arts education and/or graduate training in human services) clearly contradicts the notion that the outlook of religious workers is narrowly and exclusively confined to theology and religious concerns and conceptions. Even a greater number saw substantial areas of overlap in ultimate work goals, particularly in terms of a common focus on enhancing the well-being of individuals (cf. Borowitz, 1984). In addition, many of our respondents had already been engaged in efforts at professional liaison/networking in their own work with human service workers. We would also be remiss not to acknowledge that many human service and prevention workers recognize and value the role and importance of spiritual issues, and that there is a considerable history of trying to bridge the two domains in various contexts (for example, as in the work of Jung, Peck, Sanford, and Nouwen). As additional dialogue and mutual work projects develop within the prevention arena, it would appear plausible that misconceptions and stereotypes would recede, and be replaced by more complex, accurate understandings of the real similarities and differences between the human services and religious personnel.

SUMMARY AND IMPLICATIONS

Religious values and perspectives are clearly complex and influence individuals in manifold ways. In this chapter, based on interviews with prominent religious professionals, we have sought to articulate ideas concerning the links between religion and prevention, from the religious perspective. Our efforts were explicitly exploratory. Our interviews spawned a number of ideas which are not prominent in the religion and prevention literature to date: (1) prevention, as understood in the human services, is not an explicit goal for religious workers; (2) the work of religion is probably better viewed as promotion rather than prevention — i.e., the goal is to enhance the well-being of others, rather than to prevent specific disorders or problems; (3) religion's holistic view of people and problems results in an emphasis on enhancing holism and balance (i.e., among the material, psychological, social and spiritual elements of life) as central to promotion; and (4) at the same time, the holistic world view emphasizes many points of entry, and many pathways or methods of helping, for specific individuals with specific needs and in specific contexts.

Given the exploratory nature of this work, several caveats are in order. The views and practices of the small, select sample of workers we spoke with may not be generally representative of religion. For instance, we chose to talk with individuals in leadership positions known to be articulate and effective; as a result, we likely are presenting a view of religion at its best. Future research is necessary to ascertain the extent to which the average religious worker, even those working with such leaders, differs from those we interviewed. Furthermore, our efforts necessarily began with a small number of interviews within a limited denominational range; those from other denominations, or other religions, may differ. For instance, consistent with Spilka and Bridges (in press) we would expect that workers from the Christian fundamentalist sector of religion would differ in at least some important regards (e.g., more emphasis on the afterlife than on change in the present). Finally, we have attempted to present a model of prevention as articulated by the religious worker; we are aware, however, that in the religious as in other human enterprises there likely exists some degree of disparity between ideals and everyday practice.

While best viewed as tentative and in need of empirical examination in future research, the conclusions drawn from our interviews nonetheless appear to us to have important implications for both religious and human services workers. For example, it is clear that there is much each can learn from the other, in terms of conceptual philosophies, strategies for prevention work, and specific tactics. We hope that increased research, especially of a collaborative nature, and increased dialogue, will contribute to this mutual learning. Generally speaking, research (and dialogue) might focus on the interrelationships among two or more of the following: dimensions of religious and human services world view, intervention goals and strategy, openness to collaboration, and the nature and extent of religious influence on individuals.

Furthermore, it is clear that collaboration in the realm of action is desirable and will likely prove mutually beneficial for both religion and human services/prevention, as well as for the larger society. However, both religious and human service workers will need to be aware of those situations in which collaboration may not be a good idea — e.g., when there does not exist at least some overlap or convergence among goals, perspectives, strategies, and/or tactics. Productive collaboration, we believe, is possible in many cases, and will best be built upon a realistic, complex understanding of similarities and differences in perspective between the religious and human services domains. We hope that our work represents a step in the direction of such understanding and collaboration.

REFERENCES

Albee, G. W. (1982). Preventing psychopathology and promoting human potential. *American Psychologist, 37*, 1043-1050.

Borowitz, E. B. (1984). Explorations and responses: Religious values in a secular society. *Journal of Ecumenical Studies, 21*, 536-548.

Coughlin, B. J. (1965). *Church and state in social welfare.* NY: Columbia University Press.

Cowen, E. (1983). Primary prevention in mental health: Past, present, and future. In R. D. Felner, L. A. Jason, J. N. Moritsugu, & S. Farber (Eds.), *Preventive Psychology.* NY: Pergamon.

Duchrow, U. (1984). Struggling for justice and human dignity. *The Ecumenical Review, 36*, 50-56.

Heifetz, L.J. (1987). Integrating religious and secular perspectives in the design and delivery of disability services. *Mental Retardation, 6*, 127-131.

Magee, J. B. (1967). *Religion and modern man, a study of the religious meaning of being human.* NY: Harper and Row.

Martin, S. P. (1990). Is Catholic education providing something that public schools cannot? *America, May 26,* 520-522.

Maton, K. I., & Pargament, K. I. (1987). The roles of religion in prevention and promotion. In L. A. Jason, R. E. Hess, R. D. Felner, & J. N. Moritsugu (Eds.), *Prevention: Toward an interdisciplinary approach.* NY: The Haworth Press, Inc.

Moore, T. (this volume). The African American church: A source of empowerment, mutual help, and social change, pp. 147-167.

Sharpe, E. J. (1983). *Understanding religion.* NY: St. Martin's Press.

Spilka, B., & Bridges, R. A. (in press). Religious perspectives on prevention: The role of theology. In K. I. Pargament & K. I. Maton (Eds.), *Religion and prevention in mental health: Conceptual and empirical foundations.* NY: The Haworth Press, Inc.

Whitfield, C. L. (1985). *Alcoholism, attachments, and spirituality.* East Rutherford, NJ: Thomas W. Perrin.

Healing and Empowering
Through Community Narrative

Julian Rappaport

University of Illinois at Urbana-Champaign

Ronald Simkins

New Covenant Fellowship
Champaign, Illinois

SUMMARY. Religious and mental health organizations share a number of common goals, including an interest in prevention of future problems in living. Community narratives — the telling of stories — is one method used by religious communities to accomplish some of their goals, including public education, healing and empowerment. Narratives are increasingly recognized by cognitive psychologists, mental health professionals and theologians as powerful tools for both learning and self-understanding. Many of the assumptions of preventive psychology and empowerment, including beliefs concerning the competence of individuals, the utility of self help groups and the power of community healing, are consistent with beliefs about the healing power of communities prominent in Judeo-Christian religious narratives. These narratives, when believed, incorporated into personal stories, and acted upon, serve as a counter to the tendency of medical and mental health stories to isolate people and force reliance on scarce resources and inaccessible expertise. Several of these narratives, concerned with the value of every individual, the power of people in a community to care for one another, attributes of self, of God, of hope and of history are de-

---

Biblical quotations throughout this paper are either brief paraphrases or from the *New International Version* (1978) Grand Rapids, MI: Zondervan.

Reprints may be requested from Julian Rappaport, Department of Psychology, University of Illinois at Urbana-Champaign, 603 E. Daniel Street, Champaign, IL 61820, or Ronald Simkins, New Covenant Fellowship, 507 W. Nevada Street, Urbana, IL 61801.

215

scribed, and their functions illustrated in the context of a particular congregational community.

Stories are the style and substance of life. They fashion and fill existence . . . (However) If without stories we live not, stories live not without us.

— Phyllis Tribble (1984)

The general point of this essay is to bring to the attention of those interested in prevention of problems in living the power of community narratives — the telling of shared stories. We make three specific observations:

1. Religious and mental health institutions hold in common the social task of assisting people to live "properly." Despite other differences, including language, there is a certain degree of similarity in how these two kinds of organizations pursue their task, including an interest in healing of emotional hurts, promotion of particular lifestyles and prevention of future problems in living.
2. Many of the assumptions of preventive psychology and empowerment, including beliefs concerning self and community healing, are consistent with beliefs about the competence of individuals and the healing power of communities prominent in Judeo-Christian religious traditions. These beliefs lend themselves well to communication through narratives. Ironically, given that medicine, science and technology were historical liberators from superstition and authoritarian control imposed by traditional religion, religious stories are today a challenge to current medical-technical stories that tend to isolate people and force a reliance on scarce resources and inaccessible expertise.
3. Community narrative — the telling and retelling of shared stories — is here illustrated in the context of a particular congregational community.

The Social Tasks of Psychology and Religion

It is no stretch of the imagination to suggest that in our society social scientists and helping professionals are, sociologically speaking, the functional equivalent of theologians, priests and ministers with respect to role relationships. Historically and contemporaneously, both kinds of professionals are called upon to find answers to the questions every generation asks: Who am I? Am I living properly? Who am I in relation to others? Who am I in relation to transcendental objects—the past, the future, the universe, God? (see for example, Sarbin, 1970). While those who work within a religious framework are more likely to use words that imply moral choices, such as "character," and those who work within a secular framework are more likely to prefer words with a medical sound, such as "healthy lifestyle," the similarities are at least as striking as the differences.

The aim of a preventive psychology of mental health and human services is to reduce the likelihood that the difficulties of life will lead to future problems in living so serious as to become debilitating. It is also possible to frame the activities of prevention in more positive terms, such as the promotion of health and well being (Dunst, Trivette, & Deal, in press) or empowerment (Rappaport, 1981, 1987). Preventionists generally adopt one of two strategies: person centered or system centered (Cowen, 1985). Person centered approaches are typically designed to reach "at risk" populations (those groups of people considered to be more likely than average to experience some difficulty) so as to provide them with an "inoculation" against some future predictable or unpredictable problem in living. Predictable problems in living include the developmental transitions of childhood through adult life and ageing, most of which can be expected to occur, within a given society, in a known time frame correlated with chronological age. Programs designed to teach parents or children interpersonal problem solving skills are an example of the sort of efforts in which preventionists engage (Shure & Spivack, 1988). In the religious community many Sunday school curricula and training seminaries are concerned with teaching children and adults similar skills, often through the telling of stories.

Unpredictable difficulties include death of a loved one, divorce, job loss, natural disasters and other such events. Various programs for prevention might generally fall under the rubric of "crisis intervention," wherein the mental health professional recognizes that during times of stress and heightened anxiety people are more amenable to change; if people can be helped to quickly and successfully handle a particular crisis they are more likely to do so in the future. Pastoral training has emphasized this same reality for decades, and such thinking is quite consistent with the framework developed in the New Testament's Book of James, where readers are encouraged to consider "trials as opportunities" for new learning (James 1:2-4).

System centered approaches include efforts to change existing social institutions and to create new settings that operate by different "rules of the game." For example, rather than providing individual counselling for adjudicated teens as a condition of probation, because contact with the legal system is believed to increase rather than decrease likelihood of future legal difficulties, one might develop alternatives that bypass adjudication and probation altogether by using nonprofessional or trained volunteers as advocates (Davidson & Redner, 1988). Many religiously founded organizations, such as the YMCA, have participated in such programs, often involving the use of community volunteers who assist young people to learn new ways to think about their lives (i.e., their personal stories). Programs such as the Peace Corps and Vista, that seek to assist in community development, a staple of preventive psychology, are based on a model developed in the Mennonite tradition of voluntary service in which a community is encouraged to think about itself in new ways. Similarly, the development of models of community care, in which congregations see themselves as part of a continuous history of supportive networks for members who are disabled or dependent, have been sponsored and disseminated by the Mennonite Central committee (Kingsly & Ruth-Heffelbower, 1987; Preheim-Bartel & Neufelt, 1986).

Another strategy for prevention is to develop settings, either within traditional social institutions or as alternatives to them, designed to facilitate the empowerment of people by means of citizen participation in the decisions and activities that affect their lives (Zimmerman & Rappaport, 1988). Self- and mutual-help organizations that operate for various groups of people outside of the established mental health system (Gartner & Riessman, 1979; Jacobs & Goodman, 1989; Powell, 1990), patient controlled alternatives to the mental health system (Chamberlin, 1978), as well as neighborhood associations (Wandersman & Florin, 1990) and community run alternative schools are all within the framework of a preventively oriented social policy. It has long been recognized by sociologists and theologians such as Lenski (1962) and Berger and Neuhaus (1977) that among the mediating structures between large and impersonal social institutions and individual lives, churches, synagogues and other such voluntary associations have great potential for the empowerment of people through direct participation in the creation of their own communal stories.

Finally, both mental health and religious organizations emphasize teaching and public education as major components of their programs for prevention of problems in living. Both seek to reach as many people as possible by means of outreach workers, educational materials and public presentations. Both assume that by providing information about how to think about one's self, one's community and one's place in the world, people will be better able to live their lives in positive ways. An important vehicle for communicating such ideas is the telling of shared community stories.

SOME BASIC ASSUMPTIONS WITH RESPECT TO HEALING

Mental health professionals concerned with prevention of problems in living, empowerment of communities and promotion of positive lifestyles necessarily make implicit assumptions about the competence of individuals and the power of communities with respect to healing. Such assumptions are also basic to many religious communities. In this context, the meaning of the term "healing" should not be understood to be limited to the repair of past hurts for weak people. Healing is something that everyone needs. It is not only for the weak. Rather, the assumption is that healing is a process that is proactive as well as reactive. Everyone who experiences healing is better equipped to enter into new life challenges. Thus, healing, prevention and empowerment are interwoven products of community beliefs, attitudes and behaviors that apply to the entire community.

The religious community we discuss in the last sections of this paper holds to the belief that every individual is gifted by God with both the power for self healing, and the ability to help others. In those beliefs there is considerable similarity to the views of people in the field of mental health who hold an empowerment framework. Both communities believe that these abilities do not depend on arcane knowledge, nor are they a scarce resource. Everyone has them. They are, as Katz (1982, 1984) has suggested about empowering community activities, and Riessman about mutual assistance (1985), regenerating and synergistic. Each individual can be both a giver and a receiver of help, and the more that help is given and received the more the community is energized (see also Maton, 1987).

This implies neither encouragement nor discouragement with regard to the use of traditional medical care. Rather, medical care is seen as one of a wide range of potential resources available to people. It is neither enemy nor savior. How to make intelligent use of it in the context of one's life, or as part of a self-developed "treatment package" combining traditional medicine and religious healing techniques (Cottingham, 1985; McGuire, 1983, 1988; Tournier, 1962), rather than in a passive acceptance of the medical establishment's "rules of the game," is seen as a more important question than whether or not to follow the doctors' advice. Thus, many of the community stories we discuss below are concerned with both the value of each person in her or his own right, and the power of people in the community to care for one another. It is no accident that much of the self-help movement, mediated through the success of Alcoholics Anonymous and its many variants of "twelve step programs," are directly traceable to Judeo-Christian religious narratives.

The belief that powerful forces for change are contained within ourselves, and that these forces can be released by a relationship with God, and with significant others in our communities, is a challenge to the hegemony of professionalism. The Enlightenment and the Reformation are often presented in historical studies as the liberation of modern men and women from the dominance of church professionals. This accurately describes one half of the historical process. The layperson was freed from clerical control and domination in politics, language, science, economics and education. The belief that the common person could and should be empowered in all of these domains was a strong force in the framing of Western modernity. However, we seem to be far less conscious of the other side of the historical process.

Throughout the Western World the dominance of the priest has been replaced by the hegemony of the secular professional. The promise of empowerment for the layperson has regressed rapidly with the rise of the professional-technical "expert." Unquestioned reliance on expertise ranges from the halls of government to the surgical floors of the local hospital. Legislators, physicians, psychologists and social workers often have more to say about how people live and when they die, than the people themselves. While many religious professionals—pastors, priests, and rabbis—may similarly and willingly accept being regarded by their congregants as "experts," it is now more likely for the power of laypersons to participate in the shaping of their own destiny to be usurped by government sanctioned science and technology. This has led at least one philosopher of science to suggest that the future of freedom no longer lies in the separation of Church and State, but rather in the separation of Science and State (Feyerbend, 1978).

Much of the way in which the sanctioned helping professions obtain their power is by means of faith in experts. Writers such as Frank (1973) and Cousins (1979, 1983) have made us aware of how much the effects of any treatment are dependent on faith in the healers and their techniques. The unintended negative effects of a medical system that removes much of the power of decision making from the person whose life is in question, and of a system that isolates people as individual cases to be handled by specialists without concern for other matters occurring in a person's life have been well described (Illich, 1976; Morgan, 1983). The language of mental health, borrowed from medicine, tends to reinforce the reliance on experts. What is needed is a language of empowerment that communicates the power of people to participate in their own healing and in the healing of others. Although there are a variety of such languages possible, the language and stories of religious communities can challenge the status quo. Ironically, given that the medical model helped to break down the power of superstition and entrenched authority with respect to problems in living by reconceptualizing them as illness, many of the beliefs of traditional religion are now a challenge to the current powers that be, which are largely medical or ancillary to medicine.

Once, a wide variety of medical cures were labeled "witchcraft," and thus demeaned, were able to be ignored. Under the present dominant way of thinking, a wide variety of cures, changes and improvements in people's lives that occur outside the sanctioned medical establishment are discounted as "placebos" or as "spontaneous remission," terms which are intended to demean the contribution to healing of anything outside the control of the designated experts (McGuire, 1983, 1988; Weick, 1983). Yet in the context of places such as self and mutual help organizations, and religious communities, the healing that is attained by faith in "a power greater than ourselves" (as many twelve step organizations put it) and by the power of mutual love (agape) as many religious settings describe it, is often acknowledged.

Community Narrative: A Vehicle for Empowerment

In recent years, those who study religious communities have increasingly been emphasizing the creative and sustaining role of narrative (Alter, 1981; Campbell & Moyers, 1988; Goldberg, 1985; Hauerwas, 1983; Josipovici, 1988; McClendon, 1986). The communal narrative and faith in that narrative may play a far deeper role in sustaining a community than dogma, ritual, or charismatic leadership. This is not only true in the faith communities of religion, but in other faith communities as well. Kuhn (1970) pointed out the importance of the paradigm of reality (a communal narrative) in the faith community of the natural sciences. Likewise, in the realm of political behavior one can make a case that the recent break up of the Soviet Union has far less to do with Western success or with Eastern deprivation than it does with the loss of faith in its story.

At the individual level, the psychiatrist, Robert Coles, (1989) has described what he terms "the call of stories," as a means to understand the self presentations of his clients, as well as of his students. Recently, some psychologists have suggested that study of "the storied nature of human conduct" (Sarbin, 1986; Vitz, 1990) is promising as a means to understanding people in context and the ways in which they learn and think. Much of the content of our most cherished beliefs about ourselves and our world are communicated in the narrative form.

The Judeo-Christian heritage has at its roots powerful narratives which when believed and acted upon by a community can have a significant impact on the lives of the members of the community. The faith of the community in a common narrative may serve as a vital source of healing and empowerment. Nevertheless, perhaps a few disclaimers are necessary before pursuing these issues further.

First, we are very aware of the damage that has been caused by some applications of the Judeo-Christian narrative. The Christian story was used to justify the Crusades and the Holocaust. It has also been used by Jim Jones to justify Jonestown and by Jim Bakker to justify siphoning off millions of dollars from the estates of the elderly. Community stories are being used by both Israelis and Palestinians to fan the fires of tension and alienation in the Middle East. Obviously, faith in the community story has not only the potential to unleash healing and empowerment, but also to unleash destruction and loss.

Similarly, anyone who has visited the mental hospitals and training schools, the prisons and the public schools of our urban inner cities, all of which were developed out of the best stories that the social science, medicine and educational establishment could muster—including stories about the low intelligence of racial and ethnic minorities, the need to confine people in mental hospitals for long periods of time, and the stories told of the "mental illness" of homosexuality and the weakness of women's character—will be at best humble about the value of the stories told by social and medical science. The point here is that the method of shared community narrative is a powerful one that can be used for good or ill. Therefore, it is important that the content of the narrative be examined.

Finally, although here we will use examples we have seen in the context of one particular religious community, this is not meant to suggest that similar things do not occur in other communities of faith, nor does it mean that positive outcomes cannot follow from the stories of those outside the community of faith.

We turn now to a description, in the context of one congregational community, of how a shared common narrative is used to communicate an understanding of self in relation to others, to God, to history, and to the future.

THE NARRATIVES OF A RELIGIOUS COMMUNITY

Context of Our Observations

While many traditional, denomination based religious congregations are quite "competent communities" for their membership (Johnson & Mullins, 1990), there are also a wide variety of independent, nondenominational religious organizations that form and develop in local communities where the leadership and the internal operations emerge from and are governed entirely by the members themselves. They hold no formal connections to any national organization. The descriptions and examples used in this essay are largely from one such setting. The authors have been a part of both the original and the more recently developed setting discussed below since their founding over fifteen years ago.

The setting from which our examples are taken is solidly within the Judeo-Christian tradition, and its values, beliefs and attitudes are similar to other organizations within that tradition. However, the exact combination of beliefs and practices, particularly how they are applied, is uniquely determined by the membership. The congregation is entirely responsible, by means of voluntary contributions, for its own financial needs, including the expenditure of 25% of its budget for programs of assistance to persons and organizations that seek to assist economically and socially needy people. There is no permanent building, and meeting space is rented as needed in various locations that may change from year to year. The philosophy has been self described as a "tent community," in which members do not wish to tie up large sums of money and resources in order to maintain a building. The community recently committed itself to a policy of not renting space unless it is accessible to its physically disabled membership. The community is most recently attending to issues of inclusive language, and the roles of women in the church, attempting to reconcile traditional biblical language with current sensitivities to the lives of women.

This congregation, known as New Covenant of Champaign, Illinois, was founded in 1984 when, primarily because of a desire to keep the size of the community small enough to permit a sense of intimacy and shared interpersonal relationships, a group of about 60 adults and children began to meet separate from the founding organization which itself had formed in 1975. The original organization, which had grown to some 225 members and 100 children, has already been described in some detail with respect to basic beliefs, economic and social diversity of members, personal goals, organizational structure, sense of community and strategies for caring and sharing material and interpersonal resources (Maton, 1987;

Maton & Pargament, 1987; Maton & Rappaport, 1984). The setting that serves as a context for the observations reported here is quite similar in its demographics, and in its beliefs and intentions, to the community described in those reports. Here we are less concerned with describing the individual people or organizational structure than with describing certain of its conceptual elements as expressed in the community narratives—the ways in which the members of the setting collectively think about themselves and communicate those thoughts within the larger context of Biblical narratives—which we suggest are consistent with many of the assumptions of a psychology of prevention, empowerment and a promotion of positive lifestyles, as well as with a reading of the biblical texts.

It is, however, probably useful to know three things about this setting:

1. The basic vehicle for communication is an organizational structure that involves weekly worship services including teaching, prayer and singing, as well as small group meetings in the homes of individual members. Many members participate in a variety of outreach activities designed to be helpful to nonmembers. Each of these settings provide a regularized context for telling both community stories and personal stories.
2. The explicit goals of the settings are to create an "extended family" of people who will share their lives with one another in the context of developing their relationship with a God who is believed to be active and loving.
3. The membership is quite diverse in ethnic background, previous religious affiliation and socioeconomic status; yet they share a faith in a common set of community narratives.

The Community Stories

In using the term "community narrative," we are, for the purposes of this essay, using an inclusive definition. One could limit use of the term to an explicit story with a beginning, a middle, and an end, as well as a specific set of characters. However, a community story may also involve a set of themes, beliefs and ideas about past and present members of the community. Here we are using the term narrative in both its specific and its general sense. We are also using the term to describe both the focal community narrative and the older and larger narratives of Judeo-Christian history from which the local story flows.

The power of these stories lies in their repetition, internalization and enactment. To the extent that community stories become an adopted and conscious part of the story one tells about one's self, it may be understood to have become internalized. The power of narrative thinking and episodic memory has been discussed by cognitive psychologists such as Bruner (1986), and Tulving (1983). Sarbin (1986, p. 9) has argued that it is qualitatively different from propositional thinking, and in an extension of his earlier work on role theory (Sarbin & Allen, 1968) suggests that narrative is "an organizing principle for human action." Vitz (1990) has recently applied these observations to a discussion of moral development. In the theological realm similar insights are being expressed. McClendon (1986) argues that theological ethics are best understood in their narrative context. Hauerwas (1983) maintains that not only ethics, but community itself is an expression of narrative. Josipovici (1988) and Goldberg (1985) argue that narrative is more basic to Judeo-Christian history than any other factor.

In some respects the application of stories to one's life might be thought of as similar to the way cognitive therapists help people to adopt new ways to "talk to themselves" about their own life. In any case, one of the common methods that people in both religious communities and mutual help organizations use to understand their life is to tell each other their personal story. In what is sometimes referred to as "testimony," people have the opportunity to explain how they came to their current self-understanding. The community stories described below, made available by repetitive telling and retelling in a variety of contexts, are often seen to emerge as a part of the personal stories told by individual members. We think this is an indication of their power.

Here we are concerned with *community* narratives, that is, those that are derived from the community's historical sense of itself. They become personal when they are adopted by an individual, but the source is in the common experience of the historical community. We are not concerned here with matters of cognitive psychology, such as how and in what form these stories are learned and "stored," although that may be an interesting topic for research. Although we will claim to have seen the personal incorporation of the community narrative to have an impact on the lives of many people, our intention below is not to "prove the effectiveness," of those stories, but rather to describe some of them and the challenges they present to a community that adopts these narratives as their own. Finally, because re-telling stories takes a great amount of space, we will often need to summarize as abstract themes, Biblical themes that would be related in the community in the form of both historical and personal stories.

You are lovable and you are valuable. The Judeo-Christian paradigm of reality contains several narratives emphasizing the claim that God loves and values human beings. These stories are about people who are believed to be both real historical figures and members of the community. Whether one focuses upon the creation account (male and female in the image of God), or the choosing of Israel (not because of your productivity, but because I love you), or the birth of Jesus (God loves humans enough to choose to be present with us uniquely in our humanity), or the death and resurrection of Jesus (One of us humans, who experiences all human suffering, even death, is crowned with the glory and honor of God), or the evangelist Paul's description of his own life story, each narrative is a claim that every human is loved and valued (Genesis 1:26-27; Deuteronomy 7:7-9; Matthew 1:22-23; Hebrews 2:5-18; II Corinthians 4:6-14).

When one hears the story of Exodus told over and over again, and believes that in bringing Israel out of Egypt, God was also preparing for one's own future, a sense of being valued is established. In the telling of the exodus, the writer emphasizes that God did this for the current listener, and that each person is to consider themselves personally taken out of slavery. When one believes that God would choose to humanize himself in a son who would rather die than lose his relationship with me, a sense of value is established.

For children of the community, such stories can be a powerful force for prevention of anxiety and self doubt. Many will use the experiences of biblical figures to describe and make sense of their own life experiences. As adults, many people when asked to "tell their story" will begin by saying how hurt they had been by their parents, and conclude by speaking of the forgiveness they are now able to both feel and offer because of their current experience of being loved. This is often expressed in ways that are derived from the stories referred to above. Some will say that God has chosen them, despite their lack of worldly accomplishments. Others will describe the events of their own life as a kind of death and resurrection.

This emphasis on each person's value leading to a responsibility to care for others is concisely expressed in the phrase "Love God and love your neighbor as yourself" (Mark 12:29-31, summarizing the Torah of Moses). Its meaning is explicated in some detail by Jesus, who uses narrative to illustrate the point in the story of the "good Samaritan." He tells a story of a man who is beaten and left for dead. The man is not valued by the religious professionals, his supposed neighbors, but is cared for by a hated foreigner — the good Samaritan. The listener is at first focused on a mistreated member of the in-group, but is suddenly confronted with the goodness of a hated outsider who is sensitive enough to value others. The audience is asked, "So who do you think was a neighbor to this man?" (Luke 10:25-37). The challenge to the community is to believe and practice this narrative upon which the community is based. It is not an easy story to live. Therefore, it usually will not be practiced unless the community constantly retells the story and challenges itself to act accordingly.

We have seen this potential for healing and empowerment actualized in various ways. People who have never felt loved before, or have never experienced the intimacy of hugs and pats on the back, begin to believe that they may be lovable. Closedness and fear can begin to be replaced by openness and trust. The process and the testing of the reality are often very similar to those experienced in families adopting children. But slowly, the identity as son or daughter of God in a supportive community can begin to supersede the identity as an unloved and unlovable son or daughter. This empowers one as a potential giver of love and value.

You are a gift. Perhaps among the most powerful of the parables in the community narrative is the one told in Paul's first letter to the Corinthians. Here he likens the community of believers to a human body, made of many parts, all necessary, all important to a fully functioning life. He raises a series of rhetorical questions in which he asks what would happen if all the body parts were the same. For example, "what if the ear would say 'because I am not an eye, I do not belong to the body?'" "If the whole body were an eye, where would the sense of hearing be?" Moreover, he asserts, "the head cannot say to the feet, I don't need you" (I Corinthians 12:15-21).

In New Covenant there are people who have come to know themselves as a gift to the community who never felt like a gift at any other time in their lives. People who have heretofore seen their troubles as only burdens come to value their own "experiential knowledge" (Borkman, 1990) as a source of help for others. Some know that their prayers are a gift which the rest of the community needs and desires. They can tell Biblical narratives that assure them that sometimes they are a gift that outweighs that of the best speaker or singer. Some likewise know that their desire to care and understand is deeply appreciated. Some have learned that their love for children is crucial to the life of this community and can repeat Biblical narratives to illustrate this reality. Some have learned that their intuitive insights into the mixed motives of the people around them need not any longer be a confusing curse requiring a diagnosis, but can actually be a gift empowered with love—the stories of the prophets are also their stories. A sense of humor, a simple honesty, a persistent cynicism, or an almost naive optimism, can change from a trait that has haunted one all of one's life, to an appreciated gift in a community that has "seen it before" in its historical narratives. A community that believes that this is both God's ultimate nature and ours is consistent with the beliefs of a prevention oriented psychology that emphasizes strengths rather than deficits as the best way to be helpful to people (Saleeby, in press). The challenge for a community attempting to live this narrative of "gifts" is to honestly learn to value the unique potentials of each person, rather than to experience them as deficits which are feared and only tolerated.

We are all broken and all capable of being healed. A much maligned part of the Judeo-Christian narrative is the story of reality often referred to as "the fall" or as "sinful human nature." We would unhesitatingly agree that this narrative has been applied and practiced in some extremely destructive ways, but would maintain that it need not be so (Mowrer, 1961; Mowrer & Vattano, 1976). In fact, there is something refreshing and powerful in the Biblical narratives of human life. We are presented with men and women who are in genuine relationships with God, but who are also filled with foibles, weaknesses, false starts, and the need for new starts. The story of King David's life (I Samuel 16-II Samuel 24; Psalms. 32, 51) is but one example of a narrative that captures an important element of the shared community story. The narratives claim that even the healers and the leaders are wounded and broken people. No one is "together" (the exception in the Christian scriptures is Jesus, who nevertheless experiences brokenness). However, together we can all experience, from God and from each other, the process of healing. God is capable of healing and saving everything that makes us human (Psalm 8 and I Thessalonians 5:23-24).

Since all of us know privately that we are falling short of our human potential, public acknowledgement that this is inherent in the story of all human beings (including our "heros") makes it possible for people to incorporate that understanding into their own personal stories, without fear of condemnation. One does not need to be ashamed of one's particular weakness, nor to hide it, since we are all just under our surface appearances, more alike than not. The community to which one belongs is a community in which all of the healers are wounded healers. Nobody stands before God as better off or worse off than anyone else. All are dependent upon God's love, mercy and grace. The community is not divided into "pitiful victims" and "together helpers." Life is wasted when one insists either upon remaining a passive victim or being better than others.

The shared belief in the larger narrative which illustrates that all are broken and that everyone can experience healing, and be empowered to help others, has provided an atmosphere in which many hidden fears have been able to be shared as people learn to express their own stories. This is particularly true in the small group settings. Those addicted to alcohol and drugs have been able to say so and ask for prayer and support. Those who were sexually abused through incestuous relationships or rapes have been able to talk about this without feeling as if they are somehow more unacceptable than everyone else. Interestingly, we were hearing an amazingly large number of reports of sexual abuse and incest, several years before it became so public in popular counselling, and before individual people knew of anyone else who had ever acknowledged having this happen to them.

The variety of "secrets" that people have learned to talk about with others in this community covers most of the issues that one is likely to hear as a helping professional. Personal stories concerning homosexual orientation or behaviors, sharing concerning the difficulty of being a parent, sharing concerning one's sense of being totally unacceptable to the opposite sex, sharing concerning anger toward one's parents or someone else in the community has all been done in an atmosphere in which everyone is acknowledged to be valuable, everyone is known to be broken, and everyone has the potential to experience some healing. Many small group discussions have begun with the words, "I have never told anyone this before."

God as real, active, responsible and accessible. The stories of the Judeo-Christian Scriptures involve a community narrative about God as well as a narrative about the members. The narrative claims that God is far beyond the ability of humans to control or fully understand. Yet, the narrative also claims that God is near and lovingly engages humans in the reality of space and time; that God does things in this space and time continuum which he has created; that God takes responsibility for being God (humans do not need to create God nor to prop up God's existence — "I am who I will be"); and that God chooses to genuinely be with people, though much of God is far beyond them (some paradigm passages include Isaiah 40-53; Exodus 1-15; Psalm 8; Genesis 1-3). This description of what God is like is presented through the telling of stories about how God has interacted with people throughout history.

Since much of the stress of human life flows from attempts to understand, describe, predict and control a physical and psychological universe that is far beyond one's abilities, this narrative offers peace, but not passivity. Believers in the community narrative are free to be active, adventuresome, growing children in a reality far beyond one's wildest dreams, but need not individually nor corporately pretend to be in control. Everything does not depend upon individuals, nor the community, nor national security. One need not "keep everything under control" (see, for example, Pargament et al., 1987). There is someone to turn to who stands behind life and above history; and yet who delights in participating in this venture with people. The fact that neither I as an individual, nor we as a community, have a given answer to some important question or hurt, is an adventure toward healing and empowerment, not a dead end. Often, shared personal stories end with, "I can't wait to see what God will lead me into next."

In New Covenant we have seen several people who were beginning to take refuge in mental hospitals allowed to establish firm roots in reality as a part of the congregational community. This has occurred through participation in the community's practice of learning to depend upon God in the real world of space and time events. It involves both accepting responsibility and giving it up. For the many people in the community who are willing to be supportive friends and participants in a network of individuals willing to provide both social and material support, this narrative of a God who is both personal and "in charge" serves as a positive story through which to reach people with a history of serious emotional difficulties. Not only are several of these people living sanely in the world of relationships and work, but they are productively caring for others as well.

Self-help organizations such as Alcoholics Anonymous and mutual help organizations for former mental patients, such as GROW (Salem, Seidman, & Rappaport, 1988), have taken this part of the Biblical Narrative and reapplied it with positive results in healing and empowerment that generally outstrip those of the most elaborate hospitals and highly paid therapists. Both of these organizations have emphasized "the great paradox" that by giving up the desire to control one's life, one is more likely to find it (Luke 9:24). In some respects, these and other similar organizations may have believed and practiced the narrative borrowed from the Judeo-Christian community with a reality and a genuineness that may not be present in some churches.

God wastes nothing in moving toward the goal of building character. Perhaps a summary of the most central narrative in the Judeo-Christian story is this: no situation can stop God from making those who love and trust God more and more the people of God. This claim is at the heart of both the Exodus-Torah story and the cross-resurrection story. This narrative claims that both the individual and the corporate community have ultimate historical meaning. The individual is becoming more fully a son or daughter of God. The community is becoming the future people of God who will live with God forever as a new society filled with love, peace, creativity, trust, and joy. Although every valuable human being is broken and is constantly falling short of being in the image of God, every human can become more like God. Although the community of God's people has a very checkered history, that history is part of God's process of building a society in which humanity reaches its fulfillment. No evil, no brokenness, and no amount of injustice and suffering can ultimately thwart God's goal of making humans into his image (Psalm 8, Isaiah 61-62; Hebrews 11:13-16; Revelation 21:1-8; and Romans 8:26-39). For this reason, it is common for people in small group meetings to spend a good deal of time developing personal stories of how God refused to waste even the worst of life's difficulties.

The power of this narrative in the modern Jewish Community can be seen in the response of many Jewish people to the horror of the Holocaust. Instead of defeat and despair, we saw a community with perhaps the clearest dedication to civil and human rights since the Hebrew prophets of the 8th through 5th centuries B.C. What might well have ended the viability of the Jewish Culture instead became a new chapter in an age old narrative. It can be argued that this empowerment could only have occurred among a people who had been telling and living such stories for centuries.

When a community believes that nothing need be wasted, there is no room for one of the most destructive and disempowering of human beliefs—"We are (I am) just a victim." This paralyzing paradigm is replaced by the healing and empowering knowledge that no matter how bad things are, if I engage the situation fully and in faith, God will not let it be wasted. When a community insists upon caring and sympathy, but rejects the paralysis of despair and determinism, even the worst of situations has an aspect of expectation and adventure.

This narrative also maintains that one is always in process, and is always contributing to the process of God's community. On the one hand, this means that no one time event is going to solve everything; on the other hand, it means that no single failure or setback is going to ruin everything. Since most human hurts and problems have to be dealt with over and over again, there is tremendous potential for empowerment in believing this narrative. Perfectionism and despair, as well as self-satisfaction and laziness, are exchanged for an "in-process" view of reality. The job of the community is to applaud each new step in the process. Like the fans applaud the efforts of an athlete, or the parents applaud the first wobbly steps of their child, the community applauds each attempt to go forward; rather than to "boo" every mistake. The point is not to deny the missed shots, nor the falls after two wobbly steps; but to reinforce the growth process which God has guaranteed.

You belong to a historical community. The Judeo-Christian narratives emphasize the importance of belonging. Not only Abraham and Sarah, but their descendants are chosen with them. Not only the Jews of Moses' time, but every succeeding generation is to identify themselves as those who can say, "We were brought out of Egypt." Not only Jesus, but those who believe in him are "crucified with Christ, and raised with Christ." These are not primarily mystical claims, they are claims of community and relationship. They are claims that emphasize belonging to an historical community with deep and meaningful roots.

Particularly in Western culture where both the extended family and the small town have broken down as communities to which one can "belong," this gift of roots can provide spiritual and psychological healing and empowerment. Knowing that one is a part of something that transcends just the existential moment of the individual is important to a sense of identity and value. The powerful potential for healing and empowerment that Alex Haley (1973) captured for the African American community in *Roots* is very much a part of the biblical narratives. Both Jews and Christians claim to be "sons and daughters of Abraham and Sarah." The community that flows from this identification with the same roots has tremendous potential for overcoming much of the isolation, separation, and loneliness of the rootless world of modernity.

It is not unusual to have someone in one of the small support groups, or in a Sunday morning worship time, say, "You are my family," or "You are the nearest to family I have ever known." This is an acknowledgment of experiencing belonging or rootedness. With this experience comes a sense of identity, of being able to contribute, of being able to trust more, and of having a place in the world.

Both Christians and Jews have misused this gift of roots at times. Particularly noticeable is the tendency to become arrogant and exclusive in applications of this gift. It is easy while attempting to emphasize the shared roots to do so in a manner that demeans those "who do not belong." In this case, the sense of belonging becomes also the excuse for excluding and disliking. A healing sense of community roots is one that not only empowers one to love those with whom one shares roots, but frees one to love those who do not share these roots as well. Indeed, there is at least some empirical evidence that those who attend a church with a strong belief in this narrative may actually be more open to new ideas and tolerant of the views of others than those who attend churches with a less clear story (Pargament et al., 1987). Again, the story of the good Samaritan comes to mind (Luke 10:25 ff). Here, the narrative to be incorporated into one's own story is in response to the question asked of Jesus, "Who is my neighbor?" The answer is, "Everyone." For those who believe in this narrative the challenge is great, but the potential for building a community that serves as a setting for healing, prevention and empowerment is also great.

CONCLUSION

The stories that communities tell about themselves, their history, and their collective identity are powerful tools for communication among the members. The narratives of the Judeo-Christian tradition, some of which are described in this paper, are based on a set of assumptions about healing and community relationships that are in many respects similar to those of an empowerment and prevention oriented psychology, even though they are expressed in a different language. Given the shared social tasks of religious and mental health institutions, understanding their respective community narratives — and how they affect those who believe in them — is a topic worthy of continued serious study. In addition, the study of other communities — secular as well as religious — may benefit from a description of their shared narratives in order to appreciate the self-understanding of community members. To the extent that we are able to describe a variety of community narratives interventionists may be in a better position to borrow and apply ideas from one setting to another, and to appreciate the underlying assumptions of the contexts in which we work.

REFERENCES

Alter, R. (1981). *The art of biblical narrative*. Harper-Colophon Books.

Berger, P. L., & Neuhaus, R. J. (1977). *To empower people: The role of mediating structures in public policy*. Washington, DC: American Enterprise Institute for Public Policy Research.

Borkman, T. J. (1990). Experiential, professional, and lay frames of reference. In T. J. Powell (Ed.), *Working with self-help.* (pp. 3-30). Silver Spring: NASW Press.

Bruner, J. (1986). *Actual minds, possible worlds*. Cambridge, MA: Harvard University Press.

Campbell, J., & Moyers, W. (1988). *The power of myth*. New York: Doubleday.

Chamberlin, J. (1978). *On our own: Patient controlled alternatives to the mental health system*. New York: McGraw-Hill.

Coles, R. (1989). *The call of stories: Teaching and the moral imagination*. Boston: Houghton Mifflin.

Cottingham, J. T. (1985). *Healing through touch: A history and a review of the physiological evidence*. Boulder, CO: Rolf Institute.

Cousins, N. (1979). Anatomy of an illness (As perceived by the patient) — *Reflections on healing and regeneration*. New York: W. W. Norton.

Cousins, N. (1983). *The healing heart*. New York: Norton.

Cowen, E. L. (1985). Person-centered approaches to primary prevention in mental health: Situation-focused and competence-enhancement. *American Journal of Community Psychology, 13*, 31-48.

Davidson, W. S., & Redner, R. (1988). The prevention of juvenile delinquency: Diversion from the juvenile justice system. In R. H. Price, E. L. Cowen, R. P. Lorion, & J. Ramos-McKay (Eds.), *Fourteen ounces of prevention: A casebook for practitioners* (pp. 123-137). Washington, DC: American Psychological Association.

Dunst, C. J., Trivette, C. M., & Thompson, R. B. (In press). Supporting and strengthening family functioning: Toward a congruence between principles and practice. *Prevention in Human Services*.

Feyerabend, P. (1978). *Science in a free society*. London: NLB.

Frank, J. (1973). *Persuasion and healing* (Rev. ed.). Baltimore: Johns Hopkins University Press.

Gartner, A., & Riessman, F. (1979). *Self-help in the human services*. San Francisco: Jossey-Bass.

Goldberg, M. (1985). *Jews and Christians: Getting our stories straight*. Abingdon Press.

Haley, A. (1973). *Roots*. Garden City: Doubleday.

Hauerwas, S. (1983). *The peaceable kingdom*. South Bend: Notre Dame Press.

Illich, I. (1976). *Medical nemesis: The expropriation of health*. New York: Pantheon.

Jacobs, M. K., & Goodman, G. (1989). Psychology and self-help groups: Predictions on a partnership. *American Psychologist, 44*, 536-545.

Johnson, M. A., & Mullins, P. (1990). Community competence in religious congregations. *American Journal of Community Psychology, 18*, 259-280.

Josipovici, G. (1988). *The book of God*. Yale University Press.

Katz, R. F. (1982). *Boiling energy: Community healing among the Kalahari Kung*. Cambridge, MA: Harvard University Press.

Katz, R. F. (1984). Empowerment and synergy: Expanding the community's healing resources. *Prevention in Human Services, 3*, 201-226.

Kingsly, M. L., & Ruth-Heffelbower, D. (1987). *After we're gone: Estate and life planning for a disabled person's family: A Christian perspective*. Akron, PA: Mennonite Central Committee.

Kuhn, T. S. (1970). *The structure of scientific revolutions* (2nd ed.). Chicago: University of Chicago Press.

Lenski, L. (1962). *The religious factor: A sociologist's inquiry.* Garden City: Anchor Books.

Maton, K. I. (1987). Patterns and psychological correlates of material support within a religious setting. *American Journal of Community Psychology, 15,* 185-208.

Maton, K. I., & Pargament, K. I. (1987). Roles of religion in prevention and promotion. In L. A. Jason, R. D. Felner, R. Hess, & J. N. Moritsugu (Eds.), *Prevention: Toward a multidisciplinary approach* (pp. 161-206). New York: The Haworth Press, Inc.

Maton, K., & Rappaport, J. (1984). Empowerment in a religious setting: A multi-variate investigation. *Prevention in Human Services, 3,* 37-72.

McClendon, J., Jr. (1986). *Systematic theology: Ethics.* Nashville: Abingdon Press.

McGuire, M. B. (1983). Words of power: Personal empowerment and healing. *Culture, medicine, and psychiatry, 7,* 221-240.

McGuire, M. B. (1988). *Ritual healing in suburban America.* New Brunswick: Rutgers University Press.

Morgan, R. F. (Ed.). (1983). *The iatrogenics handbook.* Toronto: IPI Publishing Ltd.

Mowrer, O. H. (1961). *The crisis in psychiatry and religion.* New York: Van Nostrand.

Mowrer, O. H., & Vattano, A. J. (1976). Integrity groups: A context for growth in honesty, responsibility, and involvement. *Journal of Applied Behavioral Science, 12,* 419-431.

Pargament, K., Echemendia, R. J., Johnson, S., Cook, P., McGrath, C., Meyers, J. G., & Branneck, M. (1987). The conservative church: Psychosocial advantages and disadvantages. *American Journal of Community Psychology, 15,* 269-286.

Powell, T. J. (Ed.). (1990). *Working with self-help.* Silver Spring: NASW Press.

Preheim-Bartel, D. A., & Neufelt, A. H. (1986). *Supportive care in the congregation.* Acron, PA: Mennonite Central Committee.

Rappaport, J. (1981). In praise of paradox: A social policy of empowerment over prevention. *American Journal of Community Psychology, 9,* 1-25.

Rappaport, J. (1987). Terms of empowerment/exemplars of prevention: Toward a theory for community psychology. *American Journal of Community Psychology, 15,* 117-148.

Riessman, F. (1985). New dimensions in self-help. *Social Policy, 15,* 2-4.

Rosenthal, R., & Jacobson, L. (1968). *Pygmalion in the classroom: Teacher expectation and pupil's intellectual development.* New York: Holt, Rinehart, & Winston.

Saleeby, D. (Ed.). (In press). *The strengths perspective in social work practice: Power in the people.* White Plains, NY: Longman.

Salem, D. A., Seidman, E., & Rappaport, J. (1988). Community treatment for the mentally ill: The promise of mutual help organizations. *Social Work, 33,* 403-408.

Sarbin, T. R. (1970). A role theory perspective for community psychology: The structure of social identify. In D. Adelson & B. L. Kalis (Eds.), *Community psychology and mental health: Perspectives and challenges.* Scranton, PA: Chandler.

Sarbin, T. R. (Ed.). (1986). *Narrative psychology: The storied nature of human conduct.* New York: Praeger.

Sarbin, T. R., & Allen, V. L. (1968). Role theory. In G. Lindzey & J. E. Aaronson (Eds.), *Handbook of Social Psychology* (Rev. ed.). Volume I. Reading, MA: Addison-Wesley.

Shure, M. B., & Spivack, G. (1988). Interpersonal cognitive problem solving. In R. H. Price, E. L. Cowen, R. P. Lorion, & J. Ramos-McKay (Eds.), *Fourteen ounces of prevention: A casebook for practitioners* (pp. 69-82). Washington, DC: American Psychological Association.

Tournier, P. (1962). *Escape from loneliness.* Westminster Press.

Tribble, P. (1984). *Texts of terror.* Philadelphia: Fortress Press.

Tulving, E. (1983). *Elements of episodic memory.* New York: Oxford University Press.

Vitz, P. C. (1990). The use of stories in moral development. *American Psychologist, 45,* 709-720.

Wandersman, A., & Florin, P. (Eds.). (1990). Citizen participation, voluntary organizations and community development: Insights for empowerment through research. *Special Section, American Journal of Community Psychology, 18,* 41-177.

Weick, A. (1983). Issues in overturning a medical model of social work practice. *Social Work, 28,* 467-471.

Zimmerman, M., & Rappaport, J. (1988). Citizen participation, perceived control and psychological empowerment. *American Journal of Community Psychology, 16,* 725-750.

The African-American Church:
A Source of Empowerment,
Mutual Help, and Social Change

Thom Moore

University of Illinois

SUMMARY. The African-American church in America has stood between individuals and the larger society for blacks for over two hundred years. In so doing it has been a source of empowerment and mutual assistance and a center for considerable social change. An historical review of the church's development from its early form as an invisible institution during slavery to its present diverse and formal structures reveals the significant role of the church in the black community. This chapter calls attention to the function that the church played as a setting in which shared needs and hopes could be expressed and the contribution it made in forging an identity for a people removed from their homeland. In the early 1900s the church was a familiar setting for migrants making a new life in the urban industrial north. The implications of the church for human service workers are that it is a resource site for studying empowerment, mutual assistance, and social change for African-Americans and how they have mobilized for community building.

The black church as it exists today is the result of a long evolutionary process in which the forms and functions of the institution were shaped by the demands and needs of its people. The church, which today is repre-

---

The author wishes to thank Martha and Austin Moore for their contributions in the form of long dinner discussions and critical feedback to various versions of this manuscript. He would also like to remember Muhumad Abdullah, Bullah Lateff, and Hubert Brown, for their invaluable historical and present perceptions of the African-American church. Finally, he wants to thank his colleagues Julian Rappaport, Ken Maton, Mark Aber, Jean Rhodes, and Deanna Barch for their encouragement, time, and critical and scholarly advice. Reprints may be obtained from Thom Moore, Psychological Services Center, Room 329, University of Illinois, 505 East Green Street, Champaign, IL 61820.

237

sented by a variety of denominations, at times was reactive and at other times proactive. This paper will take the position that the religion of African-Americans, as practiced through the black church, has wittingly and unwittingly been an agent of mutual help, empowerment, and social change. In addition to filling the spiritual needs and expressions of the African, the church was a mechanism for the reorganization of a displaced people. As such the church was a setting which identified and sanctioned attitudes and behavior, for both individuals and the larger group, and played an active role in promoting the social, political, educational and economic life of the people it served. In its modern day form, with expanded roles, it continues to provide for its constituency.

The African-American church stands as a natural, existing institution which, when better understood, will inform our psychological knowledge of African-American communities. The first section of the paper will highlight the development of the church from slavery to the present. The influence of the social climate will serve as the backdrop for the actions of the church. In the second section, examples of the church acting as an agent of empowerment, mutual help, and social change will be emphasized. The final section will discuss the implications that the African-American church as an historical social institution has for psychology both from a research and an intervention perspective.

RELIGION AND CHURCH

For purposes of clarification religion and the church will be treated separately; religion representing a set of ideas and church representing a social organization based on religious ideas. The church is a bridge connecting individuals with a larger group and allowing the individual to experience a sense of kinship and belonging. For human service workers interested in community social structures, religion and church present rich areas of study as factors that play a major role in the lives of individuals and communities. Levine (1988) in a review of mutual help groups lists key features of mutual assistance. Throughout its history the black church has displayed these features: developing an ideology which stressed belonging, promoting a sense of community, providing role models, teaching effective coping strategies for day-to-day problems, and providing a network of social relationships. The black church has been a setting which made opportunities available that were nonexistent in the larger society for African-Americans.

Studying empowerment, mutual help, and social change as a function of the church is complicated by competing assumptions of religion and psychology, and the languages of the two disciplines. The knowledge foundation of the church, based on religious principles, is faith, while the knowledge base of psychology comes from scientific research. Uncovering the relationship between psychology and church is further hampered by their fundamental intents. The science of psychology studies human behavior, and when it is applied the intent is to change behavior. A church, on the other hand, is established to nurture the spiritual needs of an individual or individuals, and in the process has an impact on the social lives of the people involved. Evidence of the African-American church serving as a source of empowerment, mutual help, and social change has to be deduced from history, self report, case studies, and descriptions of church activities.

Definitions

Yinger (1946) says that religion is, "the attempt to bring the relative, the temporary, the disappointing, the painful things in life into relation with what is conceived to be permanent, absolute, and cosmically optimistic." Crippen (1988) says that religions are unified systems of beliefs and rituals relative to conceptions of the sacred (that which is set apart and/or forbidden) — beliefs and rituals that encourage individuals to subordinate their apparent self-interest in relation to the collectively expressed interest of sovereign organizations. Crippen concludes as Durkheim (Hammond, 1988) does that religious ceremony, symbols, and sacred references are cultural universals unifying people into particular collectives.

Spiro (1966) offers an anthropological definition, stating that religion is an institution consisting of culturally patterned interactions with culturally postulated superhuman beings. The African believed in a world in which the physical and spiritual co-existed, and the spiritual was more dominant than the physical. The spirit world was everywhere in nature and human affairs, ubiquitous and portentous. The aim of life was to live each day in dynamic harmony with the spiritual forces which lay behind and exerted control over the contingencies of existential experience in the phenomenal world (Washington & Beasley, 1988).

Dueck (1987), a church scholar and psychologist, defines the church as a concrete, historical community that is called to discern the will of God. He notes further that the church is a community with a very different worldview than that of other social institutions such as government. It is exactly in this context, that the African-American church has meaning for the human services.

The Church and Identity of a People

Following emancipation, if Africans were going to survive in America as more than property to be owned, but as a people with dignity and demanding respect, they were going to have to develop social institutions which would promote their participation in the mainstream of life. Africans faced two tasks, the first being to identify and organize around their common experiences, and the second being to exert their will to be in control of their own lives. Frazier (1974) notes that in the transition from tribal member to slave, the general and specific social legacies of Africa were lost. The Africans who were brought to America were from many different backgrounds with different languages, customs, traditions, religions and religious practices. The African, although cut off from familiar forms of worship, retained a religious belief in the harmony of things spiritual and physical (Washington & Beasley, 1988). These basic but shared religious beliefs were the foundation for creating the black church.

In Hammond's (1988) exploration of religion and identity he cites the church as one of the ways people know who they are. In further examination of the relationship between religion and ethnicity he found that involvement in the religion characteristic of one's ethnic group is strongly correlated with the strength of one's ethnic identity. Religion allows a group to celebrate its collectiveness through ceremony and symbols. As a social phenomenon, religion encompasses a set of principles which give meaning to shared experiences. It is essential, then, to understand the African's need for religious outlets and how the church became that outlet. The issue of identity is tied directly to the two tasks of African-Americans mentioned earlier, for without a religion and a church to organize around, Africans in America would have at best remained a collection of unrelated people.

CHRISTIANIZING THE SLAVE

Slave or Free

From the time of the African's arrival in America to the beginning of the 1800s the seeds of the black church were being sown. One seed was the work of the European church to Christianize the slave, and the other was the effort of Africans to develop their own forms of spiritual expression. In 1660 Charles II instructed the Council for Foreign Plantations that servants or slaves should be invited to the Christian faith. In the 1680s further instructions were sent to the colonies to facilitate and encourage the conversion of Negroes and Indians to Christianity. These instructions were followed by extensive missionary efforts from the European Christian church. From all indications the interest in converting the African was in saving his/her soul. Prior to the Civil War a number of strategies were developed to demonstrate to plantation owners the need for conversion and religious training. There are reports in the late 1700s of slaves and their owners attending the same Sunday morning church services.

Conversion by Baptism

Conversion of the African to Christianity was complicated and difficult. Religious leaders of the day were strongly committed to ministering to the spiritual needs of the slaves, but met with political, social, and economic resistance. When they received cooperation, they had to overcome the problems of language and different cultural systems. Baptism, the most obvious sign of conversion, was most often denied to the slave because plantation owners interpreted British law to mean that baptizing a person gave them freedom. Raboteau (1978) states that this law was legally vague, but widely believed. In 1664 the legislature of Maryland passed an Act that in effect exempted the African from any such freedom law (i.e., baptism would not result in freedom from slavery). Although six other states had passed similar legislation by 1706, planters remained reluctant to baptize their slaves and sent an appeal to the Crown Attorney-Solicitor General to overturn the law. The appeal was ruled in favor of the planters.

In addition to fears about freedom, there were additional reasons planters were opposed to religious conversion of the African slave. For instance, there was the problem of planters not being willing to allow time for instruction in religious matters; after all, slaves represented an economic interest. Other objections were that once slaves received baptism and religious instruction, they would be difficult to handle. In effect they would perceive themselves to be free. Bishop Thomas Secker, in an anniversary sermon in 1740, diagnosed the basic cause of the planters' opposition ". . . some, it may be feared, have been averse to their slaves becoming Christians, because, after that, no Pretence will remain for not treating them like men" (Klingberg, 1940). Planters had still other objections. One objection was that the African was nothing more than an animal, far too brutish to comprehend Christianity.

Education as a Means of Conversion

In 1742 members of the Society for the Propagation of the Gospel in Foreign Parts, an incorporated missionary and humanitarian enterprise under the direction of the Anglican Church, with the urging of Alexander Gardner, purchased two teenage slaves for the purpose of training Africans to work with Africans. Efforts to convert slaves through baptism had not been as fruitful as expected and Gardner believed that the church would instead be more successful through religious training. Furthermore, he felt that Africans should educate Africans in the Gospel. Two schools were started, one in New York City and the other in Charlestown, South Carolina. In 1705 Elias Neau, a French trader, was appointed catechist and established a school in New York City. Neau reported he had two hundred pupils by 1709. This school managed to stay in existence until sometime after the War of Independence (Klingberg, 1940; Raboteau, 1978). A similar school, The Charlestown Negro School, lasted from 1743-1764 but was not as successful as Neau's New York school.

Church Membership

Their limited success was not enough to sustain these schools. They were abandoned and efforts to convert the slaves took a different path. The Great Awakening of 1740, a religious revival movement, experienced astounding conversion results throughout the country but especially among the slaves. Baptists and Methodists tended to benefit greatly from the heightened religious fervor of the period. Conversion of the African to Christianity during this time increased the membership in these churches specifically. In 1786 Methodists reported a membership of 1,890 Africans out of 18,791 total membership. By 1790 that figure had risen to 11,682, and in 1797 blacks accounted for one fourth of Methodist membership (Raboteau, 1978). Although Baptists did not maintain as accurate records as the Methodists, it is estimated that by 1793 Africans also made up one-fourth of their total membership.

THE EVOLVING BLACK CHURCH

The Invisible Church

As noted, slaves' participation in Christian worship received mixed support from slaveholders. Some planters encouraged it and others absolutely forbid it. The slaves, however, recognizing their own need for expression, developed what became known as the Invisible Institution. Even those slaves who were fortunate enough to be allowed to attend church services wanted a service that focused more on spiritual concerns. It was not uncommon where church membership was encouraged that both blacks and whites attended services together, nor was it uncommon for a congregation to have more blacks in attendance than whites. However, slaves did not share in any meaningful way in the organizing and management of the church. Slaves complained that nothing was ever said about the gospel message—instead they received instruction about their behavior. The following is a summary by an ex-slave of a sermon.

> You slaves will go to heaven if you are good, but don't ever think you will be close to your mistress and master. No! No! there will be a wall between you; but there will be holes in it that will permit you to look out and see your mistress when she passes by. If you want to sit behind this wall, you must do the language of the text "Obey your masters." (Cade, 1934)

While slaves were integrated into some religious settings in the South, their participation was limited, inadequate and lacking of any fulfillment of their own personal and social needs. Consequently, they felt that their needs would be best met through other forms of worship. What followed for them was among the earliest empowering activities of the slaves. They began organizing their own worship services. After a day's work or on Sunday evenings, at a prearranged time they would meet in a slave's home for an evening of singing, preaching, telling of Bible stories, and praying. At other times they would meet in open fields, which became known as "hush harbors," where they could be relatively safe from detection. Security was paramount for the individual slave and for the future of such gatherings.

Slaveowners feared that any time slaves were together unsupervised they were plotting ways to kill the owners and regain their freedom; therefore, anyone caught attending these meetings was severely punished. Numerous strategies to maintain secrecy were developed. Meetings were held in secluded wooded areas. Communication was in whispers, sometimes over an open pot filled with water, or a pot would be set upside down and propped up to catch and muffle the sounds.

Raboteau (1978) concluded that these meetings of prayer and singing and hearing biblical stories were special occasions for the slave. In personal interviews ex-slaves reported that during these meetings, people were anxious to talk, "everyone's heart was in tune, and when they called on God it made the heavens ring." This was a place where the slave experienced communal support and rejuvenated his/her spirit. The organization that did exist under these conditions was different than what might be expected of a church. There were no committees, nor ministers to appoint, no need for an order of worship, and money did not exchange hands. By imagining their lives in the future, slaves gained hope in the present. Furthermore, the slave had need for private and separate worship in the hush harbors or their cabin because they knew that public prayers for freedom would be met with harsh treatment (Raboteau, 1978).

Of Levine's (1988) six features of mutual assistance groups, the Invisible Institution included three of them. Without prior planning, but through its actions, the slaves promoted the psychological sense of community, developed ideology about themselves and the need for spiritual expression, and encouraged confession, catharsis, and criticism. The slaves' intentional gathering was an unwitting step toward building a community.

The Independent Negro Church

In the latter quarter of the 18th century the development of the black church took place. Through the vision of courageous individuals, mutual agreements, and church schisms, congregations and churches for Africans and African-Americans were formed. Some of these organizations were completely black, that is conceived by and for blacks, controlled by blacks, and where styles of worship which catered to black religious expression were practiced. Others were allowed limited independence. In this latter case whites continued to maintain control through ownership of property, providing pastoral leadership, or financial support. The churches emerging during this time afforded their members a sense of freedom which did not exist in any other areas of their lives (Mays & Nicholson, 1969).

African-American church historians admit to some confusion as to when the first independent black church was established. The first black church, according to Mays and Nicholson (1969), was founded in Silver Bluff, South Carolina sometime between 1773-1775 with the help of George Liele, a slave born in Virginia. Fitts (1985) credits David George, a slave and convert of Liele's with starting an independent mission in Silver Bluff. However, Frazier (1974) notes that, "the oldest or next to the oldest Negro Baptist church," the "First Colored Baptist Church," was started in Savannah, Georgia in 1779 by George Liele and Andrew Bryan, the latter a slave baptized by Liele. The oldest urban church was established in Philadelphia in 1794 by Richard Allen and Absalom Jones. Early Baptist churches represented three forms of independent churches: the separate church under white leadership, the separate church under black leadership, and the mixed church (Fitts, 1985).

One of the more dramatic beginnings of the independent church movement occurred in the 1790s in Philadelphia, Pennsylvania at Saint George's Methodist Episcopal Church. Richard Allen, a free black preacher, and member of the congregation had a vision in 1786 for a separate church for the blacks of the city. He presented a proposal to this effect that was opposed by both black and white church members. Eventually the combined membership grew so much that the facility had to be expanded. On the day that the new facility was unveiled, black members were informed that they were no longer permitted to sit on the first floor;

they would only be allowed to sit in the balcony. Richard Allen's account conveys the courage of the African men and women who founded the independent churches.

> The meeting had begun, and they were nearly done singing, and as we got to the seats the elder said, "Let us pray." We had not been long upon our knees before I heard a considerable scuffling and low talking, I raised my head up and saw one of the trustees, H___ M___, having hold of the Rev. Absalom Jones, pulling him up off his knees and say "you must not kneel here." Mr. Jones replied, "wait until prayer is over." Mr. H___ M___ said, "No you must get up now or I will call for aid and force you away." Mr. Jones said, " wait until prayer is over, and I will get up and trouble you no more." With that he beckoned to one of the other trustees, Mr. L___ S___ to come to his assistance. He came to William White to pull him up. By this time prayer was over, and we all went out of the church in a body, and they were no more plagued with us in the church. (Mays & Nicholson, 1969, pp. 21-22)

Richard Allen and Absalom Jones were the founders of the African Methodist Episcopal Church denomination, represented by Mother Bethel Church, and the African Protestant Episcopal Church denomination, represented by Saint Thomas' Episcopal Church. These churches were not under the authority of a white structure. Their congregations purchased and owned their property, called ministers, and set up their own organizational structures.

The steps taken by Jones and Allen were followed by other African-Americans in the South as well as the North, and produced what is known as the independent church. Whereas the Invisible Institution changed the slave's thoughts and action concerning the restrictions slaveowners imposed on their practice of religion, the independent church altered the working, social relationships between Africans and whites regarding religious affairs. The significance of the institutional church goes beyond religion. Its broader impact was the order it placed on the social life of slaves and freed Africans. Wingfield (1988) concludes that, "because blacks were denied the opportunity, during and after slavery, to participate fully in the social affairs of the country, the black church came to represent the only vestige of the so-called freedoms guaranteed other Americans by the constitution." In addition to filling a spiritual void, the institution of the church became the means for blacks to organize communities and meet their needs as a people.

The beginnings of what later became new urban religions were seen following the Civil War. The independent black churches had become successful, and lost some of their zeal in leading the fight against racial discrimination and injustice. Two movements, the Sanctified and the Holiness churches emerged. The Holiness movement was an outgrowth of Methodist doctrine and was later the foundation of the Pentecostal movement of the late nineteenth century (MacRobert, 1988). The Sanctified Church arose in response to and largely in conflict with changes in worship traditions within the black community (Gilkes, 1985). The Sanctified Church employed a number of strategies of a resistance nature that gave dignity to African-Americans. It was customary for whites to address black women and men by their first name, thus depersonalizing and devaluing black people. To avoid this Sanctified Church members refused to refer to each other by first name in interracial settings, church publications, or any other public media. Gilkes' main point, however, was that the church rejected the cultural and organizational model that uncritically imitated Euro-American patriarchy; instead they elevated black women to the status of visible heroines — spiritual and professional role models for their churches.

The independent church led the way for Africans to exercise control over one aspect of their lives. Structures were developed, property purchased, community behavioral standards established, social and religious agendas were set, and leaders emerged. The church became the institution through which blacks developed an identity for themselves, and challenged the dominant social, economic, and political order. For most of the 1800s the church was involved in community building. It was designed mainly to serve a rural population.

The independent church was a completed mutual assistance group (cf. Levine, 1988). While it maintained the formulating features of the Invisible Church, it became more complete by providing meaningful social roles for its members, developing and transmitting methods for coping with problems, and finally providing a network of social relationships.

The Urban Church

By 1910 the demographics of African-Americans began to change. Failing economic conditions in the south, continued harsh social treatment, reduction in European immigration, a war, and growing labor demands in the industrial north and northeast drew thousands of blacks away from the rural south. Their new surroundings were unfamiliar and, in negative ways, similar to the communities they left. Mukenge's (1983) analysis of the condition of the church during this period centers on the church's internal problems of power, wealth, and complexity, and external problems created by competing secular organizations which took over church functions. As the black population grew over time, its needs became more diverse. The church found its material and human resources being siphoned off by secular organizations whose singular focus made them more capable of serving people's specific needs. Churches also became property holders faced with large financial debt. Much of their energy turned to maintaining large memberships who in turn would help meet mortgages and ministers' salaries.

The new urban migrants, like their rural religious ancestors who found the structure of the white church an obstacle to satisfying their spiritual needs, also found the more formal urban church practices did not suit them. They were in search of worship services with more of a rural, southern flavor. Urban congregations were not warm, migrants were not made to feel welcome, and, worst of all, the leadership was monopolized by the older residents (Baer, 1984; Frazier, 1974; Wilmore, 1972). In short, the rural southern migrant's religious experiences were discounted by established urban dwellers. Mukenge (1983) describes the urban church during this period as having gone from a race church, reaching a broader range of African-Americans, to a class church, stratified along social class lines within the congregation. Many found the church of no spiritual or social use. The migrant's experience plus the church's internal problems brought on by success led to the development of new urban black religions. These conditions were fertile ground for movements like Spiritualist, Holiness, Pentecostalism, and the Nation of Islam.

Holiness, Pentecostal and Spiritual churches placed more emphasis on meeting spiritual needs while the Nation of Islam focused on both spiritual and material needs with an emphasis on building a self-sufficient nation for African-Americans. Each of these denominations has been misunderstood, confused with each other, and, except in rare cases, not taken seriously as a force in the development of the urban black church. The Holiness, Pentecostal and Spiritual churches have their roots in the post Civil War era, but did not find sustained support until the urban migration of African-Americans in the early 1900s. The Nation of Islam appeared in the 1930s.

The Nation of Islam offered an alternative to the established independent black church. The message was one that went directly to the heart of contemporary social problems. Battle (1988) notes that the contributions of the Al-Islam are best seen in the new self-image the followers exhibited. They were taught to believe that they were important in the eyes of God. The Islamic religion, under the leadership of Elijah Muhammad, encompassed a set of religious beliefs, a social agenda and a detailed plan for making African-Americans self-reliant. The Nation of Islam acquired resources and made them available to the African-American community. For example, Elijah Muhammad proposed the idea of owning a black national savings and loan bank where black peoples' savings could be reinvested to address community problems. These visions had a personal and social empowering effect and were a force behind Muslim economic programs, such as restaurants, clothing stores, schools, farms, a bakery, a supermarket, a press, and many other operations (Pasha, 1973-74).

Clearly the African-American church's history and development exemplifies the unique factors of empowerment and mutual help. It became the institution through which slaves and, later, African-Americans recreated their identity, preserved and adapted a way of life suitable for America, and passed skills on to succeeding generations. They learned to count less and less on the generosity of slavemasters and developed faith in their own abilities to bring about change which addressed their conditions. In the context of slavery the church in small and incremental ways became a mediating structure challenging the larger social structure in the interest of the slaves. Paris (1985) notes that prior to the independent black church there was no "enduring form" for expressing the deep objection against slavery. The church was the only black institution which held hope for slaves.

CHURCH CENTERED ACTIVITIES

The African-American church has held a central role in the growth of the African-American community. Lincoln and Mamiya (1990), for example, state that, "the Black Church had no challenger as the cultural womb of the black community. Not only did it give birth to new institutions such as schools, banks, insurance companies, and low income housing, it also provided an academy and an arena for political activities, and it nurtured young talent for musical, dramatic, and artistic development" (p. 8). Taylor (1986) notes that the church is considered by many blacks to be a primary institution in the black community, second in importance only to the family. Jaynes (1989), in his comprehensive account of African-Americans, states that, "probably no other single institution has played such an important role in maintaining the cohesion of black society as the black church." The strength of the church is seen in a 1984 Gallup Report on religion in America in which 94% of blacks said that religion was very to fairly important to them while 84% of whites said the same thing. When asked about church membership, 76% of blacks as compared to 69% of whites claimed membership. Among African-Americans, the church remains an important part of their lives. One simple explanation for this is that the church is a familiar setting in which people develop meaningful relationships, and have a variety of their needs met. As a source of helpful intervention the church can lay claim to developing necessary support systems for its members. It has clearly fit the description which Levine (1988) makes of mutual assistance groups.

Further demonstration of the church's social support nature can be found in the research of Taylor and Chatters. Analyzing data from the National Survey of Black Americans, they investigated informal social support networks (Taylor & Chatters, 1988) and social and religious variables associated with informal church-based support (Taylor, 1986). Overall, they found that more than half of the people had received support from the church at sometime. Black Americans, in addition, indicated that the church had helped improve social conditions. Interestingly, Taylor and Chatters (1986) found that respondents without a best friend had less chance of receiving support from either family or church.

Evidence of the black church operating at the level of empowerment and social change has also been found. Beginning with the Montgomery bus boycott, the church filled the role of a mediating structure in the empowerment process of the civil rights movement. A mediating structure, as defined by Berger and Neuhaus (1977), is an institution which stands between the individual in his/her private life and the large institutions of public life. Rappaport (1981, 1987) and Hughes (1987) imply that empowerment means the suffering party gains control over solutions to life's problems by including their own skills and knowledge in the resolution. In the struggle for civil rights the African-American church has been a tangible and inspirational setting for the development and exercise of empowerment.

Morris (1981) has shown that the church had an historical role in the civil rights movement of the 1960s and 1970s. For example, previous interpretations of the sit-ins credited their occurrence to student spontaneity while denying that pre-existing organizations played much of a part. Morris' data demonstrates that organizational and community forces were at the core of the sit-in movement from the beginning. According to Morris, the black church was the major institutional force behind the sit-ins. He details how the black church was central to the protest movement, beginning with the Montgomery bus boycott in 1955. Churches supplied money, and organized masses, leaders, highly developed communications and relatively safe environments for planning. In such a situation the church multiplied the talents, skills, and creativity of its individual members and became a symbol and a force for change.

A second compelling example of the church operating as an agent of empowerment and/or social change is the Mendenhal Ministries, a collection of church-based programs designed to provide for the social needs of people living in a rural Mississippi town. Mendenhal is a community of approximately 3,000 residents, 1,000 of whom are African-American. The Ministries (programs) grew out of the recognization that spiritual needs are not separate from physical and material needs. The founder, a local minister, provided leadership for the creation of programs based on the available resources in the community. He emphasized that the programs originated from the church and were not government funded. They also relied on voluntary support of all kinds from a national interracial collection of churches. The Ministries consist of eight different programs based on the provision of resources, ideas of self help, and community development. There is an elementary school, an after-school program, day-care for senior citizens, legal services, a thrift shop, a farm, a summer leadership program for young people, a health center, and a summer volunteer program. Without these services the African-American citizens of this community would be virtually ignored.

IMPLICATIONS

Given that the phenomenon of religion has been viewed negatively by psychologists, the social institution of the church, likewise, has been dismissed by psychologists, perhaps in part because religion and church have been seen as synonymous. Gorsuch (1988) notes that religion has been a topic of interest to psychologists since the time of William James. However, he presents four different theories of why religion fell out of favor with psychology, and has recently made a comeback (Brown, 1985; Spilka, Hood, & Gorsuch, 1985; Tisdale, 1980).

An expression of this issue can be found in an exchange about religion between Allen Bergin and Albert Ellis. Bergin (1983) tested the pathology hypothesis of religion and behavior through a meta-analysis of 24 empirical studies from 1951-1979. He found that 77% of the obtained results were contrary to a negative effect of religion. He implies that psychology has operated from a value bias against religion and he cautions against the practice of attributing pathodynamic origins to values with which one disagrees. Ellis (1980), representing a different view of the relationship between religion and mental health, wrote a comment to Bergin's article in the form of a hypothesis that might be tested, ''The emotionally healthy individual is flexible, open, tolerant, and changing, and the devoutly religious person tends to be inflexible, closed, intolerant, and unchanging.

Religiosity, therefore, is in many respects equivalent to irrational thinking and emotional disturbance'' (p. 637). In spite of such themes, religious settings have begun to receive more positive acceptance as having psychological meaning to people.

A more positive attitude toward religion and religious settings can be found recently among psychologists with a social interventionist perspective (Johnson & Mullins, 1990; Maton & Pargament, 1987; Maton & Rappaport, 1984; Rappaport, 1981; Shinn, 1987). Shinn (1987) suggested that the prevention and empowerment efforts of community psychologists stand to be greatly enhanced by working with religious organizations, learning from them, helping them evaluate their own efforts and accomplish their goals more fully, recognizing their legitimacy for community development or community organizing, and, finally, as sites for programs without the stigma generally associated with mental health and social service agencies. This general shift in the attitude of psychologists toward religion can be transferred to the church and result in a broadening of opportunities for African-Americans and psychology for understanding and documenting the church's role in the lives of its participants.

Research

In the last two hundred years, since the beginning of the independent black church, there have been any number of church forms to address the various religious preferences of African-Americans. This variety suggests opportunities for psychologists to investigate differing empowering strategies of the church. For example the simple act of using initials in place of first names in the Sanctified Church may have given its members a way to control the amount of degradation they would tolerate. Further, prevention psychologists, without making negative value judgements, must understand how the African-American community has sustained itself to this day. Research designed in collaboration with community people, and which uses the social and cultural structures that have a history of serving people well, increases the chance for understanding and explaining the experiences and lives of African-Americans.

The relationship between help, based on Levine's (1988) features of mutual assistance, and empowerment would be informed by investigations of the African-American church. With regard to social roles and role models the church has been one of the few places that permitted African-Americans to serve in positions which made use of their talents and skills. Gilkes' (1985) recognition of the Sanctified Church's elevation of black women to the status of visible heroines introduces the notion that women in these settings may also have fared better in their everyday communities than those from other churches. Does the role of women in the Sanctified church truly differ from the role of women in other African-American churches, and does it prepare them to operate in nontraditional roles in nonchurch settings?

Taylor and Chatters have laid groundwork for additional study of social support in the church. A cross cultural comparison of what is supportive in an African-American setting versus a non African-American setting would provide useful information to researcher and interventionist alike. The work of Taylor and Chatters credits the church with being an integral part of the Civil Rights Movement. Church leaders were involved in the planning and execution of marches and protests. The church has improved the status of blacks in society through its position as an advocate for better jobs, housing, and schooling for black Americans. Very clearly church members become a network of social relationships for each other; however, the particulars of the effects of specific church related activities of African-Americans have not been empirically examined.

At a more general level the African-American church is an ideal setting for addressing questions of empowerment and social change. Researchers may very well find themselves interested in the transformation process whereby a lone individual feels that his/her abilities are worthwhile in this setting. How does the mediating process work so that an individual feels his/her contribution is valuable to the group's goals?

The church setting would permit the study of an American subculture from the perspective of that subculture. This may be accomplished through an emic research strategy often employed by anthropologists. This strategy is cultural-bound. Basically, the meaning of behavior would be understood from categories describing that behavior which emerges from the culture being studied not the culture of the researcher. Lundstrom (1990) says that the emic research approach forces researchers to shed biases, those personal and those derived from their culture, and view the world through the eyes of the individual(s) of interest. The philosophy behind this technique is that the description of the form and meaning of a culture or subculture will necessarily differ from that of an outside observer whose own culture or subculture has imparted a different set of values. Snowden (1984) notes that an emic approach reflects a more culturally sensitive way to study black environments. Further, he states that documenting cultural similarities and differences through emic approaches would not only help blacks, but would also advance the scientific interest of psychology. Researchers can experiment with both the emic and etic research methods to investigate community and the sense of community among African-Americans, and document how that interacts with mutual help, social change and empowerment.

Blackwell (1985) raised the point that, in spite of shared backgrounds and experiences, African-Americans are a diverse group of people. Far too often uses of phrases such as "the black community" or "inner city" carry with them a set of stereotypes about the people in those groups which deny their individuality. They have biological overtones to them. Blackwell's intent is to dispel the notion of the monolithic black person. The fact that there are a variety of churches which African-Americans attend suggests community diversity.

Blackwell's point is a reminder that any study of the black church should avoid assigning stereotypes. Instead, the church is a setting for focusing an investigation which would identify the shared aspects of the community. For now, the task is to understand the church as a community. That is, what values, beliefs, and behaviors do people share in a particular church? How would those values, beliefs, and behaviors compare with those of members from the same denomination, but not in the same church? Moving outside the specific church community would allow for a study of social networks and the larger community. These structural variables would be the foundation for studying the similarities and differences in African-American communities at large. It is conceivable that there are communities within communities, each sharing to some extent values, beliefs and behaviors while, at the same time, having distinct differences. As attempts are made to study positive empowering aspects of community, it is likely that negative effects of communities which manifest in the tensions between the individual and the community may emerge. The shared aspects of the black church will serve as reference points for discovering and describing differences. Finally, as psychologists become more familiar with the similarities and differences in the African-American community they will be better able to understand how, when, and to whom the church and the community act in mutual assistance and empowering manners.

Intervention

Other implications to be drawn from the history of the church by psychologists and other social interventionists are that the black community is a dynamic, active social entity that has benefited greatly from the organization of the church. African-Americans have been able to assess their conditions and create avenues for responding to them. Rappaport, Davidson, Wilson, and Mitchell (1975) proposed a strategy of intervention built on the assumption that groups have a wealth of resources and strengths which can be used to create positive alternatives for meeting the needs of people. The history of the African-American church is an example of how, over time, people develop their talents and skills and provide for themselves, thus avoiding the stigma of social programs based on a deficit model. Given a strengths model and a tangible setting in which they can be exercised, the role of an interventionist may become that of a facilitator and collaborator, rather than that of program designer and implementer. Essentially, the approach being suggested here is that interventionists adopt an orientation somewhat akin to Edwin Schur's (1973) radical non-intervention.

After reviewing the assumptions, research, and policies concerning juvenile delinquency, Schur (1973) concluded that the best intervention policy was to "leave the kids alone wherever possible." He proposed mechanisms to divert children away from the courts, and opposed various kinds of interventions by diverse social control and socializing agencies. He also asserted that major and intentional sociocultural change would help reduce the delinquency problem. His final position statement was "if the choice is between changing youth and changing the society (including some of its laws), the radical noninterventionist opts for changing the society."

These ideas easily transfer to a perspective on interventions in the African-American community. If there is a need for individually-oriented programs it may be best for communities to design and deliver them on their own. Interventionists' contributions may take the form of securing resources of a technical or monetary nature, but greater impact would result from a focus on policy and social change. Both public policy and social structures should be designed to enhance, not hinder, people's lives. In any event, a collaborative, mutually beneficial relationship should characterize the work between professionals and the community. For instance, in the case of the Mendenhal Ministries, these programs have been conceived by, organized by, and operated by members of the community for other members of the community. Specific components of the program require professionals such as lawyers and physicians, and there are people who serve in those roles. They are collaborators and not the directors.

From slavery to the present the role of the black church has been fueled by the refusal of the white church and government institutions to take a stand against the practice of slavery, racism and discrimination, to include African-Americans in the life of the church, and to be involved in meaningful social change on behalf of the African. Richard Allen, founder of the African Methodist Episcopal Church, surmised, for example, that if Methodist theology refused to be identified with solutions to social and political injustice, then it was meaningless and irrelevant to the pressing needs of black people. He concluded that a separate and independent black church, served by black clergymen, could provide the most effective mission to African-Americans by utilizing not only its physical resources of buildings, committees, and such, but by also invoking the powerful philosophical resources implicit in a theology of liberation (George, 1973). Subsequently, the newly formed church became the only institution in which blacks could accommodate their need for freedom.

The church has continually stood between individuals and the larger society. It has provided alternatives offering people a choice. For the slave the making of a choice was itself an act of empowerment. Later, participating in the church organization, developing talents, and learning new skills were empowering. In the civil rights era the church was powerful enough for the masses of African-Americans to confront the power structure and change the social relationships between blacks and the larger social setting. The church is an important place within the African-American community where psychologists can be involved to learn about black people and participate in building a society that values all of its members.

REFERENCES

Baer, H. A. (1984). *The black spiritual movement*. Knoxville: The University of Tennessee Press.

Battle, V. D. (1988). The influence of Al-Islam in America on the black community. *The Black Scholar, 19*, 33-41.

Berger, P. L., & Neuhaus, R. J. (1977). *To empower people: The role of mediating structures in public policy*. Washington DC: American Enterprise Institute for Public Policy Research.

Bergin, A. E. (1983). Religiosity and mental health: A critical reevaluation and meta-analysis. *Professional psychology: Research and Practice, 14*, 170-184.

Blackwell, J. E. (1985). *The black community: Unity and diversity* (2nd ed.). New York: Harper and Row.

Brown, L. B. (1985). *Advances in the psychology of religion*. Oxford: Pergamon Press.

Cade, J. B. (1935). Out of the mouth of ex-slaves. *Journal of Negro History, 20*, 294-337

Crippen, T. (1988). Old and new gods in the modern world: Toward a theory of religious transformation. *Social Forces, 7*, 316-336.

Dueck, A. (1989). On living in Athens: Models of relating psychology, church and culture. *Journal of Psychology and Christianity, 8*, 5-18.

Ellis, A. (1980). Psychotherapy and atheistic values: A response to A. E. Bergin's psychotherapy and religious values. *Journal of Counseling and Clinical Psychology, 48*, 635-639.

Fitts, L. (1985). *A history of black baptists*. Nashville: Broadman Press.

Gallup, G., Jr. (1984). *Religion in America*. Princeton: The Princeton Religion Research Center.

George, C. V. R. (1973). *Segregated sabbaths: Richard Allen and the emergence of independent black churches 1760-1840*. New York: Oxford University Press.

Gilkes, C. T. (1985). "Together and in harness": Women's traditions in the sanctified church signs. *Journal of Women in Culture and Society, 10,* 678-699.

Hammond, P. E. (1988). Religion and the persistence of identity. *Journal for the Scientific Study of Religion, 27,* 1-11.

Hughes, R. (1987). Empowering rural families and communities. *Family Relations Journal of Applied Family and Child Studies, 36,* 396-401.

Jaynes, G. D., & Williams, R. M., Jr. (1989). *A common destiny: Blacks and American society*. Washington, DC: National Academy Press.

Johnson, M. A., & Mullins, P. Community competence in religious congregations. *American Journal of Community Psychology, 18,* 259-280.

Klingberg, F. J. (1940). *Anglican humanitarianism in colonial New York*. Richmond: Richmond Press.

Levine, M. (1988). An analysis of mutual assistance. *American Journal of Community Psychology, 16,* 167-188.

Lincoln, C. E. (1964). The black Muslims as a protest movement. In H. M. Nelsen, R. L. Yokley & A. K. Nelsen (Eds.), *The black church in America*. New York: Basic Books.

Lincoln, C. E., & Mamiya, L.H. (1990). *The black church in the African American experience*. Durham, NC: Duke University Press.

Lundstrom, F. (1990). *Parents of young persons with special needs in transition from school to adulthood: Report for participating school districts*. Champaign, IL: Secondary Transition Intervention Effectiveness Institute, College of Education, University of Illinois.

MacRobert, I. (1988). *The black roots and white racism of early pentecostalism in the U.S.A.* New York: St. Martin's Press.

Maton, K. I., & Pargament, K. I. (1987). Roles of religion in prevention and promotion. In L. A. Jason, R. D. Felner, R. Hess, & J. N. Mortisugu (Eds.), *Prevention: Toward a multidisciplinary approach*. New York: The Haworth Press, Inc.

Mays, B. E., & Nicholson, J. W. (1933). *The negro's church*. New York: Russell & Russell.

Morris, A. (1981). Black southern student sit-in movement: An analysis of internal organization. *American Sociological Review, 46,* 744-767.

Mukenge, I. R. (1983). *The black church in urban America*. New York: University Press of America.

Paris, P. J. (1985). *The social teaching of the black churches*. Philadelphia: Fortress Press.

Pasha, A. (1973-74). *Accomplishments of Muslims in America*. Chicago.

Raboteau, A. J. (1978). *Slave religion: The invisible institution in the Antebellum South.* Oxford: Oxford University Press.

Rappaport, J. (1981). In praise of paradox: A social policy of empowerment over prevention. *American Journal of Community Psychology, 9,* 1-25.

Rappaport, J. (1987). Terms of empowerment/exemplars of prevention: Toward a theory for community psychology. *American Journal of Community Psychology, 15,* 121-145.

Rappaport, J., Davidson, W. S., Wilson, M. N., & Mitchell, A. (1975). Alternatives to blaming the victim or the environment: Our places to stand have not moved the earth. *American Psychologist, 30,* 525-528.

Schur, E. M. (1973). *Radical non-intervention: Rethinking the delinquency problem.* Englewood Cliffs, NJ: Prentice-Hall.

Shinn, M. (1987). Expanding community psychology's domain. *American Journal of Community Psychology, 15,* 555-574.

Snowden, L. (1984). Toward evaluation of black psycho-social competence. In S. Sue & T. Moore (Eds.), *The pluralistic society: A community mental health perspective.* New York: Human Sciences Press.

Spilka, B., Hood, R. W., Jr., & Gorsuch, S. (1985). *The psychology of religion: An empirical approach.* Englewood Cliffs, NJ: Prentice-Hall.

Spiro, M. (1966). Religion: Problems of definition and explanation. In M. Banton (Ed.), *Anthropological approaches to the study of religion.* London: Tavistock.

Stern, E. M. (Ed.). (1985). *Psychotherapy and the religiously committed patient.* New York: The Haworth Press, Inc.

Taylor, R. J. (1986). Religious participation among elderly blacks. *The gerontologist, 26,* 630-635.

Taylor, R. J., & Chatters, L. M. (1986). Patterns of informal support to elderly black adults: Family, friends, and church members. *Social Work, 31,* 432-438.

Taylor, R. J., Thornton, M. C., & Chatters, L. M. (1987). Black Americans' perceptions of the sociohistorical role of the church. *Journal of Black Studies, 18,* 123-138.

Taylor, R. J., & Chatters, L. M. (1988). Church members as a source of informal social support. *Review of Religious Research, 30,* 193-203.

Tisdale, J. R. (1980). *Growing edge in the psychology of religion.* Chicago: Nelson-Hall.

Washington, G., & Beasley, W. (1988). Black religion and the affirmation of complementary polarity. *The Western Journal of Black Studies, 12,* 142-147.

Wilmore, G. S. (1983). *Black religion and black radicalism.* New York: Orbis Books.

Wingfield, H. L. (1988). The historical and changing role of the black church: The social and political implications. *The Western Journal of Black Studies, 12,* 127-134.

Yinger, J. M. (1946). *Religion in the struggle for power: A study in the sociology of religion.* Durham, NC: Duke University Press.

RELIGION – HUMAN SERVICES PARTNERSHIP AND ACTION

Reciprocal Ministry: A Transforming Vision of Help and Leadership

Bruce Roberts
Howard Thorsheim

St. Olaf College

SUMMARY. Reciprocal ministry is an approach to ministry in which people know, care about, and give reciprocal support and help to one another in communities in addition to congregations.

Empowering leadership enhances reciprocal ministry. Empowering leaders "walk-with" congregation members enabling them to contribute to others through their involvement in activities — allowing each parishioner to find ways to contribute that are meaningful to their own life.

Examples of an empowering style of leadership include an active working with people to help them (1) know others better, (2) grow to care more about each other, (3) find ways to help and support

Reprints may be obtained from either author at the Department of Psychology, St. Olaf College, Northfield, MN 55057.

others, and (4) ask others for help and support for themselves. These distress-reducing dimensions of reciprocal ministry can transform our visions of both help-giving and leadership.

This is a story of a journey towards understanding how people can be helpful to others as friends, leaders, and caring professionals. It is a story of some of our wrong assumptions, our search for alternatives, and our continuing struggle to understand the implications and the meanings of our research outcomes.

The purpose for our journey lies in our concern with the growing disconnectedness between people and the reduced sense of community that people feel in their lives. Our society is quick to blame the individual for the pain that accompanies his or her loneliness, isolation and anomie. Rather than "blame the victims," we need to search for the disempowering social processes within the mediating structures in society such as families, churches, neighborhoods, schools, classrooms, work settings, and community centers (see Berger & Newhaus, 1977).

The behaviors, reflections and feelings discussed in this chapter could characterize people in any mediating context from family members and neighbors, to teachers and corporate presidents. However, since many of our research projects have focused on church congregations, it is to the leaders and members of congregations and those people who work with them (i.e., social service providers) that we aim these stories of what we have learned.

HELPFULNESS AS GIVING HELP

Helpfulness, we assumed, was doing things *for* people. Helpfulness was giving people a hand; offering to do something *for* them in their struggle. For a pastor we thought being helpful might include telling people things that they needed to know, serving as an expert on religious matters, or solving a problem for parishioners. A church benevolence program might be helpful to people who are less fortunate by giving them food, money, or clothes.

Such an assumption of the meaning of being "helpful" was our notion of social support as we developed our major field research grant (funded by the National Institute on Drug Abuse) with 10,000 people in 24 church congregations in 1980. We hypothesized that in contrast to just a focus on good alcohol information programs, congregations would have lower distress and lower alcohol abuse among their members if they focused on

(1) good alcohol information programs and also (2) developed means of giving social support to those who needed assistance.

Imagine our surprise when we evaluated the data from 2,299 church congregation members (who ranged in age from 18 to over 80) in our questionnaire research sample and found that our hypothesis was not supported empirically. Not only was support from others not helpful, but more support from friends was correlated with (1) a greater level of *Distress*[1] and, (2) an increase in alcohol abuse behaviors (i.e., gulping drinks, memory loss when drinking, drinking more than they meant to drink). The regression analysis which included *Social Support from Friends* as an independent variable revealed significant beta weight relationships with the dependent variables *Distress* = .09, $p < .001$, and *Chemical Abuse Behaviors* = .11, $p < .001$ (Thorsheim & Roberts, 1984; Roberts & Thorsheim, 1987a).

"How could that be?" we asked ourselves. "What's going on here?"

Our search to understand our unexpected results covered several years. We examined carefully our measure of social support. All of the items that people checked indicating whether they received support or not were drawn from the Barrera and Ainley (1983) ISSB measures of "one-way" support. That is, they measured social support as being support *received*. Such a view of "one-way support" was in fact the way we had been thinking about support earlier. However, as we soon learned, this was the locus of the problem.

ONE-WAY SUPPORT

One of the best examples of the dynamics of a one-way support "problem" was told to us by a pastor of an inner-city church in one of our larger midwestern cities. We have reported this story before (Roberts & Thorsheim, 1987b).

> In the affluent suburbs of a city, several white women wanted to do something to help the black women in the inner-city who seemed to be struggling so hard to care for their families. The suburban women gathered used clothes, gave money, and helped with providing food for these inner-city women.
> At first this helping hand was appreciated. But soon the women in the inner-city developed a need to reciprocate the help. The suburban women were urged to talk with the inner-city women, to learn ways that the inner-city women could do something for them in return. Could the inner-city women teach them something? Could

they give them advice about how to create community? Could they share experiences about what it is like to raise small children?

However, the suburban women could not think of anything they had to learn from the inner-city women and they refused to accept the suggestions.

As the inner-city women began to understand that the suburban women were not interested in really getting to know them and to care about what was going on in their lives, they felt diminished. Any sense of dignity that may have been developing because of the first show of support was eroded. The inner-city women felt that they were seen as second-class citizens by the suburban women — not as equals.

The story above has many counterparts in daily life. We can see *one-way support* being repeated in our role as teachers. We note one way support happening in families, as social service professionals provide help to those in need, and in government programs for the needy. Most importantly, however, much of our religious tradition seems to us to have made such one-way giving of support and help a primary virtue.

RESEARCH SUPPORT FOR OUR FINDINGS

By the mid-eighties, other research psychologists were also reporting support as being problematic when it was viewed as *one-way support*. For example, Ken Maton (1987), in his research with members of a church congregation, found that persons who only received support and those who only gave support to others were significantly lower on a life satisfaction measure than those people reporting that they both gave and received support.

Karen Rook (1984) found that when elders did not feel that they were able to be important contributors in their interactions with others (i.e., to have a significant say in what they would do, to have an equal say with their friends when they would get together), they perceived these interactions with others to be negative. Furthermore, she found that these negative interactions were more detrimental than were elders' positive interactions beneficial.

Apparently, when people just receive help, they feel in a powerless, incompetent, dependent or novice position relative to those people who are giving that help. Although being supported, cared for, or the recipient of aid may be helpful to most of us in times of crisis and special need, a longer range outcome from such one-way support is correlated in our re-search with higher distress.

Disempowerment

A way to visualize the dynamics we were uncovering is to understand that it is disempowering to have people do things for you or to you if you feel you have little ability or opportunity to reciprocate with personally meaningful contributions of your own. To be disempowered is to have a sense that you are not seen by significant people in your life (and/or by yourself) as being worthwhile and valued, and that you are not really a contributing member of your "group" (i.e., family, church, work place, community).[2] Furthermore, those who give others disempowering "help" often give the kind of help and assistance that *they* feel that the recipient of the help needs. Thus, not only do the recipients of one-way support find themselves in the bottom half of a top-down situation, but they likely find themselves receiving help that they neither asked for nor particularly need or want.

Empowerment

The empowering nature of the process actually seems to lie with those who *give* help. To be empowered is to feel worthwhile, capable and val-ued. Some examples of people who are empowered are a pastor who gives help as he counsels a distraught congregation member, a senior member of the congregation who gives help as she tells a younger member how to arrange a meeting, a social worker who gives help as she helps a client manage finances, a teacher who gives help as he instructs the youth in Biblical history, and the congregation as a whole as it gives help by donat-ing benevolence money to the homeless.

Yet there is a paradox in this side of the empowering process as well. The problem was illuminated by the research of Ken Maton discussed above. Those who help others (through counseling, telling, helping, teaching, or giving), but are not open to letting people be supportive in return, are themselves vulnerable to increased distress—and "burnout." Thus the giving of help, even though empowering, may be a relatively short term gain if there is not a reciprocity of help-giving over the long haul.

RECIPROCAL SUPPORT: THE ROOTS OF EMPOWERMENT

As we discovered that an increase in the social support we measured did not correlate with reduced distress, we searched our data for indications of what it might be that people in church congregations were doing that did correlate with lower levels of distress. We found the distress reducing characteristics we were looking for in (1) parishioners involvement in *meaningful activity*, and (2) a factor that we called *"Investment in Community."*

Meaningful Activity

We saw from the analyses of our data that it was the *activity* of doing personally meaningful things together with others in the congregation that played a key role in the distress reducing processes. The regression analyses from our Bottled Pain study in which meaningful activity was one of the independent variables revealed significant relationships between meaningful activity and the dependent variables *Distress* $= -.15$, $p < .001$, and *Investment in Community* $= .34$, $p < .001$ (Roberts & Thorsheim, 1987a; Thorsheim & Roberts, 1984).

Concern for alcohol abuse problems was the meaningful issue that served as an energizer for the congregational participants in our study. Because the people who chose to be involved were personally interested in the prevention of alcohol abuse, they eagerly worked on the congregation project with others.

Not everybody in the congregation was interested in this issue, of course. But for those who were, such an opportunity to work on an activity that was meaningful to them was the critical step. It is unlikely that the same results would be obtained if a person who had no particular personal interest in the alcohol abuse prevention issue participated because somebody else told him or her to be involved.

Investment in Community

What happens during meaningful activity that makes it a cornerstone in the empowerment process, we wondered? In the factor analysis of our questionnaire data we discovered that the factor that we initially labeled *Investment in Community* correlated negatively with *Distress* and also with *abusive use of alcohol* (that is, as respondents' *Investment in Community* score increased, their reported level of *Distress* and also their abusive use of alcohol tended to decrease).

The *Investment in Community* factor was made up of the following four questions, all positively related to the overall factor: (1) I know how to link up with others to give and receive support; (2) people in my congregation frequently ask me to help other people in our congregation; (3) it is easy for me to name seven or eight persons in my congregation who are 15 years old or younger; and (4) there are people in my congregation, other than my family, who I really care about.

As we reviewed the regression analyses, using the *Investment in Community* factor[3] as one of the independent variables, we found that it had a significant negative relationship with both *Distress* $(-.18, p < .001)$ and alcohol abuse behavior $(-.06, p < .01)$. Thus, the higher a person's *Investment in Community*, the lower was their reported *Distress* and abusive use of alcohol.

Since more of the research literature was now clearly identifying the importance of a *reciprocity* of help (cf. Gottlieb, 1988; Heller & Price, 1990) as an important ameliorator of distress, we added a fifth question, "It is difficult to ask other people to help me when I am having problems," to the four items constituting our factor *Investment in Community*. This question balanced our earlier questionnaire item, "People ask me to help them." (The new question was reversed in its scoring as we added it to the original *investment* factor questionnaire items.)

Reciprocal Ministry

We began thinking of this five-question cluster as a way to envision mutual empowerment among people in the church communities with which we were working. We also began to understand that the concept of mutual empowerment learned about in our research with congregations may be akin to an approach to ministry in which people know, care about, and give support and help to one another more generally in communities in addition to congregations. We felt that the term *reciprocal ministry* characterized this dynamic.

In a multi-year series of research projects with college students, we found that this five-question *Reciprocal Ministry* cluster was a consistent and powerful correlate with lowered distress. (With sample sizes of over 100, the correlations between *Reciprocal Ministry* and *Distress* were on the order of $-.45$ or more, $p < .001$).

We reflected carefully on the make-up of *Reciprocal Ministry*. The following six dimensions of *Reciprocal Ministry* seemed especially germane for understanding its empowering characteristics:

Reciprocity of help. Not surprisingly, we view reciprocity of help and support as the most important component of *Reciprocal Ministry* (i.e., "I know how to give and receive support," "People ask me to help them," "I can ask others to help me"). Two-way supportive dynamics are clearly among the roots of empowering connections between people.

Caring relationships. The fact that care ("I really care about others . . .") was one of the key items in the empowering factor helps us recognize that it is not the superficial or mechanical behaviors of reciprocal help that make the difference. Rather, mutual help and support that grows out of the nurturing of genuine care for each other is at the heart of the empowering process. In our research we found that to care for others is strongly correlated with being cared for in return, and for having friends that ask how we are doing and that really listen to us.[4] It is the reciprocity within caring and listening relationships that sustains and empowers us.

Personally meaningful activity. A reciprocity of help and support presupposes that what is given and received (i.e., advice, time, food, listening) is meaningful both to the giver and the receiver. It is not empowering to ask our friend to help us if our friend does not perceive that the task is truly meaningful to us (and to our friend as well).

Asking others to help us. One of the stumbling blocks on the road to empowerment is the difficulty people have in recognizing the helpfulness of asking for help—as an aid to reducing distress for themselves as well as for others.[5] Since asking others to help us is a behavior that we can initiate on our own, it is particularly critical to understand the implications of this behavior. We found that men more often than women, were not able to ask others to help them when they were having problems. Furthermore, men who were not able to ask for help tended to have higher levels of distress than men who found it easier to ask for help.

Taking time to listen to others. Listening to others is also a form of helping and being helped that is open to self-initiation. Having time to listen to others is related to increased empowerment and decreased distress for the listener as well as for the person to whom one listens.[6]

Who should know more, care more, and help more? As leaders, clergy, supervisors, teachers, or social service providers, we often have an image that a key element of our job is for us to know the names of people, to show them that we really care about them, and to be supportive in our communications. Such behaviors are surely a helpful part of *Reciprocal Ministry*.

The benefit, however, that we document in our research projects is the lowered distress within congregation members, students, or community members which is correlated with their ability to name more people, care more about others, and to contribute in meaningful ways. Activities and processes which lead to an increase in opportunities for congregation members, for example, to know more about what is happening, care more about others through intimate listening relationships, and to give and receive help, should thus be a focus of empowering efforts.

Limitations. There is, however, a limitation on the extent to which one can generalize from the developing concepts of reciprocal support and empowerment. *Reciprocal ministry* comes alive at the level of concrete situations and specific interactions between unique individuals. As a result, complex personal, interpersonal, and environmental conditions will vary over time and place, thus altering the outcomes that one might expect in a given context. In other words, we simply can not know or specify all of the ecological conditions which might limit or strengthen the beneficial nature of reciprocal support.

RECIPROCAL MINISTRY IN ACTION

Our research projects generally include qualitative evaluations as well as the quantitative measures reported above. Our project with the 24 congregations contained what we called an informal portrait in which we gathered information from:

1. The clergy whom we called periodically on the telephone to ask: (a) How is it going with the project? (b) How is it going with your congregation? and (c) How is it going with you?
2. A person we called a Congregation Steward in each congregation who agreed to watch for key changes in the congregation that they perceived were a result of the project.
3. Observations we made during our site visits to the participating congregations.

These qualitative evaluations are best presented in narrative story form in order to make clearer the meaning of what is observed to those being observed. Although we have dozens of narratives documenting empowering processes that span several of our projects, we will relate just four.

Sharing Begets Sharing

Five persons, all of whom had experienced alcohol problems, volunteered to be members of the Prince of Peace Lutheran Church research leadership team. Pastor Erik Saxvik recognized the power of story that was alive in each person.

Pastor Saxvik asked the five team members to share their stories of struggle, pain, and vigilance with him and with each other. Then, together, they decided to share their stories with the congregation — from the pulpit. As they rehearsed their stories together, supporting one another in their nervousness about revealing these untold experiences to the congregation, they grew in a supportive bonding for each other, and in an appreciation for the resources (from these important experiences) that they each had within them already.

The response of the congregation to their Sunday morning presentation was overwhelming. There was an outpouring of reciprocal openness about the struggles of people never before acknowledged — not just about alcohol problems, but about all sorts of issues from delinquent children to grief over job loss. The questions and the reach for supportive connections went to the team members and also to the pastor. The church rediscovered that sharing begets sharing.

What can we learn from this story?

First, the willingness of people to share their stories of struggle is a powerful gift to the community. It opens other people to the sharing of their own experiences that for many have been millstones around their necks preventing them from fully developing their own potential.

Second, the pastor did not assume that the five parishioners already had the skills needed to tell their story. His deliberate step-by-step process of working with ("walking-with") them as together they developed the confidence to tell their personal stories in public was a very critical part of the process. This is a lesson that should not be forgotten by leaders. Basic skills of listening actively, working with others as a team, or speaking in public are often missing and can be significant barriers to the accomplishment of what might otherwise seem to be straightforward goals.

The vulnerability in openly sharing one's story can have a negative side, however. It could have been that the people in the congregations would misunderstand the team members sharing of difficult times as a desire for sympathy, or a request for answers. Some hearers of those problems might even have criticized (blamed) the "victims" for their alcohol-related problems. These responses would have been disempowering because they would have placed the people who were honest enough to share their struggles in a position of sensing that they and their experiences were not valued or seen as worthwhile.

People who are willing to take the risk of open sharing need supportive cohorts such as these team members were for each other. Then, if they encounter judgmental or "superior" attitudes from others, they can share these negative experiences with each other and put the disempowering remarks and attitudes in perspective. Support can also come in other forms, as illustrated in the story below.

Support the Supporters

One of the tasks of our research with the 24 congregations was for us as co-directors to call the clergy of each congregation once a month or so to check on how things were going with the project, the congregation, and with them. We looked forward to these calls and anticipated that they would take about 15 minutes each.

Imagine our surprise as we found ourselves on the phone for an hour or more with our clergy friends. When we asked the question, "And how is it going with you?" the flood of concerns that tumbled out caught us by surprise.

Some of the clergy felt that the Bishop of their district, no matter how pastoral he might be, was still their supervisor. They felt that to pour out their concerns to him could reflect badly on their own capabilities as ministers and leaders. Some of the clergy said that members of their congregation expected perfection from them, so to seek solace by discussing the travails of ordinary living with congregation members would be very difficult. Finally, some of the pastors in our research project lamented that the other clergy in their region who could have been supportive were competitors (for new members); therefore, to show weakness to somebody with whom one is in competition was reported by the clergy to be almost impossible. Spouses were sometimes helpful as "listening ears," but as one pastor said, "I can't dump everything on my wife, she gets too down herself."

So because of our relative anonymity, and our willingness to listen to their stories, we found ourselves to be a critical link in the lives of some of the pastors with whom we were working. Years later, one pastor came up to us and said, "You men don't know how important you were to me that year. I don't think I could have been as supportive to my project team if you hadn't been so supportive to me by just listening."

In retrospect, as we gave listening support to the clergy (who were, in turn, the critical supporters of those in the congregation who were trying to develop helpful outreach programs), we were extending our reach manyfold. Such listening to those who are on the front line of helping others, be they parents, clergy, teachers, or youth leaders, is a powerful and important way to sustain and multiply a supportive community. We could never have been as helpful to as many people if we had tried to reach the congregation members directly ourselves, one-by-one.

The story below is another example of empowerment multiplication.

Face-to-Face Empowering Leadership:
A Story from Reverend Cheryl Kleven

My sense of leadership involves an understanding that most people are not in touch with their own gifts. I decided to offer a seminar dealing with the topic: What is God calling me to do? (Where are my gifts?) I expected four or five people and got 30. I was overwhelmed at how hungry people were to find out and discuss this topic.

One person really felt she was being called to work for peace (in the family and the world). Since I too was very interested in peace issues, I said, "Would you be willing to work on this with me? We could share leadership and see where it goes." I told her, "What you and I do could be really important to the congregation." So we worked together developing a theme around peace. More people joined us and saw themselves as being called as peace makers. We shared together our common interests and concerns. These heartfelt conversations were really important to all of us.

After some things we did in the congregation, I said to her, "How can we be a resource to the larger community?" Together we contacted pastors in the community and said, "Okay, here we are. How can we serve you busy clergy in some way for peace?" Then we developed an ecumenical group. Eventually we grew to a community-wide project! I worked along with her until she had more confidence to work with the project on her own.

Another woman in the original group had two small children, and I could tell that she was restless. She needed to understand her vocation as a Christian. She needed to gather people together to discuss parenting. So together we led a course on parenting. I went through it once with her, and spent a lot of time with her, discussing who she was, and that what she was doing that was important and significant.

It was a relationship that was personal, touching on our own experiences. We both had small children, and we shared a lot together about these common connections. Then she led the groups on her own. Her groups still are one of the more popular programs in our congregation.

Notice that the central values or issues had already been experienced by both the leader and the women she worked with. The empowering relationships were personal and connected because of who the people were, not just because of what they wanted to do. Pastor Kleven exhibited what we would call a face-to-face empowering leadership style.

A reflection on this leadership approach is provided by Pastor Kleven herself. She said, "As one person, there is no way to touch everybody in the church. So as you support people who are ready to develop themselves as more of who they are, they can grow and develop. This helps me extend my helping role manyfold. Plus it is important for me to be personally involved in those relationships. I tend to invest myself in support with others when I am supported in the process myself."

In contrast, note the differences in the connections between the empowering leader and the person being helped in the story below.

Shoulder-to-Shoulder Empowering Leadership: A Story from Dee Heier

We met biweekly for eight months and Pastor Thompson was at every meeting until the very last few months! He had read about the needs of people like me who were divorced and who were trying to put their lives back together again. He realized that there was something important here to listen to. He accepted that challenge and became very active in helping us get a group of newly divorced people started.

He learned a lot from us. He said many times, "Well I learned something new tonight." That made me feel very good. You know, in the beginning if you haven't had too many contacts with pastors you hold them at a higher level, but he was willing to learn, to make mistakes, and to be open about them. He is open so nobody feels that they have to be perfect around Merv. That is real affirming to people. For instance, he is open about saying something like, "Well, yesterday I was trying to do that, but . . ."

If he were holding himself up as a model who does not make mistakes, that sets a standard that is impossible — so when he admits to mistakes, we can all learn faster. We don't worry about what we did wrong but we can just decide to do better next time, and of course we do.

He also comes in (now that I am a staff person) and just asks what I think; what is my opinion? "How should I say this?" he will say, or, "Should I do this — or this?" He doesn't have to do that you know. The best thing was that I felt he needed my input that day. It made me feel that he valued my opinion and that he valued my role there. It was very affirming.

This is a story of empowerment even though the empowering process did not involve a personally connected relationship as was the case in the previous story with Paster Kleven. Pastor Thompson worked alongside Dee to help her find resources and strength within herself — from her own experiences in life. Pastor Thompson's openness seemed to empower Dee through his genuine acknowledgement that he was learning new things about a topic that he knew very little about. He was helping to get a new and important program started within his congregation. He traveled along the empowering road by walking with Dee — shoulder-to-shoulder.

Differences between face-to-face leadership of Reverend Kleven and the shoulder-to-shoulder leadership of Reverend Thompson may be characteristic of differences between the empowering approaches of women (face-to-face), and men (shoulder-to-shoulder). More research in this area is needed. In any case, both approaches are empowering.

LEADERSHIP IMPLICATIONS OF RECIPROCAL MINISTRY

For Clergy

Much of what clergy do involves the sending of messages, information, and understandings and the giving of help and support. Yet, a higher level of commitment from the members of the congregation can be expected for those parishioners who are themselves the ones sending, giving, and helping others. Thus, the more open and risk-taking a pastor is in allowing the congregation to be helpful and supportive to him and to others in the congregation, the greater may be the feelings on the part of the parishioners that they are an integral part of the community of the church.

Ken Pargament and his colleagues (1988), in their research on the nature of helpfulness of different visions of one's relationship with God, found that persons who think of their relationship with God as a partnership for action tended to be healthier than those who thought of God as an all powerful uni-directional force and thus adopted a passive role in response to problems. The importance of a reciprocity of support and helpfulness, versus a one-sided acceptance of help and support from others, is a core factor in successful coping with the stresses of life, even in one's relationship with God.

For Social Service Providers

An implication for social service providers also follows from our research — active involvement in meaningful and empowering activities of a church can be an excellent means for clients of social service providers to reduce many of their personal/social difficulties and can serve to help prevent subsequent problems from developing. The church is one of the few social organizations that (potentially) remains relatively open to all comers. Church congregations have the ability to expand the programs offered so that increasing the number of meaningful activities is a real possibility. Indeed, the benevolence mission of many church congregations strongly supports the involvement of parishioners in the process of helping others, and thus as we saw above, helping themselves in the process. Social service providers can work with their clients to explore opportunities within a church congregation to become active participants in activities that are meaningful to them.

There is also another role for social service providers to consider — promotion of a healthy community. It is a way to extend the helpfulness of their professional assistance. It can include:

1. Getting to know the clergy and other church leaders on an informal basis,
2. As opportunities arise, supporting church leaders through direct aid if it seems wise, but perhaps best as a trusted, confidential, listening ear concerning the issues that the pastor is facing,
3. Helping clergy understand the empowering role of meaningful involvement in activities by their parishioners, and
4. Encouraging the clergy to give permission to energetic members of their congregation to work with others to start new groups and activities which are meaningful to them and to other parishioners.

CONCLUSIONS

Reciprocal ministry develops with empowering leadership in which congregation members are encouraged to contribute to others through their involvement in activities — allowing each parishioner to find ways to contribute that are meaningful to their own life. The diversity of activities which could serve as mediating structures for empowering parishioners include the delivery of meals to shut-ins, the collection of food for the homeless, involvement in a weekly Bible study, the sharing of life stories between the generations (cf. Thorsheim & Roberts, 1990), involvement in open forums on topics of personal importance (i.e., drug abuse, the struggle for faith in everyday life, the floundering family), and service as an usher or as a participant in the Sunday worship.

As we saw in the review of our research results above, (1) knowing others better, (2) growing to care more about each other, (3) finding ways to help and support others, and (4) asking others for help and support for one's self are processes within mediating structures that can create a sense of well-being and empowerment for people. Leadership that encourages such meaningful and empowering activities is not a laissez faire leadership or a managerial delegation of responsibility. Those styles essentially involve a hands off approach on the part of the pastor. In contrast, the empowering leadership of reciprocal ministry involves an active working with people. Both the shoulder-to-shoulder and the face-to-face styles involve reciprocal approaches that are comfortable to the leader and helpful to the parishioner. Depending on the context and the goal, both empowering approaches may help the parishioners gain basic skills and facilitate their talking with other supportive people who are facing the same situations.

NOTES

1. Distress was measured by a 13 question factor consisting of items which, for example, tapped people's feelings of helplessness, conflict, low trust, and discouragement.

2. This particular cluster of characteristics (feeling worthwhile, knowing that you contribute to others, sensing that you are valued by people that are important to you) has been identified by Sarason and her colleagues as they reviewed the outcomes from multiple social support assessment instruments, as the primary ingredient of helpful social support (Sarason, Shearin, Pierce, & Sarason 1987).

3. The *Investment in Community* factor had a Cronbach Alpha Coefficient of .53. The five-question version of this factor (in a subsequent study) had a one month test-retest correlation of .80.

4. Significant correlations were found between "I really care about others" and (1) "Others care about me" $= .30, p < .01$, and (2) "Others listen to me" $= .47, p < .001$).

5. Significant correlations in the college student research projects were found between "I can ask others for help when I am having problems" and (1) *Distress* $= -32, p < .01$, and (2) "Others listen to me" $= .24, p < .01$.

6. Significant correlations in the college student research projects were found between "I have the time to *listen* to others" and (1) *Distress* $= -38, p < .001$, (2) *Reciprocal Ministry* $= .33, p < .01$, and (3) "Others listen to me" $= .31$, $p < .001$.

REFERENCES

Barrera, M., & Ainley, S. (1983). The structure of social support: A conceptual and empirical analysis. *Journal of Community Psychology, 11*, 133-157.

Berger, P., & Newhaus, R. J. (1977). *To empower people: The role of mediating structures in public policy*. Washington, DC: American Enterprise Institute.

Gottlieb, B. (1988). Support interventions: A typology and agenda for research. In S. Duck, D. Hay, S. Hobfoll, B. Ickes, & B. Montgomery (Eds.), *Handbook of personal relationships*. New York: John Wiley & Sons.

Heller, K., & Price, R. (1990). The role of social support in community and clinical intervention. In I. Sarason, B. Sarason, & G. Pierce (Eds.), *Social support: An interactional view. Issues in social support research*. New York: John Wiley & Sons.

Maton, K. (1987). Patterns and psychological correlates of material support within a religious setting: The bidirectional support hypothesis. *American Journal of Community Psychology, 15*, 185-207.

Pargament, K., Kennell, J., Hathaway, W., Grevengoed, N., Newman, J., & Jones, W. (1988). Religion and the problem solving process: Three styles of coping. *Journal for the Scientific Study of Religion, 27*, 90-104.

Roberts, B., & Thorsheim, H. (1987a). A partnership approach to consultation: The process and results of a major primary prevention field experiment. In J. Kelly & R. Hess (Eds.), *The ecology of prevention: Illustrating mental health consultation*. New York: The Haworth Press, Inc.

Roberts, B., & Thorsheim, H. (1987b). *Empowering leadership: A Brief Introduction*, Northfield, MN: Social Ecology Resources.

Rook, K. (1984). The negative side of social interaction: Impact on psychological well-being. *Journal of Personality and Social Psychology, 46*, 1097-1108.

Sarason, B., Shearin, E., Pierce, G., & Sarason, I. (1987). Interrelations of social support measures: Theoretical and practical implications. *Journal of Personality and Social Psychology, 52*, 813-832.

Thorsheim, H., & Roberts, B. (1990). Empowerment through story sharing: Communication and reciprocal social support among older persons. In H. Giles, N. Coupland, & J. Wieman (Eds.), *Communication, Health and the Elderly*. Fulbright Colloquium Series No. 8. Manchester, England: University of Manchester Press.

Thorsheim, H., & Roberts, B. (1984). *Substance abuse prevention: A social ecology approach*. Final report for the National Institute on Drug Abuse Grant # 1-RO1-DA-02671.

Congregational Consultation

H. Newton Malony

Fuller Theological Seminary

SUMMARY. Several dimensions of the interaction between religious congregations and consultants are explored. Congregations are construed as social organizations which succeed or fail in terms of society's response to the services they offer. Consultants should conceive of themselves as system-interlopers who may be received less than enthusiastically. The consultation relationship should be understood as similar in many ways to more general types of business consultation. The unique qualities of congregational consultation can be described in terms of the Ponton and Weber model which includes three aspects: external and internal Modes; direct and indirect Approaches, and process or content Dimensions. Consultants can play the role of Participant, Researcher, Resolver, or Trainer. Relationships between consultants and congregations should be encouraged because they share similar concerns for human welfare.

Thorndike and Barnhart state that "consultation" is "a meeting to exchange ideas or talk things over" (1965, p. 191). A better, less-technical definition could not be found. When professionals, such as psychologists and educators, consult with religious congregations, they do, indeed, meet to exchange ideas and talk things over. The "things" that they talk over are their common concerns for the life-fulfillment of human beings and the "ideas" they exchange are their respective perspectives on various ways to accomplish that goal.

This essay will address the several dimensions of this interaction between religious congregations and consultants who come to them to "talk things over and exchange ideas." Special emphasis will be placed on the insights which consultants need in order to be effective in this endeavor. However, congregations will find many of these ideas helpful when they engage consultants for assistance.

Reprints may be obtained from H. Newton Malony, Graduate School of Psychology, Fuller Theological Seminary, 180 North Oakland Avenue, Pasadena, CA 91182.

Initially, the consultant needs to adopt an organizational perspective about congregations. This perspective should result in consultants understanding themselves as systems interlopers. Then the consultation can be construed as similar to, but not exactly equivalent with, other non-religious professional relationships. Finally, congregations need to be encouraged to utilize consultants.

Religion needs the help that consultants can give and consultants need to identify congregations as partners in enhancing human existence. Both parties need to become aware that they share many values in common. Consultants are people helpers. Congregations exist for the enhancement of human life. In fact, their concerns may be much more congruent than either congregations or consultants had thought possible. Although congregations might express their values in theological terms while consultants might be more used to expressing theirs in psychological terms, the value of enriching human existence is very similar. In this spirit, the role of congregational consultant could best be conceived within a "resource collaborator" model (Tyler, Pargament, & Gatz, 1983) in which there is, indeed, an exchange of ideas based on mutual respect. This mutual respect should be based on an acceptance of the fact that the desired outcome of a given program might be shared while the perspective on which planners collaborate might be different — but not contradictory.

CONGREGATIONS: AN ORGANIZATIONAL PERSPECTIVE

Congregations should be perceived by consultants as social organizations. This may sound obvious, but it is not meant to be so. "Organization" is a technical term. It should be distinguished from "institution," the more common label applied to churches or synagogues. Institutions are those necessary, inevitable, required, essential, universal components of society. Like the poor, which Jesus said "you always have with you" (Matthew 26:11), institutions "just *are*."

State churches, such as those that exist in England and Norway, are good examples of "institutions." Congregations in American culture have a different type of existence. They are "organizations," not "institutions." This means they are intentionally created social groups designed to meet human needs. They are consciously established, purposefully planned, premeditatively maintained, and studiously programmed assemblies. Congregations cannot be assumed to be necessary or inevitable parts of culture, as are schools and governments. Although some of these characteristics could be said to typify state churches, little if any money from the state goes into establishing American congregations as is the case for religious buildings in England and Norway, for example. Further, it is the rare sub-division in America where land is set aside by the developers, much less the civil government, for the building of churches.

Congregations exist by interaction and interchange with the cities and towns in which they exist. They produce and sell "products and services" just as surely as do businesses like the Hallmark greeting card company, Reynolds tobacco company, and AT&T. Congregations are not indispensable. They can either succeed and survive or falter and fail. Their income must exceed their expenses. They can go bankrupt on the one hand or they can amass enough funds to build magnificent edifices on the other. They do not have the guarantee of being an institution which will always be perpetuated. If they do not survive, they become "redundant," as the sign on one Cambridge, England church suggests.

However, there is one important difference between redundant churches in England and American congregations which illustrates this difference between organizations and institutions. The English government maintains redundant churches for sentimental and historical purposes even though their doors are locked and no one worships there anymore. When American congregations fail, their buildings are bulldozed down and the land is cleared for new shopping malls. The institution of religion in society may continue, but local congregations rise and fall, come and go.

Because congregations are like businesses, they always have "maintenance" as well as "mission" concerns. Sometimes these maintenance concerns predominate over mission goals as when The First United Methodist Church of Pasadena, California conducts a five-million dollar campaign to repair damage resulting from the 1987 earthquake. Such an emphasis on housing might tend to make consultants restless unless they keep in mind that congregations are not institutions whose existence is guaranteed but are organizations which must survive. However, one role that consultants can persistently play is to help congregations keep maintenance and mission concerns in balance and place their primary concerns on the spiritual and welfare needs of persons. In the final analysis, survival will depend less on buildings and more on whether the public avails itself of the services congregations provide. This is the *prime* organizational reality. Nevertheless, resources, such as buildings, staff and supplies, must be adequate for any organization to function. This, too, is reality.

Thus, congregations should be best understood by consultants as "organizations" which only come into being if they meet a human need and only stay in business as long as there are consumers who purchase their products. Although they are religious, congregations are not *non*-profit.

No organization is. Profit, defined as an excess of income over expenditures, is necessary for any organization to survive. The uniqueness of religious congregations lies not in their being *non*-profit but in their being not-*for*-profit in that their prime reason for being is to expend their resources to meet persons' basic needs—not lay aside monies for their own benefit. The recent debacle of Jim and Tammy Bakker illustrates this distinction. They were not censored for making a profit but for using that profit to increase their own wealth instead of serving people.

Perhaps the most unique organizational feature which must be kept in mind by consultants is that congregational membership is voluntary. Although there are over a half-million paid clergy in the United States, the major work of congregations is done by volunteers. The noted management consultant Peter Drucker reportedly said that religion lived off of culture's "excess." By this he meant that while people had to work, they did not have to be religious. They belong to congregations with the time, the energy and the money they have left over after their work-to-survive is done. Because they primarily are made up of volunteers who participate out of their "excess," congregations are much more vulnerable to the fickleness of personal tastes and interests than other organizations. As has been said, members are constantly voting "with their feet and with their pocketbooks." Consultants who presume that persons *have* to participate in congregations do so at their own peril.

In sum, while congregations are just as "productive" as any businesses, they, nevertheless, are not-for-profit and are voluntary. These are essential features and paradoxes of congregations that must not be forgotten (cf. Malony, 1986a, p. 43ff). While it is obvious that the religious function congregations serve is universal, the viability of local congregations is best understood in organizational survival terms. For instance, neither New Covenant Fellowship nor River Plain Jewish Synagogue, described by Maton and Pargament (1987) in their article on "The roles of religion in prevention and promotion," would continue to exist unless they functioned as organizations which met participant needs at a certain time and at a given place. Both of these congregations were healthy organizations providing services for which members paid their money and gave their time. As had been said, ". . . perhaps the first of the Ten Commandments of effective consultation should be "know thy system." This injunction is particularly important in working with religious systems which so often have been overlooked and misunderstood by psychologists" (Pargament, Ensing, Falgout, & Warren, 1988, p. 4).

THE CONGREGATIONAL CONSULTANT:
A SYSTEMS INTERLOPER

What is a fact of consultation in general, is even more true of congregational consultation, namely, that the consultant is a systems interloper. By this is meant that the consultant is similar to a parasite that attaches itself to a tree but which never becomes a part of the main trunk. In fact, while congregations do often rely on technical advice such as is given them by plumbers, organ manufacturers, and office suppliers, organizational consultants should probably consider themselves foreign bodies who are like incompatible transplanted organs which the host body is more than likely going to reject. This appraisal may sound overly pessimistic but experience proves it often correct. The issues of interpersonal interaction are much more sensitive than the kind of concerns which pertain to building construction and usable supplies. To ignore this difference is unwise.

The reasons for the resistance and rejection with which congregational consultation is sometimes received are twofold. The first reason is a theoretical one while the second is practical. Because congregations are religious they are necessarily theoretical. To be religious means to be a part of a group of persons who believe in some theory or "theology." Congregations are theory-heavy organizations. Their existence and their functioning is based on logic or reasoning about the gods. The "gods" are those ideas people have about supernatural, transempirical forces or ideas that control the universe. Groups which are centered in such ideas feel they have become privy to special information about the meaning of life and the ways persons should live to achieve happiness and fulfillment. Unless consultants fully espouse those same beliefs, congregations tend to be suspicious of their advice. Such advice is seen as secular and as less important.

The second reason for resistance to consultation is practical. Whereas business leaders typically are trained to perceive their decisions as always imperfect and are, thus, fairly open to the kind of help consultants can give, congregational leaders often feel they have failed if they need advice from outsiders. Since they have access to supernatural knowledge through such resources as scripture and such actions as prayer, seeking help is an affront to their judgment and a challenge to their basic beliefs. They often enter consultative relationships passively resentful or covertly resistant. They become peculiarly defensive of their own opinions and often find a host of reasons not to truly attend to the advice of the consultant. They have a set to say "No!" The old anonymous poem reflects this common feeling which consultants ignore to their own peril:

> The sermon now ended, each turned and descended.
> The eels went on eeling, the peels went on peeling.
> Much delighted were they, but preferred the old way.

Most church consultants could tell a story or two about experiences such as this. For example, one consultant led a Presbyterian church through a required self-study when they were seeking a new pastor. The conclusions were that the church needed a bilingual pastor with urban experience who was about 40 years of age. The church hired a monolingual pastor in his late 50s from a rural church in Iowa. The self-study gathered dust on the shelf. In another case, the consultant was notified that her services were no longer needed after spending three painful, acrimonious months of meetings with two sides in a case of deep congregational conflict. The call ending the consultation came just as she thought the parties were beginning to negotiate with each other. She learned later that the negotiation which she thought was dependent on her efforts resulted in a coalescing of the former enemies around a rejection of her help. They resolved their differences by scapegoating the consultant — a not uncommon experience for congregational consultants. Although, not all consultations end so negatively, the possibility of such should be kept in mind by those who would do congregational consultation.

Suffice it to say, consultants should remain attuned to the fact that they are entering systems which may explicitly welcome them but implicitly reject them for theoretical and/or practical reasons which are peculiar to religious congregations. Such constant awareness of the fact that they are systems interlopers should provoke in consultants a style of cautiousness and a tentativeness that is significantly greater than that which they normally exhibit with non-religious clients. Time spent in understanding and, hopefully, affirming the core beliefs, values, and polity of congregations will reassure the sensitivities and reduce the suspicions in those to whom they consult. After all, it should be remembered that consultation is best defined as "an exchange of ideas." Congregations come to consultations with well thought out rationales about life which need to be understood and utilized. Any tendencies that consultants have to think they automatically know what is best for congregations should be tenaciously resisted if they want to be effective.

Psychologists, in particular, should remain aware of two biases that might make them be less cautious consultants than they should be. One is a bias toward anti-institutionalism and the other is a bias toward cultural adjustment. Psychological training is so focused on individual, intrapsychic processes that many psychologists subconsciously adopt an anti-institutional bias (Bunker, Miller, & Malony, 1990; Malony, 1988). They tend to feel that groups of any kind, much less religious congregations, constrain and handicap individual fulfillment. Much of psychologists' work takes place in individual counseling where they encourage persons to reaffirm their own potential in the face of social constraints. It would seem natural, therefore, that, while a large percentage of psychologists affirm the importance of spirituality (Shafranske & Malony, 1990), they tend to conceive of such spirituality more in personal than in organizational terms. This perception can lead to a type of consultation that does not respect or affirm the importance of the group orientation so essential to congregational life. Congregations are primarily "organized religion." This goes against the grain of many psychologists.

Likewise, psychologists tend to have a bias toward cultural adjustment which might make them less effective in consulting with religious congregations who traditionally have been counter-cultural. As Richard Niebuhr pointed out in his seminal volume *Christ and culture* (1951), religion has consistently been suspicious of those who simply or easily adjusted to their culture. The more common prescriptions, at least in Christianity, have been admonitions for believers to resist or transform culture—not accept and adjust to it. Psychologists, in turn, are trained to be far less critical of culture. In fact, their prime concern has been to help persons adjust to their society; to find relationships and means of livelihood within the options available in their culture. They might tend to be impatient with congregations' less than automatic approval of life-styles which might be socially functional but are not acceptable from a religious point of view. There is no doubt that these distinctions between the approaches of congregations and psychologists cannot be generalized to all situations. As Niebuhr and others have noted, mainline churches become culturally accommodated in many ways. There has been much stress experienced in many such congregations as they adjusted to the social gospel emphases of their ministers which, in the 1960s, came on the heels of massive infusions of membership based on cultural conformity during the 1950s. Furthermore, there are a growing number of psychologists who have joined the calls for social change outside the safety of their private offices.

However overdrawn the differences between individualistic and cultural values might be, there are still enough illustrations extant to say the distinction should be acknowledged. Recently, the expert testimony of a secular, non-religious psychologist reportedly included the following statement about a religious group which was accused of giving "total" answers to life's problems: "It has taken up to two years for some of the people I have counseled to readjust to society." This psychologist thought she was making a statement with which most of the public would agree, namely, that social adjustment was a preeminent value in life. She was reflecting a familiar bias among psychologists. She was also reflecting ignorance about religion which in many groups, such as the Christian Anabaptist and Jewish Orthodox traditions, is basically counter-cultural in orientation. Such questioning of cultural conformity has been a part of the Jewish/Christian tradition since the time of the 8th century prophets. It is an essential part of all of the world's great religions to one degree or another.

CONGREGATIONAL CONSULTATION: A NOT-SO-UNIQUE OPPORTUNITY

Turning next to the content of congregational consultation itself, it is important to conceive of the interaction as a not-so-unique opportunity. Congregational consultation is not-so-unique that it has to be understood as sui generis, one of a kind. Rather, essentially congregational consultation is consultation and it should follow steps which have come to be accepted and expected in the field (Galessich, 1982; Pargament, Ensing, Falgout, & Warren, 1988). These steps include entry, assessment, intervention, evaluation and termination. The importance of cautious entry and assessment has already been emphasized. The remainder of this section will consider the types of interventions available to consultants to congregations. Although these interventions are novel in some respects, they, too, are not-so-unique examples of more general consulting practices.

As a format within which to conceive these consultative interventions consider the model proposed by Ponton and Weber (1986). Figure 1 presents this model. There are three aspects to this model: a Mode aspect, an Approach aspect and a Dimension aspect. Ponton and Weber explain these aspects thusly:

> The external-internal continuum represents the consultative *mode* of psychologists, which is based on their relationship to the church (whether that be as a church member, a parishioner functioning in a professional role for a specific project, or as a contracted non-member consultant). The psychologist's *approach* can either be direct (actively implementing strategies for change) or indirect (raising issues for the consultee's consideration). The "approach" generally

depends on the model being used or the role the psychologist has assumed. Both mode and approach . . . concern themselves with two *dimensions*: process and content . . . Process refers to those activities, methods, and behavior patterns with which a church system faces environmental as well as internal demands. Content, on the other hand, refers to the values and attitudes motivating behaviors. (Ponton & Weber, 1986, p. 26, emphasis mine)

Another way to describe this process/content distinction is to say that processes are those programs which a church initiates and offers to its members and the public. Bible study classes and hunger walks to raise money for AIDS' ministries are examples. Contents are the reasons given for undertaking these deeds. For example, a congregation may explicitly state that the Bible study classes are motivated by a conviction that optimal Christian living should be deeply informed by scriptural teachings. Further, they may feel that Christ's teaching about serving those in need compels them to assist those with AIDS.

This model provides a helpful structure in which to consider the several roles a consultant might play with a congregation. For example, a psychologist who was asked to consult on parenting skills to a group of couples in a congregation might be a non-religious professor at a local college

FIGURE 1. Conceptual Paradigm

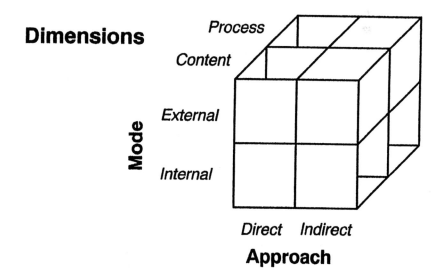

(i.e., functioning in the "external" Mode). If lectures were given on children's needs and their development phases, the psychologist would be approaching parenting skills "indirectly," i.e., assuming that parents could make their own application. The information would be focused on the "content" rather than the "process" Dimension.

As another example, psychologists who are asked to lead their own congregations in self-studies would be "internal" consultants (the Mode aspect of the model). If those psychologists actually designed and led the events in the self-study they would be utilizing the "direct" Approach. And if they focused on the interaction of the members rather than the programmatic outcomes of the events, they would be employing a "process" Dimension.

Ponton and Weber observe that, "In choosing any of these paths to consultation, the psychologist might function in a variety of roles, as well as move from one end of the continuum to the other during consultation" (1986, p. 27). And what is true for psychologists who consult with congregations is likewise true for other consultants, be they educators, social workers, counselors, psychiatrists, or nurses, to mention only a few.

Yet another format for looking at congregational consultation is to consider four possible roles that could be played. These are the roles of participant, researcher, resolver, and trainer (Malony, 1988). Increasingly congregational consultants are insiders; they are actual participants in the congregations to which they are asked to consult. This type of role poses unique advantages and novel stresses. There is no way that the consultant can be fully objective in such a role. On the other hand, there will be no outside consultant who will know better the congregation from the inside than a participant. Furthermore, there will likely be no one that the congregation would trust more than a participant.

Researcher is a role that can be fulfilled by a participant or an outsider provided there is agreement beforehand concerning the important issues to be addressed. It is important for researchers who are evaluating programs or assessing participation to investigate soft as well as hard data. In congregations, it is just as important to know whether persons' spiritual lives are being enhanced by the services of the church as it is to know how many people attended a given program. Perceptions are as important as participation. Research is a skill that congregations often lack which consultants possess.

Resolver is a strategic role for consultants to play. This often takes the form of mediating disputes. It can also involve intentionally designing discussions about issues which the consultant has identified as potentially divisive. There is no doubt that differences of opinion often arise in voluntary organizations, especially congregations. An objective third party, such as a consultant, can quiet emotions and help people solve problems rationally. Then, too, consultants have the time and resources to gather information and help congregations resolve dialogues about which decisions are best.

Training is a very common role for consultants. In a recent gathering of alumni from a graduate school that trains psychologists to be consultants to congregations, training was the most typical type of consultation reported. The type of training ranged from multi-session courses in such varied areas as parent-child rearing, controlling emotions, spiritual development, and leadership skills to one-time presentations on abused children and being a whole/holy person. Congregations consider consultants to be experts on a wide range of topics, so that this type of consultation is of immense value. Often such training consultation provides opportunity for further contacts with individuals as well as groups within the congregation.

Turning next to the reasons congregations seek consultation, two major types of problems would seem to be foci of concern: problems which can be anticipated and, thus, prevented and problems which have occurred unexpectedly and need to be resolved posthaste. An example of the former would be when a congregation might request a consultant to work with them in their adjustment to a new rabbi during the first six months he is on the job. An example of the latter would be when a congregation requested a consultant to help them resolve the turmoil resulting from the showing of a sex film on a youth retreat.

Problems that can be anticipated are called "developmental" problems. The focus here is on prevention and promotion of health-giving and cohesion-accomplishing procedures. Wise congregational leaders recognize these issues and encourage consultation. Illustrations of such developmental problems might be life-phase issues such as adolescent independence issues, retirement concerns, change of congregational locale and new leader training. The term "developmental" is used to indicate that, as in child rearing, congregational planning anticipates the needs of its members as they grow up and grow old. It further anticipates the changing societal and environmental pressures which will interface with and be the channel through which those needs are met. Such congregational planning takes into consideration the pitfalls of life within its unique setting and attempts to offer programs which both prevent problems and enhance adjustment. Consultants can be of real value in helping congregations become aware of societal trends, community resources, the effect of past programs, and the best ways to offer their preventive services. In the case of "developmental" problems, problems can be best conceived as "opportunities."

Problems which cannot be anticipated but which occur are called "accidental." Some have termed them "woodwork problems" because, like termites, they suddenly appear when they are least expected. Strong disagreements leading to deep divisions over such things as building plans, budget priorities, neighborhood changes, political differences, repair of storm damage, staff conflict, local politics, and national tragedies are illustrations of accidental problems. Although some might say that the possibility of these difficulties always existed and, to that extent, could have been anticipated, most congregations have enough other problems about which they have concrete evidence, that this depiction of certain problems as accidental is helpful. Many other illustrations of both types could be given. Wise congregational leaders acknowledge these types of problems early in the process and solicit consultation to keep them from getting worse.

In addition to the problem consultation discussed above, consultants can be of value to congregations in preventive consultation. Professional leadership is a crucial issue for congregations, particularly those that function under what is known as a "call system." The Alban Institute has designed procedures whereby they consult with churches as they undertake the selection of new ministers and stay with them throughout the first year of the new minister's tenure. There are some standard difficulties that all churches face in selecting and adapting to new leadership that an outside consultant can help congregations acknowledge and solve.

Another type of situation that is very demoralizing is when a congregation suddenly begins to lose significant numbers of members. Although, some denominations, such as the United Presbyterian Church, require a self-study each time there is a ministerial change, other churches invite consultants to lead them in self-studies on a regular basis as part of their long-range planning. This allows these congregations to consider the issues of recruitment and membership decline within a more benign atmosphere than when leadership changes or membership suddenly changes. Congregational cohesion is increased where members know they will have a chance to give feedback on a regular basis rather than having to wait until a crisis arises.

Yet another type of preventive consultation that pays off in enhanced congregational harmony is that of staff performance and staff relationships. While most congregations have standing personnel committees, these committees need periodic updating of their methods of evaluation and supervision. There is a tendency for these lay committees to often feel one-down in relation to professional staff and to be unsure of how to monitor performance of full time personnel. Where there are agreed upon regular visits by outside consultants, the functioning of these personnel committees is greatly enhanced. Congregational members, knowing of these consultations, feel able to participate in the process and influence staff functioning without the issues becoming overly personal. Thus, harmony and cohesion are enhanced.

Helping prevent conflicts from eventuating in church splits is a further way that consultants can engage in preventive work with congregations. Far too often, congregations fail to call consultants in early enough in times of conflict. Consultants can deter conflicts from getting worse plus initiate procedures for managing the difficulty without it resulting in a breakdown in communication or members leaving. There is no question but that conflicts are the most difficult problems congregations face. Personal feelings prevent most parties in conflicts from handling their differences rationally. Here is where consultants can be of immense help. And if consultants assist congregations in establishing procedures for future conflict prevention while they are handling immediate problems, their help will prove extremely valuable.

CONGREGATIONS AND CONSULTANTS: A MARRIAGE THAT NEEDS CONSUMMATING

There is one aspect of consultation that is not addressed in the above discussion. This is the option that consultants could offer their services to congregations rather than waiting to be asked. In the business world this is very common. Many consultants market themselves to business and industry but hesitate to approach congregations. Often, this hesitation has been based on the presumption that their basic beliefs would be incompatible with those of a given congregation or that congregations were so unique that they would not be interested in consultation or that there would be little monetary reward for their work. All three presumptions are, in fact, erroneous. Hopefully, the absolute uniqueness of congregations has been laid to rest by the prior discussion in this essay about understanding congregations as organizations who are attempting to meet human needs. Then again, the human needs that congregations are trying to meet are so universal that consultants can be quite confident that their values would be compatible quite apart from the specific religious beliefs of a given congregation. Further, by offering consultative service for which they might receive less than their usual fees, the consultant can possibly establish trust relationships with congregational leaders and pastors which will result in future referrals. For example, all congregations are composed of families which, in turn, have marital problems, child raising concerns, adolescent development issues, vocational changes, aging dilemmas and community crisis involvements. Further, all congregations are concerned with cohesion, program planning and leadership training.

Maton and Pargament (1987) note these commonalities between the practical values of consultants and religious congregations. Most of the helping professions are basically concerned with assisting persons to find meaningful lives within the culture in which they live. Although, as has been noted, a significant amount of religion is counter-cultural in that it calls people to ideals that supersede society, religion, nevertheless, usually calls for action that would make basic happiness available for all persons in the name of justice. Therefore, religion shares with the helping professions a concern for human welfare. It is this basic concern which unites consultants with congregations.

Consultants, then, need have no hesitation in marketing themselves to congregations. Providing periodic meetings for pastors and rabbis to discuss their counseling cases or to share their own dilemmas is an example of one thing a consultant could advertise and provide. Sending congregations announcements of parent training sessions or offering to help train lay counselors is yet another option. Furthermore, taking congregational leaders to lunch in order to become mutually acquainted while sharing brochures on services provided is perfectly admissible.

Without question, at least among applied psychologists, congregations can be a prime source for referrals. Offering one's services to churches can become an opportunity to become known to congregational leaders and members alike. For example, one psychologist moved into the city of Temelucah, California without knowing anyone. He attended the ministerial association meetings and offered to provide the ministers a free workshop on clergy malpractice. He visited each church and became acquainted with the clergy leaders. He queried them about their needs and offered to teach classes in their church schools. Although he did not perceive his offers as being cost effective, he did see these as consultative opportunities which would result in referrals for service where he would charge regular fees. His plan worked. He is now firmly established as a reputable congregational resource and consultant in that area.

The above discussion leads naturally to a discussion of the possibility of a marriage between congregations and consultants. Society needs congregations. As Maton and Pargament so forcefully stated, "As an individual and institutional force, religion represents an important resource for efforts to prevent significant personal and social problems. (In a recent survey) . . . Fifty-six percent of the population stated that religion is very important in their own lives. Fifty-eight percent reported that religion is an answer to all or most of today's problems" (1987, pp. 161-162, parentheses mine). At the very least, religion is here to stay. At most, religion may be among the most prominent of society's means by which human life can be improved. While religious participation may be voluntary and elective, the place of congregations in the "body politick" should be considered as the kind of necessity society can ill afford to do without.

Consultants should look upon congregations as allies, not obstacles, to human development. Religion provides a unique type of motivation for the living of life. It calls persons to live by ideals. This includes ideals about how individuals are to grow spiritually as well as how they are to express their spirituality in service to others. There is probably no higher motivation available to humans than that which is provided by religion. Congregations exist to make these ideals become realities. This is their mission. While it has to be granted that religion often is preoccupied with heaven and the world to come, it also has been a great force in behalf of life here and now. In most cases, society can count on congregations to respond to human pain and to be vitally interested in preventing human suffering. On the positive side, society can count on most congregations to join in efforts to promote healthy, wholesome existence for persons in almost every phase of their lives.

Toward these ends, congregations will always need consultants just as much as consultants need congregations. In another publication, it was stated that congregations should be looked upon as "organized disorganizations or disorganized organizations; pay your money, take your choice" (Malony, 1986a, p. 69). Either way you look at congregations, they need help! Consultants can give that help. In another context Malony asserted that, "The Lord's house needs built-in shrinks" (1986b, p. 211). This is not only a fact, it is a truth. This does not necessarily mean that the consultant should be a member, or on the staff, of the congregation. It does mean that congregations should adopt a "consultative attitude" in which they easily and eagerly seek the type of assistance consultants can give. This may not always be easy because of their natural resistance to seek help. But the pay-off for congregational life will be great. In fact, congregations that utilize consultants will find that their efforts to express their ideals will be greatly enhanced.

Congregations can change. As the old saying states, "that which is bad can get worse; that which is good can get better." Congregations need not stagnate and continue to do business as usual. More often than not, they need the kind of objective reflection, counsel and training which consultants can give.

Yes, the relationship between congregations and consultants is a marriage that needs courting and consummating. Congregations are a burgeoning market for consultant services. Consultants are a relatively untapped resource for congregations. Both will profit from the marriage. Most importantly, when consultants and congregations come together the welfare of persons will be enhanced, suffering will be ameliorated, pitfalls will be avoided, and problems will be prevented.

REFERENCES

Barnhart, C. L. (Ed.). (1965). Consultation. In *Thorndike-Barnhart Comprehensive Desk Dictionary*. Garden City, NY: Doubleday, p. 191.

Bunker, D., Miller, D., & Malony, H. N. (1990). *Secularization among students in Christian professional education*. Unpublished manuscript, Graduate School of Psychology, Fuller Theological Seminary.

Galessich, J. (1982). *The profession and practice of consultation*. San Francisco: Jossey-Bass.

Malony, H. N. (1986a). *Church organization development: Perspectives and processes*. Pasadena: Integration Press.

Malony, H. N. (Ed.). (1986b). *Is there a shrink in the Lord's house? How psychologists can help the church*. Pasadena: Integration Press.

Malony, H. N. (1988). Theoretical models of church consultation or "a good man is hard to find." *Newsletter: Division 36, American Psychological Association: Psychologists Interested in Religious Issues, 12*(3), 6-8.

Maton, K. I., & Pargament, K. I. (1987). The roles of religion in prevention and promotion. *Prevention in Human Services, 5*(2), 161-205.

Niebuhr, H. R. (1951). *Christ and culture*. New York: Harper and Row.

Pargament, K. I., Ensing, D. S., Falgout, K., & Warren, R. K. (1988). Consultation with churches and congregations. In P. Keller & S. R. Heyman (Eds.), *Innovations in clinical practice: A sourcebook*. Sarasota, FL: Professional Resource Exchange.

Ponton, M. O., & Weber, T. (1986). A multi-modal approach to psychological consultation with the church. In H. N. Malony (Ed.), *Is there a shrink in the Lord's house? How psychologists can help the church*. Pasadena: Integration Press.

Shafranske, E., & Malony, H. N. (1990). Clinical psychologists' religious and spiritual orientations and their practice of psychotherapy. *Psychotherapy, 27*(1), 72-78.

Tyler, F., Pargament, K., & Gatz, M. (1983). The resource collaborator role: A model for interactions involving psychologists. *American Psychologist, 38*, 388-398.

Networking Between Agencies and Black Churches: The Lay Health Advisor Model

Eugenia Eng
John W. Hatch

University of North Carolina

SUMMARY. The question of the possible, proper, or desirable relationships of churches to health and human service agencies is raised. Identifying, recruiting, and training important members of natural helping networks in the black church, who can serve as "lay health advisors" (LHA) linking and negotiating between people at risk and agency services, is one health intervention strategy for establishing a relationship between formal and informal support systems. As lay people to whom others naturally turn for advice, emotional support, and tangible aid, LHAs provide informal and spontaneous assistance. Found at many levels in a community, these persons are already helping people by virtue of their community roles, occupations, or personality traits. A lay health advisor intervention model conceptualizes the relationships between the social support functions of networks within black congregations and their expected effects on: (1) the behaviors of individuals at risk; (2) the service delivery structures of agencies; and (3) the problem solving capacities of communities. Based on this model, three types of LHA interventions are categorized in accordance with the aim of network

---

The authors are grateful for the thoughtful review and comments provided by Robert Hess, the editor of *Prevention in Human Services*, and Kenneth Pargament and Kenneth Maton, the editors of this special volume. The authors acknowledge the indispensable contributions from the public health practitioners, church leaders, and lay health advisors in North Carolina who shared their wisdom and experience from working with black congregations to promote health and human dignity. Reprints may be requested from Eugenia Eng or John Hatch, Department of Health Behavior and Health Education, School of Public Health CB #7400, University of North Carolina, Chapel Hill, NC 27599.

member involvement: (1) enhancing the total network within a church; (2) cooperative problem-solving linking networks between churches; and (3) coalition building connecting networks beyond the church. An intervention example for each of these categories is provided, including a description of the target population, support provider(s), purpose, problems addressed, network characteristics emphasized, activities used, and role of the professional. Important lessons learned from these examples are drawn, with particular emphasis given to the issues and special interests of working with natural helping networks in black congregations.

As an institutional force in the lives of black Americans, the church can exert a wide-reaching influence through changing the behaviors, attitudes, and knowledge of individual congregation members as well as through mobilizing changes in the larger social order. Notwithstanding the mission of all religious systems in fulfilling the human need for meaning and belonging, the black church has the distinction of being one of the few institutions in the U.S. controlled by black people. An estimated 70% of the black American population report membership in a church. Of these members, 65-70% belong to churches governed by black denominations, 10-15% belong to predominantly black congregations governed by white denominational conferences, and 15-20% belong to independent sects (Lincoln, 1984). To ensure a sense of connectedness, the seven major black church denominations and many smaller denominational bodies centrally produce and distribute publications to all their members. To provide support and assistance for members' needs, ranging from basic survival issues to issues involving politics and decision-making, most black congregations have organized committees and programs, each connected to the denomination headquarters through workshops and annual meetings. Even black Americans with no affiliation to a church are connected to its influence through their family and friends who are attached to the lay support system provided by the black church (Lincoln, 1984).

Caplan (1974), a community psychiatrist, defines a lay support system as:

> . . . an enduring pattern of continuous or intermittent ties that play a significant part in maintaining the psychological and physical integrity of the individual over time . . . Support systems are attachments among individuals or between individuals and groups that serve to improve adaptive competence in dealing with short-term crises and life transitions as well as long-term challenges, stresses, and privations through (a) promoting emotional mastery, (b) offering guid-

ance regarding the field of relevant forces involved in expectable problems and methods of dealing with them, and (c) providing feedback about an individual's behavior that validates his conception of his own identity and fosters improved performance based on adequate self-evaluation.

Lay support systems in the church have the similar goal of promoting the well-being of their members as that of professional service delivery systems in promoting the health of their clients (Eng, Hatch, & Cunningham, 1985; Maton & Pargament, 1987). A widely held view is that although it is important to acknowledge the separateness of the professional and lay helping systems, they may nevertheless interface in important ways by engaging in free communication, and collaborating at times to supplement each other's services. Some suggest that the relations between formal and informal helping systems can be strengthened through the promotion of what is termed a "hidden health care system" so that agencies' consideration of natural helping networks would lead to more comprehensive and long-lasting support for people in trouble (Levin & Idler, 1981; Veroff, Kulka, & Douvan, 1981). Still others go further, in that they see these natural helping networks not as replacements for services but as "mediating structures" that can in part negotiate with professional agencies for more and better quality services (Berger & Neuhouse, 1981; Service & Salber, 1979).

The question of the possible, proper, or desirable relationships of churches to health and human service agencies—whether the latter are practicing privately or publicly—is being raised with the emergence of interest in the social support functions of religion for buffering the effects of stressful life events (Glik, 1986; Kaplan, 1980; Maton, 1989; Pargament & Hahn, 1986; Veroff, Kulka, & Douvan, 1981; Zuckerman, Kasl, & Ostfeld, 1984) and in church-based networks for promoting personal and social change to improve health (Catalano & Dooley, 1980; Eng, Hatch, & Cunningham, 1985; Hatch & Lovelace, 1980). Identifying and recruiting important members of natural helping networks in the black church, who can serve as "lay health advisors" linking and negotiating between people at risk and agency services, is one health intervention strategy for establishing a relationship between formal and informal support systems.

The focus of this paper is on the authors' work in conceptualizing and implementing such a strategy to increase the health promotion capacities of natural helping networks in black congregations. The conceptual model and its application in designing three different lay health advisor interventions with black church congregations in North Carolina are described. The implementation process and effects from each intervention are examined. Finally, important lessons learned about network based interventions are drawn, with particular emphasis given to the issues and special interests of working with natural helping networks in black congregations.

LAY HEALTH ADVISOR MODEL

Figure 1 presents the conceptual model describing how members of social networks can influence professional and lay helping systems to have an effect on the health of individuals and on the development of their communities. A lay health advisor intervention based on the social support functions of networks within congregations can target change at multiple levels: (1) the behaviors of individuals at risk; (2) the service delivery structures of agencies; and (3) the problem solving capacities of communities. The relationships and their expected effects depicted by the model are drawn from several health education theories and concepts.

The uppermost section of the model represents the behavior change process at the individual level. Health behavior research and health education practice have found that an individual's health decisions and behaviors are related to his/her perceptions of risks, such as believing one is susceptible to illness and that the consequences from illness are sufficiently severe to warrant the level of effort required to change one's behavior (Hochbaum, 1970; Janz & Becker, 1984; Rosenstock, 1979). However, it has also been found that by increasing individuals' knowledge and fear of illness, such as inserting brochures on the warning signs of cancer in church bulletins, the effects may be necessary but not sufficient to motivate individuals to use a particular service, such as cancer screening, or to change a lifestyle practice, such as smoking cessation. That is, behavior change is part of a decision making process through which individuals appraise prevailing social norms and expectations toward the behavior (Azjen & Fishbein, 1971) — "Many of my buddies smoke, but my pastor is trying to quit," assess their own capacity to master the requirements of behavior change (Bandura, 1979; Strecher, DeVellis, Becker, & Rosenstock, 1987) — "I don't know if I can resist even though my church is sponsoring a Smoke-Out Sunday," and go through stages of seeking and trying out different services (Brownell, Marlatt, Lichtenstein, & Wilson, 1986; Kahneman & Tversky, 1972) — "I've tried to quit by using that special chewing gum my doctor gave me, but maybe this time the stop smoking kit that my bible study group is using will work."

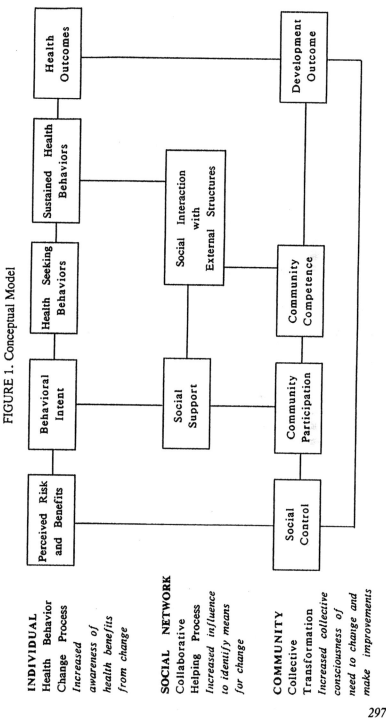

FIGURE 1. Conceptual Model

INDIVIDUAL
Health Behavior
Change Process
*Increased
awareness of
health benefits
from change*

SOCIAL NETWORK
Collaborative
Helping Process
*Increased influence
to identify means
for change*

COMMUNITY
Collective
Transformation
*Increased collective
consciousness of
need to change and
make improvements*

The middle section of the model represents how individual perceptions, appraisals, decisions, and behaviors can be influenced by people and circumstances in the person's immediate social environment (Germaine, 1979; McLeroy, Bibeau, Steckler, & Glanz, 1988; Porter, 1983). Friends, family, church leaders, members of church groups are defined sets of people who may form an individual's various social networks. Commonly accepted norms and forms of transactions that link network members to one another, such as exchanging information with neighbors but sharing domestic problems only with friends, or receiving help from the church members during a crisis but from relatives on a daily basis, can be used by professional caregivers to interpret the behaviors of the persons involved (Cobb, 1976; Gottlieb, 1985). For example, different types of support (informational, emotional, tangible assistance) may be provided by different sets of relationships (Israel, 1985). The number of people in a network, their frequency of interaction, and the degree of reciprocal helping can affect the flow of support (Caplan, 1974). The finding that perceived social support can have a significant and positive association with health status underscores the need to examine the potential of using social networks in an intervention to improve individuals' health behaviors (Broadhead, Kaplan, James, Wagner, Schoenbach, Grimson, Heyden, Tibblin, & Gehlback, 1983; Cassel, 1976; Gore, 1978; Thoits, 1983; Zuckerman, 1984).

Moreover, social networks frequently overlap and interact, thereby exerting an influence on members' perceptions, decisions, and behaviors which goes beyond the effects of more immediate kin and non-kin networks (Israel, 1985). For example, members of a church are often tied to others in the congregation on the additional basis of kinship, friendship, neighborhood, civic and social organizations, or work. These overlapping networks, therefore, can perform important social support functions to meet some need, render some service, or nurture some interest not only for their congregation but also for the members' communities. For many black communities, particularly in the rural South, church affiliation and activities can provide the social cohesion of interpersonal ties for establishing natural community boundaries that may be different from the geographic boundaries of a town or school district. Collective norms, roles, practices, and decision-making patterns structured in the black church can be reflected in the forms of social control exerted by the community to socialize individual community members to particular beliefs, lifestyles, and ways of dealing with the issues of health and survival. Thus, the church has the potential for playing an important linking role in mobilizing the overlapping networks in a community to negotiate and mediate with external structures, such as agencies, for more resources and more responsive services.

Additionally, the church can fulfill a community development role. The lower section of the model depicts the influence that can be exerted by mobilizing communities served by the church. It is a well known fact that the black church was critical to the community organizing efforts of the American civil rights movement in the 1960s. The effects from mobilizing a community to participate in planning and undertaking its own problems, combined with the effects from establishing relationships with outside agencies, can be an increased sense of collective competence (Cottrell, 1979) that will contribute toward the outcome of community growth and development (Biddle & Biddle, 1965; Brown & Margo, 1978; Eng, Hatch, & Cunningham, 1985; Florin & Wandersman, 1984; Hatch & Eng, 1983; Heller, 1989; Steuart, 1985; Tweeten & Brinkman, 1976; Uphoff & Cohen, 1979; Wellman & Leighton, 1979). Furthermore, empirical evidence exists for a positive correlation between community participation and sense of empowerment (Zimmerman & Rappaport, 1988) and between community development and improved health status (Ratcliffe, 1976). And, it is through changes in collective perceptions of social control at the community level that changes in perceptions of health risks and benefits at the individual level can occur (Suchman, 1967).

The model implies that the professional service delivery system may be considered by individuals as being separate from the support functions provided by their networks and from the problem-solving functions provided by their communities. A promising approach would be to strengthen existing helping networks and to increase the interaction between multiple networks by: (1) increasing health information and knowledge of available services for members to share; (2) improving communication techniques for members to expand their outreach; (3) teaching self-care skills to members at risk; (4) establishing linkages with agencies to negotiate a more efficient system of access and referrals; and (5) providing channels for exchanging and coordinating resources among networks experiencing common needs.

Identifying, recruiting, and training influential members of social networks as lay health advisors (LHA) to accomplish the above tasks is one intervention strategy that has emerged from the model and has been implemented in black churches. As lay people to whom others naturally turn for advice, emotional support, and tangible aid, LHAs provide informal and spontaneous assistance (Israel, 1985). Found at many levels in a community, these persons are already helping people by virtue of their community roles, occupations, or personality traits (Kelley & Kelley, 1985). LHAs based in the church can pursue a variety of goals, fulfill a variety of roles, and use a variety of activities and tactics. There is no one type of LHA intervention that will be effective in all situations. As a way of organizing the different LHA interventions that have been developed with black congregations, one typology containing three broad categories will be presented.

TYPOLOGY OF CHURCH-BASED
LAY HEALTH ADVISOR PROGRAMS

Although the typology presents three distinct types of LHA interventions, there is often overlap, and actually the third category combines elements of the other two. The three types of interventions are categorized in accordance with the aim of network member involvement: (1) enhancing the total network within a church; (2) cooperative problem-solving linking networks between churches; and (3) coalition building connecting networks beyond the church. An intervention example for each of these categories will be provided, including a description of the target population, support provider(s), purpose, problems addressed, network characteristics emphasized, activities used, and role of the professional.

Enhancing the Total Network Within a Church

The North Carolina General Baptist State Convention (GBSC) Health and Human Services Program, initially funded by the Kellogg Foundation and Z. Smith Reynolds Foundation, is an example of an LHA intervention which enhances the total network of members in a church through working with natural helpers. Such natural caregivers are lay people to whom others in a congregation naturally turn for advice, emotional support, and tangible assistance on an everyday basis. They are not necessarily formal church leaders who provide social support during a crisis, but more routinely fulfill other functions as opinion-leaders and organizers. Examples of their helping include daycare for young and old; advice and emotional support on personal, family, and financial matters; and assistance in making connections between network members by matching needs with resources or by referring them to formal agencies. The nature of the support provided by natural helpers is informal and spontaneous—so much a part of everyday life that it often goes unrecognized by natural helpers themselves. Natural helpers were most often described by GBSC church members and pastors as persons who are trusted for maintaining confidentiality, who listen with an open ear and caring heart, and who are respected for being sufficiently in control of their own life circumstances.

With the potential for reaching 400,000 adult church members, the target population for the GBSC Program was the total congregation of each participating church. This approach may be considered to be a primary prevention strategy in that the focus is on strengthening network ties of all members in a church, rather than exclusively for those members who are at risk or already experiencing health problems. For each GBSC congregation, the desired network changes from the work of LHAs were: increased skills and knowledge of natural helpers in risk reduction; increased diffusion of this knowledge and skill to network members; increased exchange of self-care resources; and increased referrals of members in need to local agency services. Particular care was needed to monitor changes in the level and quality of the social support exchanged without jeopardizing LHAs' reputation for maintaining confidentiality and without giving the impression that LHAs were being inspected and rated. To reduce the potentially negative effects from a network analysis which elicited names, less obtrusive network information was collected on the types of relationship between the LHAs and persons helped, e.g., relative, friend, co-worker, church member, neighbor, other acquaintance.

Among individuals in the congregation, desired effects from the work of LHAs were: increased awareness of health risks related to hypertension, diabetes, and maternal and child health problems; increased utilization of relevant health services; and, increased adoption of health promoting behaviors to prevent and control these problems. Selecting the health problems to be targeted was not a simple task. First, it was necessary to review and interpret with GBSC officials statewide health data broken down by race to identify the leading health problems among the black population. GBSC officials then had to consider which problems would most likely be viewed not only as a need by most of the churches but also as an undertaking for which most churches had the resources. Related to this latter point was the need to locate and review existing educational and training materials to assess their relevance to GBSC congregations. Through this process, the decision was made not to address cancer for which there was a prevailing fear but a relative lack of options other than early detection through screening. There were many more prevention and control measures for hypertension and diabetes that LHAs could be trained to learn and diffuse within their congregations. It was also decided to frame the problem of teenage pregnancy within the broader category of maternal and child health problems, given the sensitivities attached by the church to premarital sexual activity.

The desired organizational changes were: institutional adoption by GBSC to continue funding program staff and activities after the life of the grants; institutional adoption by each church of LHA health promotion activities; and institutional support from local agencies for training and supporting LHAs. During the intervention planning stage, an understanding of how GBSC as an organization is structured and operates was critical in order to negotiate these institutional expectations. The more obvious challenge presented by these desired changes was to assist GBSC to assume financial responsibilities for the long-term costs. Most initial start-up costs had to be funded by the grants. However, GBSC officials decided that through careful fundraising and gradual increments in the GBSC contribution to the program's budget, they would be able to assume full responsibility for personnel costs by the end of the funding period. After notification of funding, an additional challenge posed in institutionalizing the intervention was structural. As in any organization, including a religious based one, the GBSC governing system of boards in the headquarters and associations of churches in the various districts needed to consider how decisions and activities related to the intervention could be integrated into their existing structures of supervision and support to the various committees in each of the participating churches. During all phases of the intervention, progress reports and issues requiring decisions were placed on the agendas of GBSC board meetings, statewide and regional conferences, and district meetings of associations.

The GBSC hired three full-time public health professionals (one health administrator and two health educators) to be based in the headquarters. Working with the GBSC leadership, the staff targeted a different church region for each year. From this region, groups of 10-20 churches were selected and recruited to participate. With each church grouping, the staff played four major roles. One was to initiate the process of identifying and selecting natural helpers. To establish a set of criteria that describes the characteristics of an LHA, the staff carried out a series of open-ended interviews with the pastors of the churches and then asked for names of people who fit the criteria. Nearly all of the natural helpers initially identified by their pastors were women over 30 years of age actively involved in church committees and events. The potential problem raised by having almost no male LHAs was in not reaching men in the congregation. Consequently, project staff asked each pastor to add at least one male to the list of natural helpers. To strengthen the staff's recruitment efforts, each pastor was also asked to inform his recommended members that he had selected them for LHA training and why, in his opinion, they were natural helpers. This helped to reduce the element of surprise or self-doubt among the many natural helpers who often do not recognize themselves the support they provide to others. The final recruitment for LHA training of at least three natural helpers from each church was made following interviews to explore their interest and willingness to participate.

The second role for staff was to arrange LHA training for each group of approximately 30 natural helpers focussed on: measures for preventing and controlling hypertension, diabetes, and maternal and child health problems; techniques for communicating health assistance to individuals; and methods for organizing health promotion activities, such as health fairs, for their church. A meeting with the pastors from the participating churches was held to decide on which church and evening of the week the 10 two-hour sessions would be conducted, and by which local professionals. The staff recruited trainers from among local public and private practitioners.

Orienting the practitioners to establish a link between natural helping networks in the churches and the service delivery system was the third role for staff. The challenge was to assist providers in making a shift from viewing LHAs as clients to one of viewing them as influentials who can help people prevent and control illness and to seek appropriate services when needed. Inviting providers to share their technical knowledge with natural helpers in a church fellowship hall and to participate in the "graduation" ceremony at the end of training facilitated this process. LHAs in the security of their own surroundings and peers could interact on a more personal and social basis with providers, raising points and questions in the context of their own experiences.

The fourth role for staff was to serve as consultants to the LHAs during and after training on matters related to organizing activities with support from the church and local agencies. Blood pressure screening once a month after church, diabetes support groups, cookbooks of low fat recipes, health fairs, and parenting programs for teen mothers are examples of activities initiated by LHAs to strengthen and develop the social networks of people in need. These activities often focused on alleviating a specific problem or providing assistance in dealing with a given disease, and therefore, LHAs required some consultation from staff on how to elicit technical support from external sources.

At the end of five years, GBSC has implemented the intervention in churches representing all its districts and appears to be achieving the desired changes. Findings from the evaluation comparing pre and post indicators found significant increases in knowledge and service utilization as well as significant decreases in health risks among members of the participating congregations. On ethical grounds, GBSC decided against including congregations as a control group in the evaluation design. Staff support has been taken over by GBSC. A GBSC board has assumed responsibility for the program. Health promotion materials and diffusion have been integrated into the GBSC Christian Education Office. The GBSC has been recognized with a national award for being one of the most innovative programs in health promotion from the Department of Health and Human Services and with a state award for excellence in community service from the Governor's Office.

Cooperative Problem-Solving Linking Networks Between Churches

The Interdenominational Health and Human Services Program (IHHSP), funded by the Ruth Mott Fund and the Presbyterian Church U.S.A., is an example of an intervention to link the support networks of two or more congregations, regardless of denomination, to one another. In recognizing that some needs are more effectively met within the support system of a church, but demand commonly exceeds one congregation's ability to respond, the purpose of this type of intervention is to develop network ties between churches to respond cooperatively to these demands. This approach combines the resources of churches of different denominations, located in close geographic proximity to one another, to coordinate the services and crisis care they provide to the same general population.

Drawing a majority of their members from working class black homes in the same area of an urban center and including some professionals and low income members, three large inner-city black churches (Baptist, African Methodist Episcopal Zion, and Christian Methodist) differed very little in religious belief and social class. Nonetheless, each church had a strong sense of identity with its own denomination. Members of each church's missionary societies, who provided outreach and family counselling services, were in close contact with missionary workers from other churches of the same denomination but serving different areas of the city. Pastors, missionary workers, and other lay leaders of the same denomination were brought together through regularly scheduled meetings, retreats, and leadership workshops to sustain and encourage the services they provided. However, the responsibilities for care and outreach from churches of different denominations ministering in the same area of the city were seldom coordinated. Patterns of association among church lay leaders followed denominational lines. Their networks of helping, developed over many years, had not expanded to include church members of other denominations.

The challenge of linking the support systems of three churches of different denominations grew from a special discussion series sponsored by the Social Issues Committee in one of the churches on establishing needs and priorities. Members in the congregation who provided services on a professional or volunteer basis in health, education, law enforcement, or social welfare assisted the Committee in conducting a community survey of perceived needs among residents in what the church determined was its "catchment zone." The findings indicated that while the demand for services was significant, agency workers reported service underutilization by black people. For example, the effects from arthritis were a common disability reported by the elderly. Yet, few of them were attending any of the seven arthritis support groups organized by a local agency because none was located in a black neighborhood. The survey also showed that needs far exceeded the resources of the congregation. For example, a large proportion reported diagnosed cases of hypertension and diabetes. However, the church was not carrying out any health promotion and disease prevention activities beyond routine announcements of services offered by local agencies.

The Committee concluded that a first step toward finding a solution would be to approach the two other churches serving these residents with the survey results. On meeting with the pastors and lay leaders, they discovered that all three churches were struggling to respond to the growing service gap. A task force of representatives from the three churches was formed to investigate how cooperative action could increase their own capacity and that of local agencies to improve the quantity and quality of services offered to black residents.

It became clear to the task force from their discussions with professional service providers and church lay leaders that while many of the needs could be met by existing agencies, simply increasing an awareness of available resources would be necessary but not sufficient to encourage church members to use them. First, many members who knew about services that might meet their needs were reluctant to seek assistance from organizations perceived to be created by and for white people. Second, there existed a prevailing sense of ownership and reciprocity toward the church. That is, members supported the church in good times with the confidence that the church would not forget them during their own times of need. Third, members felt more secure in taking their problems and concerns to the church. Pastors and lay leaders involved in outreach ministries were not only well known to members as well as non-members but were also respected for "listening with an open heart" by maintaining confidentiality. Consequently, people felt more comfortable contacting them.

To improve the quality and use of available agency services, the task force recommended that each church hire a part-time health and human service coordinator to be in direct contact with agencies and thereby serving as a two-way link for the pastor and lay leaders to provide information about services needed by church members. To reduce the strain from overutilization of church resources, the task force recommended that the three churches jointly employ one full-time health and human service professional to develop a cooperative program of services that would respond to the needs shared by all three congregations, but not met by agencies. As a result, the three churches combined the budgets from their Welfare Ministries and jointly sought outside funding to establish the Interdenominational Health and Human Services Program (IHHSP).

During the first year, the IHHSP director played a major role in assessing the availability and accessibility of agency services to members of the three congregations, supervising three part-time staff to coordinate LHAs, and organizing three weeks of technical training for them. The three women had been active church volunteers and brought years of experience to their role as LHA coordinators. One was a retired clerical worker. Another had taught in the public schools for 25 years. The third was a homemaker returning to school as a part-time student in the local technical college. There were problems initially in clarifying relationships and responsibilities between the pastors and director. In assuming a more centralized role of supervising and evaluating coordinator activities, the director was frustrated when pastors directly handled problems and emergencies encountered by the coordinators. At the end of the year, the director resigned to accept another job and was replaced by a person willing to play a more enabling support function. By this time, the coordinators had gained confidence in their skills and began to play a more proactive role in making direct contacts with the agencies.

During the second year, health professionals from private agencies and local universities were training LHAs to serve as counsellors for teens and home visitors for the elderly. Sunday school teachers who work with youth, home missionary workers who visit home-bound elders, and other congregation members serving these two population groups were recruited. The training from local professionals focussed on the social and psychological aspects of the particular life stage, and on the services and resources usually needed by teens and elders. For example, staff from a local teen development program conducted a session on the services they provide related to adolescent sexuality.

Support groups for elders with arthritis or hypertension were being established by LHAs. LHAs were also organizing evening classes on topics such as smoking cessation and weight control. Some congregation members remained skeptical toward the merits of receiving these services in a church other than their own. Thus, the director needed to be careful in ensuring that each church had equal numbers of services scheduled in its building.

There is general agreement among the IHHSP board of directors (composed of three members and the pastors of each church and five members at large) that the program is more efficient and comprehensive than what each church was able to accomplish on its own. The church representatives on the board define the scope of health action to be taken by IHHSP more biomedically than the at-large members, but have become more community oriented in understanding the problems than they were before the program began. Movement toward self-financing and evaluation has not been easy, given the modest level of available resources. Nonetheless, the board feels that the program could be expanded to two or three additional churches. The current director projects that with one additional full-time staff member IHHSP could coordinate and monitor the effectiveness of services for up to 12 churches. The estimated cost would be $10,000 per congregation, an amount that could be realistically generated by the larger churches. The likelihood of this happening will depend heavily on the value that the pastors and lay leaders place on the service. The board is currently searching for mechanisms to reach those church members who influence budgetary decisions to solicit foundation support with an increasing match from the participating churches.

Coalition Building Connecting Networks Beyond the Church

The Shaw-Speaks Center (SSC) risk reduction education project, organized by the Cape Fear Conference of the African Methodist Episcopal Zion (AMEZ) Church in North Carolina, is an example of an intervention to connect church-based support networks to civic, business, and political networks in the surrounding communities. In recognizing that some problems are often beyond the church's ability to control, e.g., employment, inadequate housing, and participation in the political life of the region, the purpose of this type of intervention is to build coalitions through strengthening supportive ties across the various networks to which church members belong. This approach is based in one black denomination, but extends the arena of action to black and white congregations of other denominations found in the same communities.

The more general interfaith church council model in which an interdenominational group of churches combines resources to prevent crises is not common among black denominations. In large part this is due to the communal ethos of the black church and its rural roots in "taking care of our own" which is both a strength and a weakness. Many black churches contribute as much as 20% of their budgets to provide immediate and intensive support on a case by case basis, to respond to crises. However, the capacity to mobilize population based resources to prevent crises collectively, such as more services for families or improved public safety, is limited.

Thus, in the early 1960s the AMEZ Church organized the SSC as a more culturally appropriate alternative to the interfaith church council to curtail the negative impact of rapid social change and uncontrolled development in the eastern coastal region of the state. Low and modest income communities living in this 13 county area had low levels of formal education and few support services to help residents cope with the shift from labor intensive agriculture to an industrialized service based economy. Black residents were disproportionately represented among those negatively affected by these changes.

The stated goal of the SSC was to increase bi-racial cooperation and understanding. To move black social networks toward greater interaction with white social networks, the AMEZ Bishop began by recruiting black and white opinion leaders to serve as SSC board members and advisors. These included local black and white elected officials, senior business leaders and professionals, and university administrators. Many of them were members of AMEZ churches, but the predominant criterion was their reputation for supporting the interests of low and modest income communities. To overcome the traditional boundaries between the agenda of black communities and the development agenda of the region, SSC board members and advisors were assigned two tasks. First, they were to identify and discuss the specific needs of black communities within the wider context of social, political and economic forces influencing regional growth and development. Second, as problems of special concern to black people were identified, they were to assist the AMEZ Bishop in organizing a task force for each issue. Typically, task force members included black and white clergy, civic leaders, political influentials, educators, grassroots community leaders, and service providers representing social networks that, if linked together, could successfully carry out cooperative problem-solving activities and exert greater influence over decision-making and access to resources in the region.

Within this type of intervention there are at least five different organizing processes that could be used to stimulate interaction among several networks. These processes are: community development, social planning (citizen participation), social action, public advocacy, and consciousness-raising. Detailed descriptions of each of these processes can be found elsewhere (Freire, 1976; Kahn, 1978; Rothman, 1981), but it is useful to consider a few dimensions along which they differ: the focus on changing community groups, agencies, controllers of resources, policy makers, or individuals in need; the professional as a facilitator, mediator, catalyst, advocate, or consciousness-raiser; and, the types of techniques used such as working toward consensus, placing citizens on agency boards, non-violent civil disobedience, lobbying, or non-formal education. The selection of the organizing process or combination of processes used are based on factors such as the needs of the network members, their history of collective action, the social, political and economic context, and the skills and preferred role of the professional.

In 1986 an SSC task force was formed around the issue of health. An operating assumption for the members was that organizing several opinion leaders to join the forces of their respective networks to act on their own behalf could in itself be health promoting. That is, improved mental health would be realized from increasing actual and perceived collective competence in undertaking problems that they themselves have identified, and from a strengthened sense of belonging to a wider support system. Thus, the target population was not limited to the people in need, but included the members of their support networks.

To determine the extent of the health problems faced by the target population, the members of this task force used the social planning organizing technique of convening a public hearing from 100 persons representing civic, church, civil rights, and service organizations located in the five counties surrounding the largest urban center in the eastern region. The director of the State Office of Health Statistics was invited to prepare a statement on health needs in these five counties for discussion. The president of the regional chapter of the National Medical Association and an expert in self-help action provided suggestions on the challenges and opportunities for mobilizing community resources. Sub-standard housing, hypertension, and cancer in these black communities emerged as the major health concerns that the participants decided to emphasize.

After the hearing, the SSC health task force provided each participant with a written summary of the meeting for them to report to their respective organizations and communities. As a direct result, the task force was able to engage local participation for planning three self-help risk reduction education projects to promote housing safety for the elderly, cardiovascular health, and cancer screening. Funding was secured in 1987 from the Ruth Mott Foundation to hire a full time SSC health program director and a program assistant to implement the projects. However, the major resource for implementation was the combined pool of volunteers already playing service roles in their respective churches. Among these volunteers, staff recruited and trained LHAs as outreach workers extending agency-based risk reduction services directly to community groups and organizations. A county health department provided free office space for the SSC health program director. Working through the director, LHAs arranged screenings and group education sessions for civic, social, and commercial organizations in their communities. Local physicians, nutritionists, nurses, and health educators volunteered their time to conduct these activities. Three county health departments referred clients to the SSC risk reduction education and screening projects.

Hiring a core professional team to plan and execute mobilizing activities to increase the interaction among civic, religious, and political networks with traditions of volunteer service appears thus far to be a strategy that works for black churches. An evaluation of its impact on health has yet to be conducted. This appears to be a function of assigning priorities to service when faced with limited resources. Continued financial support for the three projects is currently secured through donations from local charities and members of the local AMEZ Church Conference. A fourth project to address the needs of single parent families is being explored.

The leadership role played by the AMEZ Bishop and the predominance of over 80 AMEZ church members on SSC boards and committees permitted the projects to be easily launched and fully integrated into a denominational structure. However, financial commitments from other black denominations have been weak and the professional staff are more closely identified as employees of the AMEZ Church. The success of the SSC in its role as a social change agency rests in part in its failure to gain strong support from black churches of other faiths. There are few models among black churches of interdenominational cooperation in the domain of health and human services. Structural differences, such as the strong centralized control found in black Methodist churches and the black Baptist system of strong congregational autonomy, do not fit well. The long-term survival of an intervention bringing together loosely associated networks to build a wider base of resources, power, and control will depend on the abilities of an umbrella organization, such as the SSC, to modify the structure it inherited from the sponsoring organization.

The tendency toward denominational autonomy appears quite strong. Replicating this type of intervention will require fairly long-term external support. The most successful example is the nationally known Southern Christian Leadership Conference (SCLC). This group has, however, confined its activities to mobilization for political action and has not undertaken the task of using its organizational base to focus on health and human service needs. Nonetheless, local chapters of SCLC draw their membership from many faiths serving the black population. These might be more closely examined for their potential in carrying out health promotion and disease prevention programs.

BARRIERS AND LIMITATIONS
OF NETWORK INTERVENTIONS

Network interventions, like other kinds of strategies, cannot be viewed as a panacea solution for all problems and situations. There are limitations to their effectiveness, and the barriers can come from a variety of factors. Based on the experience of implementing the above LHA interventions within and across black churches, the following is a summary of the major issues that can arise in working with religious institutions.

Natural helpers, lay leaders, and opinion leaders in a church usually provide social support from a spiritual point of reference, whereas health professionals are usually motivated by self-care and direct service considerations. If these differences are not clarified through a process of open exchange, then the focus of the intervention can become overly client-centered and categorical, not responding to the broader based needs of the network. Thus, it is important for agency staff to have the skills, attitudes, and values necessary to work through these differences.

Given the above, the entry phase of a church based network intervention can be time consuming and is unlikely to be cost-effective in the short-run. For sponsoring health agencies or funding foundations, this can be problematic. Also, accounting for and measuring the effects from the activities of natural helpers, lay leaders, and other church volunteers can be difficult. Striking a fine balance between the need for reliable and valid data to evaluate effectiveness and the need not to undermine the functions of a church's natural support system is a continual challenge.

Administrative support, funds, and skilled and reliable volunteers from the church are valuable resources that are needed to carry on existing programs for the congregation. Although the pastor and lay leaders may look with favor on a proposed health intervention, it is especially important to avoid competing for these scarce resources. Integrating a health intervention into the agenda and activities of a long-standing church group or committee can be less of a strain or threat than organizing a new committee structure. In many congregations, existing committees have stated missions that are sufficiently broad to graft on the promotion of health.

When health interventions "borrow" the reputation of a church to take advantage of a support system that is respected and trusted by the people it serves, the program can also take on any negative identities associated with a particular church. Prior actions of the church's clergy or lay leaders may have alienated some members of the wider community to such a degree that health professionals collaborating with the church could be viewed with suspicion.

Interventions that require cooperative action among churches, either of the same or different denominations, are at times viewed with caution by pastors. This is more likely to occur when the lay leaders from different churches form a coalition to carry out a project. A pastor can become threatened with the possibility that his membership might develop notions of lay decision-making that could conflict with his leadership style.

History and traditions of responsibility and service along congregational or denominational lines can prevent churches from expanding their mission to include the broader universe of community and society. It is important, therefore, that the health focus of an intervention be congruent with the church's interpretation of its mission.

Agency policies which place too much emphasis on self-help and direct services may constrain larger scale coalition building by diverting churches' attention away from political and economic inequities which are root causes of most health problems. Rivalries and problems of "turf" can also result, thereby undermining the development of new supportive and reciprocal ties between churches and the service delivery system to bring about needed changes in the service system itself.

To overcome most of these barriers, health and human service providers need to consider modifying their frame of reference for "helping." This includes: not having to be in complete control; working with people who have different norms and approaches for providing help; relating to colleagues who may not understand or value church-based network interventions; and not receiving immediate feedback or recognition from the lay system. Then it will be possible to recognize, learn from, and draw upon the lay expertise from the support system of the church.

When sustainability is as important as replicability, then it may be less efficient in the long-term to organize interventions around a particular set of health problems. That is, interventions designed to use the structures and functions of existing support systems are more likely to encourage participation and mobilize resources for a range of health problems that go beyond those originally targeted. In planning a church-based program, the LHA model can provide a useful conceptual rationale for: (1) determining expected levels of outcome; (2) selecting network intervention strategies; (3) identifying formal and informal structures to be linked; and (4) defining LHA characteristics, roles, and activities that contribute to the above. A wide range of health problems can be addressed within this conceptual model, constrained only by the church's framework of values. The three LHA interventions described were based in the black church, not because it is a convenient place to reach people with a specific health problem, but because of the caregiving and problem-solving relationships that are formed among members of the congregation. Moreover, it is through this black religious system of social support that linkages to the professional service delivery system can shift the dynamics from a provider-client mode to a group-collaborator mode. The LHA model represents a mediating strategy between people and their environments to secure the basics for health; information and life skills; opportunities for making healthy choices; and physical, social, and economic conditions of living which enhance health.

REFERENCES

Azjen, I., & Fishbein, M. (1977). Attitude-behavior relations: A theoretical analysis and review of empirical literature. *Psychological Bulletin, 84*(5), 888-918.

Bandura, A. (1977). *Social learning theory*. Englewood Cliffs, NJ: Prentice-Hall.

Berger, P., & Neuhouse, R. (1977). *To empower people: The role of mediating structures in public policy*. Washington, DC: American Enterprise Institute for Public Policy Research.

Biddle, W., & Biddle, L. (1965). *Community development process: The rediscovery of initiative*. New York: Holt, Rinehart & Winston.

Broadhead, W. E., Kaplan, B. H., James, S. A., Wagner, E. H., Schoenbach, V. J., Grimson, R., Heyden, S., Tibblin, G., & Gehlback, S. H. (1983). The epidemiologic evidence for a relationship between social support and health. *American Journal of Epidemiology, 117*(5), 521-537.

Brown, E. R., & Margo, G. E. (1978). Health education: Can the reformers be reformed? *International Journal of Health Services*, *8*(1), 3-26.

Brownell, K. D., Marlatt, G. A., Lichtenstein, E., & Wilson, G. T. (1986). Understanding and preventing relapse. *American Psychologist*, *41*(7), 765-782.

Caplan, G. (1974). *Support systems and community mental health*. New York: Human Sciences Press.

Cassel, J. (1976). The contribution of the social environment to host-resistance. *American Journal of Epidemiology*, *104*, 107-122.

Catalano, R., & Dooley, D. (1980). Economic change in primary prevention. In R. Price, R. Ketter, B. Bader, & J. Monahan (Eds.), *Prevention in mental health: Research, policy and practice*. Beverly Hills: Sage Publications.

Cobb, S. (1976). Social support as a moderator of life stress. *Psychosomatic Medicine*, *38*, 300-314.

Cottrell, L. (1976). The competent community. In B. H. Kaplan, R. N. Wilson, & A. H. Leighton (Eds.), *Further explorations in social psychiatry*. New York: Basic Books.

Eng, E., Briscoe, J., & Callan, A. (1990). Participation effect from water projects on EPI. *Social Science and Medicine*, *30*(12), 1349-1358.

Eng, E., Hatch, J., & Cunningham, A. (1985). Institutionalizing social support through the church and into the community. *Health Education Quarterly*, *12*(1), 81-92.

Florin, P. R., & Wandersman, A. (1984). Cognitive social learning and participation in community development. *American Journal of Community Psychology*, *12*(6), 689-708.

Germaine, C. (1970). *Social work practice: People and environments: An ecological perspective*. New York: Columbia University Press.

Glik, D. (1986). Psychosocial wellness among spiritual healing participants. *Social Science and Medicine*, *22*(5), 579-586.

Gore, S. (1978). The effects of social support in moderating the health consequences of unemployment. *Journal of Health and Social Behavior*, *19*, 156-165.

Gottlieb, B. H. (1985). Social networks and social support: An overview of research, practice, and policy implications. *Health Education Quarterly*, *12*(1), 5-22.

Hatch, J., & Eng, E. (1984). Community participation and control: Or control of community participation. In V. Sidel & R. Sidel (Eds.), *Reforming medicine: Lessons of the last quarter century*. New York: Pantheon Books, 223-244.

Hatch, J., & Eng, E. (1983). Health worker roles in community oriented primary care. In E. Connor & F. Mullan (Eds.), *Community oriented primary care*. Washington, DC: National Academy of Medicine Press, 138-158.

Hatch, J., & Lovelace, K. (1980). Involving the southern rural church and students of the health professions in health education. *Public Health Reports*, 95.

Heller, K. (1989). The return to community. *American Journal of Community Psychology*, *17*(1), 1-15.

Hochbaum, G. H. (1970). *Health behavior*. Belmont, CA: Wadsworth Publishing.

Israel, B. (1985). Social networks and social support: Implications for natural helper and community level interventions. *Health Education Quarterly, 12*(1), 65-80.

Israel, B. (1988). Community-based social network interventions: Meeting the needs of the elderly. *Danish Medical Bulletin, 6,* 36-44.

Janz, N., & Becker, M. (1984). The health belief model: A decade later. *Health Education Quarterly, 11*(1), 1-47.

Kahneman, D., & Tversky, A. (1974). Prospect theory: An analysis of decisions under risk. *Econometrica, 47,* 263-291.

Kaplan, B. H. (1980). *Deviant behavior in defense of self*. New York: Academic Press.

Kelley, P., & Kelley, V. R. (1985). Supporting natural helpers: A cross-cultural study. *The Journal of Contemporary Social Work*, June, 358-366.

Levin, L., & Idler, E. L. (1981). *The hidden health care system: Mediating structures and medicine*. Boston: Ballinger Publishing.

Lincoln, C. E. (1984). *Race, religion and the continuing American dilemma*. New York: Hill and Wang.

Maton, K. I. (1989). The stress-buffering role of spiritual support: Cross-sectional and prospective investigations. *Journal for the Scientific Study of Religion, 28*(3), 310-323.

Maton, K., & Pargament, K. (1987). The roles of religion in prevention and promotion. *Prevention in Human Services, 5*(2), 161-205.

McLeroy, K., Bibeau, D., Steckler, A., & Glanz, K. (1988). An ecological perspective on health promotion programs. *Health Education Quarterly, 15*(4), 351-377.

Pargament, K., & Hahn, J. (1986). God and the just world: Causal and coping attributions to God in health situations. *Journal for the Scientific Study of Religion, 25,* 193-207.

Porter, R. A. (1983). Ecological strategies of prevention in rural community development. *Journal of Primary Prevention, 3*(4), 235-243.

Ratcliffe, J. (1978). Social justice and the demographic transition: Lessons from India's Kerala State. *International Journal of Health Services, 8*(1), 123-144.

Rosenstock, I. M. (1974). The historical origins of the health belief model. *Health Education Monographs, 2,* 354-395.

Service, C., & Salber E. J. (1979). *Community health education: The lay health advisor approach*. Durham, NC: Duke University Health Care Systems.

Steuart, G. (1985). Social and behavioral change strategies. In H. T. Phillips & S. A. Gaylord (Eds.), *Aging and public health*. New York: Springer Publisher.

Strecher, V., DeVellis, B., Becker, M., & Rosenstock, I. M. (1987). The role of self-efficacy in achieving health behavior change. *Health Education Quarterly, 13,* 73-92.

Suchman, E. A. (1967). Preventive health behavior: A model for research on community health campaigns. *Journal of Health and Social Behavior, 8,* 197-209.

Thoits, P. A. (1983). Dimensions of life events that influence psychological distress: An evaluation and synthesis of the literature. In B. H. Kaplan (Ed.), *Psychosocial stress: Trends in theory and research.* New York: Academic Press.

Tweeten, L., & Brinkman, G. (1976). *Micropolitan development.* Ames, IA: Iowa State University Press.

Uphoff, N., Cohen, J., & Goldsmith, A. (1979). *Feasibility and application of rural development participation: A state of the art paper.* Rural Development Committee. Ithaca, NY: Center for International Studies, Cornell University.

Veroff, J., Kulka, R. A., & Douvan, E. (1981). *Mental health in America: Patterns of help-seeking from 1957-1976.* New York: Basic Books.

Wellman, B., & Leighton, B. (1979). Networks, neighborhoods and communities: Approaches to the study of the community question. *Urban Affairs Quarterly, 14*(3), 363-390.

Zimmerman, M., & Rappaport, J. (1988). Citizen participation, perceived control, and psychological empowerment. *American Journal of Community Psychology, 16*(5), 725-750.

Zuckerman, D. M., Kasl, S. V., & Ostfeld, A. M. (1984). Psychological predictors of mortality among the elderly poor: The role of religion, well-being, and social contacts. *American Journal of Epidemiology, 119,* 710-723.

Preventing Homelessness: Religious Organizations and Housing Development

Evan Cohen

Michigan Department of Mental Health

Carol T. Mowbray

Wayne State University

Vicki Gillette

National Association of Community Development Loan Funds

Elizabeth Thompson

Michigan Department of Mental Health

SUMMARY. Homelessness in America has emerged as a national problem of increasing breadth and complexity, one that must be addressed by private and public sectors to effect a solution. Research results describing the homeless population and its subgroups indicate the need for broad-based housing and support service initiatives which are client preference-based and provide involvement with relational communities. Several examples are offered of religious organizations' traditional social service role with the homeless. More recent and proactive roles are highlighted, describing social action in arenas of advocacy, finance, and housing development. Finally, the possibilities and challenges of improved collaboration between religious and human service organizations are discussed, with suggestions for next steps.

Homelessness has perhaps existed in America ever since individuals had to rely on the actions of others for their shelter. Religious organiza-

---

Reprints may be obtained from Evan Cohen, Department of Mental Health, Lewis Cass Building, Lansing, MI 48913.

317

tions have frequently taken a leading role in sponsoring shelters for the homeless. However, the current dimensions and complexity of the homeless issue have changed, as well as its social circumstances. It is now recognized that simply building shelters for the homeless may be part of a new and dehumanizing way of isolating the poorest among us. Developing permanent housing and providing support services to prevent homelessness and/or to shorten its debilitating course is the preferred solution.

In *Economic Justice for All* (1986), the Catholic Bishops recognized that the allocation of income, wealth, and power must be evaluated in light of its effects on persons whose basic material needs are unmet. The Second Vatican Council stated:

> The right to have a share of earthly goods sufficient for oneself and one's family belongs to everyone. The fathers and doctors of the Church held this view, teaching that we are obliged to come to the relief of the poor and to do so not merely out of our superfluous goods.

Housing is an absolute necessity for human life. If persons are to be recognized as members of the human community, then the community, including its religious institutions, have an obligation to help fulfill these basic needs, unless an absolute scarcity of resources makes this strictly impossible. No such scarcity has been established for the United States today. Community-based religious institutions can be catalysts for sustained action on social and economic justice issues. This significant potential for affecting housing and homelessness issues should be recognized.

WHO ARE THE HOMELESS?

It has been argued that homelessness is an increasing national problem. Economic forces, such as unemployment, loss of low income housing stock, an expanding poverty level population, and rising housing costs, are continuing to draw broader segments of the nation's population into homelessness (Solarz, Mowbray, & Dupuis, 1986). Research indicates that the homeless population is now younger than a decade earlier, with greater numbers of women and children, as well as significant numbers of persons with disabilities (Partnerships for the Homeless, 1989).

A synthesis of NIMH-funded studies of homeless adult populations (Tessler & Dennis, 1989) found disproportionately high numbers of young adults, minorities, Vietnam era veterans, and male substance abusers among the homeless. Homeless adults had higher unemployment and arrest rates, and far less education and contact with or help from friends or relatives than did low-income, housed adults. Most did not receive benefits for which they were eligible and had no health care despite prevalent medical problems (33%-50%) and mental illness (28%-37%). Similarly, homeless children have been found (Homelessness Information Exchange, 1988) to present far more developmental problems, chronic health problems, abuse, neglect, absence from school, and acute emotional problems than comparable, housed children.

WHAT ARE THE LONG-TERM HOUSING AND SUPPORT NEEDS OF HOMELESS INDIVIDUALS?

The aggregate picture is one of tremendous heterogeneity, vulnerability, and estrangement from any personal sense of belonging as well as from any formal connection to the larger society. Furthermore, within any one person or family, this multiplicity of needs may interact to compound the already severe challenge of finding and keeping affordable housing. These needs do not point to one uniform model of housing and support services but rather to a broad range of highly adaptable alternatives.

Research demonstration project results also support the need for heterogeneous housing and support arrangements, even within the subpopulations of mentally ill homeless individuals. Five New York City programs for homeless mentally ill individuals (Barrow, 1988; Barrow, Hellman, Lovell, Plapinger, & Struening, 1989; Plapinger, 1988) accessed a wide variety of living arrangements and found that more than two-thirds of clients seen in six months were successfully housed. Half the clients were housed in independent settings (low-cost, non-serviced with access to off-site support services) and half were housed in support settings. Of these, 74% were in "low demand" single room occupancy (SRO) hotels with varying degrees of voluntary on-site services and 26% were in more structured settings, such as group homes or treatment based residences.

The New York project data also suggest that long stability of housing may require a selection process that prioritizes and responds to clients perceptions of their own needs, i.e., that stable living arrangements may well be chosen living arrangements. Twenty-one percent of all clients housed were no longer in their housing *after* six months. Departures after only a brief stay were clearly related to disagreement between the client and provider with respect to amount of on-site supervision, structure of the housing, or other specific requirements (e.g., turning over control of one's money, participating in treatment programs) (Plapinger, 1988).

It has been argued (Carling, 1989; Ohio Department of Mental Health, 1988; Solarz, Mowbray, & Dupuis, 1986) that affordable permanent housing will be more successful if people have meaningful choices from a full range of normal options, including renting, owning, and cooperative living, and that these options be linked with real opportunities for community participation. For people with disabilities and/or special needs, this would entail both individualized assistance with daily life in their housing, reciprocal opportunities to work and contribute, and the chance to share in the long term process of community change.

This view of community integration (Taylor, Biklen, & Knoll, 1987) is consistent with Heller's (1989) analysis of the kinds of social ties or "relational communities" that can transcend geographic transience. He argues that such community experiences are now less likely to be available via extended family or neighborhood and *more* likely to occur through informal peer groups, voluntary organizations, and other networks of like-minded people with shared agendas and destinies. These group attachments address personal needs while integrating the individual into the larger society. Provided they have the requisite traditions and skills, such "relational communities" can function as interest groups, achieving consensus and building coalitions on the pathway to collective power.

Religious institutions, often a vastly underestimated resource (Pargament, Silverman, Johnson, Echemendia, & Snyder, 1983), would appear to be a prime source of relational communities, as described above. Congregational potential for social action and social service activity can be identified (Pargament & Maton, in press) and utilized. In fact, for many communities, a religious organization may represent the *only* system capable of bringing people together around a community problem.

HISTORICAL ROLES IN HELPING THE HOMELESS

Throughout most of our nation's history, the homeless have been cared for by religious and other voluntary organizations. Their role has been and continues to be aimed at rehabilitating the individual, both physically and spiritually (Cooper, 1987; Stoil, 1987; Volunteers of America, 1987). This approach is consistent with a "social service" pathway of religious influence in society (Pargament & Maton, in press), which seeks to ameliorate social problems by aiding underserved individuals rather than working towards fundamental systemic changes ("social action" pathway).

Caring for one's neighbors in America can be traced to the religious traditions of the first settlers, pilgrims and puritans, and to a reliance on mutual help that was dictated by early hardships (Cooper, 1987). During the 1800s, waves of immigration stimulated development of a wide range of religious and ethnic self-help and service organizations (YMCA in 1851; National Conference on Social Welfare in 1873). Evangelistic services for homeless alcoholics gained public recognition as early as 1880, when "Ash Barrell" J. (Jemmy) Kemp was "saved" by the Pioneer Party of the Salvation Army in New York City (Stoil, 1987). Transitional residential and rehabilitation programs grew rapidly between 1880 and 1900; Commander F. Booth Tucker reported that the Salvation Army in the United States had "rescued" at least 100,000 alcoholics during its first 25 years.

This rapid growth in Salvation Army services is attributed to several factors (Stoil, 1987). First, the Christian Temperance movement, with spokesperson Mrs. "Lemonade Lucy" Rutherford B. Hayes, had already established popular and philanthropic support for work with skid row populations. Second, the Army adapted to the cultural diversity of the homeless by forming corps that were identified with local ethnic communities (Swedish, Norwegian) and by forming missions that spoke the language of local immigrant communities (German, Russian). Finally, local Army units used aggressive community outreach, scouring the streets for public inebriates on designated "Boozers' Days."

The primary reliance on organized voluntary efforts continued into the early twentieth century, with resources increasingly exceeded by expanding needs (Cooper, 1987). After the Great Depression and consequent collapse of voluntary and local funds, the federal government assumed substantive responsibility for the poor and handicapped. A primary federal role continued for forty years until the early 1970s when the War on Poverty programs were gradually eliminated. Over the next decade, the federal role in housing and social services continued to shrink while the voluntary sector faced rapidly increasing numbers of homeless individuals with more diverse and complex needs than had ever been confronted before.

THE CURRENT SITUATION IN HOMELESSNESS SERVICES

In 1983, Congress finally perceived a need for coordinated, federal assistance to help address the homeless "emergency." The Emergency Jobs Appropriations Act (1983) included a grant of $100 million to the Federal Emergency Management Agency (FEMA) to distribute to nonprofit groups, half routed via state governors and half via a National Board of nonprofit organizations, the Emergency Food and Shelter National Board Program (EFSP). The $50 million for EFSP was intended as a one-time only response to recession; consequently, its distribution network was set up to use existing service providers, rather than create a new federal system. The focus was on non-profits, including mostly church-related organizations, who were seen as knowledgeable and experienced, and who had also acted as advocates for this federal funding. Later, with belated recognition that homelessness was *not* a one-time only crisis, programs were expanded in other federal agencies to provide additional shelter space, food, and limited help with rents, mortgages, and utility costs.

The 1987 McKinney Homeless Assistance Act, PL 100-77, authorized 20 different funding programs and appropriated 1.1 billion dollars over three fiscal years. The Act affirmed a public-private partnership for service delivery. Most of the competitive grant programs for shelter creation and expansion, supportive services, and health care are available only to private non-profits. Issues of constitutional separation of church and state have been resolved in two ways: a focus on the services provided rather than the provider; and the requirement that churches and religious organizations create a separate non-profit entity to own real property. The McKinney Act is the major vehicle through which the federal government provides homeless assistance. This new funding should be viewed in the context of the precipitous decline in federal spending for low-and moderate-income housing through the last decade, from 25 billion dollars to less than 8 billion dollars — a decrease that cannot be addressed through the resources of state and/or local government agencies.

In the exhausting struggle to compensate for Reagan era cutbacks, religious and other voluntary institutions have outstripped the federal government in resources committed to homeless services, despite the federal appropriations through FEMA and the McKinney Act. U.S. News & World Report (Chaze, 1985) found that more than 50 voluntary groups raised half a billion dollars per year for homeless service projects. In 1986, the Salvation Army reported treating about 60,000 alcoholics per year in over 150 different transitional programs with an annual budget of $200 million, financed almost entirely from the private sector (Stoil, 1987). These programs included at least 31 facilities that were designed specifically for the skid row population. A 1988 HUD study indicated that 63% of operating expenses for all shelters nationwide was from private sources, largely religious institutions. A more recent EFSP study (National Alliance to End Homelessness, 1990) of model homeless programs found that 35% to 89% of *all* actual expenses were covered by private funds.

The traditional commitment of many religious organizations to a "social service" approach continues to the present and entails a wide range of program models:

The Harbor Light program model (Stoil, 1987) for homeless alcoholics includes detoxification; emergency food and shelter; vocational preparation and placement; personal counseling; medical care; social fellowship; and spiritual training and voluntary service.

The Metropolitan Inter-Faith Association (MIFA) of Memphis, Tennessee (Cooper, 1987) offers a religious-secular partnership model for transitional housing. Sixteen churches and local community organizations and government agencies jointly developed a two month transitional program for homeless families. In its first year, MIFA leased ten HUD houses, utilized Community Development Block Grant funds for renovation, and donated furnishings, appliances, and supplies. MIFA also provided guest families counseling, referrals, and assistance with finding other housing. The ten houses served 51 families per year while an equal number were turned away.

Michigan has over 200 emergency shelter providers. They all are private non-profit organizations, usually church-based or with a strong participation by local religious organizations. Emergency shelter and food are provided in most settings, with a few having resources to offer some transitional housing along with limited advocacy to address unemployment, lack of education, health care, and substance abuse problems.

Public and private service providers are increasingly recognizing limits to each organization's ability to assist homeless clients, because of their clients' broad range of needs. Groups are beginning to examine the long-term needs for training, education, job development, and permanent housing. In order to meet these service needs, and to avoid competing for scarce resources (a tendency exacerbated by the structure of the McKinney Act which awards most funding on a competitive basis), service providers are developing networks to coordinate efforts and build support for more resources. In recent years, some religious institutions have also stepped beyond the traditional "social service" pathway onto one of "social action" attempting to address the aggregate needs of homeless individuals and families by working towards fundamental systemic change.

PROACTIVE ROLES FOR RELIGIOUS ORGANIZATIONS

Housing is increasingly seen as not just an economic commodity, but as a basic human right. This perspective is also seen in religious literature, as demonstrated in Pope John II's writing on the tragedy of homelessness (1987):

> We are convinced that a house is much more than a simple roof over
> one's head. The place where a person creates and lives out his or her
> life, also serves to found, in some way, that person's deepest iden-
> tity and his or her relations with others.

Virtually all housing issues relate to inadequacies in affordability, quality, and availability (both the quantity of units and accessibility to them).
Easing the squeeze on any of these helps move toward the ultimate goal of
safe, decent, and affordable housing for everyone. Often the most effective community projects addressing these housing issues have a church or
other religious organization or coalition at their base, providing strength,
personnel, vision, stability, continuity, and intellect to that effort.
Churches, and other religious institutions are promoting incremental
change in housing and homelessness through three methods: advocacy,
finance, and development (Appel, Gillette, & Christian, 1989). They are
described here in order of their increasing requirements for commitment,
involvement, skill, energy investment and risk. While these descriptions
are offered with optimism and hope, they should not be misconstrued as a
final solution for eliminating — or even reducing the incidence and prevalence of — homelessness. As long as these "thousand points of light" are
surrounded by federal darkness, then the growth rate of the homeless population may stay ahead of the rate at which people can be housed and
stabilized. No amount of voluntary sector commitment, regardless of the
promise and potential it offers, can substitute for significant federal investments in affordable housing and serious, national response to poverty.
The examples that follow offer a place to begin, not to end.

Housing Advocacy

Advocacy, at its simplest, is the process through which concerns are
conveyed about an issue in order to effect needed changes. In housing
advocacy, community and congregation awareness is raised so that
changes may be made in the quality, availability or affordability of housing. Examples include lobbying elected officials to enact needed legislation; monitoring the effectiveness or enforcement of current policies; organizing housing coalitions; setting up educational or election forums on
affordable housing; and scheduling a housing film series. Or advocacy can
be simply informing friends, family and colleagues of the need for housing and correcting misperceptions.

Advocacy efforts may be directed at local-level service improvements
or at systemic change. Raising money for emergency shelter helps a few
families; advocacy to increase welfare shelter allowances helps thousands
of families. If it is the current political, social, and economic realities

which make housing too expensive, changes in these systems may be the most effective means of creating affordable housing. This type of advocacy has been recognized by the Episcopal House of Bishops (1987, p. 3) as a "moral imperative," by the Catholic Church as the "pursuit of economic justice" (U.S. Catholic Bishops, 1986, p.xv), and by the Lutheran Church as "God's advocacy." Several examples of effective models for church advocacy can be identified (Appel, Gillette, & Christian, 1989):

Core City Neighborhoods. Housed in a former convent and staffed by Catholic nuns, Core City Neighborhoods believes that housing is central to broader goals of social and economic justice. It works in a well-defined 3-1/2 square mile area of Detroit and its board is composed of community residents (from a variety of denominations) as well as representatives from area businesses and institutions. Since its beginnings in 1984, Core City projects have included crime prevention, garbage removal, mowing overgrown weeds, and housing development, including creating a redevelopment plan through community meetings; a street by street survey with a city building inspector to document external building code violations; demanding demolition of the most deteriorated buildings; and a city-funded program to mow 300 acres (4,000 lots) of vacant land so adjacent residents would have an incentive to keep up occupied units.

Coalition for Block Grant Compliance. The Coalition was begun in 1974 by Detroit-area citizens to monitor the use of federal Community Development (CDBG) funds, especially within some 25 suburban communities. It was funded by six different denominations as well as contributions from local parishes and congregations in the region, whose members volunteered their time. The coalition has been able to deny CDBG funds to suburbs who were using them for discriminatory housing and to influence HUD standards for the metro area.

Religious institutions and people of faith frequently take advantage of their considerable clout and their politically protected status when joining and organizing efforts for social and economic justice. The Lutheran Resources Commission (1983) viewed local churches of all denominations as being "of the community" and uniquely suited to mediate between quality of neighborhood life on the one hand and mainline financial institutions on the other.

Housing Finance

The problem of affordability is well-illustrated by a concrete example. A single mother with two children will earn $8,000 annually at a minimum wage job. For her, affordability (defined as 30% of household income) equates to $200 per month, including utilities. The possibilities of obtaining a quality, acceptable, two to three bedroom apartment at that price are almost nonexistent. The Detroit/Wayne County Homeless Strategy Coalition estimates that half of their county's public assistance recipients spend 60 percent or more of their income on housing.

Housing affordability is improved by *lowering* the monthly amount people pay for rent or mortgages. This can be accomplished through several mechanisms — lowering the actual cost of acquisition, construction or purchase; or by lowering interest rates or other loan terms. Of these choices, changing the method of financing holds the greatest possibility. For example, if the mortgage term is longer, the monthly payment is smaller and becomes affordable to more families.

The cost of credit itself (interest rates and fees or points, if any) also affects affordability. When people and institutions, in recognition of the need for social and economic justice, make investments in housing and accept lower interest rates, that capital can make housing affordable for those with limited incomes. The monthly payment on a $40,000 mortgage, for example, drops from $286 to $162 when the interest rate is reduced from 11% to 5%. On a $1 million apartment building project with 40 units, the rent drops from $308 to $202 when the 1-year construction loan interest is reduced (from 15% to 5%) and the 30-year permanent mortgage interest is reduced (from 12% to 7%).

There is a growing awareness of the value of social investing, i.e., voting with dollars. This has been pursued by means of boycotting consumer products as well as public debate over how and where retirement funds are invested. Churches have recognized the "crucial moral dimensions" of such investment and management decisions (U.S. Catholic Bishops, 1986). It has been said that capital is the building block of communities, and credit is its lifeblood. A deficiency of either can devastate a neighborhood, as well as a family. Without capital and credit, homes cannot be built, sold, purchased or repaired — and the results are predictable. In the housing area, the social investment strategy is reflected in the growing number of community loan funds capitalized with money from religious institutions. The community loan fund serves as an intermediary between lenders and borrowers, assuring judicious review of loan applications and faithful monitoring of the outstanding loans for the lenders. The community loan fund makes loans for housing and business development born of community initiative. It also frequently serves as a technical advisor to borrowers, assisting with the packaging of their loan from the fund with donations and loans from other sources.

The Michigan Housing Trust Fund is a good example. The Fund was created with technical support, start-up costs, and initial funding for staffing provided by the Michigan State Housing Development Authority. It secured its loan capital from religious organizations — investors who were committed to the Fund's goal of providing loan capital and technical assistance to developers of housing for families below the poverty level. Since it began lending in 1987, the Michigan Housing Trust Fund has made 13 loans to support the development of 166 housing units. Many of these projects have been in Detroit, but there have also been loans to projects in outstate urban and rural areas, as well. Of the $424,546 in cumulative loan commitments made to date, $108,867 has already been repaid to the Fund and is available to lend out again. All but $50,000 of the Fund's load capital comes from regional and national religious institutions.

Housing Development

Housing may be lost to a variety of factors: poor maintenance, fires, downtown and industrial development, commercial encroachment, abandonment and disinvestment. As housing becomes more costly to build, inner-city and rural communities cannot replace housing that is lost. So new development is needed of housing that is affordable to the increasing numbers of people with minimum wage jobs, the unemployed, or single mothers with young children.

Housing development requires juggling many variables and managing many processes. These include studying the market, finding sites, assembling financing, getting public approvals, developing the design and the specifications for the work, improving the site, actual construction, finding people to live in the sites who can pay to rent or own, and finally, paying back loans. Because housing production for poor people is not a highly profitable venture, more and more of such work is through non-profit sponsors.

Examples of non-profit corporations that engage in housing development activities include: human service agencies with minor or emergency home repair programs, community action agencies with weatherization programs, public housing authorities who manage single and multi-family low-income housing, and Indian tribes who form public housing authorities to develop housing on trust land. And finally, there are the churches, hospitals, and neighborhood organizations that become involved because of social justice concerns or because of a need in their neighborhoods.

Community development corporations are frequently formed out of coalitions or partnerships between local churches, neighborhood organizations, hospitals, and small business owners who come together with the goal of revitalizing a neighborhood. Community-based non-profit developers have done everything from operating $500 per unit minor home repair programs for single family homeowners to carrying out $40,000 per unit new construction of multi-family rental housing. This is not a new endeavor for churches and religious institutions. Congregations have played many roles in organizing community development corporations and in contributing staff services, volunteers, meeting space, equipment and cash (Zalent, 1983).

What particularly distinguishes community-based housing development from conventional efforts is the motivation and process for doing it: the determination that neighborhood revitalization be done to benefit the people who live there and involving those people in the development process. Such self-determination has theological underpinnings, e.g., "efforts that enable the poor to participate in the ownership and control of economic resources are especially important" (U.S. Catholic Bishops, 1986). Community-based organizations are democratic and accountable to the communities in which they are working. Some consciously use the development process as a new way to empower residents of low-income communities, to provide them opportunities for voicing their dreams, and for developing the skills necessary to help bring those dreams about.

Many successful non-profit housing developers have church support for their efforts through leadership and/or funding. The key motivations behind church involvement include the sense of moral outrage at homelessness, and the deterioration of the community's housing. It may be an emergency that propels a congregation into action. Other churches see the need to stabilize the neighborhood as an investment in their own future. Churches exist within communities, and their long-term stability may depend on the vitality of the community.

Churches are special in their involvement both because they have unique talents to offer and a level of commitment that is beyond that of other voluntary institutions. They have special capacities which arise from and depend upon the theologies which inspire them, and the ways they choose to express those theologies through their ministries in the world (Zalent, 1983).

There is no such thing as a single "church role" in housing development. The following descriptions (Appel, Gillette, & Christian, 1989) show that anything is possible, from efforts initiated by a single church, to ecumenical church groups, to collaborative church-community organization partnerships.

Single church initiatives. Church of the Messiah Housing Corporation (CMHC), located in a 77 square block area in Detroit, is a subsidiary of the church created in 1978 to address housing deterioration, abandonment and the lack of quality management. The church supplied the first board members, paid the first staff persons, and contributed office space. Their first project was in response to an emergency—the apartment building across the street from the church had a fire and several tenants were being housed temporarily by church members. The 24 unit building was acquired and renovated over a period of 4 years. CMHC then worked with residents of the newly-named Mustard Tree Apartments to develop their management capability. In 1984, the residents, members of the Mustard Tree Cooperative Association, were able to buy the building from CMHC. CMHC has since rehabilitated (rehabed) and now manages the 36 unit St. Paul Manor, and owns and manages the 73 unit El Tovar apartments. They have rehabed 5 duplexes, and sold 6 of those 10 units. They are beginning to renovate (rehab) the Kingston Arms, a 24 unit building. CMHC also provides construction management services to other Detroit non-profit housing organizations.

Ecumenical church groups. Dwelling Place of Grand Rapids, Inc., was formed in 1980 by the church community in downtown Grand Rapids. They were concerned with displacement resulting from redevelopment, and the adequacy and availability of housing for the low-income people being displaced. The churches formed a partnership primarily to provide financial support. Dwelling Place constructed and manages 19 units for the mentally ill. They have also done substantial rehab to convert two warehouses into 190 units of housing, have done one moderate rehab of a 16 unit building, and operate an SRO (single room occupancy facility) for 89 recipients of General Assistance and Social Security payments (SSI).

Collaborative church-community efforts. Reach, Inc. was founded in 1986 by the leaders of Twelfth Street Missionary Baptist Church in Detroit. They cultivated partnerships with community residents, government, lenders, businesses, and other churches and supplemented the effort with financial and in-kind contributions. The church's pastor is president and the church provides free office space for the organization. In addition, it covers shortages in the operating budget and the rental program, where rents frequently don't cover costs. Reach has rehabilitated 11 houses; 5 have been sold to low and moderate-income families and others are rented to low-income people. Over 100 more vacant homes in the area are on the list for future rehab and resale. There are also plans for moving houses to vacant lots. Reach also has a home-ownership training program and a "share-a-life" program, in which senior citizens train teens in home repair skills. Once trained, the teens provide these services to seniors who need help.

COMPLEMENTARY ROLES FOR HUMAN SERVICE AND RELIGIOUS ORGANIZATIONS

The contribution of religious institutions and the voluntary sector towards the care and housing of the homeless continues to surpass that of the public sector. The range of social roles for religious institutions is highly developed and warrants further study and familiarity on the part of human service professionals charged with serving the homeless. The commitment and capabilities of religious institutions, together with some federal willingness to identify a government role, suggest opportunity for expanding the complementary roles which could be played by voluntary and public sector agencies in addressing homelessness. These possibilities include individual (social service) and systems-level (social action) initiatives. However, we found few current examples of this happening. In this final section, we will describe possible complementary roles at both levels, but also suggest the barriers impeding these activities. It is our hope that presenting this information may be useful in creating change.

Collaborative Social Service Pathways

Research on the individual needs of homeless persons indicates a heterogeneity of problems as well as lack of social supports and community ties. The involvement of religious organizations in human service programs for the homeless can help address both of these issues, through the *broad range* of supports they may offer, including spirituality, and the sense of connection they can provide to a *relational community*. In turn, many human service professionals working with the homeless have developed knowledge and techniques on how to best engage those who are chronically homeless, who have been disenfranchised and isolated for long periods of time. A consultative relationship could impart this learning to those religious organizations offering social services to homeless individuals and families. This could expand the population served to include more behaviorally challenging people. The success of such consultation would hinge on increments of trust that human services staff can earn by demonstrating flexibility, responsiveness, and sensitivity over the long term (Cohen, Murphy, Rosalik, & Cooper, 1988).

Collaborative Social Action Pathways

Partnerships between human service agencies and religious organizations are also indicated at the social action (systemic) level. The unique credibility of religious organizations as advocates for social change could be complemented by human services expertise in services research and evaluation that produces valid empirical ammunition. Similarly, the quest for new homeless funds rewards community partnerships. The need to compete for funding from a variety of sources, such as contracts from state agencies, grants from foundations, awards from the federal government, private gifts and in-kind assistance, has required the development of name recognition and trust building in the community, and among potential contributors. Linkage to broader networks, such as the membership of religious organizations, is crucial in providing both credibility and access to resources. Finally, it has long been argued that responsibility for the homeless and disabled homeless populations rests with the entire community rather than exclusively with one sector or agency (Cooper, Murphy, & Cohen, 1987).

However, complementary and coordinated activity at the system level is not without problems, as well. While it is understandable that many church-based efforts are aimed at an immediate geographic locale, many homeless individuals have, by definition, already lost such "neighborhood" ties. The examples provided of religious organizations' proactive efforts to develop housing and address homeless prevention have mainly been limited to "their own" — their own parishioners, neighborhoods, or at most, poorer congregations of the same denomination in proximal geographic areas. Church writings ascribe to religious organizations a potentially larger role — affirming the basic human right to quality housing for *all* people, speaking for the voiceless, defending the poor and vulnerable, and advancing the common good. Many homeless individuals, whose vulnerabilities have targeted them for public sector attention, are least likely to be seen by local religious communities as "their own." The public sector faces the challenge of how to broaden religiously based community development efforts to include more vulnerable individuals. This may require long-term developmental strategies within individual congregations, i.e., gradually branching out to other groups over time, as well as across congregations and voluntary agencies, city or regional coalition-building. Perhaps the simple accumulation of experience will promote the realization that a larger group remains in need and that homelessness and housing problems cannot be fully addressed until all God's children are sheltered.

NEXT STEPS

Community involvement and coalition building are essential if public and private service providers are to move toward the ultimate goal of eliminating homelessness. This entails developing a broad and preference-based range of decent, affordable housing with flexible supports as well as effectively reaching and engaging vulnerable subgroups of the homeless population. Increasingly it is the private sector, churches and religious organizations, who must be called upon to assist our communities in accepting the responsibility of housing the homeless.

The first step on pathways to collaborative social service and social action is to acknowledge that responsibility for homelessness rests with the entire community and is not the exclusive province of any one sector or institution, public or private. The second step is commitment to enhanced communication among all sectors of the local community. Human service and religious organizations must come together at the local level to share their goals, capabilities, and problems with one another. This can yield a shared and rich understanding of the community's homeless and housing problems as well as a shared appreciation of resources available from each sector. This process can be initiated through any local institution, but participation must be invited from the full range of human service and religious leaders. Initial explorations need to be flexible, allowing a range of possible contacts and involvement, and need to be "out in the open," acknowledging prior misadventures as well as current doubts and biases. The actions and priorities will have to reflect the unique housing/homeless needs of the local community as well as the mandates and capabilities of the participating organizations. Although a full range of partnerships and activities are possible, as our discussion has indicated, none can be realized without the commitment of local institutions, public and private, to understand one another and to seek complementary roles in addressing the larger needs of their communities.

REFERENCES

Appel, M., Gillette, V., & Christian, S. (1989). *A resource guide for effective housing ministries.* Lansing, MI: Michigan Housing Coalition.

Barrow, S. M. (1988). *Linking mentally ill homeless clients to psychiatric treatment services: The experience of five CSS programs.* New York: New York Psychiatric Institute.

Barrow, S. M., Hellman, F., Lovell, A. M., Plapinger, J., & Struening, E. L. (1989). *Effectiveness of programs for the mentally ill homeless.* New York: New York Psychiatric Institute.

Carling, P. J. (1989). Access to housing: Cornerstone of the American dream. *Journal of Rehabilitation*, July/August/September, 6-8.

Chaze, W. L. (1985). Helping the homeless: A fight against despair. *U.S. News & World Report*, 16 January, 55.

Cohen, E., Murphy, M., Rosalik, B., & Cooper, S. (1988). *Shelter case consultation: A historical case study.* Presented at Eastern Psychological Association Annual Meeting, Buffalo, New York.

Cooper, M. A. (1987). The role of religious and nonprofit organizations in combating homelessness. In R. D. Bingham, R. E. Green, & S. B. White (Eds.), *The homeless in contemporary society.* Milwaukee: Sage Publications and Urban Research Center, University of Wisconsin.

Cooper, S., Murphy, M., & Cohen, E. (1987). *Partnerships for homelessness.*

Presented at National Council of Community Mental Health Centers Annual Meeting, Miami.

Episcopal House of Bishops. (1987). *Economic justice and the Christian conscience.*

Heller, K. (1989). The return to community. *American Journal of Community Psychology, 17,* 1-16.

Homeless Information Exchange. (1988). *Family and child homelessness.* Washington, DC: Homelessness Information Exchange.

Lutheran Resources Commission. (1983). *The local church and community-economic development.*

National Alliance to End Homelessness. (1990). *Checklist for success: Programs to help the hungry and homeless.* Washington, DC: Emergency Food and Shelter National Board Program.

Ohio Department of Mental Health. (1988). *Housing-as-housing discussion paper.* Columbus, OH: Ohio Department of Mental Health.

Pargament, K. I., & Maton, K. I. (in press). Religion in American life: A community psychology perspective. In J. Rappaport & E. Seidman (Eds.), *Handbook of community psychology.* New York: Plenum.

Pargament, K. I., Silverman, W., Johnson, S., Echemendia, R., & Snyder, S. (1983). The psychosocial climate of religious congregations. *American Journal of Community Psychology, 11,* 351-381.

Partnerships for the Homeless, Inc. (1989). *Moving forward: A national agenda to address homelessness in 1990 and beyond.* New York.

Plapinger, J. D. (1988). *Progress service goals: Service needs, service feasibility, and obstacles to providing services to the mentally ill homeless.* New York: New York Psychiatric Institute.

Pope John Paul II. (1987). *Letter on the tragedy of homelessness.*

Solarz, A., Mowbray, C. T., & Dupuis, S. (1986). *Life in transit: Homelessness in Michigan.* Lansing, MI: Michigan Department of Mental Health.

Stoil, M. (1987). Salvation and sobriety. *Alcohol Health and Research World, 11(3),* 14-17.

Taylor, S.J., Biklen, D., & Knoll, J. (1987). *Community integration for people with severe disabilities.* New York: Teachers College Press.

Tessler, R. C., & Dennis, D. L. (1989). *A synthesis of NIMH-funded research concerning persons who are homeless and mentally ill.* Rockville, MD: NIMH.

U.S. Catholic Bishops. (1986). *Economic justice for all: Pastoral letter on Catholic social teaching and the U.S. economy.* Washington, DC: Office of Publishing Services, U.S.C.C.

U.S. Department of Housing and Urban Development. (1989). *A report on the 1988 national survey of shelters for the homeless.* Washington, DC.

Volunteers of America. (1987). *Proceedings of symposium on homelessness.* Metarie, LA: Volunteers of America.

Zalent, K. (1983). *Religious institutions as actors in community based economic development.* New York: A Seedco Report prepared for the Lilly Endowment.